YES, I'M A CHRISTIAN!
So What Do I Believe?

Yes, I'm A Christian!
So What Do I Believe?

Ralph William Moore

KGI Publishing
Las Vegas

YES, I'M A CHRISTIAN!
So What Do I Believe?
By Ralph William Moore

First Edition, January 2003

KGI Publishing
2232 South Nellis Blvd., Suite #103
Las Vegas, Nevada 89104
"Knowing God Intimately"

ISBN 1-932006-50-8

Library of Congress Control Number: 2002104092

Unless otherwise indicated,
All Scripture taken from the NEW AMERICAN STANDARD BIBLE(r),
© Copyright 1960, 1962, 1963, 1968, 1971, 1972, 1973, 1975, 1977, 1995 by
The Lockman Foundation. Used by permission. (www.Lockman.org)

The information and advice offered in this book are true to the best of the author's knowledge. The advice and counsel of true Christians who have demonstrated a complete surrender of this life to Jesus Christ, while displaying an ability to handle the Word of God correctly, should always be sought. The author assumes absolutely no liability for anyone misunderstanding or misusing this information, but rejoices greatly in the continuing fruit God has produced in many lives to His glory.

To David Peters, P.W.E.,
Whose prayers, love and advice have made this work possible.

Contents

Illustrations and Tables

Acknowledgments

First and foremost, I would like to thank the Lord God Almighty for answering my prayers to know His ways in order to know Him more intimately.

I would also like to thank my family, not the least my mother Delores J. Moore and my sister Pam Moore, for their support, encouragement and prayers.

Thanks to Kay Stevens, Gregg Burg, Jeff Rhoades and the gang at Thompson-Shore for all of their help, and Irene Archer of Archer Graphics for the cover design.

I am indebted to my many friends in Christ who have read the manuscript and offered constructive criticism, namely David Peters, Grant Lada, Paul and Gena Suarez, Julius Amman, and Ralph and Kelly Kroll.

Special thanks to Grant Lada for his prayers, encouragement and cover photography.

May the Lord Jesus Christ be glorified greatly by this effort.

1

Introduction:
An Eye-Opening Encounter

Matt was impressed. The quick service at his favorite fast-food restaurant presented him with a feast of tacos and burritos. A dedicated Christian in his college sophomore year, Matt was taking a well-deserved lunch break from his studies. As he brought his tray into the dining area, he noticed another student reading a Bible and taking detailed notes. Intrigued, Matt asked if he could join him.

Upon sitting, Matt asked the athletic-looking student if he was a Christian. "No," Rick replied, "I'm reading the Bible for my 'Bible As Literature' class, and I have to write a term paper on the subject, 'What Christians Believe, and Why.'"

Seizing upon a unique opportunity to share his faith, Matt identified himself as a Christian, and offered to explain any Bible passages and answer any of Rick's questions. Rick was delighted with such a fortunate situation, as this interview would give a personal perspective to his essay.

"So, if I understand Christianity correctly, you hold this Bible to be God's infallible Word. This book is the standard by which you live your life, and the doctrine taught in its pages you regard as absolute truth," Rick began.

"Correct," answered Matt.

"Were you always a Christian? In other words, were you a Christian from birth?"

"No," Matt explained. "Even though my father and mother are Christians, being a Christian cannot be inherited from one's parents. Every person is born with a sinful nature, which we did inherit from our forefather, Adam, the first human. When he sinned against God's commandment, part of God's punishment was that every person born from human males would be born with a sin nature."

"So how did you overcome this sin nature and become a Christian?" asked Rick, probing a little deeper.

"I attended church with my parents my entire life, but was never really interested in the kinds of songs that they sang or the preacher's talks," Matt recalled. "At a healing service about four years ago, the pastor asked if anyone wanted to come down to the front and give his heart to Jesus Christ. I felt an intense stirring within me, though at the time I did not understand what God was doing. I chose to go down and accept Jesus Christ as my personal Lord and Savior. At that moment, I was born again into the family of God."

"Are you saying," Rick examined, "that you—an unbeliever—accepted Jesus Christ as your Lord and Savior, and that you made the choice to do that, and that this action caused you to become a Christian?"

"Yes. I chose of my own free will to accept Jesus as my Savior." An immediate look of confusion crept across Rick's face. "What's wrong?" asked Matt.

"Well, I've been studying this Bible to write my paper," Rick said. "And this Bible, which you claim is your standard for truth, says the exact opposite."

"What?" Now Matt was confused. He looked at Rick's Bible, and it was the New American Standard version, an excellent and extremely accurate English translation. "I don't understand. What do you mean?"

"Well, let me refer to my notes here," Rick answered. "Read this verse from the Apostle Paul's First Letter to the Corinthians."

Matt read:

> But a natural man does not accept the things of the Spirit of God, for they are foolishness to him; and he cannot understand them, because they are spiritually appraised. (1 Corinthians 2:14)

"What confuses me," Rick continued, "is that you claim that this book is God's Word. This book specifically says that an unbeliever 'does not accept the things of the Spirit of God.' It also says that these things of God 'are foolishness' to the unbeliever, and that the unbeliever 'cannot understand them.'

"You say that you were born an unbeliever. So my question is, how is it that, as a naturally-born unbeliever, you accepted Christ as your Savior, if God says in His Word that this does not happen?"

Matt did not have an answer. He thought about telling Rick that 'God just performed a miracle,' but that would not answer the problem. Matt understood that he was claiming something that God's own Word said does not happen.

"And I have another question," Rick said, interrupting Matt's thoughts. "You said that you chose to make the decision to accept Christ as your Savior. But these next verses in the Apostle John's Gospel say the exact opposite. Here, read them."

Matt read:

> But as many as received Him, to them He gave the right to become
> children of God, *even* to those who believe in His name,
>   who were born, not of blood nor of the will of the flesh nor of the will
> of man, but of God. (John 1:12,13)

"These verses say that children of God are 'born again,' as you call it, 'not of blood nor of the will of the flesh nor of the will of man,'" repeated Rick. "You were right on one point: one cannot inherit Christianity, for Christians are not born again through blood-relative ties, as it says here.

"But it also says you cannot be born again by your will, or in other words, your choice or decision. But you said that, as an unbeliever, you accepted Christ—which the Bible says a natural man does not do—and that it was your choice to do so, which the Bible refutes word for word.

"Also, I was reading Paul's Letter to the Romans, where in chapter 9, the Apostle explains how people become true children of God. He writes: 'So then it does not depend on the man who wills or the man who runs, but on God who has mercy' (Romans 9:16). I can see that the Apostle John completely agrees with the Apostle Paul on how one does *not* become a Christian, as well as how one does become 'born again'.

"The book you claim to be God's Word states clearly that becoming a child of God has nothing to do with man's will or man's actions. This Bible explicitly says that people become children of God by God's will alone, totally excluding man's choices and man's deeds. But you say that you became a child of God by your choice to go down to the altar, and by your accepting Christ as your Savior. I don't understand."

Matt was at a loss for words.

"You claim to have made your decision to accept Christ by your own 'free will'?" Rick inquired.

"Yes," Matt replied.

"But this Bible, which you hold as God's Word, says the exact opposite again. Here, read these verses."

Matt read:

> The Lord's bond-servant must not be quarrelsome, but be kind to all,
>   able to teach, patient when wronged,
>   with gentleness correcting those who are in opposition, if perhaps God
> may grant them repentance leading to the knowledge of the truth,
>   and they may come to their senses *and escape* from the snare of the
> devil, having been held captive by him to do his will. (2 Timothy 2:24-26)

"The Bible expressly declares here that those 'in opposition' to Christianity—those not 'born again'—are 'held captive' by the devil to do the devil's will," Rick expounded. "So, the will of an unbeliever is not free, but is enslaved to the devil. Is it the devil's will that you accept Christ as your Savior?"

"Absolutely not!" Matt replied. "The Lord Jesus said that the devil's aim is to steal, kill and destroy—not save."

"Then how could you choose Christ if, according to your Bible, your will as an unbeliever is held captive by the devil to do the devil's will?" questioned Rick.

Matt was totally at a loss for an explanation.

"Did you say that this happened at a 'healing service?' What is that?" Rick asked.

"Well," Matt responded, a little shaken, "it is a church service where the focus is on praying to God to heal those that are sick."

"Do these people become well instantly, like the ones Jesus healed here in the Bible?"

"Not instantly," Matt answered, "at least none that I have personally witnessed. But I have heard reports of instant miraculous healings in other places, like Africa."

"So then, God does not answer these prayers for healing—at least most of them. Do Christians then believe that it is not God's will for the majority to be healed?" Rick asked.

"Oh no!" Matt replied. "God loves His children, and He does not want them to suffer."

"What?" Rick asked in disbelief. "That is the exact opposite of the Apostle Paul's words. Here, read them."

Matt read the passages in Rick's notes:

> The Spirit Himself bears witness with our spirit that we are children of God, and if children, heirs also, heirs of God and fellow heirs with Christ, if indeed we suffer with Him in order that we may also be glorified with Him. (Romans 8:16,17)

> For to you it has been granted for Christ's sake, not only to believe in Him, but also to suffer for His sake. (Philippians 1:29)

> Therefore do not be ashamed of the testimony of our Lord, or of me His prisoner; but join with me in suffering for the gospel according to the power of God. (2 Timothy 1:8)

"These verses explicitly say that suffering is an expected part of being a child of God," Rick stated. "Is your God totally good?"

"Absolutely," Matt replied.

"How do you know?" Rick asked.

"God describes Himself that way in the Bible," answered Matt.

"Where?"

"Well, I can't show you exact verses," Matt stammered.

"Then how do you know that God is totally good?" Rick questioned. "If you are relying on what people have told you, they could have lied and told you the exact opposite of what the Bible actually teaches—just like all of these issues we were just discussing! Do Christians believe that God is all-powerful?"

"Yes," Matt said.

"How do you know?" Rick asked as Matt looked with a blank stare. "One would think that a totally good God would eliminate suffering, if He had the power to do so. Why then would the totally good, all-powerful God of Christianity want people to suffer—especially His own children?"

Matt sat there without an answer.

"Oh, look at the time!" Rick jumped up, gathering everything into his book bag. "I must get to class. Thanks for the interview." Rick rushed out of the restaurant as Matt smiled and gave him a courteous nod.

"Wow," Matt thought to himself. "I've been going to church for four years and reading my Bible almost every day. Almost everything that I have been taught about the Christian faith seems to be the exact opposite of the Word of God. How can that be?

"Yes, I'm a Christian—I know I'm a Christian! So, what do I believe? I need to get into a Bible study where I can find the true answers to those deep questions! The 'milk' is no longer good enough. I need the 'meat' of God's Word explained to me.

"Heavenly Father, help me to find a book, a teacher—anything—with the deep knowledge of Your Word. I need to understand Your ways, so that I may know You and love You more intimately. In Jesus' Name I pray, amen."

Matt's situation is all too common in the church today. Millions of Christians who have been going to church for years—for decades—are longing to understand God's ways. These sincere Christians desperately need to know what they should believe, and why.

Finding a resource that can help can be difficult. Delving into thousands of theological volumes can find one inundated with words almost impossible to pronounce. Reading countless writings of church fathers to systematically explain the Bible just does not seem to be an option.

This work is designed to answer the deep questions of God's ways directly from God's holy Word, the Bible. God's Word is replete with clear, consistent answers to questions like:

Who is God?

What is God's real purpose for the universe?

If God is totally good and powerful, why do evil and suffering exist?

What is God's purpose for this life?

Does man really have a free will?

How are men really saved from God's wrath against sin?

Can such salvation ever be lost?

Which Law does God expect man to obey?

This book examines the teachings in the modern church—where they agree with God's Word, and where they directly contradict it. The clear messages of God's Word are the major focus, making the many cited passages indispensable. It also addresses knowledge learned in seminary, and gleans from the writings of Christians whom God used mightily to transform His church throughout history. It is written as a story, in conversational language, making difficult doctrines easy to read and understand.

May God bless every reader with new insight into His ways, so that the reader may come to know and love Him more. This book hopefully will be an answer to Moses' prayer, which should be in the heart and on the lips of every child of God. Paraphrased from Exodus 33:13:

Lord,

If I, as Your child, have found favor in Your sight,

Let me know Your ways,

So that I may know and love You intimately,

And may forever find favor with You.

Let this life bring exceedingly great glory to You,

For otherwise it is not worth living.

2

Conversion

"Hey Dave! Wake up! I have to talk to you!"

Nick pounded on the dormitory room door with the tenacity of a thunderous jackhammer. Dave opened the door and stared into the face of a person who looked like he had just seen a ghost.

"I'm sorry if I woke you, Dave, but I have to talk to you!"

"No problem, Nick," Dave replied in a quiet manner. "Come on in."

"I hope I didn't wake you," Nick said as he plopped down in the chair by the desk, a desk that looked like all of the desks in all of the rooms in Gammage Hall.

"No, I wasn't sleeping. I had just finished praying for the guys on our floor...praying for you, as a matter of fact." Dave was searching Nick's face to find a clue to his urgency.

"Look, the weirdest thing just happened to me, and I need your help to figure it all out. I was doing some homework for an English class, and the most incredible thing happened!"

"From doing English homework? On a Friday night?" Dave was totally baffled.

Nick began a tale that would change his world. "I was feeling kind of low, and didn't feel like going out with the guys. So I stayed in, and thought I'd get some reading done for my English class. The class covers the works of C.S. Lewis...you know—*The Chronicles of Narnia: The Lion, The Witch and The Wardrobe*—that stuff."

Dave's eyes suddenly brightened. He knew C.S. Lewis' writings very well, being raised in a Christian family. Lewis' works are classics, telling the story of Jesus Christ, and explaining God's plan for mankind and His universe.

"Well, we have to read a book called *Mere Christianity* by next week, so I figured I'd get a good jump on it," Nick explained. "But as I read about God and His view of man, an intense feeling of horror and dread came over me. For the first time in my life, I could see that I am an extremely filthy person. For some reason, I knew that if I died and went into the presence of God for judgment, I was in deep, deep trouble!"

Dave sat quietly but listened carefully to every word Nick spoke.

"As I continued reading, this feeling of dread grew so bad I thought I was going to die! Finally, when I just couldn't take any more of it, I cried out, 'God, help me!' Then a really strange feeling swept over me. It was like ten million pounds were lifted off of my shoulders! I felt so light I thought I could fly! The dread of certain judgment was gone! It was like a light went on in my brain, and I knew God was real! He's alive, but I don't know anything about Him! Dave, what is going on here?"

"Praise God! Nick, you have been born again!" Dave exclaimed. Dave now understood the reason Nick came to see him. Dave was known as the dorm's "Born-again Christian," a title he treasured.

"What?" Nick asked, completely puzzled. "I've heard guys call you a 'born-againer,' but I never knew what they were talking about. So, what are you talking about?"

"Well," Dave began, "I guess it's best I explain everything from the start."

Nick nodded. That sounded logical to him.

"In the beginning, God created the heavens and the earth. He then created the first man, Adam, and the first woman, Eve. He created them just to love them and have a deep, personal relationship with them. Not that God needed them, for God is perfectly complete in and of Himself in every respect. But He wanted to show His deep love for them. He wanted a family."

Nick was hanging on every word Dave spoke, so he continued.

"God created a beautiful garden in which they could live, and told them that they could eat from any tree in the garden except one—the 'tree of the knowledge of good and evil.' Here, let me show you in the Bible, the Book of Genesis, chapter two."

Dave pulled off the desk a brown, leather-bound New American Standard Bible and began leafing through the thin pages. Nick recognized it immediately. It seemed that every time he saw Dave in the halls or on campus, he was carrying that book.

"Here we go," Dave said, finding the verses for which he was searching. "Read this, verses 16 and 17." He handed over the Bible, and Nick cradled it in his hands like a new father holding his newborn son.

Nick read:

> The LORD God commanded the man, saying, "From any tree of the
> garden you may eat freely;
> but from the tree of the knowledge of good and evil you shall not eat,
> for in the day that you eat from it you will surely die." (Genesis 2:16,17)

God's Standard for Entering Heaven

Nick felt a strange exhilaration reading the words, but he could not explain it.

"Adam and Eve, however, disobeyed God's commandment and ate from the forbidden tree. Because of this sin they died spiritually, meaning that their sin of disobedience destroyed their intimate relationship with God, the Giver of life," Dave proceeded. "God is perfectly holy, and will not tolerate sin in His family. Absolute perfection is God's standard for living in heaven with Him. Read the words of the Lord Jesus Christ in Matthew 5, verse 48."

Nick read, ""**Therefore, you are to be perfect as your heavenly Father is perfect**.""

"God drove Adam and Eve out of His paradise because of the Fall," explained Dave. "In order to live in heaven with God, one must be as perfect as the infinitely holy Almighty God is perfect. That is God's standard for entering heaven, and it does not change for anyone."

"Why is that?" asked Nick.

"Well, God made everything and sustains the very existence of everything. Therefore, He owns everything," Dave explained. "Since everything belongs to God, God makes the rules. But the reason one must be perfect to be in the presence of the eternally and perfectly holy God can be easily illustrated.

"Remember science class in high school? The teacher showed us a tube filled with pure oxygen. What happened when any impurity was introduced into the tube?"

"The impurity burned up," recalled Nick.

"Exactly," Dave responded. "Whenever the slightest impurity comes into the presence of pure oxygen, the impurity burns up. The same is true with the infinitely holy, pure Almighty God. Any person dying and going before God's throne had better be absolutely perfect as God is perfect, or that person will burn.

"In God's eyes," continued Dave, "Adam was the head—the legal representative—of all of mankind. As the father of the human race, as it went with Adam, so it went with all of Adam's descendants. Adam's disobedience not only ended his stay in the garden, but it caused an infinite break from the only holy Source of Life for all of his descendants as well.

"God's just punishment declared that every person born from Adam—which then involves any descendant of a human male—is credited with the 'original sin' of Adam on his or her soul at conception. Therefore, every human being born from a human male is imperfect from conception, separated from God's love, and subject to His condemnation for not meeting the standard of perfection."

"Wow," Nick grievously replied. "Where does it say that in there?"

"Read the words that God had inspired King David to write about himself in Psalm 51, verse 5," Dave answered, finding the page while Nick held the Bible.

"'Behold, I was brought forth in iniquity, and in sin my mother conceived me.'"

"Also, read the words God inspired the Apostle Paul to write in First Corinthians 15, verses 21 and 22." Dave was getting pretty fast at finding scriptures, and Nick was silently impressed.

"'For since by a man came death, by a man also came the resurrection from the dead. For as in Adam all die, so also in Christ all shall be made alive.'"

"The Book of Romans—chapter 5, verse 17—says about Adam and his descendants: 'by the transgression of the one, death reigned through the one.'" Dave hoped he was not going too quickly, but Nick seemed hungry for more. "Here, read the third verse in the second chapter of the Letter to the Ephesians, and verses 17 and 18 in the Apostle Peter's First Epistle."

Nick read:

Among them we too all formerly lived in the lusts of our flesh, indulging
the desires of the flesh and of the mind, and were by nature children of
wrath, even as the rest. (Ephesians 2:3)

If you address as Father the One who impartially judges according to
each one's work, conduct yourselves in fear during the time of your stay *on
earth*;
knowing that you were not redeemed with perishable things like silver
or gold from your futile way of life inherited from your forefathers.

(1 Peter 1:17,18)

"The 'original sin' of Adam, resulting in our 'futile way of life,' was inherited through our
fathers," Dave explained. "Adam's sin makes all of his posterity 'by nature children of wrath.'"

"So all of us are doomed to the wrath of God from the get-go because of the sin of Adam
on our souls," reasoned Nick. "There is no way I, or anyone else—being mere finite men with
sinful natures—can be as perfect as the infinitely perfect God. What hope is there?" Nick
definitely grasped the gravity of the human condition.

"Well, God did not create the human race just to throw every man and woman into the
fires of hell," Dave reasoned. "As I've said, God created man for deep, loving relationships...a
family.

"But mankind rebelled against God, and instead of serving God, we decided to serve
ourselves. We were created to worship and serve the Creator, but we worshiped and served
ourselves instead. This rebellion against God is called ***sin***, a heinous crime of disobedience
against the eternal holiness of God, punishable by eternal torture in hell.

"We made the deadly assumption that this life was ours to do with as we pleased. We
foolishly assumed that we owned our lives because we were in control. But one only owns what
one creates, buys, or is given as a gift.

"We had nothing to do with creating our lives. We had no part in being born, for we were
not even around. We never bought this life, for God never put it up for sale. Contrary to
modern thought, God never gave us this life as a gift to do our own thing.

"We are like a cab driver who hires on with a taxi company. Though we drive the cab, and
are totally responsible for the decisions we make while driving, we don't own the cab. We didn't
create the cab, nor did we buy it. The cab company bought the cab, and, as its owner, reserves
all rights to its use. In the same way, we don't own this life. God owns all life, because He
created and sustains all life, and thus reserves all rights to the use of all life.

"But in our rebellion, we stole this life for our own selfish purposes. God gave us life in
order to love, serve and glorify Him. But with our sinful natures, we rebelled against God, using
this life to love and serve ourselves. Thus, everything we do is sin, including breathing, thinking,
speaking and acting. Therefore, everything we do deserves God's righteous judgment. Isaiah the
prophet boldly says, 'For all of us have become like one who is unclean, and all our righteous
deeds are like a filthy garment' (Isaiah 64:6).

"This is the dread that God was revealing to you as you read through *Mere Christianity*.

Your sin is the incredible weight you felt on your soul as God opened your eyes to your total depravity. If God had left you in that condition, in the moment you died you would have gone before His judgment throne with sin on your account.

"Since the standard for going to heaven is to be as perfect as God is perfect, you would have been declared guilty of sin, and would have been rejected for entrance into heaven. You would have been left to pay for your sins—your heinous crimes of rebellion against God—by eternal conscious torture in hell."

Dave was gauging Nick's facial expressions. Understanding the severity of one's sinful condition before God is critical to understanding one's desperate need to be saved from His wrath.

"As a result of being born with a selfish, sinful nature," Dave maintained, "everything we do in this life, no matter how good it looks from the outside, is tainted by sin. We were made to worship and serve God, but we chose to worship and serve ourselves. Therefore, all of our deeds are tainted by our total depravity—even 'good' works like giving to charity, or what we would consider 'service to God,' such as going to church."

Being completely honest with himself, Nick had to admit this was true in his life. "So, even if I lived a 'perfect life' in man's eyes, or even a 'good life' where my 'good deeds' outweighed my bad ones, I would still be found guilty before God because of the 'original sin' on my soul."

"Correct," Dave affirmed. "God is not only perfectly holy, He is perfectly just. *Justice* means perfect adherence to a standard, and corresponding punishment for failure. God's standard for being in His family and entering heaven is to be as perfect as He is perfect (Matthew 5:48). One cannot be perfect with the 'original sin' of Adam on his soul."

"So how can God save me from hell—a sentence I know I deserve?" Nick asked.

Aaah, the most crucial question anyone could ask, thought Dave.

All for the Honor of God the Son

"Before He made the universe, God had His perfect plan for His creation. The entire purpose of this plan was, is, and ever will be **the glory of God**. God is to be adored and worshiped by all of His creation because He deserves it. He is the Almighty Creator who gives existence to everything, and sustains the existence of everything.

"Without God, we would not exist. Also, you, and I, and everything else continue to exist, and take our next breaths, only because God ordained it in His plan that He set before the creation of His universe.

"At that time, God the Father chose some people to be in His family for **God's ultimate purpose: to honor and glorify God the Son, Jesus Christ**. To ensure the supremacy of Christ's honor, God, in His infinite wisdom, subjected His entire creation, including the human race, to slavery to evil. The only way out of that slavery would be through God the Son, Jesus Christ. Christ Jesus would then receive all the glory as the only Savior of the universe—the only way of escape from slavery to the devil. Read these two passages I have marked."

Nick read:

> For the anxious longing of the creation waits eagerly for the revealing of the sons of God.

> For the creation was subjected to futility, not willingly, but because of
> Him who subjected it, in hope
>   that the creation itself also will be set free from its slavery to corruption
> into the freedom of the glory of the children of God.
>   For we know that the whole creation groans and suffers the pains of
> childbirth together until now. (Romans 8:19-22)

> The Lord's bond-servant must not be quarrelsome, but be kind to all,
> able to teach, patient when wronged,
>   with gentleness correcting those who are in opposition, if perhaps
> God may grant them repentance leading to the knowledge of the truth,
>   and they may come to their senses *and escape* from the snare of the
> devil, having been held captive by him to do his will. (2 Timothy 2:24-26)

"All humans conceived from a human father are born spiritually dead in sin, separated from God, the only Source of life," Dave continued. "We are in dire need of rescue from slavery to the devil, and desperate for a Savior to clear our 'rap sheet' of crimes. But no one who was born of a human male could pay for your sin or mine, because he himself would already have the 'original sin' of Adam on his soul, and would be just as guilty as you or me!

"So, God determined to pay for all of the sins of all of His people—those whom He chose to be in His family—by Himself! God would become a man, though always still being God, for the Eternal God can never stop being God! God the Son, Jesus Christ, would add humanity to His divinity!"

"But how does God becoming man make me as perfect as God is perfect?" questioned Nick.

"There are only two ways a being can be as perfect as God is perfect," Dave replied. "The first is to be God Himself. Any sane human being would admit that he is not the God of the Bible, who created the universe; is fully present everywhere at all times in that universe; and has all knowledge of past, present and future.

"The only other way to be perfect as God is perfect is for God Himself to pay the penalty for your sins, and to legally transfer to your account His perfection! Remember, God is eternally just and must punish sin. God simply cannot just ignore our crimes against His law, or God Himself would sin against His own standard of perfect justice.

"God, eternally perfect and without sin, is the only one able to pay the just penalty for your sin to wipe your slate clean. The just punishment for sinful rebellion against the Source of Life is death. God the Son—who has never and can never sin—would die in man's place!

"Since the worth of God's life is infinite, His death can pay for all of the sins of all of His people. Though the number of those sins is vast, it is still a finite number! God legally transfers the sin of every person He chose to be in His family to Christ on the cross!

"God then transfers to the account of every chosen person the perfect, sinless life that God the Son Jesus Christ lived while on earth as a man! Because Jesus Christ *is* God, His perfect life transferred to your account makes you as perfect as God is perfect!

"It is as if you caused a fatal auto accident, and you died as well. The judge demands that you pay the victim's family for the damage and suffering you caused. But you cannot pay, for you are also dead—utterly helpless to make any amends. To clear your name, your brother asks to pay the legal judgment, and the judge agrees to this plan. When the payment is made, though you were totally guilty, your name is now completely cleared.

"In like manner, God legally transfers all of your sin—past, present and future—to Christ. God the Son pays the penalty for them in His death on the cross. God also legally transfers God the Son's perfect righteousness to your account, so that, even though you still have a sin nature, you are now *legally* as perfect as God is perfect! Christ dies for you, and makes you alive in Christ! How about that for an amazing solution?" Dave asked.

"Incredible! God would die for me? He would take on my death sentence? Your death sentence? What love! But how could God become a man and avoid the 'original sin' of Adam?" Nick was addressing a critical issue.

"Great question!" Dave was impressed with Nick's ability to reason through essential doctrines of the Christian faith. "Back in the Book of Genesis—chapter three, verse 15—God promised a fallen Adam that He would bring a Savior who would be of 'the seed of a *woman*,' not the seed of a man. God used His prophet Isaiah to give more details 700 years before the Savior would be born. Here, read Isaiah 7:14."

"'Therefore the Lord Himself will give you a sign: Behold, a virgin will be with child, and bear a son, and she will call His name Immanuel (which means "God is with us").'" Nick enjoyed reading the passages selected by Dave.

"To avoid the 'original sin' of Adam, the Savior had to be born without the involvement of a human male. To be the Savior of humans, He had to be a human, and thus had to be born of a human," concluded Dave. "God's amazing plan included the virgin Mary giving birth, something never before seen in human history, and never to be repeated! God the Father sent God the Son to earth to become a man and pay the price for the sins of His people!"

"What a plan! Only God Himself could come up with that one!" Nick exclaimed.

"Right! God the Son, Jesus Christ, in obedience to God the Father, left His glorious throne in heaven, and gave up infinity, in order to take on the limits of human flesh. Though He was still fully God, the Lord Jesus voluntarily laid aside His rights and privileges as God as an example for us in totally depending on God the Father for everything," Dave explained.

"God left His throne, and gave up infinity, and gave up His life for us? That's astounding! Absolutely amazing! And up until tonight, I could not have cared less! And all for me, a guy who only looked out for himself! Now that is what I would call true love!" Nick asserted.

"Yes!" Dave agreed. "Read Ephesians 2:4 and 5."

Nick read:

> But God, being rich in mercy, because of His great love with which He
> loved us,
>> even when we were dead in our transgressions, made us alive together
> with Christ (by grace you have been saved). (Ephesians 2:4,5)

Nick began reciting, "'Amazing grace, how sweet the sound, that saved a wretch like me!' I remember the words of that song from my childhood."

"Yes, God's grace is amazing! God the Son, Jesus Christ, lived a perfect, sinless life," Dave continued. "He declared that He was God Almighty, the Messiah, the Savior of His people, who had come in the flesh. Jesus asserted in John 14:9: '"He who has seen Me has seen the Father."'

"But the religious leaders—who were pretending to serve God while really serving themselves—rejected Jesus' claim to be God Almighty, and demanded proof.

"So Jesus told the religious leaders that He would allow them to kill Him, and then He would do something ordinary man could never do: He would raise Himself from the dead, thereby proving to be God! Here, read Jesus' words in the Gospel of John, chapter 10, verses 17 and 18."

Nick read:

> "For this reason, the Father loves Me, because I lay down my life that
> I may take it again.
>
> "No one takes it away from Me, but I lay it down on My own initiative.
> I have authority to lay it down, and I have authority to take it up again. This
> commandment I received from My Father." (John 10:17,18)

"Wow," Nick remarked, "If Jesus brought Himself back to life from a corpse, He would have to be God. No man can do that. Harry Houdini, the famous magician, promised his wife he would communicate with her from the afterlife if it was at all possible, but he never did."

"Good point," Dave agreed. "The Lord Jesus, however, came back physically with the same scars from His crucifixion. He also ate breakfast with seven disciples on the shore of the Sea of Galilee. The last chapter of each of the four Gospels, as well as the first chapter of the Book of Acts, detail many historical accounts of the resurrected Christ.

"Then the Lord Jesus ascended into Heaven where He sits at the right hand of the Father. He now intercedes for the saints, or, in other words, prays to the Father on our behalf."

"But why did He have to leave?" asked Nick.

"Well, for two reasons. First, remember Jesus gave up being only an infinite spirit to take on a finite, physical human body. By staying, He could only be in one place at one time.

"Secondly, Christ promised to send the Holy Spirit to indwell His children, empowering us to love and serve God. The Holy Spirit can be anywhere and everywhere He desires, and His chief mission is to glorify Christ. Here, read Jesus' words in John 16, verses 7, 8, and 13."

Nick read:

> "But I tell you the truth, it is to your advantage that I go away; for if I
> do not go away, the Helper will not come to you; but if I go, I will send Him
> to you.
>
> "And He, when He comes, will convict the world concerning sin, and
> righteousness, and judgment;
>
> "But when He, the Spirit of truth, comes, He will guide you into all the
> truth." (John 16:7,8,13a)

"It is the Holy Spirit who raises spiritually-dead corpses to life," claimed Dave. "It was the Holy Spirit who opened your eyes to your sin tonight. Otherwise, you never would have even considered that you were heading to eternal torture for your sin against God."

"That's true," Nick agreed.

"The term is **regeneration**. That's a fancy word meaning 'born again.' You were born physically the first time with the 'original sin' of Adam on your soul. You were born again spiritually tonight when God placed the Holy Spirit within you and forgave you of all of your sins," Dave explained. "Read Second Corinthians 5:17."

"'Therefore, if any man is in Christ, he is a new creature; the old things passed away; behold, new things have come,'" quoted Nick.

"To be 'in Christ,'" Dave clarified, "means that God has transferred to your account the perfect, sinless life that Christ lived on earth! You are now a member of God's family, and you are legally perfect in His eyes. The 'old things' that have 'passed away' are your sins that have now been forgiven. Remember the weight that you felt being lifted from you? Christ was taking your sins upon Himself, relieving you of the guilt and condemnation of living in disobedience to God!"

"Awesome," Nick mused. "It's so incredible, that if it wasn't true, I could never believe it!"

"Yes, our God is awesome!" agreed Dave. "Now, let's go back over the answer to your question of what happened to you tonight."

"Please do!" begged Nick. "That's a lot of stuff!"

Dave began summarizing.

"First and foremost, God is the awesome Creator who deserves all glory and honor because He made and sustains everything that exists.

"The Father's entire purpose for creation is to honor and glorify God the Son, Jesus Christ.

"God desired a family that would honor Him, and for you to be a part of that family.

"The Almighty is perfectly holy and will tolerate no sin in His family. In order to live with Him in heaven, God's standard is to be as perfect as He is perfect.

"God set up the condition where humans would desperately need a Savior by subjecting His creation to slavery to evil.

"That condition was brought about by the sin of Adam.

"God's ingenious plan to enslave creation to evil assured the total glory and honor of God the Son, Jesus Christ, by making Christ the only way out of that slavery.

"God's justice declared that Adam's 'original sin' would be imputed, or credited, to the account of everyone born of a human male. This created a desperate need for every human to be saved from His wrath.

"Next, God the Son, Jesus Christ, left His throne and took on humanity without 'original sin' by being born of a virgin woman.

"The Lord Jesus came to His people announcing that He was God Almighty in the flesh, the one-and-only Savior of mankind, and man rejected Him.

"To prove He was God, Jesus allowed man to crucify Him, and then He raised Himself from the dead.

"Because the value of God's life is infinite, His death paid for all of the sins of all of the people He would choose to be in His family. He died in their place, satisfying the perfect justice of God.

"Jesus then ascended back to His throne in Heaven, and sent the Holy Spirit into the world to convict it of sin, righteousness and judgment.

"God, at the exact moment that He had ordained it, placed His Holy Spirit in you to raise you from your spiritual death, open your eyes to your sin and depravity, instill in you your desperate need to be saved from God's wrath, and give you the power to cry out to Him for help.

"God the Holy Spirit had freed you from enslavement to your sinful nature and captivity by our enemy the devil, and brought you into His family.

"As a family member, Jesus Christ's death paid the penalty for all of your sins—past, present and future. God transferred all of your sins to Christ on the cross.

"As a family member, God imputed—credited, or legally transferred—to your account Christ's perfect life, thus making you as perfect as God is perfect—because Jesus *is* God.

"Nick, you have been born again...born from above...born of God. Welcome to the family of God!" Dave exclaimed.

"Wow! Thank you, God! Thank you, Jesus! Thank you, Dave, for explaining all of this to me!" Nick could hardly contain his excitement.

"Repent and Believe!"

"Now, there are two critical parts to beginning your walk with Christ. The first is **repent**, and the second, **believe**. I can't emphasize enough the importance of understanding these two terms."

"Okay," Nick replied, "I'm listening."

"The first words of Jesus in the Gospel of Mark are these: '"The time is fulfilled, and the kingdom of God is at hand; repent and believe in the gospel"' (Mark 1:15). Jesus defines the word 'repent' in Mark 8:34 and 35. Here, read His words," Dave directed as he pointed to the verses.

Nick read:

> And He summoned the crowd with His disciples, and said to them, "If anyone wishes to come after Me, he must deny himself, and take up his cross and follow Me.
>
> "For whoever wishes to save his life will lose it, but whoever loses his life for My sake and the gospel's will save it." (Mark 8:34,35)

"To **repent** means much more than to change one's mind about God," Dave explained. "It means to change one's master. Before we were saved, we thought we were the masters of our lives. But we were dead in our sinful rebellion against God, having stolen this life to serve ourselves. Unable to do anything to fix the broken relationship with the only Source of Life, we were destined for hell. Now God has raised you up from spiritual death to life in Christ by placing His Holy Spirit within you.

"Once you are spiritually alive with the indwelling Holy Spirit, the Lord Jesus requires you to embrace His deal. God's command is this: You give this life back to Him, its rightful owner, for whatever He desires to do with it. Christ can make you president, or He can put you in a prison cell to be tortured—whatever He desires.

"You give up this life—your opinions, your goals, and your ideas of what you think is true.

You give this life back to Christ, who truly created, sustains, and owns it, for whatever He decides to do with it. In return, His death pays for all of your sins, you are credited with His perfect life, and you will live forever with Him in heaven!

"But if you hold on to this life—your opinions, your goals, your desires—and live it for yourself, you will lose your life and pay for your own sins in hell," Dave warned.

"Now, let me get this straight," Nick pondered. "I give up this life—these 70 or so years—to Christ, for whatever He wants to do with it. In return, He forgives all of my sins and I get to live in absolute paradise for eternity?"

"That is God's deal," Dave responded. "It's called **repentance**, which means changing your mind about who really owns this life, and giving this life back to Christ—it's rightful owner—for whatever He desires to do with it.

"To repent is a life-or-death matter. Listen to Jesus' responses to the crowd talking about the news of the day:

> Now on the same occasion there were some present who reported to Him about the Galileans whose blood Pilate had mixed with their sacrifices.
>
> And Jesus said to them, "Do you suppose that these Galileans were *greater* sinners than all *other* Galileans because they suffered this *fate?*
>
> "I tell you, no, but unless you repent, you will all likewise perish.
>
> "Or do you suppose that those eighteen on whom the tower in Siloam fell and killed them were *worse* culprits than all the men who live in Jerusalem?
>
> "I tell you, no, but unless you repent, you will all likewise perish."
>
> (Luke 13:1-5)

"Jesus tells two **parables**—stories with moral lessons—in the Gospel of Luke, chapter 14, about counting the cost of giving this life back to Him. Let me read them to you."

"Okay," answered Nick.

Dave read:

> Now large crowds were going along with Him; and He turned and said to them,
>
> "If anyone comes to Me, and does not hate (by comparison of his love for Me) his own father and mother and wife and children and brothers and sisters, yes, and even his own life, he cannot be My disciple.
>
> "Whoever does not carry his own cross and come after Me cannot be My disciple.
>
> "For which one of you, when he wants to build a tower, does not first sit down and calculate the cost to see if he has enough to complete it?
>
> "Otherwise, when he has laid a foundation and is not able to finish, all who observe it begin to ridicule him, saying, 'This man began to build and was not able to finish.'
>
> "Or what king, when he sets out to meet another king in battle, will not first sit down and consider whether he is strong enough with ten thousand

men to encounter the one coming against him with twenty thousand?

"Or else, while the other is still far away, he sends a delegation and asks for terms of peace.

"So then, none of you can be My disciple who does not give up all his own possessions." (Luke 14:25-33; *parenthesis from margin*)

"To repent—giving back this life to Christ for whatever He desires to do with it—is a very serious commitment. It will cost you everything you have—your family, your possessions, even your own earthly life. To repent means to give it all up to Christ. God may give it all back to you and more. He may also take it all away. To hold on to anything means you have not repented."

"But from what you just explained to me—" reasoned Nick, "what God has done for me, and what Jesus promises me, I'd be a fool not to embrace His deal. He can have this life—these measly 70 or so years on this earth! I just want to live with Him forever in His glorious heaven!"

"Great!" exclaimed Dave. "The second part of the start of your walk with Christ is to **believe**. This does not mean that you know about God, or believe that He exists. The Apostle James says that even the demons believe in God, but they are not going to heaven (James 2:19)! Many, many people claim to 'believe in God,' but that is not even close to what the Lord Jesus means here.

"To '**believe in Christ**' requires that you now commit, or entrust, your entire spiritual well-being to Him. You put zero faith in your abilities, deeds, and any future accomplishments to get you into heaven.

"To '**believe in Christ**' means to place total trust in Christ's two-part perfect work for your salvation: His death on the cross to pay for your past, present and future sins; and His perfect life that was imputed, or legally credited, to your account. Here, read Romans 5:8-10."

Nick read:

> But God demonstrates His own love toward us, in that while we were yet sinners, Christ died for us.
>
> Much more then, having now been justified by His blood, we shall be saved from the wrath *of God* through Him.
>
> For if while we were enemies we were reconciled to God through the death of His Son, much more, having been reconciled, we shall be saved by His life. (Romans 5:8-10)

"You are perfect in God's eyes not because you are a good person, or do good works, but only because God chose to forgive your sins and credit your account with the perfect life of Christ to cover your imperfection. Adding anything of yours to God's salvation would only taint Christ's two-part perfect work credited to your account, and then you would no longer be as perfect as God is perfect! Do you understand?"

"You are saying that in order to live with God I must be absolutely perfect as He is perfect. Since I am not, I must trust totally in Christ's two-part perfect work—His death on the cross to pay for my sins, and His perfectly sinless life credited to my account—which God gives to me when I am born again," Nick figured.

"Excellent!" Dave replied. "To *repent* means to totally give this life back to Christ, its rightful owner, for His use. To *believe* is to totally trust in Christ's perfection credited to you and nothing else for salvation! **Christ's commandment requires *both* responses to His salvation**. Do these terms make sense?"

"Yes, I think so," answered Nick.

"Many people claim they 'believe in God' or 'believe in Jesus,' and they think they are going to heaven," warned Dave. "But their meaning of 'believe' must be the same meaning that Jesus applied to the word—total trust in His work alone for salvation. I may 'believe' that the President of the United States exists and has great power, but I most certainly do not trust in him for salvation from the wrath of God due to me for my sins.

"Both responses to the Lord Jesus' deal must be obeyed as proof that Christ's perfection was applied to a person's account. One may not simply repent. One must also believe in Christ, relying on *His* perfect work alone, and not adding any personal merit or good deeds into the mix. One may not simply trust in Christ's two-part perfect work for salvation. One must also repent—giving up this life totally to Christ—or Jesus insists that person will perish.

"Why don't we pray to God and thank Him for giving you new life in Christ, and solidify the deal with Him?" Dave asked.

"Okay," Nick responded somewhat nervously, "but I've never prayed seriously before. Maybe you could start."

"Sure," Dave said. "Remember, even though God is holy and deserving of the utmost respect, He is now our Father, and He loves us dearly, and He greatly desires that we come to Him in prayer. Let's join hands."

Dave reached over and took Nick's hands into his.

"Dear Heavenly Father, thank You for Your great love for us! Thank You for sending Your Son to die for us and pay for our sins against You! Thank You for Your resurrection, Lord Jesus, and for raising us up from spiritual death! Thank You for sending Your Holy Spirit to be with us forever, and to guide us into Your truth!

"Heavenly Father, I thank You for giving Nick, my new brother in Christ, eternal life! Thank You for opening his eyes to his sin and his dire need for You! I ask that You would bless him abundantly in his first steps as a Christian, and pour out Your Spirit upon him! Protect him from the enemy, and give him an overwhelming desire to know You and love You! Teach him Your ways, Lord, and let him glorify You by his life!"

Dave squeezed Nick's hands, signaling him to begin praying.

"Dear God," he began somewhat nervously, "I am truly sorry for my sins. You gave up everything for me and I didn't even care. All I cared about was myself. Forgive me. I give up this life to You for You to use any way You want. I put all of my trust in You—Your gift of perfection and Your death on the cross—for my salvation. I desire to know You and love You with all my heart. Help me to do what You want. I can't thank You enough for what You did for me."

Dave finished, "In Jesus' Name we pray, amen!"

"Amen!" Nick echoed.

The Four Basics

Dave got up and embraced his new brother. "You asked God to help you to do what He wants," Dave said, "so here are **The Four Basics**: Pray every day, study the Bible every day, go to church to worship God as often as possible, and fellowship with committed Christians."

"Pray," Nick repeated, "every day. Study the Bible every day. Go to church to worship God, and fellowship with Christians."

"Praying means talking to your loving Heavenly Father, just like we did," Dave explained. "You should start every day by talking to God first. You give each day to Him for His use, asking Him to fill you with His Holy Spirit who empowers you to glorify God.

"Here is a Bible of your very own," continued Dave, pulling down *The NASB Study Bible* from the bookshelf over his desk. "Read it every day without fail. Start here in the Gospel of Matthew. This is your spiritual food, and not reading God's Word will result in spiritually starving yourself. You wouldn't miss eating meals, would you?"

"No way," assured Nick, "not often anyway!"

"I know your schedule...it's similar to mine. Why don't we get together every Tuesday afternoon after lunch and study the Bible together?" asked Dave. "That way you can ask me any questions you may have."

"Great!" Nick responded. "I was hoping you would help me out there."

"My pleasure. Can you go with me to church on Sunday?" Dave was making sure Nick started his walk with Christ by committing to do The Four Basics for Christian growth. "I'll be teaching the College & Career Sunday school Bible study before the worship service. The goal of our Bible study—and of our Christian lives—is to know God intimately, and enjoy Him forever as our Father. In fact, I'm giving them a pop quiz on the Bible!"

"Wow," Nick thought out loud, "I haven't been to church in ages. But if that is what God wants me to do, I'll make it for sure!"

"Here, read it for yourself," encouraged Dave. "The Letter to the Hebrews, chapter 10, beginning with verse 23."

Nick read:

> Let us hold fast the confession of our hope without wavering, for He
> who promised is faithful;
> > and let us consider how to stimulate one another to love and good deeds,
> > not forsaking our own assembling together, as is the habit of some,
> but encouraging *one another*; and all the more as you see the day drawing
> near. (Hebrews 10:23-25)

"We go to church first and foremost to worship our faithful God who saved us," Dave explained. "Second, God gives us gifts and talents to share with the church, the body of Christ. We need the church, and the church needs us! Third, we hear the Word of God read and explained by the pastor, and participate in the Sacraments the Lord established. And last but not least, we meet committed Christians there for fellowship, the fourth of The Four Basics."

"The Sacraments?" Nick asked.

"Christ Jesus established two very important Sacraments for His church to observe: Baptism and The Lord's Supper, sometimes called Holy Communion," explained Dave. "We will be partaking in The Lord's Supper during the church worship service. It's a solemn occasion to remember the awesome sacrifice Christ made on the cross for our sins.

"Baptism is a physical testimony to the church that you have died and have buried the old Nick, and that you have emerged from that 'watery grave' a new person in Christ. Have you ever been baptized?"

"No, I don't think so."

"Would you like to be baptized as a new believer in Christ? It is an important step of obedience to God, and we can arrange it with the pastor at church this Sunday," informed Dave.

"Okay," answered Nick. "Whatever the Lord wants of me. This is His life now!"

"That is the perfect Christian attitude!" Dave applauded. "Every Christian who struggles with his walk with Christ is inevitably disobeying God by not concentrating on doing The Four Basics. Since we desire to obey God and receive His blessings, The Four Basics must be at the center of our attention. Repeat them for me, so I know you have them."

"'Pray every day, study the Bible every day, go to church to worship God as often as possible, and fellowship with committed Christians,'" quoted Nick. "I can't wait to go to church to worship my God who saved me!"

"Great!" Dave said. "Meet me here Sunday morning at nine, and we'll go together. Remember to read your Bible beginning from the Gospel of Matthew, where I marked it. And pray to God—praising Him for saving you, and asking Him to help you understand His Word.

"Come Tuesday, I'm sure you'll have lots of questions. We'll start studying the Bible and learning the essentials that God wants every believer to know. You are beginning the most exciting adventure possible by walking with Almighty God, the Creator and Sustainer of the universe!"

"This is awesome!" Nick exclaimed. "I'll start reading the Gospel of Matthew in the morning, and I'll see you here Sunday morning!"

"Welcome to the family of God, brother," Dave said, embracing Nick at the door. "If you need me, I'll be around most of the day tomorrow. Have a great night's sleep!"

"If I can get to sleep! I'm still buzzing from what God has done for me! I'll call you tomorrow," Nick said as he exited. "Praise God!"

"Yes!" Dave echoed. "Praise God!"

3

What A Mighty God We Serve

"Surprise! Surprise!"

Dave shouted over the pleasant noise of fellowship ringing through the Sunday school room at Grace Chapel. His unusual greeting caught the attention of the College & Career class, and they made their way to their respective seats, quieting down.

"Yes, ladies and gentlemen!" Dave exclaimed as he took his place at the front of the class with paper in hand. "It's a pop quiz!"

A collective groan echoed through the classroom, followed by laughter. The forty or so students ranged in age from 17 to 39, and were equally numbered in gender. Some have been Christians for decades, while others, like Nick, were recent converts.

"One particular issue in the New Testament Gospels really raised the ire of the Lord Jesus," Dave proposed as he began passing out the quizzes. "Does anyone know what that was?"

"Giving pop quizzes?" Paul asked as he grabbed the papers from Dave's hand. The room exploded in laughter, and a big grin formed on Dave's face.

Ed, sitting near the back of the room, raised his hand and said, "Well, Jesus made a whip and began driving the sellers and cashiers from the Temple."

"Very good," Dave replied, "and that altercation was just a symptom of a grievous sin being committed in Israel. Anna, turn to Mark 7, and read verses 6 through 13 please."

Anna, sitting near the front, flipped the pages of her Bible and found the passage as Dave finished passing out the quizzes. He usually chose Anna to read the longer excerpts because she never became nervous reading to a group.

Anna read:

And He said to them, "Rightly did Isaiah prophesy of you hypocrites, as it is written:

'THIS PEOPLE HONORS ME WITH THEIR LIPS,
> BUT THEIR HEART IS FAR AWAY FROM ME.

'BUT IN VAIN DO THEY WORSHIP ME,
> TEACHING AS DOCTRINES THE PRECEPTS OF MEN.'

"Neglecting the commandment of God, you hold to the tradition of men."

He was also saying to them, "You are experts at setting aside the commandment of God in order to keep your tradition.

"For Moses said, 'HONOR YOUR FATHER AND YOUR MOTHER'; and, 'HE WHO SPEAKS EVIL OF FATHER OR MOTHER, IS TO BE PUT TO DEATH';

but you say, 'If a man says to *his* father or *his* mother, whatever I have that would help you is Corban (that is to say, given *to God*),'

you no longer permit him to do anything for *his* father or *his* mother;

thus invalidating the word of God by your tradition which you have handed down; and you do many things such as that." (Mark 7:6-13)

"Thank you, Anna," Dave acknowledged. "The heinous sin of setting aside God's holy Word in favor of man-made traditions is rampant in the church today. This sin was one of the foremost reasons the Jews missed the long-awaited visitation of their Messiah. It is also one of the foremost reasons the modern church is so anemic and confused.

"Ever watch people trying to find a ripe watermelon at the grocery store?" Dave asked. "Some people thump it with their hand, thinking the sound might give them a clue. Some pick it up and shake it, and still others put it up to their ears! I'm not sure *what* they are doing!

"But agriculture experts say the correct way to tell if a particular watermelon is ripe is to look at the underside, and if there is yellow coloration, it's ready to eat!

"The modern church is very much like those shoppers," Dave continued. "There are many man-made traditions being taught, and then there is God's eternal Word. We listen to sermons on Christian radio, watch preachers on television, read books by Christian authors, and hear the Word expounded during the Sunday worship service—and they all use the Bible! Can we really tell which teachings are the man-made traditions, and which are truly the Word of God?"

Dave looked around at the faces of his students. He could tell that his subject was causing deep thought throughout the room.

"Only God's originally intended meaning conveyed through the writers that He inspired is God's holy Word. All other interpretations are mere man-made speculations, and God does not support speculation. God supports truth. *Truth* is reality according to the all-knowing, eternally righteous Creator God. Truth is not reality according to the perceptions of fallible, finite man.

"Language, and the meaning of words, change over time. For example, a teenager hearing his favorite song may exclaim, 'That was *bad!*' The term 'bad' here has the exact opposite meaning of its original usage!

"When we assign meaning to the terms in God's Word according to our modern understanding, we can come up with teachings that are the exact opposite of God's intentions! If we then hold to our understanding instead of determining God's original meaning, we can be disobeying God while claiming to believe in the Bible! Over time, these misunderstandings can become accepted teachings, which then become cemented as tradition.

"The Lord Jesus scolded the Pharisees and scribes for their hypocrisy in setting aside the Word of God for their traditions. This sin is obviously very grievous to God," Dave explained, "because it leads to man-made error, and still more error, until the truth is gone.

"The Pop Quiz today is a test of some of the things you may have heard taught or preached. Some or all of the statements may be biblical, and therefore true. Some or all of the statements may be traditions of men.

"As you read through each statement, place an 'X' on the line before the number if you think the statement is supported by God's Word as truth. At the end of the quiz, add up all of the 'X's' that you marked on all pages and write the total at the bottom of the last page. Ready? Go!"

The College & Career group tore into the test like a grandma looking through a grocery store bin for the ripest watermelon for the annual family picnic. Immediately questions began to arise. Jennifer raised her hand, and Dave acknowledged her with a nod.

"So, what do you mean by—"

"Just take the statements for what they say," interrupted Dave with a smile. He obviously anticipated the questions. "There is no need to read anything into them. We'll discuss the statements after everyone has finished taking the quiz."

"Okay," Jennifer said, as she went back to work on the task at hand. The class seemed to be moving along at a decent rate, as the sound of rustling pages became more and more frequent throughout the room.

Pop Quiz on Biblical Teachings

Please place an "X" in the space before each sentence if the statement is true. Please note that how you feel about a concept is not being asked, but if the statement is supported by God's holy Word, and therefore true. At the end, please add up all "X's" on all pages and write the total on the line provided.

____ 1. In creating the universe, God set up the laws of nature to run it and He does not intervene.

____ 2. God is all-loving and all-forgiving.

____ 3. God loves all sinners but hates their sins.

____ 4. God loves everyone and has a wonderful plan for each life.

____ 5. God did not plan the Fall of Adam before creation.

____ 6. When Adam sinned, he gave ownership of this world to Satan.

____ 7. Salvation is a gift of God, but, like any gift, we must reach out and take it.

____ 8. God would never violate man's "free will" to accept or reject Christ, for that would be unloving.

____ 9. Man is born with a "free will," which means he possesses the ability to accept or reject Christ as his Savior.

___10. Predestination means that God, before creation, looked down the corridors of time to see who would choose Jesus as Savior, and God then chose those ones to be saved.

___11. Salvation is a decision each person is responsible to make.

___12. No one can come to Jesus unless the Father draws, or woos, him.

___13. God is always fair.

___14. By dying on the cross for man's sins, Jesus only made salvation possible.

___15. Jesus' death on the cross paid for all of the sins of all of mankind.

___16. God is not willing for anyone to perish, but for everyone to come to repentance.

___17. In the Bible, the word "all" always means "all without exception."

___18. In the Bible, the phrase "the whole world" always means "everyone living on the face of the earth."

___19. All people are children of God and are part of His family.

___20. All that is necessary to be saved is to confess with your mouth Jesus as Lord and believe in your heart that God raised Him from the dead.

___21. Jesus stands at the door of the sinner's heart, just waiting for him to let Him in.

___22. The essence of the gospel is to accept Jesus Christ as your personal Lord and Savior in order to be saved from your sins.

___23. In the process of salvation, faith is man's responsibility—to believe the gospel of Jesus Christ.

___24. Jesus did all He could do on the cross in paying for man's sins—now it's up to man.

___25. Salvation is like God giving a man mountain-climbing gear, but it is up to the man to climb to the top to be finally saved.

___26. A person who is truly born-again (saved) can lose his salvation.

___27. The doctrine "Once saved, always saved" results in "greasy grace," where a person can sin all he wants and still be saved.

___28. Christians are still under the authority of the Law of Moses.

___29. Christians are still under the authority of the Ten Commandments.

Thank you for your participation. Please add up all the X's and write the number below.

———————

(Before reading on for the answers, take the quiz yourself!)

The last person to put down his pencil was Ed. "Whew! That was tougher than I thought it would be!" he remarked, as Dave took his place at the front of the class.

"Not to embarrass anyone, for you don't know the answers...by a show of hands, how many people had more than 15 'X's'?" Dave asked, as about half of the students in the room raised their hands. "How many had five to 15 statements marked?" About a third of the class raised their hands. "Anyone have less than five marked?" Six students raised their hands.

Dave turned and approached the blackboard at the front of the class and picked up a piece of chalk. "The correct answer for the number of statements that are true, supported by God's holy Word—" Dave proceeded as he drew a large "O" on the board, "is zero."

Most of the class looked on in disbelief. "Which means," Dave continued, "that every one of the statements are man-made traditions that God's Word specifically *rejects.*"

"I can't believe that!" Matt, sitting next to Anna, declared somewhat loudly. "Surely numbers 3, 4, 5 and 7 are biblical!"

"During the next couple of weeks, we will cover each statement and investigate what the Bible really has to say on each subject," Dave assured the class. "And we will begin with the first one today. You may keep your quizzes and do some investigating on your own during the week.

Who Is God?

"We have already found that one of the most heinous sins committed by man in the Bible—one that really irked Jesus—was setting aside the Word of God in favor of man-made traditions. Can anyone tell me the most common sin in the Old and New Testaments—the sin with the greatest consequence?"

"That would have to be idolatry," answered Anna as she raised her hand. "God was constantly warning Israel against this sin, and it ultimately led to slavery in Babylon."

"Correct! The number one, all-time, most heinous crime against our holy Almighty God is idolatry. Setting aside God's holy Word in favor of man-made traditions is a form of idolatry.

"*Idolatry* is the worship of anything other than the Lord God Almighty Himself," Dave replied, "which includes, by the way, the 'Lord God Almighty' of our imaginations."

"I don't understand," said Nick, sitting at the far table by the windows.

"Well, many people have different ideas about God and who He is," explained Dave, "and these ideas can be shaped by our parents, society, or the condition of the world—even the condition of our health.

"For example, many people relate to God the Father as they related to their earthly fathers. If they had a very loving relationship with their fathers, trusting that God is loving would come easily. However, if anyone came from a home with an abusive, alcoholic father—like myself, for instance, and sadly many others—believing that God is loving and trustworthy might be difficult."

"But, if we impose our personal ideas upon the character of God," Anna reasoned, "doesn't God then become a god of our own making?"

"Exactly, Anna," agreed Dave. "**God is who *God* says He is, not who *we* say He is.**

"So it is critical that we find out how God describes Himself in His own Word. We are to let go of any self-made idols—our ideas about God—and embrace the God of the Bible. Only the one, true God of the Bible is able to save us from His wrath against our sins.

"Many cults today claim they know God, and some even use the Bible as their reference. But true Christians indwelt by the Holy Spirit know that cultists are in grave error—that they will die in their sins and be subject to the wrath of the true God. Therefore, it is crucial that true Christians do not fall into the same error, and worship a 'god of their own making,' instead of the one, true God of the Bible.

"This is how God introduced Himself to His people, the nation of Israel, in Deuteronomy 5:6-10:

> I am the LORD your God who brought you out of the land of Egypt, out of the house of slavery.
>
> You shall have no other gods before Me.
>
> You shall not make for yourself an idol, *or* any likeness *of* what is in heaven above or on the earth beneath or in the water under the earth.
>
> You shall not worship them or serve them; for I, the LORD your God, am a jealous God, visiting the iniquity of the fathers on the children, and on the third and the fourth *generations* of those who hate Me,
>
> but showing lovingkindness to thousands, to those who love Me and keep My commandments. (Deuteronomy 5:6-10)

"God was pretty clear about worshiping no other god than Him," Nick stated.

"Right!" Dave answered. "One of God's favorite analogies is to compare Himself to a potter, and His creation to the clay in the potter's hand. Grant, would you please read Jeremiah 18:1 through 6?"

"Okay," replied Grant as he turned in his Bible to the passage.

> The word which came to Jeremiah from the LORD saying,
>
> "Arise and go down to the potter's house, and there I will announce My words to you."
>
> Then I went down to the potter's house, and there he was, making something on the wheel.
>
> But the vessel that he was making of clay was spoiled in the hand of the potter; so he remade it into another vessel, as it pleased the potter to make.
>
> Then the word of the LORD came to me saying,
>
> "Can I not, O house of Israel, deal with you as this potter *does?*" declares the LORD. "Behold, like the clay in the potter's hand, so are you in My hand, O house of Israel." (Jeremiah 18:1-6)

"With your quiz, each person was given a scripture on a piece of paper. Look at the scripture and turn to the passage in your Bible now. Beginning with Matt here in the front, let's go around the room and read how God describes Himself in His Word.

"Please mention the scripture reference before the passage and repeat it after the passage so

the next person knows to begin. Since it looks like everyone has found the assigned verses, sit
back and listen to what God says about Himself, and we will discuss it afterward."

Dave motioned toward Matt, and he began reading. These are the verses read by the class:

The LORD has established His throne in the heavens,
>   And His sovereignty rules over all. (Psalm 103:19)

The LORD is righteous in all His ways
>   And kind in all His deeds. (Psalm 145:17)

For I know that the LORD is great
>   And that our Lord is above all gods.
Whatever the LORD pleases, He does,
>   In heaven and in earth, in the seas and in all deeps.
>   (Psalm 135:5,6)

"Woe to *the one* who quarrels with his Maker—
>   An earthenware vessel among the vessels of earth!
Will the clay say to the potter, 'What are you doing?'
>   Or the thing you are making *say*, 'He has no hands'?"
>   (Isaiah 45:9)

On the contrary, who are you, O man, who answers back to God?
The thing molded will not say to the molder, "Why did you make me like
this," will it?
>   Or does not the potter have a right over the clay, to make from the
same lump one vessel for honorable use and another for common use?
>   (Romans 9:20,21)

Also we have obtained an inheritance, having been predestined
according to His purpose who works all things after the counsel of His
will. (Ephesians 1:11)

For by Him all things were created, *both* in the heavens and on earth,
visible and invisible, whether thrones or dominions or rulers or
authorities—all things have been created through Him and for Him.
>   He is before all things, and in Him all things hold together.
>   (Colossians 1:16,17)

And He is the radiance of His glory and the exact representation of
His nature, and upholds all things by the word of His power. When He
had made purification of sins, He sat down at the right hand of the
Majesty on high. (Hebrews 1:3)

"The God who made the world and all things in it, since He is Lord of heaven and earth, does not dwell in temples made with hands;

nor is He served by human hands, as though He needed anything, since He Himself gives to all *people* life and breath and all things;

and He made from one *man* every nation of mankind to live on all the face of the earth, having determined *their* appointed times and the boundaries of their habitation,

that they would seek God, if perhaps they might grope for Him and find Him, though He is not far from each one of us;

for in Him we live and move and exist, as even some of your own poets have said, 'For we also are His children.'" (Acts 17:24-28)

The lot is cast into the lap,
But its every decision is from the LORD. (Proverbs 16:33)

Many plans are in a man's heart,
But the counsel of the LORD will stand. (Proverbs 19:21)

The king's heart is *like* channels of water in the hand of the LORD;
He turns it wherever He wishes. (Proverbs 21:1)

Then Job answered the LORD and said,
"I know that You can do all things,
And that no purpose of Yours can be thwarted." (Job 42:2)

"Who then is he that can stand before Me?
"Who has given to Me that I should repay *him?*
Whatever is under the whole heaven is Mine." (Job 41:10b,11)

Let all the earth fear the LORD;
Let all the inhabitants of the world stand in awe of Him.
For He spoke, and it was done;
He commanded, and it stood fast.
The LORD nullifies the counsel of the nations;
He frustrates the plans of the peoples.
The counsel of the LORD stands forever,
The plans of His heart from generation to generation.
(Psalm 33:8-11)

But our God is in the heavens;
He does whatever He pleases. (Psalm 115:3)

But the LORD is the true God;
    He is the living God and the everlasting King.
At His wrath the earth quakes,
    And the nations cannot endure His indignation.
                                                      (Jeremiah 10:10)

God is not a man, that He should lie,
    Nor a son of man, that He should repent;
Has He said, and will He not do it?
    Or has He spoken, and will He not make it good?
                                                      (Numbers 23:19)

The LORD has made everything for its own purpose,
    Even the wicked for the day of evil. (Proverbs 16:4)

For You are not a God who takes pleasure in wickedness;
    No evil dwells with You.
The boastful shall not stand before Your eyes;
    You hate all who do iniquity.
You destroy those who speak falsehood;
The LORD abhors the man of bloodshed and deceit. (Psalm 5:4-6)

The LORD tests the righteous and the wicked,
    And the one who loves violence His soul hates. (Psalm 11:5)

Thus says the LORD, your Redeemer, and the one who formed you
from the womb,
    "I, the LORD, am the maker of all things,
        Stretching out the heavens by Myself
        And spreading out the earth all alone." (Isaiah 44:24)

"I am the LORD, and there is no other;
    Besides Me there is no God.
    I will gird you, though you have not known Me;
"That men may know from the rising to the setting of the sun
    That there is no one besides Me.
"I am the LORD, and there is no other,
    The One forming light and creating darkness,
    Causing well-being and creating calamity;
    I am the LORD who does all these." (Isaiah 45:5-7)

"You are My witnesses," declares the LORD,
"And My servant whom I have chosen,
 So that you may know and believe Me
 And understand that I am He.
"Before Me there was no God formed,
 And there will be none after Me.
"I, even I, am the LORD,
 And there is no savior besides Me.
"Even from eternity I am He,
 And there is none who can deliver out of My hand;
 I act and who can reverse it?" (Isaiah 43:10,11,13)

"See now that I, I am He,
 And there is no god besides Me;
 It is I who put to death and give life.
 I have wounded and it is I who heal,
 And there is no one who can deliver from My hand."
            (Deuteronomy 32:39)

The LORD said to him, "Who has made man's mouth? Or who makes *him* mute or deaf, or seeing or blind? Is it not I, the LORD?"
            (Exodus 4:11)

"Remember the former things long past,
 For I am God, and there is no other;
 I am God, and there is no one like Me,
"Declaring the end from the beginning,
 And from ancient times things which have not been done,
 Saying, 'My purpose will be established,
 "And I will accomplish all My good pleasure.'"
            (Isaiah 46:9,10)

"Thus says the LORD, the King of Israel
 And his Redeemer, the LORD of hosts:
 'I am the first and I am the last,
 And there is no God besides Me.'" (Isaiah 44:6)

"I am the Alpha and the Omega, the first and the last, the beginning and the end.
"I, Jesus, have sent My angel to testify to you these things for the churches. I am the root and the descendant of David, the bright morning star." (Revelation 22:13,16)

Jesus said to him, "I am the way, and the truth, and the life; no one comes to the Father but through Me." (John 14:6)

Jesus said to her, "I am the resurrection and the life; he who believes in Me will live even if he dies." (John 11:25)

Then Jesus again spoke to them, saying, "I am the Light of the world; he who follows Me will not walk in the darkness, but will have the Light of life." (John 8:12)

This is the message we have heard from Him and announce to you, that God is Light, and in Him there is no darkness at all. (1 John 1:5)

The one who does not love does not know God, for God is love.
(1 John 4:8)

For our God is a consuming fire. (Hebrews 12:29)

"Are not two sparrows sold for a cent? And *yet* not one of them will fall to the ground apart from your Father. But the very hairs of your head are all numbered. So do not fear; you are more valuable than many sparrows."
(Matthew 10:29-31)

Your eyes have seen my unformed substance;
And in Your book were all written
The days that were ordained *for me,*
When as yet there was not one of them. (Psalm 139:16)

Oh, the depth of the riches both of the wisdom and knowledge of God! How unsearchable are His judgments and unfathomable His ways!
For WHO HAS KNOWN THE MIND OF THE LORD, OR WHO BECAME HIS COUNSELOR?
Or WHO HAS FIRST GIVEN TO HIM THAT IT MIGHT BE PAID BACK TO HIM AGAIN?
For from Him and through Him and to Him are all things. To Him *be* the glory forever. Amen. (Romans 11:33-36)

"Well! God sure has a lot to say about Himself!" Kelly said at the "amen."

"Yes," Dave replied, "and these few verses just scratch the surface! Can anyone define for us the heresy of deism?"

"What's a 'heresy'?" Nick asked.

"A *heresy* is the deliberate act of choosing to oppose or contradict the truth taught in God's holy Word," Dave explained. "A heretic, then, is the one who commits heresy. So, can anyone define the heresy of deism?"

"Wasn't that popular around the time of the American Revolutionary War, and weren't some of the founding fathers of the United States deists?" Anna queried.

"Correct," affirmed Dave. "The heresy of **deism** is the belief in a god who created the universe and its laws of operation, but since then has no interest in interfering with his creation supernaturally. It would be as if God wound up the universe like a big alarm clock and then went away, and whatever happens in the world happens."

"But most of the verses we just read contradict that," said Pam, sitting directly behind Anna.

"Exactly!" Dave rejoiced that God's description of Himself began to sink into their minds.

The Sovereignty of God

"The God of the Bible," Dave summarized, "says that He rules over all, that He works all things according to His will, that He upholds all things by the word of His power, and that in Him all things hold together!

"The God of the Bible says that He owns all of creation, and He does with it whatever pleases Him! The God of the Bible says that there is no other God besides Himself, and there never was nor ever will be any other God—He alone is the Creator and Sustainer of everything!

"The God of the Bible says He sovereignly declares the end from the beginning, and that He knows the future because He ordained it to occur!

"The God of the Bible says He is the way, the truth, and the life. The God of the Bible says He is righteous, He is love, and He is a consuming fire.

"The God of the Bible says that His counsel shall stand in the affairs of men and kings. He is the potter and man is the clay, and He makes man to serve His own purposes. Again, the God of the Bible says that He works all things after the counsel of His own will, including 'causing well-being and creating calamity!'

"Finally, the God of the Bible says that not one sparrow falls to the ground apart from Him, and that the very hairs of your head are numbered. The Lord Jesus here is not simply talking about sparrows and hairs, or the lack thereof," Dave maintained.

"Yes, I have been known to lack several sparrows," quipped Paul, as the class chuckled.

"Jesus is stating the essential principle that Almighty God is sovereign," Dave declared. "God's **sovereignty** means that God had His plan for creation from eternity, and everything that happens or exists in creation—down to the smallest detail—has been ordained by God."

"Even sin?" asked Anna.

"What was the greatest sin ever committed by man?" questioned Dave.

"Obviously, the crucifixion of Christ," Anna answered.

"Correct, Anna," Dave assented. "And what does God say in His Word about the crucifixion? Turn to the Book of Acts, chapter 2, and read verses 22 and 23 please."

Anna read:

> Men of Israel, listen to these words: Jesus the Nazarene, a man attested
> to you by God with miracles and wonders and signs which God performed

through Him in your midst, just as you yourselves know—

this *Man*, delivered over by the predetermined plan and foreknowledge
of God, you nailed to a cross by the hands of godless men and put *Him* to
death. (Acts 2:22,23)

"Thank you, Anna," Dave said. "The crucifixion of Christ was the most heinous sin ever
committed. It was the murder of the God-man, the only guiltless human being that ever lived.
Christ's crucifixion was idolatry's most vicious moment, and it was done by the predetermined
plan of God. This sin was infinitely heinous, and if God predestined this sin to occur, any other
sin pales by comparison.

"Everything that happens or exists in creation has been ordained by God. He says so in His
Word, in Ephesians 1:11, which we just read, and in many other places. Read Ephesians again,
please, Kelly."

"In Him also we have obtained an inheritance, having been predestined according to His
purpose who works all things after the counsel of His will," Kelly recited.

"God works *all* things after the counsel of His will, not some things, or not just the 'good'
things," Dave asserted. "The axiom to remember is: **God ordains what He hates in order
to accomplish what He loves**."

"Does this make God the author of sin?" Paul asked.

"A great question!" Dave replied. "Paul, you work in the computer field, right? Let's say I
was a publisher, and I wanted to publish a book on computers. So, I go to Paul the computer
expert, and I sign Paul to author a book on computers. I provide him with money, a place in
which to study, a secretary to help him type, and everything else needed for this book to become
a reality. Barring the return of Christ Jesus, this book on computers will be written, because I
have made it certain.

"However, when that book is published, my name will not appear in the author's space.
Only Paul's name will be there. Why? Because, even though I 'ordained' the book, I did not
actually put the words on paper. Paul did the actual writing. Therefore, Paul is the author, and
I am the cause.

"God must be the First Cause of everything," Dave concluded, "because nothing existed
before He created, and nothing can continue to exist unless He sustains it. God says that He
creates and sustains everything according to His perfect plan, or counsel, that eternally existed
in His mind before creation. God's rule is, though He ordained everything that occurs in
creation, the person who actually commits the transgression is guilty of the sin.

"It's like a city mayor who orders the installation of a traffic light because of increased traffic
at an intersection that used to be a four-way stop. If a drunk driver runs a red light and causes
an accident, are we to blame the traffic light for being red, or even the mayor who ordered that
it be put there? Of course not.

"The guilt and punishment belong to the one who actually committed the crime. No one
forced the man to get drunk—he desired to do it. No one forced the man to drive while
drunk—he insisted on it. The sinner is known as the Secondary Cause. Since he totally
concurred with committing the sin, he is totally guilty."

"You are not saying that God takes an innocent person and makes him sin, are you?" asked Chelsea, sitting in the center of the room next to Jennifer.

"Good question," Dave answered. "This is a common assumption that most people make which causes them to come to false conclusions about God's sovereignty. God never takes good people and has them do bad things, because **there are no good people**. God simply directs the evil intentions in the hearts of all people born with a sin nature to fulfill His eternal plan."

"There are no good people?" Chelsea repeated.

"Well, what does the Bible say?" Dave replied. "Chelsea, please read Luke 18:19, Romans 3:9 through 12, and Romans 7:18 and 19."

Chelsea read:

> And Jesus said to him, "Why do you call Me good? No one is good except God alone." (Luke 18:19)

> What then? Are we better than they? Not at all; for we have already charged that both Jews and Greeks are all under sin;
> as it is written,
> "THERE IS NONE RIGHTEOUS, NOT EVEN ONE;
> THERE IS NONE WHO UNDERSTANDS,
> THERE IS NONE WHO SEEKS FOR GOD;
> ALL HAVE TURNED ASIDE, TOGETHER THEY HAVE BECOME USELESS;
> THERE IS NONE WHO DOES GOOD,
> THERE IS NOT EVEN ONE." (Romans 3:9-12)

> For I know that nothing good dwells in me, that is, in my flesh; for the willing is present in me, but the doing of the good *is* not.
> For the good that I want, I do not do, but I practice the very evil that I do not want. (Romans 7:18,19)

"Thank you, Chelsea," acknowledged Dave. "Both the Lord Jesus Christ and the Apostle Paul affirm in God's holy Word that there are no good people. God and only God is good. All people born of a human father are born with a sin nature that desires only selfishness and evil continually, despite all outward appearances. Thus, any person born of a human father who claims to be a 'good' person is simply denying the Lord Jesus Christ and His truth in God's Word, the Bible.

"So, God does not take good people and, against their wills, cause them to do evil—because there are no good people. God takes evil people already filled with selfish desires and, with their full cooperation and approval, appoints their actions for His purposes. God does not tempt people to sin—He doesn't have to! We sinful humans willingly sin! Kelly, please read Psalm 5:4 and James 1:13-17 for us."

Kelly read:

> For You are not a God who takes pleasure in wickedness;
> No evil dwells with You. (Psalm 5:4)

> Let no one say when he is tempted, "I am being tempted by God"; for
> God cannot be tempted by evil, and He Himself does not tempt anyone.
>
> But each one is tempted when he is carried away and enticed by his own
> lust.
>
> Then when lust has conceived, it gives birth to sin; and when sin is
> accomplished, it brings forth death.
>
> Do not be deceived, my beloved brethren.
>
> Every good thing given and every perfect gift is from above, coming
> down from the Father of lights, with whom there is no variation or
> shifting shadow. (James 1:13-17)

"Thank you, Kelly," acknowledged Dave. "Most people believe that 'man is basically good.' This is because sinful man is looking at himself and other people through selfish, self-preserving, sin-marred eyes. But the Lord Jesus directly refutes this grave error, declaring that, '"no one is good except God alone."' God's Word repeatedly declares this bold truth that man consistently denies: every person born of a human male has a selfish, sinful nature, and 'there is none who does good...not even one.'

"God is neither the source of evil nor temptation. He is absolute goodness and righteousness. God takes no pleasure in the wickedness in the heart of man, but He directs it toward fulfilling His eternal purposes. God says that He 'works all things after the counsel of His will' (Ephesians 1:11). Again, God's *sovereignty* means that God has ordained everything that happens or exists in creation according to His perfect eternal plan."

"So that must mean that God planned the first sin of Adam in the Garden of Eden," Matt mused.

"Well, what does the Scripture say?" Dave responded. "Matt, read Ephesians 3:10-12 and 2 Timothy 1:8 and 9 please."

Matt read:

> ...so that the manifold wisdom of God might now be made known
> through the church to the rulers and the authorities in the heavenly *places*.
> *This was* in accordance with the eternal purpose which He carried out in
> Christ Jesus our Lord, in whom we have boldness and confident access
> through faith in Him. (Ephesians 3:10-12)
>
> Therefore do not be ashamed of the testimony of our Lord or of me His
> prisoner, but join with *me* in suffering for the gospel according to the power
> of God,
>
> who has saved us and called us with a holy calling, not according to our
> works, but according to His own purpose and grace which was granted us in
> Christ Jesus from all eternity. (2 Timothy 1:8,9)

"Thank you, Matt," appreciated Dave. "God's plan is an eternal plan, which means it never had a beginning. God's purpose for all of His creation always existed in His mind. God was not surprised by Adam's sin, and then had to work out 'Plan B.' That thought is heresy, denying

God's ability to know all things past, present and future. God's saving grace 'was granted us in Christ Jesus from all eternity.'

"God's eternal purpose, also known as His eternal plan which He had before creation, involved the dispensing of His grace toward those He chose to be in His family. His people are sinners who were granted salvation in Jesus the Savior from eternity past, before the creation of the universe. If Jesus was deemed the Christ, the Savior, from all eternity past, then God's plan had to include a sinful people that needed saving from His wrath from all eternity past.

"Pam, please read Romans 11:36 and Colossians 1:16 and 17 for us."

Pam read:

> For from Him and through Him and to Him are all things. To Him *be* the glory forever. Amen. (Romans 11:36)

> For by Him all things were created, *both* in the heavens and on earth, visible and invisible, whether thrones or dominions or rulers or authorities—all things have been created through Him and for Him.
> He is before all things, and in Him all things hold together.
> (Colossians 1:16,17)

"Thank you, Pam," Dave responded. "The Scriptures declare from Genesis to Revelation that this creation is God's thing, not man's thing. He is working out His plan for His glory. God did not create for man's convenience, man's comfort or even man's salvation. All things were made by God first and foremost for the glory and honor of God.

"Again, God's entire purpose for making the universe is **the glory of God**, because He planned, created and sustains it all," reasoned Dave. "The Father subjected His creation to slavery to sin so that God the Son, Christ Jesus, gets all the honor and glory for being the only way out of this bondage (Romans 8:19-22)!"

God's Sovereignty and Man's Responsibility

"Does this mean that we are not responsible for our sin?" Jennifer asked.

"Another great question!" Dave exclaimed. "Scripture clearly states that both God's sovereignty and man's responsibility co-exist simply because God set it up that way. This is God's creation, and He makes the rules. Remember the story of Joseph and his multi-colored tunic in the book of Genesis?"

"Oh yes," said Grant, who sat next to Ed. "I was just reading that section in my personal study time. Jacob loved Joseph more than his other sons because he was the son of his old age, and Jacob gave him a multi-colored cloak. His older brothers resented Joseph, and when Joseph related to them a dream that they would bow down to him, they sought to kill him.

"But Reuben, the oldest brother, intervened. So they threw Joseph into a pit. When a caravan going down to Egypt passed by, they sold Joseph to the traders as a slave. In Egypt, God gave Joseph great favor with the ruler Pharaoh, because God enabled Joseph to tell Pharaoh his troubling dreams and interpret them.

"So Pharaoh made Joseph his second-in-command, and Joseph implemented God's plan to save grain during years of plenty for the coming years of famine. During the drought, all the surrounding peoples went to Joseph to buy grain, including the sons of Jacob. When Joseph revealed himself to his treacherous brothers, he forgave them and brought his father down to Egypt to live as Pharaoh's honored guest."

"Excellent recap, Grant!" Dave said. "The words of Joseph to his brothers are most critical here. Anna, please read Genesis 50:17-20."

Anna found the passages and read:

> "'Thus you shall say to Joseph, "Please forgive, I beg you, the transgression of your brothers and their sin, for they did you wrong."' And now, please forgive the transgression of the servants of the God of your father." And Joseph wept when they spoke to him.

> Then his brothers also came and fell down before him and said, "Behold, we are your servants."

> But Joseph said to them, "Do not be afraid, for am I in God's place?

> "As for you, you meant evil against me, *but* God meant it for good in order to bring about this present result, to preserve many people alive."
>
> (Genesis 50:17-20)

"Thank you, Anna," Dave said. "The brothers were totally responsible before God for their evil actions against Joseph, and they knew it. Joseph agreed that they were responsible. But he looked beyond the finite sphere of man's interactions to God's infinite sphere. Joseph recognized that God was working His eternal plan by directing the evil to accomplish His purposes. So, in answer to your question, Jennifer, we are still responsible for our actions even though God has sovereignly ordained everything that happens in the universe according to His eternal plan."

"Isn't that a contradiction, and thus illogical?" Paul asked.

"No," Dave answered. "*The Law of Non-contradiction* states that something cannot be both true and not true at the same time and in the same sense (or relationship). God's sovereignty and man's responsibility are both true at the same time, but not in the same sense, or relationship. Look at this diagram.

God (infinite) ———

Man (finite) inside
smaller sphere

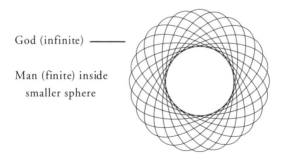

"God has set up reality like two concentric spheres—a smaller one inside a larger one. The outer sphere is God with His sovereign plan, controlling everything inside of it. This outer sphere is reality from God's point of view—the true, infinite, complete and reliable point of view. The inner, finite sphere is reality from man's point of view. This finite sphere exists only because the power of God sustains it. Man does not have access to God's point of view unless God reveals it to man.

"God set up man in a finite, three-dimensional universe—the smaller sphere—where man makes real decisions with real consequences within that finite sphere. For every decision, man will give an account to God on the day of judgment. Life in this 'time and space' creation is real, but it is finite and subordinate to the infinite.

"So God's sovereignty operates in the infinite sense, or sphere, whereas man's responsibility operates in the finite sphere. The infinite sphere totally controls the finite sphere.

"There is no contradiction here, because we are talking about two distinct beings operating in two different relationships, or senses. For a contradiction, the Bible would have to claim: 'God is sovereign, and not sovereign, at the same time and in the same sense;' or, 'Man is responsible for his choices, and not responsible for his choices, at the same time and in the same sense.' But the Bible does not say these things.

"The Bible declares that God is sovereign and that man is responsible for his decisions. This does not fulfill the definition of a contradiction, because the senses in which they are true are different. The relationship of God to man is completely different than the relationship of man to God. God ordains and controls all. Man lives this life in finite space and time, making real decisions with real consequences, while knowing only the fraction of reality that God reveals.

"As a result, every decision we make in this finite sphere will fall perfectly into the perfect plan of the infinite God which He had from all eternity, because, as we read earlier: 'Many plans are in a man's heart, but the counsel of the LORD will stand' (Proverbs 19:21).

"Revisiting Christ's prophecy regarding His crucifixion, the Lord Himself outlined God's intention for the coexistence of God's sovereignty and man's responsibility. Jennifer, would you read for us Luke 22:20-22 please?" Dave asked.

Jennifer read:

> And in the same way *He took* the cup after they had eaten, saying, "This cup which is poured out for you is the new covenant in My blood.
>
> "But behold, the hand of the one betraying Me is with Mine on the table.
>
> "For indeed, the Son of Man is going as it has been determined; but woe to that man by whom He is betrayed!" (Luke 22:20-22)

"Thank you, Jennifer," Dave said. "Christ Himself declares that God indeed ordained His betrayal and crucifixion." But Christ also condemned Judas for betraying Him, and added in Mark 14:21: "'*It would have been* good for that man if he had not been born.'" God made and sustains everything that exists or happens in His creation. Thus, everything belongs to Him, so He makes the rules. The Almighty set up reality having both God's sovereignty over all, and man's responsibility for his actions in this world, as His rule."

"Well, where does God's sovereignty end and man's responsibility began?" asked Ed.

"That's a false question, because it does not accurately reflect reality," answered Dave. "It's like asking, 'Have you stopped kicking your dog upon coming home from work?' Well, if you've never kicked your dog, answering the question 'yes' or 'no' is a false answer. Try it.

"Responsibility and authority do not have to end and begin—they coincide. Picture the owner and president of a construction company, who hires a general foreman, who, in turn hires shift foremen, who, in turn hire laborers. The president's authority and responsibility for the building project do not end at the general foreman's level. The president's authority covers the entire company, including all projects and personnel.

"The president then delegates authority and responsibility to his general foreman, who, in turn delegates part of his authority and responsibility to his foremen, who delegate part of their authority and responsibility to their workers. Authority and responsibility do not end and begin at each level, but are an extension of the power of the preceding level, covering everything beneath.

"God delegates to man the authority to make decisions with real consequences within the finite three-dimensional sphere of the universe. God also assigns man the responsibility '"to be perfect, as your heavenly Father is perfect"' (Matthew 5:48). God's authority does not end at man's will, but covers everything beneath Himself. God's responsibility to Himself to work His perfect plan to its completion will be fulfilled, because He is all-powerful and has all authority.

"Part of the problem in understanding how God's sovereignty and man's responsibility line up is bad teaching. God's sovereignty and man's responsibility are not two equal, opposing concepts. God's 'sovereignty rules over all' (Psalm 103:19b), and man's responsibility is but a small area over which God rules. Man's responsibility is totally subject to God's sovereignty.

"Man is totally responsible for his actions, though God ordained all of them. Why? Because God set it up that way. It is God's universe, and He can set it up any way He desires. Since man is born enslaved to evil, evil man is totally in agreement with doing evil continuously. God simply directs man's evil to accomplish His plan, and decrees that man is responsible for actually committing the evil crimes he would have done anyway.

"God is under no obligation to reveal any part of Himself or His eternal plan to anyone! But, He has blessed us by sending His beloved Son to reveal part of Himself to man, and has given us His holy Word to reveal part of His plan as well! God's holy Word declares that God ordains beforehand everything that exists or occurs in creation. God's Word also declares that, for every decision man makes, he is totally responsible.

"This is how our all-powerful, infinite God set up reality," Dave concluded.

"But how does He do that?" Matt asked.

"How?" Dave echoed. "Matt, please read Mark 6:47-50."

Matt read:

> When it was evening, the boat was in the middle of the sea, and He was alone on the land.
>
> Seeing them straining at the oars, for the wind was against them, at about the fourth watch of the night He came to them, walking on the sea; and He intended to pass by them.

But when they saw Him walking on the sea, they supposed that it was
a ghost, and cried out;

for they all saw Him and were terrified. But immediately He spoke
with them and said to them, "Take courage; it is I, do not be afraid."

(Mark 6:47-50)

"Thank you, Matt," said Dave. "Well, how did Jesus walk on the sea? Did He suspend gravity? If He did, one would think the water would rush skyward. So, how did He do it, Matt?"

"I don't know," Matt answered, "but I believe it happened because God's Word says it did."

"Exactly," Dave commended. "If God declares something to be true in His Word, it is true whether or not we, with our finite minds, can understand it or how He does it. God is not limited by our understanding. Two critical points must be made here.

"First, logic exists because it is part of God's holy character. Thus, God's holy Word will be perfectly logical and never contradict itself. However, our ability to use logic and reason is severely marred by our sinful natures. Therefore, we must exercise great care when an apparent contradiction occurs.

"We may be misunderstanding God's intended meaning of a passage. Or, the apparent contradiction is indeed not a contradiction, because it does not fulfill all of the requirements of the definition of a contradiction. For a *contradiction* to occur, the same thing must be declared true and not true at the same time and in the same sense (or relationship). If it does not fulfill all of these requirements, it's not a contradiction. Maybe it is just a mystery that we as finite beings cannot, or never will, understand. That does not mean it's a contradiction.

"Second, we must be very careful not to commit the heinous crime of idolatry here," warned Dave. "There is nothing contradictory about Jesus being able to walk on water when we can't do likewise. There is also no contradiction in God's sovereignty and man's responsibility just because we can't figure out how God does it.

"If God declares something to be true, it is the abhorrent sin of idolatry to say: '*I* can't understand this, so it must not be true, and I refuse to believe it.' We commit a heinous sin when we set up our limited, sin-marred reason as an idol, and expect God to bow to it. Could we do anything more despicable?

"Much of who God is, what God does, and how He does it, is a mystery to our finite minds. That is only logical, being that, by definition, the finite could never completely grasp the infinite. But upon the truths which God does reveal, we can and do stake our eternal lives. Jennifer, please read Deuteronomy 29:29."

Turning to the scripture, Jennifer stated: "'The secret things belong to the LORD our God, but the things revealed belong to us and to our sons forever.'"

"Thank you, Jennifer," recognized Dave. "All of the scriptures we read earlier about God declare His absolute sovereignty. However, we also have plenty of passages declaring man's responsibility. Anna, please read Jesus' words in Matthew 12:36 and the Apostle Paul's words in Romans 14:12 for us."

Anna read:

"But I tell you that every careless word that people speak, they shall give an accounting for it in the day of judgment." (Matthew 12:36)

So then each one of us will give an account of himself to God.
(Romans 14:12)

"Thank you, Anna," acknowledged Dave. "God's holy Word thus declares both to be true: God sovereignly ordains everything that exists or occurs in creation according to His eternal counsel, also known as His eternal plan. Also, man is responsible for, and will give an accounting for, every one of his decisions on the day of judgment.

"I once saw a 'Christian' bumper sticker that clearly expressed the heinous crime of idolatry in elevating man's understanding to the level of God's holy Word. It said: 'God said it. I believe it. That settles it.' Yes, heresy even comes on bumper stickers today.

"God's holy Word declares: 'God said it. That settles it. So I had better believe it.' God and God alone is the standard of truth, not our sin-marred, finite minds.

"So let us review the main points of today's Bible study, and then I will emphasize the major point and its practical application," Dave summarized.

"First, a sin that really irked Jesus was the setting aside of God's eternal Word for man-made traditions.

"Only God's originally intended meaning that He conveyed through the writers that He inspired is God's holy Word. All other interpretations are mere man-made speculations.

"A heresy is the deliberate act of choosing to oppose or contradict the truth taught in God's holy Word.

"The number one all-time most common crime against our holy Almighty God is idolatry.

"Idolatry is the worship of anything other than the Lord God Almighty Himself, a sin that comes with grave consequences.

"Setting aside God's holy Word in favor of man-made traditions is a form of idolatry, placing the opinion of man over the truth of God.

"God is who God says He is, not who we say He is.

"We are to let go of any self-made idols—our ideas about God—and embrace the God of the Bible who alone is able to save us from our sins.

"It is crucial that true Christians do not fall into error and worship a 'god of their own making' instead of the true God of the Bible.

"The God of the Bible says that He rules over all, that He works all things according to His will, that He upholds all things by the word of His power, and that in Him all things hold together.

"The God of the Bible says that all of creation is His, and He does with it whatever pleases Him! The God of the Bible says that there is no other God besides Himself, and there never was nor ever will be any other God—He alone is the Creator and Sustainer of everything!

"The God of the Bible says He declares the end from the beginning, and that He knows the future because He ordained it to occur!

"The God of the Bible says He is the way, the truth, and the life. The God of the Bible says

He is righteous, He is love, and He is a consuming fire. He is all of these things!

"The God of the Bible says that His counsel shall stand in the affairs of men and kings. He is the potter and man is the clay, and He makes man to serve His own purposes. The God of the Bible says that He works all things after the counsel of His own will.

"Almighty God is sovereign. He knew His plan before creation, and everything that happens or exists in creation—down to the smallest detail—has been ordained by God.

"The crucifixion of Christ, the most heinous sin ever committed—idolatry's most vicious moment—was done by the predetermined plan of God.

"God ordains what He hates in order to accomplish what He loves.

"God must be the First Cause of everything, because nothing existed before He created, and nothing can continue to exist unless He sustains it.

"God's rule is, though He ordained everything that occurs in creation, the person who actually commits the transgression is guilty of the sin.

"God never takes good people and has them do bad things, because there are no good people. God simply directs the evil intentions in the hearts of all people born with a sin nature to fulfill His eternal plan.

"The entire purpose of creation is for the glory of God, because He planned and created and sustains it all.

"God the Son, Jesus Christ, is to receive all of the glory by being the only Savior of creation.

"Scripture clearly states that both God's sovereignty and man's responsibility co-exist simply because God set it up that way.

"To have a contradiction, the same thing must be declared true and not true at the same time and in the same sense, or relationship. All requirements must be met for a contradiction to exist.

"God's sovereignty operates in the infinite sense, whereas man's responsibility operates in the finite sense—so there is no contradiction.

"We must avoid the heinous sin of idolatry when, as God declares truth in His Word, we refuse to believe it because our finite, sin-marred minds cannot understand it.

"Our imperfect use of logic and reason must be subservient to God's holy Word, which alone is the standard of truth for all of creation.

"And the critical, overarching message of all of these truths—what the Scriptures declare from Genesis to Revelation—is that this creation is God's thing, not man's thing. Almighty God is working out His plan for His glory. God's sovereign power, which rules the infinite and finite spheres of reality, ensures that His glory is and always will be supreme.

"What does God's sovereignty mean to us, His children? First and foremost, it means that whatever circumstances we face were ordained by our loving heavenly Father. We can approach problems with a view to learning God's purposes for them instead of crumbling in despair. This is God's life now, for whatever He desires, to bring honor to His Name. God's sovereignty means that we are not puppets to circumstance, but that He has the power to fulfill His promise to us in Romans 8:28: 'And we know that God causes all things to work together for good to those who love God, to those who are called according to *His* purpose.'

"Also, God's sovereignty gives us the power to be joyful when suffering. The Apostle James gives us this command: 'Consider it all joy, my brethren, when you encounter various trials, knowing that the testing of your faith produces endurance' (James 1:2,3). This command from God's Word would be almost laughable if not for God's sovereign power—which enables us to not just endure suffering, but to glorify Almighty God through it.

"And lastly, God's sovereignty guarantees that He will bring every one of His children home to His glorious heaven! This is our real hope and true home, not this evil world, just as Jesus promised in John 6:37-40 and 65:

"All that the Father gives Me will come to Me, and the one who comes to Me I will certainly not cast out.

"For I have come down from heaven, not to do My own will, but the will of Him who sent Me.

"This is the will of Him who sent Me, that of all that He has given Me I lose nothing, but raise it up on the last day.

"For this is the will of My Father, that everyone who beholds the Son and believes in Him will have eternal life, and I Myself will raise him up on the last day.

"For this reason I have said to you, that no one can come to Me, unless it has been granted him from the Father." (John 6:37-40, 65)

"Only a sovereign God who has ordained the beginning through the end of creation can guarantee such promises. We don't have to find our way through the maze of this world and keep ourselves saved. We just need to fall head-over-heels in love with our heavenly Father, who first loved us with an unending love, and chose us to be in His family before He created the universe.

"Paul, would you please close our Bible study with prayer?" Dave concluded. "I hope studying the Scripture concerning the sovereignty of God has painted for you just how awesome, how powerful, and how loving our heavenly Father really is toward us. Everything God does in creation is first and foremost for His glory, and secondly, for His children. He truly loves us with an unending love!

"Go and worship our God with all of your heart, strength, mind and soul! Paul?"

"Dear heavenly Father, we praise You and worship You. You are the sovereign God, the only God, the ruler of the universe—and you have desired to share Your infinite love with us, Your children. Thank You, Lord, for Your love.

"Pour out Your love within our hearts, so that we may love You and others with Your incredible love. Give us Your Spirit of worship, so that we may now go and worship You as You deserve, with all that You have given us. Thank You for Your glorious promises, and we long to see Your face! Bless us as we go, in Jesus' holy Name. Amen!"

4

Our Father Who Art In Heaven

Tuesday came quickly, and Nick dropped by Dave's room after lunch. Nick was absorbing everything he could learn about God. The worship of God in the church service left him in awe. The pastor's message about unwavering commitment to God, regardless of the circumstances, left Nick hungering for more.

"Hey, Dave!" Nick said with a beam on his face as he looked through the open door. Dave looked up from his studies at the desk and greeted his brother with a smile.

"My brother in Christ! Come on in! I see you have your sword with you!" Dave noted, embracing his friend and offering him a seat.

"My what?"

"Your sword—your Bible!" Dave explained.

"Oh, yeah. I've been reading it constantly since Friday night. Since I've given this life back to God, I want to know everything about Him!" said Nick. "But why do you call it a 'sword'?"

"Here, read Hebrews 4:12," Dave answered, taking Nick's Bible and opening it to the fourth chapter of the Epistle to the Hebrews.

Nick read:

> For the word of God is living and active and sharper than any two-edged sword, and piercing as far as the division of soul and spirit, of both joints and marrow, and able to judge the thoughts and intentions of the heart.
>
> (Hebrews 4:12)

"I've felt that sword cutting through my thoughts as I read the Gospels. God has shown me a lot about myself and my opinions that He wants to change."

"Awesome!" Dave exclaimed. "The Holy Spirit is moving in your life to make you more and more like Jesus!"

"Yes, God is awesome!" Nick agreed.

"So let's go over the important points of Friday night's discussion," said Dave. "But first let's ask God our Father to bless our time studying His Word."

"Okay."

"Holy Father, we praise You for who You are, the Awesome Creator of the universe! We thank You for bringing us into Your family through Jesus Christ, Your Son! Thank You, Lord, for Your death to pay for our sins, and Your resurrection, so we can live eternally with You!

"Pour out Your Holy Spirit upon us, I pray, so that He may guide us into Your truth. We thank You for the promise of Your presence here with us in a special way, and ask that You would teach us about Yourself so that we may love You more and more! In Jesus' Name we pray, amen!"

"Amen!" Nick agreed.

"Almighty God is the Creator and the Sustainer of all that exists or will exist," Dave said, jumping right in to the subject at hand. "However, He is not the Father of every person. He becomes our Father when He raises us from spiritual death and brings us into His family."

"That's what He did for me Friday night," asserted Nick.

"Exactly!" Dave agreed. "So what do we do now as a member of His family?"

"Great question! I'll bet the answer is somewhere in His Word!" said Nick.

"Right! Read Jesus' answer to that very question in John 6:29." Dave let Nick find the Gospel of John on his own.

"'Jesus answered and said to them, "This is the work of God, that you believe in Him whom He has sent,"'" read Nick. "Friday night, you said that to believe and to repent were the two critical responses that Christ commanded in the Gospel of Mark."

"You have an excellent memory!" encouraged Dave. "This is how it all comes together: A spiritually-dead sinner can do nothing whatsoever toward bridging the infinite gap between a perfectly holy God and himself—because he's spiritually *dead*. Paul the Apostle confirms this state in his Letter to the Ephesians: 'And you were dead in your trespasses and sins' (Eph. 2:1).

"The spiritually-dead can't do anything towards reconciliation with God. They cannot desire God, seek God, reconcile with God, reach out for God, accept God or choose God. They're *dead*.

"Anyone born of a human male, which includes you and me, comes into this world a spiritually-dead sinner. The sinner actively suppresses the knowledge that God exists so that he can continue in his rebellion. This is explained in the Book of Romans, chapter 1, verses 18 and 19. Read them."

Nick read:

> For the wrath of God is revealed from heaven against all ungodliness and unrighteousness of men, who suppress the truth in unrighteousness,
>
> because that which is known about God is evident within them; for God made it evident to them. (Romans 1:18,19)

"God has placed the knowledge that He exists within every human being," Dave explained. "But the rebellious sinner loves his sin. So, in order to continue in his wickedness, he must suppress that inward knowledge of God—much like an ostrich sticking its head in the sand as the lion approaches.

"If God had chosen before creation a certain rebellious person to become a member of His family," Dave continued, "then, at the precise moment God had ordained it, He puts His Holy Spirit into the sinner and raises him from spiritual death to spiritual life.

"Though the sinner may have previously thought of himself as a sinner, and maybe even bragged about it, he now experiences great remorse for offending his holy Creator. This is not simply remorse, for everyone feels remorse when making adverse decisions. This is remorse specifically for offending God and His holiness."

"I remember knowing that I was destined for God's judgment, and felt like I was going to die!" recalled Nick.

"Yes. Remorse for offending the holy character of God with one's heinous sin is the first evidence that the Holy Spirit has made a sinner spiritually alive. A sinner that has no remorse, specifically for offending God and His perfect holiness, doesn't recognize any need to be saved from the wrath of God due him for his rebellion."

"That's true," agreed Nick. "I lived like that my entire life!"

"Only a spiritually-dead sinner who has been made spiritually alive by God has remorse for offending the holiness of God. Only a sinner in whom God has placed His Holy Spirit is able to respond to the gospel of God. The Holy Spirit first has to raise the spiritually-dead to spiritual life, and open his eyes to his sin. God the Holy Spirit gives him the power to repent, along with the desire and faith to come to Christ.

"**The gospel** is the good news that God the Son died on the cross and paid the penalty for sinners whom He would choose to be in His family," Dave reiterated, "and that God transferred Christ's perfect life to these sinners' accounts. This legal transfer makes them perfect as God is perfect, and able to live with God forever in heaven! Read Jesus' words in John 6:65."

Nick flipped over to the passage and stated, "'And He was saying, "For this reason I have said to you, that no one can come to Me, unless it has been granted him from the Father."'"

"The choice of who comes to Christ for salvation, as Jesus Himself says, belongs to God alone," Dave expounded, "because spiritually-dead sinners can't choose. They're *dead*.

"There are two immediate biblical responses required by God when He makes the sinner spiritually alive. When the Holy Spirit shows a sinner his heinous sin, God's first two commands are to 'repent and believe.' With His first words, the Lord Jesus commanded in Mark 1:15: '"The time is fulfilled, and the time is at hand; repent and believe in the gospel."'

"Many people throughout the years have invented other formulas for a sinner to be saved, such as 'take Jesus along in your life'; or 'try Jesus'; or 'accept Jesus as your personal Lord and Savior'; or 'pray a sinner's prayer'; or 'respond to an "altar call"'. But these responses to God's gospel are nowhere to be found in Scripture."

"I've heard some of those before," said Nick.

"To the one the Father grants spiritual life in Christ, God's commanded response—spelled out in His Word so it cannot be missed—is to 'repent *and* believe.' As you may recall from our discussion Friday night," Dave continued, "to **repent** means to change masters, giving back total control of this life to Christ, its rightful owner, for whatever He desires to do with it. To **believe** means to trust totally in Christ's two-part perfect work—His death on the cross to pay for your sins, and His perfect life credited to your account—for your salvation."

"Yes, I remember that." Nick was beginning to put the pieces together.

"All of this can happen within seconds, and be accompanied by little emotion—or, as in your case, great emotion," clarified Dave. "When God makes a spiritually-dead sinner spiritually alive, so he can respond to the gospel and believe in Christ's perfect work, that person is justified."

"Justified?" Nick queried. "You mean perfect?"

"**Justification** is the act of God that credits Christ's perfect work and Christ's perfect life to a sinner's account. This sovereign act makes the sinner free from the guilt and penalty of his sin, becoming perfect in God's eyes. Romans 8:33 says, 'Who will bring a charge against God's elect? God is the one who justifies.' Beginning with Romans 4:25, it says Jesus 'was delivered up because of our transgressions, and was raised for our justification. Therefore, having been justified by faith, we have peace with God through our Lord Jesus Christ!'

"God declares us legally perfect in His sight, justified by faith in Christ. '**Faith in Christ**' means to believe, or trust totally in the two parts of Christ's perfect work for our salvation: His death on the cross which paid for our sins, and His perfect life credited to our account. This true faith is not found within ourselves, but it is given to us as a gift by the Holy Spirit," Dave explained.

"So I repent by giving back this life totally to Christ for His use. And I believe—or trust totally in both parts of Christ's perfect work—to be declared as perfect as God is perfect, or, in other words, justified," summarized Nick.

"You've got it!" Dave exclaimed. "Justification is a once-in-a-lifetime event when God raises a spiritually-dead sinner to eternal life in Christ. And, by definition, eternal life can never end, or it is not eternal. The sinner raised to eternal life can never again be judged guilty of any sin, because the punishment for his sins—past, present and future—was taken by Christ on the cross, and he is credited with Christ's perfect life. Read Jesus' words in John 5:24."

Nick turned to the Gospel of John, and read:

"Truly, truly, I say to you, he who hears My word, and believes Him
who sent me, has eternal life, and does not come into judgment, but has
passed out of death into life." (John 5:24)

How Does One Know if He Is a True Christian?

"Praise God!" exclaimed Nick. "That's an awesome promise! So, how do I know if I'm a true Christian, or if I'm just deceived?" asked Nick.

"Excellent question! Just as God gives the unbeliever the knowledge that He exists," answered Dave, "God the Holy Spirit also gives His true child the knowledge that the believer now belongs to God. Read Romans 8:14-16."

Nick read:

> For all who are being led by the Spirit of God, these are sons of God.
>
> For you have not received a spirit of slavery leading to fear again, but you have received a spirit of adoption as sons by which we cry out, "Abba! Father!"
>
> The Spirit Himself testifies with our spirit that we are children of God. (Romans 8:14-16)

"God the Holy Spirit affirms the adoption by God the Father to the true believer's heart," Dave said. "But, to an unbeliever just going through the religious motions, one could ask oneself *The Three Burning Questions*:

1. Has this life been so radically changed that I now consider what God wants above and before what I want?
2. Have I given this life back to Christ, its rightful owner, for whatever He wants to do with it?
3. Am I totally trusting in Christ's work to make me acceptable to God, not adding anything of mine into the mix?

"The answer to all Three Burning Questions must be unconditionally 'Yes!' if one is a true child of God," Dave warned.

"A true believer has gone from spiritual death to abundant life. He is a new creation, having been born again. Thus, if one cannot point to such a radical change in one's life, then no such change has occurred. The unbeliever always considers first and foremost, 'What's in it for me?' But obeying God, and considering His commands over and above anything—even one's life—is the mark of a true Christian.

"The unbeliever still foolishly claims ownership to this life. He calls the shots, he lives by his own warped opinions, and thinks that his understanding *is* God's Word on the subject. There is no remorse for continually offending this life's True Owner. The real believer willingly declares that he is God's slave, living to bring honor and glory to God by whatever means God decides. The real Christian submits to God's Word and God's true definitions of His terms, rejecting his own sin-marred, finite opinions of truth.

"The false Christian says that Christ's work was sufficient for his salvation, but then adds his own 'good' works to 'keep himself saved.' He feels he must do this or that, instead of totally relying on what Christ has already done. The true believer rests in Christ's perfection, realizing that 'all our righteous deeds are like a filthy garment' (Isaiah 64:6b). The real Christian knows that he must be as perfect as God is perfect, and that anything he adds to Christ's perfect work would only taint it, disqualifying him for heaven.

"So, if you answered the Three Burning Questions with any conditions to a 'yes' response, then you may accurately question the validity of your salvation experience," Dave maintained.

"Great explanation!" affirmed Nick. "I answer 'yes' to all three questions. I know I have been born again. I have repented, giving this life back to Christ for whatever He desires. I have believed only in Christ's work for my salvation—His dying on the cross to pay for my sins, and His perfect life credited to my account to make me as perfect as God is perfect! Thank You, Jesus!"

God's Will for His Children

"Yes, thank You, Lord! While we were yet sinners, God sent His Beloved Son to die on the cross and pay the price for our justification!" Dave exclaimed. "Getting back to the original question, so what do we do now as a member of God's family?"

"I can't wait to find out!" answered Nick.

"Well," Dave said, "Jesus gives us the most important commandment of all of God's commandments in Matthew 22. Read verses 37 through 40."

Nick read:

> And He said to him, "'YOU SHALL LOVE THE LORD YOUR GOD WITH ALL YOUR HEART, AND WITH ALL YOUR SOUL, AND WITH ALL YOUR MIND.'
>
> "This is the great and foremost commandment.
>
> "The second is like it, 'YOU SHALL LOVE YOUR NEIGHBOR AS YOURSELF.'
>
> "On these two commandments depend the whole Law and the Prophets." (Matthew 22:37-40)

"God's entire revelation of Himself to the nation of Israel up to the time of Christ hinged on these two commandments," Dave expounded. "But a great error arises in the minds of many Christians when they read the Lord's words here. They assume that, because God has made them spiritually alive and part of His family, they have automatically fulfilled the first commandment. 'Sure, I love God,' they would say here.

"So, they look to move on to the second commandment, and begin doing good works in God's Name toward their neighbors. But we are not to do *our* wills in God's Name, we are to do *God's* will in God's Name! Read Jesus' words at the beginning of The Lord's Prayer."

Dave flipped Nick's Bible to Matthew 6 and pointed to verse 9. Nick read, "'"Pray then in this way: 'Our Father who art in heaven, Hallowed be Thy name. Thy kingdom come, Thy will be done, On earth as it is in heaven.'"'"

"Jesus tells us to ask the Father that His will be done on earth, not our wills," explained Dave. "So the obvious question is, 'What is God's will for me?'"

"Exactly!" Nick assented.

"The answer is found in that first commandment that was so quickly discarded. God desires that we love Him deeply and intimately. As He says, He wants us to love Him with all of our hearts, all of our souls, and all of our minds—not just parts of them.

"A great friend of mine tells an excellent story to illustrate this point," Dave continued.

> Picture a father of a little boy. The father is sitting in his living room chair. He's been working all day, so he hasn't seen much of his son. All the while, the little boy is running here and there, doing things that he knows should please his father. He runs and picks up his toys in the family room, then runs to straighten up his bedroom, yelling 'Hi Dad!' to his father as he scurries through the living room.
>
> Now, what the father really desires is that his son would come and climb up on his lap, hug him, kiss him, laugh with him and spend time talking with him. Not that the things the boy was doing were bad, because such tasks

must be done. But they pale in comparison to the greatest desire of the father: hours of quality time with his son developing a deep, intimate, personal relationship.

"The greatest desire of God the Father is that we, His children, climb up on the Lap of God and spend quality time developing a deep, intimate, personal relationship with Him. There is a reason why Jesus called this 'the great and foremost commandment.' The first commandment is to be done first! Here, read Luke 10:38 through verse 42."

Nick began reading:

> Now as they were traveling along, He entered a village; and a woman named Martha welcomed Him into her home.
>
> She had a sister called Mary, who was seated at the Lord's feet, listening to His word.
>
> But Martha was distracted with all her preparations; and she came up *to Him* and said, "Lord, do You not care that my sister has left me to do all the serving alone? Then tell her to help me."
>
> But the Lord answered and said to her, "Martha, Martha, you are worried and bothered about so many things;
>
> "but *only* one thing is necessary, for Mary has chosen the good part, which shall not be taken away from her." (Luke 10:38-42)

"Almighty God can instantaneously accomplish all of the good works that all of the Christians in all of the world could dream up—with one movement of His little finger," Dave asserted. "But He desires first and foremost that His children know Him deeply and intimately, and become well acquainted with His ways.

"According to Jesus, Martha was busy doing good things for God, but she was doing Martha's thing, so she became irritated and exhausted. Mary sat at the Lord's feet and listened to His word. Mary 'got on the Lap of God,' so to speak, which Jesus said is the 'one thing' that is necessary to please God.

"Listen to the heart-cry of Moses, God's servant, after leading the children of Israel out of slavery in Egypt—even after performing miracle after miracle and witnessing God's awesome power: '"Now therefore, I pray You, if I have found favor in Your sight, let me know Your ways that I may know You, so that I may (continue to) find favor in Your sight"' (Exodus 33:13)."

"Wow, what an intense prayer!" Nick replied.

"This should be the cry of our hearts every single day," answered Dave, "to know God deeply and intimately, and to know His ways. When we make God's greatest desire our greatest desire, then He blesses us by allowing us to participate in His plan. Read Ephesians 2:10."

"'For we are His workmanship, created in Christ Jesus for good works, which God prepared beforehand, that we should walk in them,'" Nick read.

"We are to do the 'good works which God prepared beforehand,' not those we ourselves can think up," Dave explained. "God wants us to do His works, not because He can't, but because He wants us to participate in His plan.

"Not one of us was around before time began, when the Almighty Eternal God ordained His plan for all of creation. He does not need our help for anything. We are not Jesus' eyes, hands and feet—He has His own eyes, hands and feet! And He actively holds all of creation together (Colossians 1:17)! But, as a good friend puts it, God wants us to 'get in on it!' God has ordained for each of His children a heavenly estate, a reward for walking in His good works. Read Ephesians 1:11."

Nick found the passage and read, "'In Him also we have obtained an inheritance, having been predestined according to His purpose who works all things after the counsel of His will.'"

"Please notice that God predetermined our inheritance based on His own purposes. But, it all starts with getting on the Father's Lap, and building a deep, intimate, personal relationship with Him," Dave exhorted. "Running around doing our wills in God's Name only ends in exhaustion and man-made, temporary results. But, when God works His plan through us, the results are eternal and nothing short of miraculous!

"When getting on the Father's Lap becomes the most important part of our day—that which we cannot live without—then the Father reveals His plan for this life to us. Then we become anything but lazy. We become totally effective Christians! But most Christians are not willing to put aside their other interests to seek the Father's will at any cost. Thus, they live entire lives always wondering what God's will is for them.

"Many preachers run away from the one thing Jesus said was necessary to please the Father: getting on His Lap. They are afraid that it will make the church body even more lazy than it is. O, the foolishness of man-made 'wisdom'!

"What the sinful nature does not understand is that most Christians 'serve God' like a slave under a harsh, legalistic taskmaster. Thus, it's a great burden to serve God, 'but sacrifices must be made!' O, the abject foolishness of man-made 'knowledge'!

"Some say, 'the church doesn't do anything'; or 'the church doesn't pray'; or 'the church doesn't give'; or 'the church doesn't obey!' This is not an action problem, it's a *love* problem! Man will exhaust himself, and even die, for the one he truly loves! But we hound Christians with man-made 'wisdom' to get out there and 'do, do, do!'...just like Martha. It's no wonder the exhausted church doesn't want to be involved.

"Christians don't pray, give, or obey God because they are not head-over-heels in love with God," Dave contended. "They don't love their heavenly Father because they don't know Him deeply and intimately.

"God's wisdom says: 'Sit at My feet and learn of Me! Get on My Lap, my child, and fall deeply in love with Me. I will then either bring to you the ones I want you to touch, or I will pave the way for you to go where I want you. Fall deeply in love with Me first. Then you will want to obey Me more than anything else in the universe, instead of just feeling that you have to obey Me. Get on My Lap and intimately learn My ways, and I will cause your enemies to be at peace with you, or I will fight them Myself and destroy them!'"

"That's where I want to be—on my heavenly Father's Lap!" exclaimed Nick.

"Amen!" agreed Dave. "Many of God's children, unfortunately, find themselves running around on the outskirts, away from the Father's Lap. Some even try to fight the devil, our enemy, out there on the fringes. Believe it or not, to face the enemy, they turn their back to the

Father, the Source of power, and attempt to engage our extremely cunning, insidious and invisible foe in spiritual warfare."

"Not very smart," chimed Nick.

"Right! The place the Father supremely desires for us is right on His Lap, deeply and intimately in love with Him. Then He will fight our battles, and He will work His plan through us.

"When we concentrate on fulfilling the first commandment, God will then use us to fulfill the second commandment by His power. He will bring about the situations for us to love our neighbor, even if 'our neighbor' is our enemy. In Luke 10, Jesus tells the parable of the Good Samaritan, a story you probably have heard (*see page 225*)."

"I've heard people call those that help others in need 'Good Samaritans,'" answered Nick.

"Exactly. Here the Lord Jesus clearly details the true meaning of the second commandment: sacrificially loving and caring for those in need. This simply cannot be done consistently and effectively without first doing 'the great and foremost commandment.'

"When we spend time on the Father's Lap loving Him, He prepares us for the ministry that He wants accomplished. Then, when God strongly plants a work in our minds, or brings people in our paths for ministry, we boldly walk through the open door. We forge ahead with faith in God and His power, and do not hesitate. If the work is not of God, He will close the door.

"And when we are loving and serving our neighbor with God's love and power, we find we are simultaneously loving and serving God as well by doing what He wants accomplished! Getting on and staying on the Lap of the Father is the will of God, for every child of God, for every moment of life."

How to Pray

"Awesome! But, as I'm spending time on our Father's Lap, what am I to do there? How do I get closer and more deeply in love with Him?" Nick asked.

"A relationship with God is not like an ABC formula—do it this way, and God responds that way. No. It's a relationship; it is active and alive, and grows with time and effort. Every free moment of every day, immerse yourself in getting to know and love your Father by any means possible," Dave responded. "Jesus said: '"But seek first His kingdom and His righteousness, and all these things will be added to you"' (Matthew 6:33).

"Prayer is God's main method of communication. Just as in human relationships, intimate communication is critical for a deeper relationship and a deeper love. Prayer is talking to our heavenly Father, and there are many levels of prayer. Picture yourself as His child, climb up on His Lap, love Him and have a deep Father-son talk.

"Since Jesus Himself is our example in prayer, read Luke 5:16 and 6:12."

"'But He Himself would often slip away to the wilderness and pray,'" Nick quoted, and then flipped to the second verse. "'And it was at this time that He went off to the mountain to pray, and He spent the whole night in prayer to God.'"

"Beginning each day in prayer is critical to the Christian walk," Dave maintained. "Since we have given this life back totally to God for His use, it is crucial to recognize God for who He is, and dedicate the entire day to Him. Here is a good outline to follow in prayer.

"First—**Gospel**: Remind yourself every morning that, when you were dead in sin and rebelling against our holy Father, He sent His Son to die on the cross to pay for your heinous crimes. This reminder will keep you humble, remembering you deserved eternal torture in hell, but God had mercy on you, and loved you, and chose you to be in His family despite your sin. Here we confess any sins we may have committed recently that would hinder our intimacy with God.

"*Confession* of sin simply means to agree with God that we have wronged Him. If God through His Word says my action or attitude is sin, I do not try to hide or justify my position. I simply, humbly agree with God that I have offended His holiness, and apologize. As true believers, our sins—past, present and future—have been paid for and forgiven by God at the cross of Christ.

"Second—**Thanksgiving**: Spend time thanking God for His mercy and love towards you and for choosing you to be in His family. Thank Him for sending Christ Jesus to earth to reveal to you the Father. Thank the Lord Jesus for dying on the cross for your sin, and for His resurrection life. Thank Him for sending the Holy Spirit to make you spiritually alive and teach you God's truth. Thank the Holy Spirit for continually remaking you into the likeness of Christ.

"Third—**Worship**: Sing songs of praise to God that you learn in church. Turn to the Psalms and create your own melodies to the words of praise in God's Word. Spend time worshiping our awesome Creator just for who He is...God Almighty!

"Fourth—**Intercession**: Pray for others, beginning with foreign nations, and then this nation, its leaders, and state and local leaders (1 Timothy 2:1-2), people in your family, friends, and especially the leaders in your church. Ask God to convict the sinners and bring salvation. Also ask Him to strengthen those in the family of God, and protect them from the evil one.

"Fifth—**Petition**: Bring all of your specific personal cares and requests before Him. Begin here with asking God to pour out His Holy Spirit upon you, and pour out His love into your heart so that you may fall more deeply in love with Him. Pray Moses' prayer! Then ask Him for specific personal needs that you have, no matter how small, because you will not receive unless you ask (James 4:2; Matthew 7:7-11).

"Finally—**The Word**: Pray God's Word back to Him, asking Him to fulfill His specific promises in you. For example, if you are reading Jesus' words in Matthew 5:44, '"But I say to you, love your enemies, and pray for those who persecute you,"' make those words personal to you. Ask God to show you how you might love an enemy at work or school, and how to pray for someone who has rejected you for sharing the gospel."

"What a great outline! It seems to cover everything! But how could I possibly remember all of it?" asked Nick.

"Here. I've written the six areas on this index card with a brief explanation of each area. You can keep it with you when you pray. After a while, it will come naturally," encouraged Dave. "And you can pray, or talk to God, anywhere and at any time!"

"Thanks, bro!" Nick exclaimed. "I'll sure thank God for bringing you into my life!"

"Excellent! Now let's sum up the answer to today's question of what the children of God are to do with the lives God gave them."

"Okay," agreed Nick. "First, always have your sword with you!"

"Correct!" Dave assented. "The Bible is Almighty God's revelation of Himself to man, that He is the Eternal Creator and Sustainer of all that exists or will exist!

"Next, anyone born of a human father has the sin nature of Adam, and therefore is a sinner, dead to the things of God. A spiritually-dead sinner cannot desire God, seek God, reconcile with God, reach out for God, accept God or choose God. He is dead, and the dead can't do anything because they are dead.

"If God has chosen a spiritually-dead sinner to be part of His family, He puts His Holy Spirit into the sinner to make him alive, so that he recognizes that his sin is a heinous crime of rebellion against his Holy Creator, deserving of judgment. For the first time, a sinner has true remorse for offending God and His perfect holiness.

"When God makes a sinner alive, making him a family member and saving him from God's wrath, the biblical response is to repent and believe in the gospel.

"To repent means to change masters, giving up our false ownership of this life that we have stolen from God; and giving this life totally back to Christ, its rightful owner, for His use.

"To believe, or 'faith in Christ,' means to trust totally in the two parts of Christ's perfect work for salvation.

"The two parts of Christ's perfect work are: His death on the cross to pay for your sins, and His perfect life credited to your account.

"Because Christ is Almighty God the Son, 'faith in Christ' results in being 'perfect as your heavenly Father is perfect'—or justification.

"Justification is the act of God to credit Christ's perfect work to the sinner's account, making him perfect as God is perfect, and able to be in God's family. This is a once-in-a-lifetime event and is irrevocable, because the sinner has passed out of death and into eternal life.

"God the Holy Spirit affirms the adoption by God the Father to the true believer's heart. But, an unbeliever just going through the religious motions could ask himself The Three Burning Questions:

1. Has this life been so radically changed that I now consider what God wants above and before what I want?

2. Have I given this life back to Christ, its rightful owner, for whatever He wants to do with it?

3. Am I totally trusting in Christ's work to make me acceptable to God, not adding anything of mine into the mix?

"The answer to all Three Burning Questions must be unconditionally 'Yes!' if one is a true child of God

"The great and foremost commandment is, '"YOU SHALL LOVE THE LORD YOUR GOD WITH ALL YOUR HEART, AND WITH ALL YOUR SOUL, AND WITH ALL YOUR MIND."' This is God the Father's supreme desire for His children.

"The Lap of the Father is where God wants His children to be, loving Him, spending time with Him, and learning His ways. The first commandment is to be done first.

"On the Father's Lap, we communicate with God mainly through prayer. Every moment possible we are to immerse ourselves in getting to know our heavenly Father better.

"We as Christians must begin our day in intimate prayer with God, since we have given this life totally to Him for His use, and this is His supreme desire.

"A good outline for praying is: Gospel, Thanksgiving, Worship, Intercession, Petition and The Word.

"As we develop a deep, intimate, personal relationship with our heavenly Father, He shows us His ways, and uses us to get in on His eternal plan by doing the good works He has prepared for us to do.

"Only after doing the first commandment can we possibly fulfill the second, '"LOVE YOUR NEIGHBOR AS YOURSELF."' As we develop a deep, intimate relationship with God, He gives us His love and His power with which to love others, even our enemies.

"God Himself brings about the good works He desires to be done—we do not invent them.

"The eternal, sovereign Almighty God does not need our help for anything. But He desires to give us an inheritance, a reward for doing the good works He prepared for us. He wants us to 'get in on it!'—to get in on the works God is doing.

"And that is God's will for His children—to get on and stay on His Lap—and develop a deep, intimate, personal relationship with Him!" concluded Dave.

Love and Suffering

"Our God is so awesome!" Nick exclaimed. "He created us, He sustains us, He died for our sins, He raised Himself for our justification, He makes us alive when we are dead in rebellion, He forgives our sins, He enables us to love Him, He gives us eternal life with Him, He gives us His love and His power to love others, and He ordains for us an inheritance to boot!"

"How much does God love you? This much," Dave said as he extended his arms, "and He spread out His arms and He died."

The acting out of the crucifixion brought a tear to Nick's eye. "I've never known a love so deep," Nick confessed, "and it's what I've been searching for all of my life."

"I love you, bro," Dave said, embracing his friend. "And the amazing thing about God's love is that we can never exhaust it. His love for us is infinite, and it just gets deeper and deeper and better.

"But God promises suffering and great pain, as well as great love, when we walk with Him. But it is His love and His power that enables us to endure to the end."

"Suffering?" questioned Nick.

"Aaah, yes...suffering," Dave solemnly avowed. "In the Kingdom of God, deep love and deep suffering are mysteriously intertwined. You can't have one without the other. Never believe the lie that once you become a Christian your troubles are over. Read Jesus' words in John 15:13."

"'"Greater love has no one than this, that one lay down his life for his friends."' I don't understand," pondered Nick.

"Just as we cannot know light unless we know darkness into which the light shines, we cannot know deep love unless we know deep suffering.

"The Christian walk," Dave explained, "can be separated into four parts: the honeymoon, the testing, the refining, and the hope. Read Romans 5:3-5."

Nick read:

> And not only this, but we also exult in our tribulations, knowing that
> tribulation brings about perseverance;
>> and perseverance, proven character; and proven character, hope;
>> and hope does not disappoint, because the love of God has been
> poured out within our hearts through the Holy Spirit who was given to us.
>
> (Romans 5:3-5)

"First is the 'honeymoon' stage, or childhood, where God weans you on His love and care, and He feeds you with the milk of His Word," Dave began. "That's where you are now.

"Second is the 'testing of your faith,' where God uses tribulation to rock your world, crumbling all of your crutches, and leaving nothing but Himself for security. Here the question, 'Did you really give up this life totally to Me for whatever I desire?' is answered. Many professing Christians never get past this step, fighting God tooth and nail, because they refuse to totally give up their claims to this life.

"Third is the 'refining of your character.' When God becomes your only security, He concentrates on melting your character with suffering in order to get rid of the dross, or garbage, or rubbish.

"Fourth is the anchor of hope. Coming out on the other end of the first three steps, you realize that the only reason you are still a Christian is because God Himself brought you through it. You have suffered excruciating loss in the flesh, but God has carried you through by His Spirit.

"This solidifies pure hope in your soul, that God really is faithful to complete His work in you, and bring you to Himself. You now have the pure gold of the love of God in your heart—true hope and comfort to share with your brothers and sisters in Christ who themselves may be suffering."

"Wow," Nick replied somberly, "I'm sure glad that God is the one who will get me through this. Where does it say this in the Bible?"

"Let me read scripture after scripture, so that you get the whole counsel of Scripture—not just an isolated verse out of context," offered Dave. "This is always a good idea when studying any one particular topic."

"Okay. I'll just listen and absorb it all." Nick shut his eyes to concentrate on the words of God that Dave began reading.

"Romans 8:16 and 17: 'The Spirit Himself bears witness with our spirit that we are children of God, and if children, heirs also, heirs of God and fellow heirs with Christ, if indeed we suffer with Him in order that we may also be glorified with Him.'

"Philippians 1:29: 'For to you it has been granted for Christ's sake, not only to believe in Him, but also to suffer for His sake.'

"Philippians 3:7 and 8: 'But whatever things were gain to me, those things I have counted as loss for the sake of Christ. More than that, I count all things to be loss in view of the surpassing value of knowing Christ Jesus my Lord, for whom I have suffered the loss of all things, and count them but rubbish in order that I may gain Christ.'

"Philippians 3:10 and 11: '...that I may know Him, and the power of His resurrection and the fellowship of His sufferings, being conformed to His death; in order that I may attain to the resurrection from the dead.'

"2 Timothy 1:8: 'Therefore do not be ashamed of the testimony of our Lord, or of me His prisoner; but join with me in suffering for the gospel according to the power of God.'

"2 Timothy 3:12: 'And indeed, all who desire to live godly in Christ Jesus will be persecuted.'

"Hebrews 12:6: 'For those whom the Lord loves He disciplines, and He scourges every son whom He receives.'

"1 Peter 2:21 and 23: 'For you have been called for this purpose, since Christ also suffered for you, leaving you an example for you to follow in His steps...and while being reviled, He did not revile in return; while suffering He uttered no threats, but kept entrusting Himself to Him who judges righteously.'

"1 Peter 4:12 through 14: 'Beloved, do not be surprised at the fiery ordeal among you, which comes upon you for your testing, as though some strange thing were happening to you; but to the degree that you share the sufferings of Christ, keep on rejoicing; so that also at the revelation of His glory, you may rejoice with exultation.'

"1 Peter 4:19: 'Therefore, let those who suffer according to the will of God entrust their souls to a faithful Creator in doing what is right.'

"1 Peter 5:10: 'And after you have suffered for a little while, the God of all grace, who called you to His eternal glory in Christ, will Himself perfect, confirm, strengthen and establish you.'

"The goal of the sufferings that God brings is to perfect us, confirm us, strengthen us and establish us in His family," Dave concluded. "God is directing the 'fiery ordeals,' and has not abandoned us in the furnace, but loves us greatly at this time. And the crowning jewel is the Apostle Paul's towering promise to us in Romans 8:18: 'For I consider that the sufferings of this present time are not worthy to be compared with the glory that is to be revealed to us!'"

"That is a towering promise!" Nick exclaimed. "If our suffering in this life is great, the glory of God waiting for us in heaven must be phenomenal!"

"Exactly!" Dave confirmed. "And it is God, and God alone, who will carry us through this process to His glory. Read Philippians 1:6."

"'For I am confident of this very thing, that He who began a good work in you will perfect it until the day of Christ Jesus.' Now that's a promise in which I can trust regardless of my circumstances or problems!" Nick exulted.

"Amen brother!" agreed Dave. "We are 'awaiting eagerly the revelation of our Lord Jesus Christ, who shall also confirm you to the end, blameless in the day of our Lord Jesus Christ. God is faithful, through whom you were called into fellowship with His Son, Jesus Christ our Lord' (1 Corinthians 1:7-9). Our faithful God Himself will complete His perfect work in us and bring us to His eternal home."

"Thank you Lord! I know I couldn't survive the test unless He brings me through it," confessed Nick. "Thank you God for Your faithfulness!"

"Why don't you close our Bible study with prayer?" Dave asked.

"All right," Nick replied, as he joined hands with Dave and closed his eyes. "Almighty, faithful, heavenly Father, we thank You for Your love, Your faithfulness, and Your awesome promises. We thank You for the privilege to climb up on Your Lap and love You, and have a deep, intimate, personal relationship with You—the Creator and Sustainer of the universe!

"We thank You that it is You who brings us through the suffering in this life; and it is You who will bring us to our heavenly home—where we can praise and worship You while basking in Your glory! I thank You for my brother Dave, for the wisdom You have given him, and his willingness to share Your Word with me. Bless him beyond all he could contain, Lord!

"Thank You for Your Word. Continue to shine Your light on us so we can know You more, and love You deeper still. In Jesus' Name we pray, amen."

"Amen!" Dave echoed. "I'll see you at dinner tonight...and don't forget church on Sunday!"

"I wouldn't miss it for the world!" Nick asserted as he closed his Bible and headed toward the door, stopping to embrace his brother in Christ. "And thanks for everything—all the time and effort you spend to teach me."

"My pleasure," Dave said. "See you later!"

"Praise Him!" Nick shouted as he walked down the dormitory hallway, lifting his hands to the sky.

"Yes!" Dave answered. "Praise Him!"

5

Questions & Answers

"It's time for answers!" Dave chimed as the Sunday school College & Career class came to order. "So, I certainly hope that there are questions!"

"You bet! Tons of them!" replied Matt, as several others nodded in agreement.

"I guess that means that we have looked at the Pop Quiz from last week, and have done some investigating," Dave assumed. "Today, we will explain why the first six questions are mere man-made traditions, which God's holy Word specifically rejects. Ed, would you please open our Bible study with prayer?"

"Dear heavenly Father," Ed began, "we praise You just for who You are—the glorious, sovereign Almighty God of the universe. We thank You that You have sent Your Son Jesus to die on the cross, paying the penalty of our sins, so that we may become Your children. Fill us now with Your Holy Spirit and teach us Your holy Word, so that we may know You intimately and understand Your ways. Thank You for Your infinite love. In Jesus' Name we pray. Amen."

"Thank you, Ed. Grant, would you please read the first quiz question?"

"Okay. Number One: 'In creating the universe, God set up the laws of nature to run it and He does not intervene,'" recited Grant.

"Thank you, Grant," Dave responded. "Last time we discussed the heresy of deism, and referred to several scriptures showing that God created the universe and actively works in it, upholding everything and sustaining it all. Anna, please read the first three scriptures I have written on the chalkboard."

Anna read:

Also we have obtained an inheritance, having been predestined
according to His purpose who works all things after the counsel of His will.
(Ephesians 1:11)

For by Him all things were created, *both* in the heavens and on earth,
visible and invisible, whether thrones or dominions or rulers or
authorities—all things have been created through Him and for Him.
He is before all things, and in Him all things hold together.
(Colossians 1:16,17)

And He is the radiance of His glory and the exact representation of His
nature, and upholds all things by the word of His power. When He had
made purification of sins, He sat down at the right hand of the Majesty on
high. (Hebrews 1:3)

"Thank you, Anna," Dave said. "The Bible makes it very clear that Almighty God not only
created everything, but actively works all things and sustains everything at all times."

"But the world certainly looks like it runs by 'the laws of nature'—science depends on it,"
offered Matt.

Judging Reality Correctly

"God is most definitely the God of order," Dave replied, "and good science can only
observe this order. God reveals the source of this order in His Word—Himself!—and that He
actively works all things and sustains everything at all times.

"One of the biggest traps to avoid is looking at reality and judging it from man's finite
viewpoint. *Truth* is reality as perceived by God, from God's infinite viewpoint, which He reveals
to us in His Word. Matt, read the Lord Jesus' words in John 7, verses 16, 17, 18 and 24,
please."

Matt found the passage and read:

So Jesus answered them and said, "My teaching is not Mine, but His
who sent Me.

"If anyone is willing to do His will, he will know of the teaching,
whether it is of God or *whether* I speak from Myself.

"He who speaks from himself seeks his own glory; but He who is seeking
the glory of the One who sent Him, He is true, and there is no
unrighteousness in Him.

"Do not judge according to appearance, but judge with righteous
judgment." (John 7:16-18,24)

"Thank you, Matt," Dave said. "The Lord Jesus first defines the True and Righteous One
as God the Father. The Lord then commands us to judge with righteous judgment—or, in other
words, to judge from God's point of view. In order to look at something from God's viewpoint,

we must first know what God declares in His eternal Word to be true.

"We often greatly err when judging according to appearance, or judging from our marred viewpoint. Our point of view is always marred by our sinful nature. More importantly, the Lord Jesus commands us *not* to judge according to appearance.

"To do so is sin for two reasons: first and foremost, it disobeys Christ's command; and secondly, one who judges according to his own opinion 'seeks his own glory.' In other words, that person attempts to elevate his own man-made opinion to the level of God's truth. To set aside God's holy Word in favor of man-made tradition or opinion, as we have already discovered, is blatant idolatry which God condemns.

"Therefore," concluded Dave, "the only correct judgment is that which is made according to God's holy Word. **God's holy Word** is only the originally intended meaning that God gave, not the finite sin-marred interpretations that man invents."

"I don't understand this," said Nick. "I read Jesus' words in the Sermon on the Mount, and He said not to judge. But here He says to judge. What's going on here?"

"Great question," Dave replied. "In Matthew 7, Jesus is saying the exact same thing He is saying here in John 7. Read the first six verses there, Nick."

Nick read:

> "Do not judge so that you will not be judged.
>
> "For in the way you judge, you will be judged; and by your standard of measure, it will be measured to you.
>
> "Why do you look at the speck that is in your brother's eye, but do not notice the log that is in your own eye?
>
> "Or how can you say to your brother, 'Let me take the speck out of your eye,' and behold, the log is in your own eye?
>
> "You hypocrite, first take the log out of your own eye, and then you will see clearly to take the speck out of your brother's eye.
>
> "Do not give what is holy to dogs, and do not throw your pearls before swine, or they will trample them under their feet, and turn and tear you to pieces." (Matthew 7:1-6)

"Thank you, Nick," Dave responded. "This is one of the most misused passages in the entire Bible, because it is quoted outside of the context in which Jesus speaks it. Jesus cannot be saying not to judge at all, because He commands us in verse 6 not to 'give what is holy to dogs' or 'swine.' In order to obey the command, we have to make a judgment to determine who are 'dogs' or 'swine'!

"Jesus is not saying not to judge at all, but not to judge according to our flawed viewpoint or opinions. We all have logs in our eyes, a sinful nature that mars our ability to see clearly. This is why in John 7 Jesus commands us to judge according to God's perfectly and infinitely righteous Word, because God's Word is the only standard of truth by which correct judgments may be made in this universe."

"That makes sense," reasoned Nick.

"We as Christians are commanded by God's Word to make judgments. The Lord Jesus ordered us to judge whether people are 'dogs' or 'swine' in order to avoid sharing God's glorious truths with sinners who absolutely do not want the truth. Jesus also commands us to judge a fellow Christian if he has been caught committing sin. As well, the Apostle Paul commands us to judge those who claim to be Christians, but live in sin, in order to forsake fellowship with them. Pam, would you please read Matthew 18:15-17 and 1 Corinthians 5:9-12?"

Pam read:

"If your brother sins, go and show him his fault in private; if he listens to you, you have won your brother.

"But if he does not listen *to you,* take one or two more with you, so that BY THE MOUTH OF TWO OR THREE WITNESSES EVERY FACT MAY BE CONFIRMED.

"If he refuses to listen to them, tell it to the church; and if he refuses to listen even to the church, let him be to you as a Gentile and a tax collector." (Matthew 18:15-17)

I wrote you in my letter not to associate with immoral people;

I *did* not at all *mean* with the immoral people of this world, or with the covetous and swindlers, or with idolaters, for then you would have to go out of the world.

But actually, I wrote to you not to associate with any so-called brother if he is an immoral person, or covetous, or an idolater, or a reviler, or a drunkard, or a swindler—not even to eat with such a one.

For what have I to do with judging outsiders? Do you not judge those who are within *the church*? (1 Corinthians 5:9-12)

"Thank you, Pam," commended Dave. "For a person living in sin to complain to a Christian that he is judging him is a foolish and indefensible position. God's Word commands Christians to judge, but to judge according to God's standards, not according to appearances, or our own flawed opinions. Situations that appear questionable are only to be judged after digging deeper and determining all of the facts. These facts are then to be taken and lined up to God's holy Word, the only standard of truth by which correct judgments may be made in this universe!

"Facts about anything, not just people, must be lined up with God's Word for truthful judgment—especially 'scientific facts.' This universe may look from all appearances to be running on its own according to 'the laws of nature.' But God says He is actively and intimately involved in personally working His eternal plan, including even the smallest of details in the universe.

"We would completely miss this truth, as many bad scientists do today, if we relied on our flawed and limited understanding instead of God's perfect, infinite Word to make judgments. **Good science** observes reality as it is, and then forms conclusions. **Bad science** first forms its desired conclusions, and then slants its observations to fit its lies."

"Okay, I understand now that just observing reality may not tell us the whole story, and that our perception of reality may be flawed, or even fooled," Matt assented. "Since God is invisible, we need His Word to explain reality, and His involvement in it, from His viewpoint."

"Excellent," praised Dave.

"What I don't understand," Matt continued, "is why you say God must be involved in even the smallest of details. Why can't He just ordain the laws of nature and let them run things?"

"For I, the LORD, do not Change!"

"Awesome question!" Dave resounded. "I can see you are trying to think things through. Keep it up! The answer to your question, though, may actually shock you. Matt, did you know that the square root of 289 is 17?"

"Huh? Uh, no...but I do now!"

"Exactly!" Dave responded, as the looks on the faces of the class showed utter confusion. "Matt, read Psalm 102:25-27, Malachi 3:6, and James 1:17 for us, please."

Matt read:

> "Of old You founded the earth,
>> And the heavens are the work of Your hands.
> "Even they will perish, but You endure;
>> And all of them will wear out like a garment;
>> Like clothing You will change them and they will be changed.
> "But You are the same,
>> And Your years will not come to an end." (Psalm 102:25-27)

> For I, the LORD, do not change; therefore you, O sons of Jacob, are not consumed." (Malachi 3:6)

> Every good thing given and every perfect gift is from above, coming down from the Father of lights, with whom there is no variation or shifting shadow. (James 1:17)

"Thank you, Matt," Dave replied. "In His holy Word, Almighty God declares, about Himself, that He never changes. This is one of God's eternal attributes; part of His holy character. Theologians call the absolute unchangeableness of God's character and God's plan ***immutability***.

"Two minutes ago, you did not know the square root of 289. Now, you do. Since you have learned something, you have changed. You are not the same as you were two minutes ago, because now you have knowledge that you did not possess then.

"God Almighty says He never changes. Therefore, it is impossible for Him to learn anything, or He would change—and would no longer be ***omniscient***, or all-knowing. Thus, He must know all things from eternity past through eternity future. God knows all things at all times because He has ordained all things for all time in His eternal plan which He formed before creation.

"Ed, please read Psalm 147:5, Romans 11:33 and Hebrews 4:13 for us."

Ed read:

>   Great is our Lord and abundant in strength;
>   His understanding is infinite. (Psalm 147:5)

>   Oh, the depth of the riches both of the wisdom and knowledge of God!
>   How unsearchable are His judgments and unfathomable His ways!
>   (Romans 11:33)

>   And there is no creature hidden from His sight, but all things are open
>   and laid bare to the eyes of Him with whom we have to do.
>   (Hebrews 4:13)

"The knowledge and understanding of Almighty God are infinite and unfathomable!" Dave exclaimed. "God does not look down the corridors of time, see something happen, and then figure out what to do. If He has not ordained absolutely everything that exists or occurs from eternity past through eternity future, then God learns something. And that is impossible, for then He would change!

"It is blasphemy to hold the position that God sees a future event and then determines His actions."

"What is blasphemy?" asked Nick.

"**Blasphemy** is the heinous crime of saying or doing anything pertaining to God that does not give Him proper worship and respect," Dave explained.

"Saying that God needs to see a future event and then determine His plan of action is blasphemy, because it profanes God's holy character. The divine attributes of unchangeableness (immutability) or all-knowingness (omniscience) are just as vital a part of God's character as His holiness or justice or goodness.

"No true Christian would ever say, 'God is not holy today'; or, 'God is not just'; because God describes Himself in His Word as having those characteristics eternally. Thus, to say those things profanes Him, and is blasphemy.

"It is equally blasphemous to say 'God does not know all things'; or, 'God learns from future events in order to make His plans'; or, 'God is not immutable, because He learns from the future and grows in understanding.' God knows all things because He has ordained whatever exists or happens. If God looks to the future to discover something, then He is not omniscient—contradicting the scriptures we just read. All of the attributes of God's character are eternal and perfect.

"Therefore," Dave concluded, "God's immutability and omniscience demand that He knows where every sub-atomic particle is because He appointed it to be where it is at every single moment. That is how intimately involved God must be in His creation! For, if one atom were outside of His plan, God would learn something, and would change, and thus could not be God—'"For I, the LORD, do not change"' (Malachi 3:6)!"

"Wow!" Nick exclaimed. "How awesome is our God!"

"This is why Anna read the earlier scriptures that said: 'in Him all things hold together'

(Colossians 1:17); and that 'He upholds all things by the word of His power' (Hebrews 1:3); and that 'God works all things after the counsel of His will' (Ephesians 1:11). For God to be God," Dave asserted, "He must rule sovereignly, and have ordained everything that exists and occurs—even the smallest of details!"

"Awesome is right!" Matt echoed Nick. "I did not realize how much of reality absolutely depends on God Himself and who He says He is."

The Kindness and Severity of God

"Well, the next few Quiz questions are also related to God and who He says He is," said Dave. "Kelly, would you please read questions two, three and four?"

"'God is all-loving and all-forgiving,'" Kelly recited. "'God loves all sinners but hates their sins,' and 'God loves everyone and has a wonderful plan for each life.'"

"Thank you, Kelly," acknowledged Dave. "'God is all-loving and all-forgiving.' True or false? Biblical, or man-made tradition?"

"Well, you've already told us that it's false," Jennifer granted, "but it sure sounds like it ought to be true."

"Just like judging the physical universe by appearances will lead to error," Dave responded, "judging teachings on spiritual matters by personal opinion will always lead you astray and into heresy. We humans—true Christians included—have a sinful nature that deceives our minds if we are not continually exposed to the truth.

"The only standard of truth by which correct judgments may be made is God's holy Word. Remember last week, Jennifer, we found that God is who He says He is, not who we think He ought to be?"

"Yes, I remember," she replied. "We agreed to give up our idols of what we thought of God, and embrace what God says about Himself in His Word."

"Excellent," commended Dave. "Anna, would you please read the next four verses written on the chalkboard for us?"

Anna read:

> In this is love, not that we loved God, but that He loved us and sent His
> Son *to be* the propitiation for our sins.
>
> Beloved, if God so loved us, we also ought to love one another.
>
> (1 John 4:10,11)

> For You are not a God who takes pleasure in wickedness;
>> No evil dwells with You.
> The boastful shall not stand before Your eyes;
>> You hate all who do iniquity.
> You destroy those who speak falsehood;
>> The LORD abhors the man of bloodshed and deceit.
>
> (Psalm 5:4-6)

> The LORD tests the righteous and the wicked,
>> And the one who loves violence His soul hates. (Psalm 11:5)

> And not only this, but there was Rebekah also, when she had conceived
> *twins* by one man, our father Isaac;
>
> for though *the twins* were not yet born and had not done anything good
> or bad, so that God's purpose according to *His* choice would stand, not
> because of works but because of Him who calls,
>
> it was said to her, "THE OLDER WILL SERVE THE YOUNGER."
>
> Just as it is written, "JACOB I LOVED, BUT ESAU I HATED."
>
> (Romans 9:10-13)

"Thank you, Anna," Dave said. "God loves His children with such an awesome love, that He sent His precious Son from His glorious throne to be spat upon and beaten by His own creation...and then to be put to death to pay our penalty for our sins. Jesus loved us so much that while we hated and reviled Him, He still died for us. That is incomprehensible love.

"The Father loves His true child so deeply, that He wants His child to come sit on His Lap as often as possible to enjoy each other's company. The Father gave up His precious, only Son—the One of infinite worth—in order to gain His true children for eternity!

"But clearly God says in His Word that He does hate as well as love. 'God is love,' as it says in 1 John 4:8; *and* 'God is a consuming fire,' as it says in Hebrews 12:29! God is all of these things!

"To take bits and pieces of Scripture about God Himself, and to leave out the parts we don't like, is the same heinous crime as setting aside God's Word in favor of our man-made opinions. The sin of *idolatry* begins with rejecting some or all of the passages in which God describes Himself. Idolatry is completed by replacing the one true God with a god of our own making—an idol that fits comfortably with our depraved, sinful nature.

"Therefore, to make an innocuous statement like 'God is all-loving' simply discards what God says in His Word about Himself. The same goes for the statement 'God is all-forgiving.' Ed, would you please read the next two passages from Jesus' own words?"

Ed read:

> "Enter through the narrow gate; for the gate is wide and the way is
> broad that leads to destruction, and there are many who enter through it.
>
> "For the gate is small and the way is narrow that leads to life, and there
> are few who find it." (Matthew 7:13-14)

> Then He began to denounce the cities in which most of His miracles
> were done, because they did not repent.
>
> "Woe to you, Chorazin! Woe to you, Bethsaida! For if the miracles had
> occurred in Tyre and Sidon which occurred in you, they would have
> repented long ago in sackcloth and ashes.
>
> "Nevertheless I say to you, it will be more tolerable for Tyre and Sidon
> in *the* day of judgment than for you.
>
> "And you, Capernaum, will not be exalted to heaven, will you? You will
> descend to Hades; for if the miracles had occurred in Sodom which occurred
> in you, it would have remained to this day." (Matthew 11:20-23)

"Thank you, Ed," acknowledged Dave. "Clearly Jesus says that not everyone will be forgiven of their sins. In fact, He states that the great majority of mankind, including the inhabitants of these three cities, will descend to hell to pay for their sins.

"Therefore, God only forgives the sins of 'the few' on the narrow road, so He is not 'all-forgiving.' God never claimed to be 'all-forgiving,' but to be perfectly just, bestowing His grace and mercy on whomever He desires.

"Question 3: 'God loves all sinners but hates their sins.' The two Psalms that Anna had just read clearly shows that this is a man-made tradition that the Word of God specifically rejects. Psalm 5:5, speaking of God, says: 'You hate all who do iniquity.' Psalm 11:5 says: 'And the one who loves violence His soul hates.' The Apostle Paul quotes God, declaring: 'JACOB I LOVED, BUT ESAU I HATED' before they were even born! God declares in His Word that He not only hates sin, but sinners who love their sin."

"What about the saying, 'Hate the sin but love the sinner?'" questioned Nick.

"Well, that's exactly what it is, a man-made saying," Dave replied. "Not to say that the saying is wrong, but its truthfulness must be determined by the only standard of truth in the universe: God's holy Word.

"God can hate sinners, because He alone is the eternal righteous Judge who must punish His evil enemies. We, however, are commanded by God to love. As we have seen, we are to love God first and foremost with all of our hearts, minds and strength. God then fills us with His love with which to love our neighbors, our brothers and sisters in Christ...even our enemies.

"We are to bring glory to God by loving a fallen world. In our finite sphere, we are to 'hate the sin but love the sinner.' In God's infinite realm, being perfectly righteous, He must judge the unrighteous."

"I see," Nick mused. "So, in this case pertaining to humans, the man-made saying is biblical, and therefore true. But I should always test man-made sayings by the Word of God, because they may not always be true."

"Excellent!" Dave encouraged. "And such is the case with our next Quiz question, 'God loves everyone and has a wonderful plan for each life.' As we have just seen, God does not love everyone. But, God most definitely has a plan for the life of every person, as He has ordained the exact number of days of every life. The question is whether the description can be biblically considered as 'wonderful,' promising a sort of 'heaven on earth.' Paul, please read the next two passages on the chalkboard."

Paul read:

> Your eyes have seen my unformed substance;
>   And in Your book were all written
> The days that were ordained *for me,*
>   When as yet there was not one of them. (Psalm 139:16)

> Women received *back* their dead by resurrection; and others were tortured, not accepting their release, so that they might obtain a better resurrection; and others experienced mockings and scourgings, yes, also chains and imprisonment.

They were stoned, they were sawn in two, they were tempted, they were put to death with the sword; they went about in sheepskins, in goatskins, being destitute, afflicted, ill-treated (*men* of whom the world was not worthy), wandering in deserts and mountains and caves and holes in the ground. (Hebrews 11:35-38)

"Thank you, Paul," recognized Dave. "God has ordained the days of every life He creates, and every detail of that life. In Hebrews 11, 'The Hall of Faith' of great saints is presented. These believers accomplished great things on earth, and obtained the resurrection from the dead into God's glorious heaven. For many, however, being a true child of God on earth meant ill-treatment, torture, and even death—some by being sawn in two!

"God does not promise 'a wonderful plan' to anyone for this earthly life. On the contrary, as we have seen, we are to totally give up this life to Christ for whatever He desires to do with it. The Lord Jesus commanded this step of repenting as part of the agreement for salvation, and He commanded it after John the Baptist was thrown into prison! Kelly, please read the next three passages on the chalkboard."

Kelly read:

Now after John had been taken into custody, Jesus came into Galilee, preaching the gospel of God, and saying, "The time is fulfilled, and the kingdom of God is at hand; repent and believe in the gospel."

(Mark 1:14,15)

"He who loves his life loses it, and he who hates his life in this world will keep it to life eternal.

"If anyone serves Me, he must follow Me; and where I am, there My servant will be also; if anyone serves Me, the Father will honor him."

(John 12:25,26)

The Spirit Himself testifies with our spirit that we are children of God, and if children, heirs also, heirs of God and fellow heirs with Christ, if indeed we suffer with *Him* so that we may also be glorified with *Him*.

(Romans 8:16,17)

"Thank you, Kelly. This world is not our home," Dave explained. "We have a glorious paradise awaiting us in heaven! We are to totally give up this life to God and serve Him. This may result in a 'wonderful life' from a human perspective, but God does not promise glory until we are home with Him.

Why Do Evil and Suffering Exist?

"As we have seen, this Christian life is more often than not marked with suffering. God's purpose for saving sinners and bringing them into His family was not to give them a comfortable life here on earth. God's purpose for His children is to glorify Him in the midst of an evil world.

The Apostle Paul states in God's Word that suffering is an integral part of being a child of God, so we should not be surprised or dismayed by affliction.

"Why? Because Paul also says: 'For I consider that the sufferings of this present time are not worthy to be compared with the glory that is to be revealed to us' (Romans 8:18). The Apostle also states: 'And we know that God causes all things to work together for good to those who love God, to those who are called according to *His* purpose' (Romans 8:28)."

"Amen!" Nick shouted.

"The problem of the existence of evil and suffering, and the belief that God is totally good and totally powerful, has perplexed philosophers and theologians, Christians and non-Christians for centuries," Dave observed. "But, it is totally a problem of perspective.

"The debate involved the ideas that, if evil and suffering exist, which they do—either God is good but does not have the power to stop them, or that God is all-powerful, but not good, because He allows such evil and suffering to continue.

"Well, evil and suffering are not the same. Evil causes suffering. Evil is not an entity in and of itself. *Evil* is the total absence of good or truth. Evil is the perversion of that which was good. That perversion is a very powerful force, much like a vacuous black hole that sucks everything into it.

"God pronounced everything He created 'very good' (Genesis 1:31). Adam was created good, but pridefully disobeyed God, plunging him and his posterity into death. Men that do evil are committing acts utterly devoid of any good. Even Satan was created the most beautiful angel and the lead worshiper of God (Ezekiel 28:12-19), but was cast down to earth when he succumbed to the sin of pride.

"Sin, Satan, evil and suffering are not surprises to God! God ordained them as part of His eternal plan to bring total honor to Christ Jesus! Almighty God tells us specifically in His Word that He subjected all of His creation to slavery to evil, so that God the Son, Christ Jesus, would receive all the glory as creation's only Savior—creation's only way out of the slavery to evil! Chelsea, please read for us Romans 8:19 through 22, and John 8:31, 32 and 36."

Chelsea read:

> For the anxious longing of the creation waits eagerly for the revealing of the sons of God.
>
> For the creation was subjected to futility, not willingly, but because of Him who subjected it, in hope
>
> that the creation itself also will be set free from its slavery to corruption into the freedom of the glory of the children of God.
>
> For we know that the whole creation groans and suffers the pains of childbirth together until now. (Romans 8:19-22)

> So Jesus was saying to those Jews who had believed Him, "If you continue in My word, *then* you are truly disciples of Mine;
>
> and you will know the truth, and the truth will make you free.
>
> "So if the Son makes you free, you will be free indeed."
>
> (John 8:31,32,36)

"Thank you, Chelsea," acknowledged Dave. "Why does evil exist? God subjected all of creation to it so that, in longing for freedom from evil's vicious claws, all glory and honor would be given to creation's only Savior, God the Son Jesus Christ. The glory of God is God's entire purpose for creating the universe and ordaining everything that occurs.

"The truth sets us free from evil's merciless grip. Christ Jesus declared: '"I am the way, and the truth, and the life"' (John 14:6a). God's truth, the Lord Jesus Christ, makes us free indeed—really and actually free—from imprisonment and slavery to evil!

"I would never want to trivialize the agony of a person's suffering, because I have known deep suffering myself—before and after conversion to Christ. But I have found that the best way to understand and deal with anything, especially suffering, is to know and trust in God's truth.

"Yes, suffering is excruciating and painful, but that does not necessarily make it evil. Imagine going to your doctor and being diagnosed with a serious flu virus requiring an antibiotic vaccination.

"Imagine your doctor saying, 'A shot will clear up this life-threatening illness. But, because the shot would cause you pain—however momentary—I refuse to administer it.' You would *demand* to suffer, for the momentary affliction is worth the lasting benefits!

"Nothing gets a person's attention quite like suffering. From God's eternal, infinite and perfect perspective, suffering is extremely effective in drawing Christians and non-Christians closer to Himself. Jennifer, please read Jesus' words in Matthew 16, verses 24, 25 and 26."

Jennifer read:

> Then Jesus said to His disciples, "If anyone wishes to come after Me, he must deny himself, and take up his cross and follow Me.
>
> "For whoever wishes to save his life will lose it; but whoever loses his life for My sake will find it.
>
> "For what will it profit a man if he gains the whole world, and forfeits his soul? Or what will a man give in exchange for his soul?"
>
> (Matthew 16:24-26)

"Thank you, Jennifer," Dave responded. "The Lord Jesus, as always, explains reality from God's perspective. What good is it for a man to live his entire life, eighty or so years, in splendor and ease—only to be tortured forever in hell? If suffering can be used to jar a person out of his self-centered rebellion against God, or to draw a devout Christian closer to God, suffering then becomes a very beneficial thing."

"But suffering can also embitter one against God," added Paul.

"So true," Dave assented, "which is why Jesus began this passage with three commands that define His true followers: '"deny yourself, take up your cross, and follow Me."' In other words, **repent**. Change your mind about who is master of this life, and give this life back to Christ, its rightful owner. Since God created and sustains your existence, He owns this life.

"What does one do on a cross? He dies! We are to deny our selfish desires and die to our opinions and goals. The person who retains his rights to this life, and feels that God is unjust to have him suffer, has not repented. Thus, by definition, the unrepentant sinner cannot be Christ's disciple, and will pay for his sins in hell.

"Jesus charges that the true Christian denies his rights in this life, dies to himself on his cross, and obeys whatever Christ wants of this life. The person who loses this life for Jesus' sake seeks to draw closer to God and glorify Him, even through suffering. These commands of Christ are agonizing and extremely difficult for us, because they require putting to death our vicious human pride. But that is precisely God's goal in making us like Christ!

"If the truth be told, many—not all, but many—modern Christians suffer unnecessarily due to disobedience to God's commands. A true Christian that has lost his way, and his joy, undoubtedly is not obeying God by doing *The Four Basics*—praying daily, studying God's Word daily, going to church as often as possible, and spending their social time with committed Christians (Acts 2:42).

"God says: 'Do it My way, for it is good for you, and I will bless you.' But we sinfully answer: 'But I want to do this my way.' When our lives inevitably fall apart, we cry out to God, asking Him what is happening. God says: 'Do it My way and I will bless you.' But we stubbornly answer: 'But I want to do this my way.' And when we reach the bottom, crying out to God in total desperation—finally agreeing to whatever God wants—our loving heavenly Father lifts us up out of the mud again.

"God disciplines His children for their good, even to the point of death (1 John 5:16,17). A good father disciplines his child out of love, and our heavenly Father is infinitely the best father. But all such suffering could have been avoided by just obeying God in the first place.

"Also, as we just read in Romans 8, Christ our Savior suffered with the excruciating weight of our sins upon Himself!" reminded Dave. "Since God's goal for us in this life is to become like Christ, then we too must suffer as we follow Him, entrusting our souls to our infinitely good and loving heavenly Father. Suffering tears us away from this world and draws us closer to God, the Source of Life and Love. When we get on the Father's Lap, God Himself will give us His power, not only endure the agony, but to glorify Him through it.

"The Bible gives many examples of Christians suffering for Christ's sake. Consider the Apostle Paul and his companion Silas, who were beaten and imprisoned for preaching the gospel. Paul, please read Acts 16:22-25 and Hebrews 12:4-11 for us."

Paul read:

> The crowd rose up together against them, and the chief magistrates tore their robes off them and proceeded to order *them* to be beaten with rods.
>
> When they had struck them with many blows, they threw them into prison, commanding the jailer to guard them securely;
>
> and he, having received such a command, threw them into the inner prison and fastened their feet in the stocks.
>
> But about midnight Paul and Silas were praying and singing hymns of praise to God, and the prisoners were listening to them. (Acts 16:22-25)

> You have not yet resisted to the point of shedding blood in your striving against sin;
>
> and you have forgotten the exhortation which is addressed to you as sons,

"MY SON, DO NOT REGARD LIGHTLY THE DISCIPLINE OF THE LORD,
     NOR FAINT WHEN YOU ARE REPROVED BY HIM;
     FOR THOSE WHOM THE LORD LOVES HE DISCIPLINES,
     AND HE SCOURGES EVERY SON WHOM HE RECEIVES."

It is for discipline that you endure; God deals with you as with sons; for
what son is there whom *his* father does not discipline?

But if you are without discipline, of which all have become partakers,
then you are illegitimate children and not sons.

Furthermore, we had earthly fathers to discipline us, and we respected
them; shall we not much rather be subject to the Father of spirits, and live?

For they disciplined us for a short time as seemed best to them, but He
disciplines us for *our* good, so that we may share His holiness.

All discipline for the moment seems not to be joyful, but sorrowful; yet
to those who have been trained by it, afterwards it yields the peaceful fruit of
righteousness. (Hebrews 12:4-11)

"Thank you, Paul," Dave replied. "It used to be a great honor to suffer for the Name of
Christ. Sadly, these days—and I am the greatest culprit—our comfort and convenience seem to
come first. But which of us during affliction asks, 'Why me, Lord?'—instead of asking God how
He might be glorified through the experience? May God give us the strength to get on our
Father's Lap and praise His holy Name when we suffer, as Paul and Silas did. Only God the
Holy Spirit can provide such strength, and we must seek Him diligently for it!

"But the greatest sin of the modern comfortable church is the idolatrous crime of living as
if this life is our life—as if God gave us this life as a gift to do with as we please. God never says
anything like that! God owns everything in His creation, including the life of every person.

"The heinous idea that 'God has a wonderful plan for my life' assumes that *I own* 'my life.'
On the contrary, I only own what I have created, bought, or have been given as a gift to keep
for myself. This life does not meet any of those criteria. The gospel demands that we repent by
giving this life back to Christ—its rightful owner—for *His* use. God never created life for our
wonderful comfort, convenience and blessing. God's holy Word declares that God gave us this
life to love, worship and serve Him!

"Summing this up, God never promises us a wonderful 'heaven-on-earth' existence during
this lifetime. Modern man thinks that life should be perfect, and that periods of suffering are an
aberration and should never happen. God's truth is that He subjected all of creation to futility,
the utter inability to do anything good.

"Thus, suffering is everywhere in this life, and God mercifully grants us times of blessing
in order to endure. Through all of our suffering, as excruciating as it may be, we as Christians
are to draw closer to God for His love, strength, mercy and comfort. Finally, we rest in the hope
of His Word, where the Apostle Paul declares:

Therefore we do not lose heart, but though our outer man is decaying,
     yet our inner man is being renewed day by day.

For momentary, light affliction is producing for us an eternal weight of glory far beyond all comparison,

> while we look not at the things which are seen, but at the things which are not seen; for the things which are seen are temporal, but the things which are not seen are eternal. (2 Corinthians 4:16-18)

Why Do Sin and Satan Exist?

"Grant, please read the next Quiz question," Dave asked.

"Question 5: 'God did not plan the Fall of Adam before creation,'" cited Grant.

"Thank you, Grant. Last week," Dave continued, "we read scriptures declaring that Jesus Christ became our Savior from eternity past. Ed, would you read the next two passages on the board for us, please?"

Ed read:

> ...so that the manifold wisdom of God might now be made known through the church to the rulers and the authorities in the heavenly *places.*
>
> *This was* in accordance with the eternal purpose which He carried out in Christ Jesus our Lord, in whom we have boldness and confident access through faith in Him. (Ephesians 3:10-12)

> Therefore do not be ashamed of the testimony of our Lord or of me His prisoner, but join with *me* in suffering for the gospel according to the power of God,
>
> who has saved us and called us with a holy calling, not according to our works, but according to His own purpose and grace which was granted us in Christ Jesus from all eternity. (2 Timothy 1:8,9)

"Thank you, Ed," Dave said. "God's purpose—also known as His eternal plan—to save us from our sin 'was granted us in Christ Jesus from all eternity.' To be the Savior from eternity past, God the Son needed a people that required saving from eternity past. Thus, the Fall of Adam was a necessary element in the eternal plan of God.

"As we have seen, the purpose of creation is to glorify God—to give Christ Jesus, God the Son, the supremacy in all things. God, in His infinite wisdom, decreed that all of creation would be in bondage to sin through the Fall of Adam, so that Christ and Christ alone would have the supremacy as creation's only way of salvation. Ed, would you please read again for us these scriptures on the chalkboard?"

Ed read:

> For the anxious longing of the creation waits eagerly for the revealing of the sons of God.
>
> For the creation was subjected to futility, not willingly, but because of Him who subjected it, in hope
>
> that the creation itself also will be set free from its slavery to corruption into the freedom of the glory of the children of God.
>
> For we know that the whole creation groans and suffers the pains of childbirth together until now. (Romans 8:19-22)

> He is before all things, and in Him all things hold together.
>
> He is also head of the body, the church; and He is the beginning, the firstborn from the dead, so that He Himself will come to have first place in everything. (Colossians 1:17,18)

"Thank you, Ed," said Dave. "The plan of God was to ensure that God the Son had 'first place in everything' by being creation's only Savior. Or, in other words, that the glory of God would be supreme, the entire purpose of creation. So, as beloved children of God, we cry out with the Apostle Paul: 'Wretched man that I am! Who will set me free from the body of this death? Thanks be to God through Jesus Christ our Lord!' (Romans 7:24,25).

"Grant, please read Quiz question 6 for us, the last question we will tackle today."

"Question 6: 'When Adam sinned, he gave ownership of this world to Satan,'" Grant read. "I've heard preachers on the radio actually make this statement. Doesn't the Bible say that Satan is 'the ruler of this world?'"

"Great question," answered Dave. "Let's read what God's holy Word says about our enemy. Anna, please read the next three scriptures on the board."

Anna read:

> Jesus answered and said, "This voice has not come for My sake, but for your sakes. Now judgment is upon this world; now the ruler of this world will be cast out." (John 12:30,31)

> And even if our gospel is veiled, it is veiled to those who are perishing, in whose case the god of this world has blinded the minds of the unbelieving so that they might not see the light of the gospel of the glory of Christ, who is the image of God. (2 Corinthians 4:3,4)

> And you were dead in your trespasses and sins, in which you formerly walked according to the course of this world, according to the prince of the power of the air, of the spirit that is now working in the sons of disobedience.
>
> (Ephesians 2:1,2)

"Thank you, Anna," Dave replied. "God's holy Word describes Satan as 'the ruler of this world'; 'the god of this world'; and 'the prince of the power of the air.' The devil may be holding the entire unbelieving world hostage in his evil grip, but he owns nothing!

"But we know the owner of this world, the sovereign Almighty God of the universe, and the King of kings who is Lord over all lords and princes! Let's read what God says about Himself in His holy Word. Jennifer, would you please read the next five passages I have on the chalkboard?"

Jennifer read:

> "Who then is he that can stand before Me?
> "Who has given to Me that I should repay *him?*
> *Whatever* is under the whole heaven is Mine."
>
> (Job 41:10b,11)

> The LORD has established His throne in the heavens,
> And His sovereignty rules over all. (Psalm 103:19)

> *He is* clothed with a robe dipped in blood, and His name is called
> The Word of God.
> And on His robe and on His thigh He has a name written, "KING
> OF KINGS, AND LORD OF LORDS." (Revelation 19:13,16)

> And Jesus came up and spoke to them, saying, "All authority has been
> given to Me in heaven and on earth." (Matthew 28:18)

> *These are* in accordance with the working of the strength of His might
> which He brought about in Christ, when He raised Him from the dead
> and seated Him at His right hand in the heavenly *places*,
> far above all rule and authority and power and dominion, and every
> name that is named, not only in this age but also in the one to come.
> And He put all things in subjection under His feet, and gave Him as
> head over all things to the church. (Ephesians 1:19b-22)

"Thank you, Jennifer," recognized Dave. "Almighty God is the owner of everything! He never gave ownership of anything to anybody! Almighty God sovereignly rules the universe, and He rules over the 'sub-rulers' of the world, including the devil himself. Satan may be 'the prince of the power of the air,' but Jesus Christ is 'the King of all kings and the Lord of all lords!'

"'Your adversary, the devil, prowls around like a roaring lion, seeking someone to devour,' the Apostle Peter warns us in 1 Peter 5:8, but he cannot touch the truly born-again children of God unless God Himself gives him permission. We see this principle in the Book of Job, where, in the first two chapters, Satan accuses the children of God before the throne of the Almighty. But it is God who determines the extent, if any, of Satan's evil."

"God uses the devil to bring evil?" Nick asked.

"Absolutely," Dave asserted. "Satan is nothing more than a slave of God, a pawn in the Almighty's eternal plan. But, in his insanity, of course, Satan does not admit to this fact. God uses the devil as a king uses slaves.

"For example, King Solomon, who ordered the first Temple built in Jerusalem, says to God, 'I have built You a lofty house, and a place for Your dwelling forever' (2 Chronicles 6:2). King Solomon does not mean he *himself* did the physical labor, but that he, as king, issued the decree, and sent forced labor to do the actual building (2 Chronicles 2:17,18).

"God uses the devil in the exact same way to accomplish His purposes. Over and over again, when Israel had forsaken God, He would incite the surrounding evil empires to ravish the nation as punishment. Ed, would you please read 2 Samuel 24:1 and 1 Chronicles 21:1?"

Ed read:

> Now again the anger of the LORD burned against Israel, and it incited
> David against them to say, "Go, number Israel and Judah."
>
> (2 Samuel 24:1)

> Then Satan stood up against Israel and moved David to number Israel.
>
> (1 Chronicles 21:1)

"Thank you, Ed," Dave responded. "Here are two biblical passages talking about the same event. Israel continuously disobeyed God's command to '"have no other gods before Me"' (Exodus 20:3,4). They worshiped idols instead of the true God, so the Lord punished their heinous sins by sending Satan to influence King David to do evil and bring calamity upon the nation.

"We find this again when King Saul, Israel's first human king, continually disobeyed God. In the Book of First Samuel, we read: 'Now the Spirit of the LORD departed from Saul, and an evil spirit from the LORD terrorized him' (1 Samuel 16:14).

"Now, we know from the scriptures about God that we read last week that: 'No evil dwells with You' (Psalm 5:4b). So, God simply ordered an evil spirit to go terrorize the disobedient Saul.

"Satan and his fallen angels, called demons, are simply pawns in God's eternal plan," Dave explained. "Where God decrees calamity, usually in response to heinous sin, He simply dispatches Satan and his demons to do what the Lord Jesus said they do best—'"steal, kill, and destroy"' (John 10:10)."

"So Satan and God are not somewhat equal forces fighting for control over this world?" asked Jennifer.

"Not even close," answered Dave with a smile. "Satan is a created being, infinitely below the sovereign, infinite, Almighty God, who is the Master of the universe. The devil simply does the will of God, though, like I said, he would never admit to that. This is not to falsely conclude that the devil has no power, for his mission is to steal, kill and destroy. He is cunning, deceitful, and totally evil, not to mention invisible to the human eye, and is bent toward our destruction.

"All people born of a human father are hostages of the devil from conception because they are enslaved to a sinful nature. Kelly, please read 2 Timothy 2:24 through 26 for us."

Kelly read:

> The Lord's bond-servant must not be quarrelsome, but be kind to all,
> able to teach, patient when wronged,
>   with gentleness correcting those who are in opposition, if perhaps God
> may grant them repentance leading to the knowledge of the truth,
>   and they may come to their senses *and escape* from the snare of the
> devil, having been held captive by him to do his will.
>
> (2 Timothy 2:24-26)

"Thank you, Kelly. The unregenerate sinner, everyone born of a human male, is held captive by Satan to do his will," expounded Dave. "All that natural man does is the will of the devil, which is only evil continually, regardless of outer appearances. And we've all read the warnings of Jesus about judging by outward appearances.

Resisting the Devil

"God's holy Word gives specific instructions for God's children in handling the devil. It should be totally obvious to anyone that only a fool would attempt to attack an invisible foe. But, as incredible as it may seem, such foolishness is written about and preached throughout the world in the modern church.

"God is not ambiguous on this matter. God absolutely forbids His children to attack the devil, and commands us to resist him. Anna, please read the next three scriptures on the chalkboard."

Anna read:

> Yet in the same way these men, also by dreaming, defile the flesh, and reject authority, and revile angelic majesties.
>
> But Michael the archangel, when he disputed with the devil and argued about the body of Moses, did not dare pronounce against him a railing judgment, but said, "The Lord rebuke you!"
>
> But these men revile the things which they do not understand; and the things which they know by instinct, like unreasoning animals, by these things they are destroyed. (Jude 8-10)

> But He gives a greater grace. Therefore *it* says, "GOD IS OPPOSED TO THE PROUD, BUT GIVES GRACE TO THE HUMBLE."
>
> Submit therefore to God. Resist the devil and he will flee from you.
>
> Draw near to God and He will draw near to you. Cleanse your hands, you sinners; and purify your hearts, you double-minded.
>
> (James 4:6-8)

> Therefore humble yourselves under the mighty hand of God, that He may exalt you at the proper time,
>
> casting all your anxiety on Him, because He cares for you.
>
> Be of sober *spirit,* be on the alert. Your adversary, the devil, prowls around like a roaring lion, seeking someone to devour.
>
> But resist him, firm in *your* faith, knowing that the same experiences of suffering are being accomplished by your brethren who are in the world. (1 Peter 5:6-9)

"Thank you, Anna," acknowledged Dave. "Not even the prince of angels, Michael, dared to attack or revile the devil—and the Apostle Jude writes this for our instruction! Jude declares in God's holy Word that those who pronounce judgment against the devil are fools—'unreasoning animals'—and are destroyed. The Lord is the Judge of the devil.

"We are commanded to 'resist the devil.' The original Greek word, *anthistemi,* as well as the English word, **resist**, means to withstand. This communicates a defensive posture, not an offensive attack, because the verb is used in the Middle, or Passive Voice. In dealing with the devil, God commands His children to withstand the onslaught without reviling or attacking."

"So how do we withstand Satan's attacks without fighting him?" Paul asked.

"Excellent question," Dave replied, "and the answer is in the context of the last two passages we just read. When God commands us to resist the devil, what does He tell us to do first?"

"Well," Paul mused, "it looks like both passages involve humbling one's self and drawing near to God."

"In other words, get on the Lap of the Father!" Dave exhorted. "Before the command to withstand the devil, we are to first humble ourselves, submitting our wills to the will of the Father. Secondly, we are to cast our anxiety upon Him. We do this by drawing near to God, getting on the Father's Lap and staying there, trusting Him to protect us and fight for us!

"Only on the Father's Lap can we 'resist the devil!' We turn our attention away from the satanic attack and towards our all-powerful, sovereign, loving Father, and seek Him to vanquish the enemy! The absolute worst thing we could do is turn our backs to the Father, the Source of life and protection, and attempt to engage an invisible foe in spiritual warfare!

"In the Old Testament, every time the nation of Israel tried to fight a greater enemy in their own strength, they were routed. But when they fell on their faces and cried out to God, the Lord fought the battle for them and destroyed the enemy!

"God gave us the Old Testament as a physical example of what we now face as His children in the spiritual realm. The principle always applies: **Do it God's way, and even if you mess up, He will still bless you. Do it your way, and even if you do it perfectly, God will frustrate your plans!** And God's will for His children is for them to get on His Lap, fall intimately in love with Him, learn of His ways, and stay there!"

"What about taking the offensive and casting out demons, like Jesus and the apostles?" Nick asked.

"Good question," Dave responded. "But that is a different matter entirely. There, an *unbeliever* is *possessed* by a demon or demons. Here, we are talking about the biblical response of *Christians* to satanic **oppression**—an attack from the outside on believers possessed by the Holy Spirit. How did the Apostle Paul handle demonic oppression when God sent it to him? Nick, please read 2 Corinthians 12:7-10 to us for God's Word to believers on satanic attack."

Nick read:

> Because of the surpassing greatness of the revelations, for this reason, to keep me from exalting myself, there was given me a thorn in the flesh, a messenger of Satan to torment me—to keep me from exalting myself!
>
> Concerning this I implored the Lord three times that it might leave me.
>
> And He has said to me, "My grace is sufficient for you, for power is perfected in weakness." Most gladly, therefore, I will rather boast about my weaknesses, so that the power of Christ may dwell in me.
>
> Therefore I am well content with weaknesses, with insults, with distresses, with persecutions, with difficulties, for Christ's sake; for when I am weak, then I am strong. (2 Corinthians 12:7-10)

"Thank you, Nick," Dave replied. "So, what did the Apostle Paul do—a man who performed many miracles, healed the sick, and even raised the dead by the power of God? Did he rant and rave against the devil, commanding the demon 'to leave in the Name of Jesus?' Did Paul say, 'I bind you and send you back to the abyss from where you came?' How did the Apostle react?

"No, Paul would never revile the devil like an 'unreasoning animal.' He never addressed the messenger of Satan at all! Not once did he ever attack or confront the evil one! Some preachers today would be astounded, and maybe even deride Paul's character as a 'weak Christian!'

"The Apostle Paul, as God's example to His children, went straight to the Lap of the Father and asked the Father for relief. The source of the Apostle's power to withstand the torment of the enemy, in Paul's human weakness, was in going straight to the throne of God his Father. Paul got on the Lap of the Father and received the grace and the power of God to endure the devil's onslaught."

"What about putting on 'the full armor of God' as the Apostle Paul commands in his Letter to the Ephesians, chapter six?" asked Ed.

"Great question!" Dave commended. "What is armor for? One does not don a one-hundred-pound metal suit to become more agile and quicker on the attack! If you've ever seen an actual coat of mail, one could barely move in that thing! The idea of the armor is for defensive protection, not offensive strikes. Read Ephesians 6:10-17 for us please, Ed."

Ed read:

> Finally, be strong in the Lord and in the strength of His might.
>
> Put on the full armor of God, so that you will be able to stand firm against the schemes of the devil.
>
> For our struggle is not against flesh and blood, but against the rulers, against the powers, against the world forces of this darkness, against the spiritual *forces* of wickedness in the heavenly *places.*
>
> Therefore, take up the full armor of God, so that you will be able to resist in the evil day, and having done everything, to stand firm.
>
> Stand firm therefore, HAVING GIRDED YOUR LOINS WITH TRUTH, and HAVING PUT ON THE BREASTPLATE OF RIGHTEOUSNESS,
>
> and having shod YOUR FEET WITH THE PREPARATION OF THE GOSPEL OF PEACE;
>
> in addition to all, taking up the shield of faith with which you will be able to extinguish all the flaming arrows of the evil *one.*
>
> And take THE HELMET OF SALVATION, and the sword of the Spirit, which is the word of God. (Ephesians 6:10-17)

"Thank you, Ed," Dave said. "We are to 'be strong in the Lord' with 'the strength of His might.' How do we access the strength and power of God? By getting on the Lap of the Father. Three times the Apostle Paul proclaims to 'stand firm,' not run and attack. The Apostle Peter says 'resist him, firm in your faith.' Faith in who? In God our Father, who is able to protect us with 'the shield of faith'—faith in God!

"But aren't we supposed to overcome the devil?" asked Paul.

"Absolutely not," Dave answered. "The truly born-again child of God *has already overcome*

Satan and his demons in Christ! Paul, please read these four scriptures on the board."

Paul read:

> "These things I have spoken to you, so that in Me you may have peace. In the world you have tribulation, but take courage; I have overcome the world." (John 16:33)

> By this you know the Spirit of God: every spirit that confesses that Jesus Christ has come in the flesh is from God;

> and every spirit that does not confess Jesus is not from God; this is the *spirit* of the antichrist, of which you have heard that it is coming, and now it is already in the world.

> You are from God, little children, and have overcome them; because greater is He who is in you than he who is in the world. (1 John 4:2-4)

> For whatever is born of God overcomes the world; and this is the victory that has overcome the world—our faith.

> Who is the one who overcomes the world, but he who believes that Jesus is the Son of God? (1 John 5:4,5)

> And the great dragon was thrown down, the serpent of old who is called the devil and Satan, who deceives the whole world; he was thrown down to the earth, and his angels were thrown down with him.

> Then I heard a loud voice in heaven, saying,

> "Now the salvation, and the power, and the kingdom of our God and the authority of His Christ have come, for the accuser of our brethren has been thrown down, he who accuses them before our God day and night.

> And they overcame him because of the blood of the Lamb and because of the word of their testimony, and they did not love their life even when faced with death." (Revelation 12:9-11)

"Thank you, Paul," Dave said. "We have already overcome the evil one in Christ, because God the Son is infinitely greater than the devil!

"If we have died to ourselves, we have given up this life totally to Christ for His use—in other words, we have truly **repented**. If, by our testimony, we have totally trusted in the death of Christ—the shedding of His blood for our sin, and His perfect life credited to our account—we have **believed** in Him. Only then are we 'in Christ,' true children of God, and have overcome Satan because Christ our Savior overcame through the resurrection from the dead!"

"Amen!" Nick exclaimed.

"Well, we've covered a lot of ground today," Dave summarized, "so let me hit the highlights.

"First, God is the source of all order in the universe and actively works in it, upholding everything in it, and sustaining it all.

"Second, one of the biggest traps to avoid is looking at and judging reality from man's finite viewpoint instead of from God's infinite viewpoint, which He reveals to us in His Word.

"Third, God's Word is the only standard of truth by which correct judgments may be made in this universe.

"Next, the immutability and omniscience of God are essential attributes of God's character.

"'Immutability' means God can never or will never change in His character or purpose.

"It is impossible for God to learn anything, or He would change. If God learned anything, He would no longer be omniscient—or all-knowing—another of God's essential attributes of His character.

"'Omniscience' means God knows all things at all times because He has ordained all things for all time in His eternal plan which He formed before creation.

"'Blasphemy' is the crime of saying or doing anything pertaining to God that does not give Him proper worship and respect.

"Judging teachings on spiritual matters by personal opinion will always lead you astray and into heresy.

"Because our personal opinions and perceptions are severely flawed by our sinful nature, God's Word is the only standard of truth by which correct judgments may be made in this universe.

"Jesus loved us, His children, so much that while we hated and reviled Him, He still died for us to pay the penalty for our sin.

"Clearly God says in His Word that He does hate as well as love.

"Keeping bits and pieces of God's holy Word, and leaving out the parts we don't like—especially involving Almighty God—is the same heinous crime as setting aside God's Word in favor of our man-made opinions. It is the sin of idolatry.

"God only forgives the sins of 'the few' on the narrow road, so He is not 'all-forgiving.' He never claimed to be 'all-forgiving,' but to be perfectly just.

"God declares in His Word that He not only hates sin, but sinners who love their sin.

"In God's infinite realm, being perfectly righteous, He must judge the unrighteous.

"We, however, are commanded by God to love our neighbors, our brothers and sisters in Christ...even our enemies.

"Always test man-made sayings by the Word of God, because they may not always be true—no matter how true they sound.

"God most definitely has a plan for the life of every person, as He has ordained the exact number of days and every detail of every life. But, He never promises 'heaven on earth.'

"God never gave us this life to own and do with as we please. God gave us this life to love, worship and serve Him!

"An example of man-centered, philosophical blindness is: If evil and suffering exist, which they do—either God is good but does not have the power to help, or that God is all-powerful, but not good, because He allows such suffering to continue.

"The truth is that God subjected His creation to slavery to evil so that Christ Jesus would be given all honor and glory as the only way out of that slavery.

"Suffering is excruciating and painful, but that does not necessarily make it evil.

"If suffering can jar a person out of his self-centered rebellion against God, or draw a devout Christian closer to God, suffering then becomes very beneficial for life in eternity.

"The person who retains his rights to this life—and feels God is unjust to have him suffer—has not repented, is not His disciple, and will pay for his sins in hell.

"If God's goal for us in this life is to become like Christ, who suffered unto death, then we too must suffer, and entrust our souls to our infinitely good and loving heavenly Father.

"God's purpose, or plan, to save us from our sin 'was granted us in Christ Jesus from all eternity' (2 Timothy 1:8,9).

"The Fall of Adam was a necessary element of the eternal plan of God, because, to be the Savior from eternity past, God the Son needed a people that required saving from eternity past.

"The purpose of creation is to glorify God—to give Christ Jesus, God the Son, the supremacy in all things.

"God's holy Word describes Satan as 'the ruler of this world,' 'the god of this world,' and 'the prince of the power of the air.'

"Almighty God is the owner of this world, the sovereign Lord of the universe, and the King of kings who is Lord over all 'gods' and princes!

"Although they would never admit to it, Satan and his fallen angels, called demons, are simply pawns in God's eternal plan.

"Satan is cunning, deceitful, totally evil and extremely powerful, not to mention invisible to the human eye, and is bent toward our destruction.

"Satan is a created being, infinitely below the sovereign infinite Almighty God, who is the Master of the universe.

"Even the thought that Satan and God are equal but opposing powers is a foolish lie of the devil. Such foolishness is blasphemy against the holy, omnipotent, sovereign Almighty God.

"All people born of a human father are hostages of the devil from conception, because they are enslaved to a sinful nature.

"The only thing an unregenerate man is able to do is the will of the devil, which is only evil continually, regardless of outward appearances.

"God's holy Word gives specific instructions for God's children in handling the devil; and it should be totally obvious to anyone that only a fool would attempt to attack an invisible foe.

"God absolutely forbids His children to attack the devil, declaring that those who pronounce judgment against the devil are fools—'unreasoning animals'—and are destroyed (Jude 8-10).

"We are commanded to 'resist the devil' (James 4:6-8; 1 Peter 5:6-9).

"'Resist' means to withstand, a defensive posture, not an offensive attack.

"In order to withstand the devil, we are commanded by God to do two things: first, we must humble ourselves, submitting our wills to the will of the Father.

"Secondly, we must draw near to God—getting on the Father's Lap—and stay there, trusting Him to protect us and fight for us!

"We turn our attention away from the satanic attack and towards our all-powerful, sovereign, loving Father, and seek Him to vanquish the enemy!

"The absolute worst thing we could do is turn our backs to the Father, the source of our life and protection, and attempt to engage an invisible foe in spiritual warfare!

"The Apostle Paul is our perfect example under oppression, as he never even addressed the demon, but went straight to the Lap of God for His grace and power.

"Do it God's way, and even if you mess up, He will still bless you. Do it your way, and even if you do it perfectly, God will frustrate your plans!

"The idea of the armor of God in Ephesians 6 is for defensive protection, not offensive strikes.

"We access the strength and power of God by getting on the Lap of the Father.

"The truly born-again child of God has already overcome Satan and his demons in Christ, because God the Son is infinitely greater than the devil!

"Finally and most importantly, Christ triumphed over Satan by His power through the resurrection from the dead!

"I trust we have a better grasp of the infinite power of our holy and righteous God the Father, and of the overcoming glory of God the Son, Jesus Christ, and of the work of God the Holy Spirit to make us more and more like Christ!" Dave concluded. "Grant, would you close our Bible study with prayer, please?"

"Dear heavenly Father, we praise You and honor You for the awesome Almighty God that You are—the Creator and Sustainer of the universe! You chose us in Christ Jesus our Savior to be Your children, and we thank You for sending the precious Holy Spirit to glorify Your holy Name.

"Draw us to Your Lap and protect us from the evil one, O Lord. We thank You that Your plan is for our good, no matter what circumstances come our way. Fill us with Your Spirit now, Father, so that we may go and worship You with all of our hearts. In Jesus' holy Name we pray, amen!"

6

The One True God

Tuesday afternoon found Nick bounding down the dormitory hall toward Dave's room with his "sword" in his hand.

"Hey, bro!" greeted Nick as he came upon the open door that revealed Dave sitting at his desk, flipping through the Bible.

"A man armed with the 'Sword of the Spirit!'" Dave embraced his brother in Christ and offered him a seat. "How's it going, my brother?"

"The Lord is blessing me abundantly beyond all that I could expect!" Nick exclaimed. "I am learning so much about Him through the College & Career class, the worship services, and our fellowship! And, it seems the more I learn about our awesome God, the hungrier I get!"

"Excellent! Well then, let's not waste any time! Would you open our Bible study with prayer?"

"I'd be honored," Nick replied, taking Dave's hands. "Dear heavenly Father, you are all-together holy, eternally just and completely righteous. Yet You have condescended to be merciful to sinful, depraved men in order to bring them into Your family. Thank You for Your awesome plan of salvation through Jesus Christ Your Son, who died to pay for our sins. Thank You for crediting His perfect life to our accounts.

"We bow before You in utter gratitude as Your servants, and ask that You be with us in a special way as we desire to know You and love You more and more intimately. In Jesus' Name we pray, amen."

The Trinity

"In the last Sunday school class, we touched on some of the eternal attributes of God's character," Dave began. "Do you remember any of them?"

"Oh yes!" beamed Nick. "Immutability and omniscience—God never changes in His character or plan, and God knows all things for all of eternity because He ordained everything that comes to pass."

"Outstanding!" praised Dave. "Today we will cover some of the other important attributes of God. But first, it is absolutely critical to understand the doctrine of the Trinity.

"It is so crucial to understand who God says He is, that all of Christianity stands or falls on this one doctrine. An *essential of the Christian faith* is any doctrine to which a person absolutely must adhere in order to obey God's eternal truth.

"I really need to know the essentials," Nick responded, "so that I keep my thinking straight, and don't wander off into heresy."

"Correct," assented Dave. "The principle of the Trinity is an essential doctrine of the Christian faith. The doctrine of *the Trinity* declares that there is ONE and only ONE God, and that ONE God is made up of three distinct persons—the Father, the Son and the Holy Spirit.

"The Godhead is one in essence (or substance), and three in person. The one God is indivisible in substance, yet He is made up of three separate and distinct persons. The Father is fully God, the Son is fully God, and the Holy Spirit is fully God at all times. This is the best expression of the eternal and infinite God."

Contradiction vs. Mystery

Nick scratched his head. "Isn't there a contradiction in there somewhere, saying that God is one and not one?"

"Do you remember, from the last College & Career class, the definition of a contradiction?" asked Dave. "The definition gives all of the requirements necessary for a contradiction to exist."

"If I remember correctly," Nick recalled, "a *contradiction* is declaring something true and not true at the same time and in the same sense."

"Exactly!" Dave applauded. "The doctrine of the Trinity declares that God is one *in substance*, but three *in person*. So, God is one and not one at the same time, but not in the same sense, or relationship. There is one 'what,' but three 'who's.' Therefore, the doctrine of the Trinity does not fulfill all of the requirements to be a contradiction. Thus, no contradiction exists."

"You're right!" agreed Nick. "But, it still seems confusing to me."

"And this is why," Dave responded. "Confusion is inevitable when we, as finite beings, attempt to fit an infinite being into our mold of reality. By definition, the finite could never contain or grasp the infinite. This is obvious. So, trying to fit the infinite into our finite framework of reality will always result in confusion.

"When we see a man across the street, we see one being. We always equate that *one being* with *one person*, because that has been our finite experience of reality from day one. But the eternal, infinite, Almighty God is not limited to our finite experience, nor our sphere of reality.

God can be one being with three Persons, when man can only be one being with one person.

"As I have shown, there is no contradiction to the Trinity. What there is, however, is a great mystery here. It should be logically obvious that if a finite being is introduced to an infinite being, the infinite being will be well beyond anything the finite being could even imagine. If that were not the case, then one might surmise that the infinite being was simply contrived by the mind of the finite being."

"That's true," Nick agreed.

"A contradiction is always illogical: 'The ball is round and not round at the same time and in the same sense.' Here the very same roundness of the ball is both affirmed and denied. This and all contradictions are pure nonsense, and thus cannot be true.

"Another example is the saying, 'There is no absolute truth.' If that statement were true, the statement itself would be an absolute truth. Therefore, it contradicts itself, it is illogical, and cannot be true.

"But much of who God is, what He does, and how He does it is a mystery," Dave continued. "A *mystery* is truth—which thus cannot be a contradiction—that the finite cannot explain, but which can be resolved if all of the pieces of the puzzle were revealed.

"Again, a mystery is true. Therefore, a mystery cannot be a contradiction, because contradictions are never true. What confuses us as finite beings is that we cannot explain a mystery in terms of our finite experience. But this fact by no means makes a mystery false or contradictory—particularly those mysteries proclaimed by God's holy and inerrant Word! This is especially true when finite man looks into the infinite realm, and even more so when finite man attempts to understand Almighty God!

"In fact, because God is infinite—and the finite can never grasp the infinite—all of who God is and what He does is beyond what man can comprehend! The only reason we know what we know about God is that He, being infinite, can and does reveal parts of Himself and His plan to man. Read Isaiah 55:8 and 9, please."

Nick read:

> "For My thoughts are not your thoughts,
>> Nor are your ways My ways," declares the LORD.
> "For *as* the heavens are higher than the earth,
>> So are My ways higher than your ways
> "And My thoughts than your thoughts." (Isaiah 55:8,9)

"God declares here what should be obvious to anyone: He is infinitely beyond finite man in who He is, what He thinks, and what He does," Dave expounded. "But the cultist and the unbeliever reject the Christian doctrine of the Trinity simply because they cannot understand it.

"They set up their finite minds as idols, and expect the infinite Almighty God to bow down to their limited capacities of understanding. But the Almighty God has a response for them. Please read Psalm 2:4 through 6, and Romans 3:3 and 4."

Nick read:

He who sits in the heavens laughs,
> The Lord scoffs at them.
Then He will speak to them in His anger
> And terrify them in His fury, saying,
"But as for Me, I have installed My King
> Upon Zion, My holy mountain." (Psalm 2:4-6)

What then? If some did not believe, their unbelief will not nullify the faithfulness of God, will it?

May it never be! Rather, let God be found true, though every man *be found* a liar, as it is written,

> "THAT YOU MAY BE JUSTIFIED IN YOUR WORDS,
> AND PREVAIL WHEN YOU ARE JUDGED." (Romans 3:3,4)

"The Lord God Almighty laughs and scoffs at the unbelievers, for they will come before His great and terrible throne for judgment, and He will 'terrify them in His fury,'" warned Dave. "But, as believers, we should know better than to worship the idol of our own finite minds. We have seen how much God hates idolatry.

"God's holy Word is the only standard of truth in the universe. Thus, when God says something is true—whether we can understand it or not—we had better believe it. For God can only speak what is true. But man, born with a sinful nature, desires to falsely put himself in the place of God by elevating his sin-marred reason above God's truth.

"Yes, the doctrine of the Trinity is a mystery. But God declares it throughout His word to be true. Let's begin with the scriptures that declare that there is only one God. First, read Isaiah 45:5-7 and 46:9. Then read the words of Jesus, quoting Deuteronomy 6:4, in Mark 12:29."

Nick read:

> "I am the LORD, and there is no other;
> > Besides Me there is no God.
> > I will gird you, though you have not known Me;
> "That men may know from the rising to the setting of the sun
> > That there is no one besides Me.
> > I am the LORD, and there is no other,
> "The One forming light and creating darkness,
> > Causing well-being and creating calamity;
> > I am the LORD who does all these." (Isaiah 45:5-7)

> "Remember the former things long past,
> > For I am God, and there is no other;
> > *I am* God, and there is no one like Me." (Isaiah 46:9)

Jesus answered, "The foremost is, 'HEAR, O ISRAEL! THE LORD OUR GOD IS ONE LORD.'" (Mark 12:29)

"Despite what critics say in their confusion, Christianity is definitely **monotheistic**. That is a term that means there is only one God," asserted Dave. "God declares this in Deuteronomy 6:4, and Jesus reaffirms this truth in the great and foremost commandment. But throughout the Old Testament, God portrays Himself as a plurality of persons. Read John 1:1-3 and verse 14 for context; and then read Genesis 1:1-3, Genesis 1:26 and 27, and finally Isaiah 48:12, 13 and 16."

Nick read:

> In the beginning was the Word, and the Word was with God, and the Word was God.
>
> He was in the beginning with God.
>
> All things came into being through Him, and apart from Him nothing came into being that has come into being.
>
> And the Word became flesh, and dwelt among us, and we saw His glory, glory as of the only begotten from the Father, full of grace and truth. (John 1:1-3,14)

> In the beginning God created the heavens and the earth.
>
> The earth was formless and void, and darkness was over the surface of the deep, and the Spirit of God was moving over the surface of the waters.
>
> Then God said, "Let there be light"; and there was light.
>
> (Genesis 1:1-3)

> Then God said, "Let Us make man in Our image, according to Our likeness; and let them rule over the fish of the sea and over the birds of the sky and over the cattle and over all the earth, and over every creeping thing that creeps on the earth."
>
> God created man in His own image, in the image of God He created him; male and female He created them. (Genesis 1:26,27)

> "Listen to Me, O Jacob, even Israel whom I called;
>   I am He, I am the first, I am also the last.
> "Surely My hand founded the earth,
>   And My right hand spread out the heavens;
> "Come near to Me, listen to this:
>   From the first I have not spoken in secret,
>   From the time it took place, I was there.
> "And now the Lord GOD has sent Me, and His Spirit."
>
> (Isaiah 48:12,13a,16)

"In John 1, Jesus is identified as being the Word of God, as being with God in the beginning, and as being God Himself," Dave declared. "Jesus is also identified as the one through whom all of creation came into being.

"In Genesis 1, the Bible opens with the three persons of the Godhead creating. God the Father purposed creation; God the Holy Spirit was moving in creation; and God spoke His Word, resulting in creation.

"Also in Genesis 1, God speaks of Himself in the plural in the creation of man. He says, 'Let Us make man in Our image, according to Our likeness.' God cannot be talking with angels here. Angels do not create. According to Isaiah 45:7, which we read earlier, the Lord God alone does all creating. Also, man is not made in the image of angels, but in the image of the one God alone.

"Arriving at Isaiah 48, God just spent eight chapters declaring over and over again that there is only one God, and that He alone is that one God. Then we find this interesting passage.

"The Speaker here claims to have created the heavens and the earth, which was done by God alone. The Speaker then says that the Lord God sends Him and His Spirit to fulfill God's prophecies. This Old Testament passage is utterly unintelligible without understanding God as the Trinity."

"Wow! I never realized the Old Testament spoke of the Trinity," Nick confessed.

"There are many other instances where the messenger of the Lord visits people like Abraham; or the messenger of the Lord appears with the children in the furnace in the Book of Daniel; and the messenger is identified as the Lord. But the above scriptures will suffice," Dave added. "Now we move into the New Testament.

"Many New Testament scriptures demonstrate the Trinity by placing the Three Persons on a par with one another. I've made a list. Let's read them one by one."

They read:

> After being baptized, Jesus came up immediately from the water; and behold, the heavens were opened, and he saw the Spirit of God descending as a dove *and* lighting on Him,
>
> and behold, a voice out of the heavens said, "This is My beloved Son, in whom I am well-pleased." (Matthew 3:16,17)

> And Jesus came up and spoke to them, saying, "All authority has been given to Me in heaven and on earth.
>
> "Go therefore and make disciples of all the nations, baptizing them in **the name** of the Father and the Son and the Holy Spirit."
>
> (Matthew 28:18,19; *emphasis mine*)

> *There is* one body and one Spirit, just as also you were called in one hope of your calling;
>
> one Lord, one faith, one baptism,
>
> one God and Father of all who is over all and through all and in all.
>
> (Ephesians 4:4-6)

> "All things that the Father has are Mine; therefore I said, that He (the Holy Spirit) takes of Mine, and will disclose *it* to you."
>
> (John 16:15; *parenthesis mine*)

> The grace of the Lord Jesus Christ, and the love of God, and the
> fellowship of the Holy Spirit, be with you all. (2 Corinthians 13:14)

> Peter, an apostle of Jesus Christ,
> To those who reside as aliens, scattered throughout Pontus, Galatia,
> Cappadocia, Asia, and Bithynia, who are chosen
> according to the foreknowledge of God the Father, by the sanctifying
> work of the Spirit, to obey Jesus Christ and be sprinkled with His blood:
> May grace and peace be yours in the fullest measure. (1 Peter 1:1,2)

"These are great examples of God the Father, God the Son, and God the Holy Spirit being placed together on the same par, working the same plan that only God could work," Dave expounded. "The Apostles Peter and Paul, in their greetings and benedictions to the churches, place the Three Persons together with qualities and attributes belonging only to God.

"Remember, we just read the Lord speaking through the prophet in Isaiah 46:9: 'I am God, and there is no one like Me.' God is an infinite, eternal being in a class totally by Himself. But the Father, Son and Holy Spirit are placed on a par with each other in these passages.

"The Three Persons are present at the baptism of Jesus. And when Jesus commands His disciples to baptize believers, it is in **the name**—singular—not 'the names'—of the Father and the Son and the Holy Spirit. Thus, the Three Persons must, in some sense, be one in Name and authority. The Apostle Paul tells us that the sense in which the Three Persons are one is that there is only ONE God:

> Yet for us there is *but* one God, the Father, from whom are all things
> and we *exist* for Him; and one Lord, Jesus Christ, by whom are all things,
> and we *exist* through Him. (1 Corinthians 8:6)

The Lord Jesus Christ Is God

"The Bible states over and over that 'there is but one God,' and inside of that one God there are three distinct Persons. Unbelievers may admit that the Bible states that there is only one God, and that the Three Persons are presented together *in purpose*," Dave continued, "but that does not prove that Jesus is God and that the Holy Spirit is God.

"So, we present the many scriptures that declare that Jesus is indeed fully God, and that the Holy Spirit is indeed fully God. I have written these down for us to read. We have shown above that the Apostle Paul emphatically states that for Christians 'there is but one God.' If we demonstrate that Jesus is also that one God, and that the Holy Spirit is also that one God, we then have the mystery of the doctrine of the Trinity."

About the deity of Jesus, they read:

> Jesus said to him, "Have I been so long with you, and *yet* you have not
> come to know Me, Philip? He who has seen Me has seen the Father; how *can*
> you say, 'Show us the Father'?" (John 14:9)

For in Him all the fullness of Deity dwells in bodily form,

and in Him you have been made complete, and He is the head over all rule and authority. (Colossians 2:9,10)

But of the Son *He says*,

"YOUR THRONE, O GOD, IS FOREVER AND EVER,

AND THE RIGHTEOUS SCEPTER IS THE SCEPTER OF HIS KINGDOM."

(Hebrews 1:8)

For I could wish that I myself were accursed, *separated* from Christ for the sake of my brethren, my kinsmen according to the flesh,

who are Israelites, to whom belongs the adoption as sons, and the glory and the covenants and the giving of the Law and the *temple* service and the promises,

whose are the fathers, and from whom is the Christ according to the flesh, who is over all, God blessed forever. Amen. (Romans 9:3-5)

And we know that the Son of God has come, and has given us understanding so that we may know Him who is true; and we are in Him who is true, in His Son Jesus Christ. This is the true God and eternal life.

(1 John 5:20)

"For I did not shrink from declaring to you the whole purpose of God.

"Be on guard for yourselves and for all the flock, among which the Holy Spirit has made you overseers, to shepherd the church of God which He purchased with His own blood." (Acts 20:27,28)

In the beginning was the Word, and the Word was with God, and the Word was God.

He was in the beginning with God.

All things came into being through Him, and apart from Him nothing came into being that has come into being.

And the Word became flesh, and dwelt among us, and we saw His glory, glory as of the only begotten from the Father, full of grace and truth. (John 1:1-3,14)

Jesus spoke these things; and lifting up His eyes to heaven, He said, "Father, the hour has come; glorify Your Son, that the Son may glorify You.

"Now, Father, glorify Me together with Yourself, with the glory which I had with You before the world was." (John 17:1,5)

"I and the Father are one."

The Jews picked up stones again to stone Him.

Jesus answered them, "I showed you many good works from the Father; for which of them are you stoning Me?"

The Jews answered Him, "For a good work we do not stone You, but for blasphemy; and because You, being a man, make Yourself out *to be* God." (John 10:30-33)

> "Thus says the LORD, the King of Israel
> > And his Redeemer, the LORD of hosts:
> > **'I am the first and I am the last,**
> > And there is no God besides Me.'" (Isaiah 44:6; *emphasis mine*)

"**I am** the Alpha and the Omega, **the first and the last**, the beginning and the end.

"**I, Jesus**, have sent My angel to testify to you these things for the churches. I am the root and the descendant of David, the bright morning star." (Revelation 22:13,16; *emphases mine*)

The Holy Spirit Is God

About the deity of the Holy Spirit, they read:

> But Peter said, "Ananias, why has Satan filled your heart to lie to the Holy Spirit and to keep back *some* of the price of the land?
>
> "While it remained *unsold*, did it not remain your own? And after it was sold, was it not under your control? Why is it that you have conceived this deed in your heart? You have not lied to men but to God."
>
> (Acts 5:3,4)

> But just as it is written,
> > "THINGS WHICH EYE HAS NOT SEEN AND EAR HAS NOT HEARD,
> > AND WHICH HAVE NOT ENTERED THE HEART OF MAN,
> > ALL THAT GOD HAS PREPARED FOR THOSE WHO LOVE HIM."
>
> For to us God revealed *them* through the Spirit; for the Spirit searches all things, even the depths of God.
>
> For who among men knows the *thoughts* of a man except the spirit of the man which is in him? Even so the *thoughts* of God no one knows except the Spirit of God. (1 Corinthians 2:9-11)

> Now the Lord is the Spirit, and where the Spirit of the Lord is, *there* is liberty.
>
> But we all, with unveiled face, beholding as in a mirror the glory of the Lord, are being transformed into the same image from glory to glory, just as from the Lord, the Spirit. (2 Corinthians 3:17,18)

"One thing is for sure: Believe it or don't believe it, but the Bible definitely teaches that there is one and only one God; and that the Father, the Son, and the Holy Spirit are that one God," Nick concluded.

"Absolutely," agreed Dave. "That is the mystery of the Christian doctrine of *the Trinity*. The Godhead is one in essence (or substance), and three in person. The one God is indivisible in substance. Yet inside of God, or under the 'umbrella' of the Godhead, there are three separate and distinct persons. At all times and for eternity, the Father is fully God, the Son is fully God, and the Holy Spirit is fully God.

"Almighty God, being infinite, goes well beyond anything we as finite beings could even imagine. With Him, there can be one being having three distinct persons. No contradiction exists here. The doctrine of the Trinity is indeed a great mystery. We bow our finite and extremely limited understanding to the glorious, infinite Almighty God, and worship Him in awe just for who He is."

"Amen!" echoed Nick.

"Theologians like to emphasize different roles for each of the three Persons in the Godhead in order to fortify the distinction between the three Persons. This is so they are not confused with being just three modes or facades of God," Dave continued. "For example, the Father is said to be the Creator; the Son, the Redeemer; and the Holy Spirit the Sanctifier of believers.

"But, though these distinctions are true, assigning these 'concrete' roles is inaccurate and misleading. God is indivisible, and all three Persons are present and involved in every aspect of God's plan. We saw this in creation, where, in Genesis 1, the Spirit is moving and the Father speaks the Word. Yes, the Father sends the Son into the world to become a man; the Son does not send the Father. But Jesus repeatedly attests:

> "He who has seen Me has seen the Father; how *can* you say, 'Show us the Father'?
>
> "Do you not believe that I am in the Father, and the Father is in Me? The words that I say to you I do not speak on My own initiative, but the Father abiding in Me does His works." (John 14:9b,10)

"The Father is present in Christ, and Christ in the Father, and the Holy Spirit is in Christ performing His works. We also see the indivisibility of the Godhead in the resurrection of Christ from the dead. Read Galatians 1:1, John 10:17 and 18, and Romans 8:11."

Nick read:

> Paul, an apostle (not *sent* from men nor through the agency of man, but through Jesus Christ and God the Father, who raised Him from the dead)...
>
> (Galatians 1:1)

> "For this reason the Father loves Me, because I lay down My life so that I may take it again.
>
> "No one has taken it away from Me, but I lay it down on My own initiative. I have authority to lay it down, and I have authority to take it up again. This commandment I received from My Father." (John 10:17,18)

But if the Spirit of Him who raised Jesus from the dead dwells in you,
He who raised Christ Jesus from the dead will also give life to your mortal
bodies through His Spirit who dwells in you. (Romans 8:11)

"We see here all three Persons directly involved in the same act, the resurrection of Jesus Christ," expounded Dave. "God is indivisible. There are not three different Gods running around doing their respective parts of God's plan. Where one Person of the Trinity is involved, the other two Persons must, by definition of the word 'indivisible,' be fully there also.

"During the incarnation, Jesus added finite humanity to His infinite divinity. And, in the resurrection, Jesus was raised with a glorified human body. But—always being God—His Spirit was, is, and always will be infinite. Though He is seated at the right hand of the Father in heaven, His infinite Spirit is able to be omnipresent—that is, fully present everywhere in the universe!"

"Wow!" Nick exclaimed. "The more I learn about God and who He is, the more awesome He becomes to me!"

False Teachings on the Trinity

"Me, too!" Dave agreed. "But beware! There are two heresies that pervert the true definition of the Trinity. They are tritheism and modalism.

"**Tritheism** says the Three Persons of the Trinity are actually three different Gods who are one in purpose, not in being. The analogy tritheists typically use to explain this unexplainable mystery is that of the egg. The one egg has three parts—the white, the yolk and the shell.

"But the Three Persons of the Trinity are not different *parts* of God where, together, they make up the whole of God. No. The Father is 100% God, the Son is 100% God, and the Holy Spirit is 100% God everywhere and at all times.

"We cannot understand this if we try to put it in terms of the finite realm. But this is possible with the infinite God with no problem whatsoever. One plus One plus One does not equal One. But One times One times One does equal One. This is a weak analogy of the difference between the finite realm and the infinite. Only the infinite realm holds the pieces to the puzzle which can easily explain any mystery.

"Remember, there is no contradiction here. God is one in essence (or substance), and three in person. These are two completely different senses in which God is one and not one."

"I got it," said Nick. "Trying to stuff the infinite into the finite with three-dimensional analogies is simply impossible. I guess any finite analogy would fail to explain the mystery of the infinite Trinity. And why would anyone try? You said that, by definition, a *mystery* is truth which cannot be explained by the finite mind, but can be resolved with all pieces revealed."

"Excellent!" Dave applauded. "We study God's holy Word and make certain exactly what He is saying. Reading what the Holy Spirit has revealed to the saints during the history of the church is very helpful to avoid heresy. We then believe God's truth, even if He has not explained every detail, and even if our finite minds can't figure out how God does it.

"The second heresy to avoid is **modalism**. Modalists pervert the doctrine of the Trinity by saying the Three Persons are simply different modes, functions, or guises of the one God. They would say that God shows Himself as the Father here, the Spirit there, and the Son during His incarnation.

"The analogy they typically use is that of water. Water is liquid in its natural state, ice when it is freezing, and steam when it is boiling.

"But, again—the one God does not show Himself in different guises at different times. No. The Father is 100% God, the Son is 100% God, and the Holy Spirit is 100% God everywhere and at all times.

"The biblical doctrine of the Trinity declares that there is ONE and only ONE God, and that the ONE God subsists in three distinct persons—the Father, the Son and the Holy Spirit.

"The Godhead is one in essence (or substance), and three in person. The one God is indivisible in substance, yet He is made up of three separate and distinct persons that subsist under the one being of God. The Father is fully God, the Son is fully God, and the Holy Spirit is fully God—everywhere and at all times.

"The doctrine of the Trinity is an essential of the Christian faith. It is so crucial to understand who God says He is, that all of Christianity stands or falls on this one doctrine. Any and all cults and belief systems that deviate from the essential doctrine of the Trinity cannot be Christian, and are subject to the wrath of the one true God."

"I can see now that knowing who God says He is becomes critical to salvation," Nick mused. "Believing anything else is not believing in the one true God at all."

"Precisely," Dave assented. "All other gods are simply idols constructed in the finite, sin-marred minds of men, who suppress the knowledge of the one true God in order to continue in their sin.

"Our goal is to love the one true God with all of our being, and to become intimately acquainted with His ways. I hope explaining the Trinity has helped you understand how God describes Himself in His holy Word."

"Yes," replied Nick. "And I'm glad you explained the meaning of 'mystery' versus 'contradiction.' Otherwise, I would have been trying to find ways to explain the infinite God in finite terms—and would have failed miserably!"

"I've tried that many times," Dave related. "I know now that much of who God is will be a mystery to my finite understanding. But everything He reveals about Himself is true—and I must bank this life on it—whether I know how He does it or not! As Moses prophesied to the people of Israel: 'The secret things belong to the LORD our God, but the things revealed belong to us and to our sons forever' (Deuteronomy 29:29).

"Let's take a break and get a soda. When we return, we'll dive into the holy character of our God, and all of His attributes."

"Sounds great!" answered Nick.

7

Holy, Holy, Holy

Dave and Nick returned from their sojourn down the hall. Each with a cold soda in hand, they resumed their respective seats.

"Let's continue our study of God by detailing the attributes of God. We've mentioned some already," Dave prompted, "such as God's immutability and His omniscience. I've prepared an outline for us to follow. Since our God is infinite and eternal, there are many attributes to cover.

"Our goal is to love God intimately with all of our hearts, strengths, minds and souls. To love anyone more and more, we must know more and more about that person. Otherwise, that person remains a stranger, or simply an acquaintance.

"This is the reason we study God and His attributes: so that we may know His ways, and love Him more deeply. As we go through the perfections of God's magnificent character, don't get bogged down in all of the theological terms. Focus in on the majesty of our God, and the glorious splendor of His perfections!"

"Excellent idea!" Nick agreed.

"*The attributes of God* are the perfect, eternal elements of His character which dictate His actions," defined Dave. "God is not under the authority of any law, because that law would then become God. **God is a law unto Himself**, meaning that He operates according to the perfections of His own glorious character, not according to any law above or outside of Himself.

"First and foremost, God is *holy*," Dave stated. "God's holiness envelopes all of the other attributes of God. God's holiness is what makes Him so beautiful in all respects.

The Attributes of God
The eternal, perfect elements of God's magnificent character

HOLINESS

- **TRANSCENDENCE**—*Qualities That God Alone Possesses*

  ✧ *Incomprehensibility* (Unfathomable Depths)
  - God's Thoughts are Self-validating
  - God's Thoughts Create from Nothing
  - God's Thoughts are Immediate

  ✧ *Indivisibility*
  - One God in Unity and Diversity
  - Simplicity—Not A Compound of Parts

  ✧ *Immutability*
  - Eternal Character
  - Eternal Purpose (or Plan)

  ✧ *Independence*
  - Self-existence
  - God Alone is Free

  ✧ *Infinity*
  - Omnipotence
  - Omnipresence
  - Omniscience

- **GOODNESS**—*Qualities God Shares With His Creatures*

  ✧ *Purity and Uprightness*
  - Eternality
  - Love
  - Hatred
  - Truth
  - Justice/Righteousness
  - Wrath
  - Grace
  - Mercy/Lovingkindness
  - Patience
  - Faithfulness
  - Logic/Reason

"In ancient literature, when the writer wanted to emphasize a point, he would repeat a word or phrase to draw attention to the importance of his words. Jesus often did this, saying 'truly, truly.' For example, in the Gospel of John: 'And He said to him, "Truly, truly, I say to you, you will see the heavens opened and the angels of God ascending and descending on the Son of Man"' (John 1:51).

"The only word repeated three times in Scripture is, 'Holy, holy, holy.' Four living creatures surrounding the throne of Almighty God do not cease to praise Him by saying, 'Holy, holy, holy is the Lord' (Revelation 4:8)! Truly, truly, our God—and our God alone—is thrice holy!"

"Amen!" shouted Nick.

"We have seen in history man's exercise of power without holiness—in the 20th century German dictator Adolph Hitler, for example. But the holiness of God governs even His hatred and His wrath, causing the psalmist to greatly desire His beauty and to live with Him forever. Let's read the scriptures I have marked down here on the holiness of God."

They read:

Then the LORD spoke to Moses, saying:

Speak to all the congregation of the sons of Israel and say to them, 'You shall be holy, for I the LORD your God am holy. (Leviticus 19:1,2)

He (Jesus) opened His mouth and *began* to teach them, saying,

"Therefore you are to be perfect, as your heavenly Father is perfect."

(Matthew 5:2,48)

One thing I have asked from the LORD, that I shall seek:

That I may dwell in the house of the LORD all the days of my life,

To behold the beauty of the LORD

And to meditate in His temple. (Psalm 27:4)

Who is like You among the gods, O LORD?

Who is like You, majestic in holiness,

Awesome in praises, working wonders? (Exodus 15:11)

The LORD reigns, let the peoples tremble;

He is enthroned *above* the cherubim, let the earth shake!

The LORD is great in Zion,

And He is exalted above all the peoples.

Let them praise Your great and awesome name;

Holy is He.

Exalt the LORD our God

And worship at His footstool;

Holy is He.

Exalt the LORD our God

And worship at His holy hill,

For holy is the LORD our God. (Psalm 99:1-3,5,9)

In the year of King Uzziah's death I saw the Lord sitting on a throne, lofty and exalted, with the train of His robe filling the temple.

Seraphim stood above Him, each having six wings: with two he covered his face, and with two he covered his feet, and with two he flew.

And one called out to another and said,

"Holy, Holy, Holy, is the LORD of hosts,

The whole earth is full of His glory." (Isaiah 6:1-3)

Out from the throne come flashes of lightning and sounds and peals of thunder. And *there were* seven lamps of fire burning before the throne, which are the seven Spirits of God;

and before the throne *there was something* like a sea of glass, like crystal; and in the center and around the throne, four living creatures full of eyes in front and behind.

And the four living creatures, each one of them having six wings, are full of eyes around and within; and day and night they do not cease to say,

"HOLY, HOLY, HOLY IS THE LORD GOD, THE ALMIGHTY, WHO WAS AND WHO IS AND WHO IS TO COME." (Revelation 4:5,6,8)

And they sang the song of Moses, the bond-servant of God, and the song of the Lamb, saying,

"Great and marvelous are Your works,

O Lord God, the Almighty;

Righteous and true are Your ways,

King of the nations!

"Who will not fear, O Lord, and glorify Your name?

For You alone are holy;

"For ALL THE NATIONS WILL COME AND WORSHIP BEFORE YOU,

FOR YOUR RIGHTEOUS ACTS HAVE BEEN REVEALED."

(Revelation 15:3,4)

"Truly our God is most holy!" Nick exclaimed.

"Amen!" Dave agreed.

God's Holy Transcendence

"**Holiness** has two distinct meanings, and our God perfectly and eternally radiates both of them," Dave continued. "The primary definition of God's holiness is God's ***transcendence***. The second idea involving God's holiness is that of His ***perfect goodness***, or ***purity***.

"God's ***transcendence*** means that He is set apart—separate and distinct from all of His creation. God is 'wholly other' than anything else in existence. God is in a class totally by Himself. God's ***transcendence*** means that He exists beyond, or exceeds, man's finite experience.

"God is not like us—in fact, God is nothing like us. He is infinitely greater than man in His glory, majesty, splendor and magnificence. Please read Isaiah 55:8 and 9 again. Then read the scriptures on God's transcendence."

Nick read:

> "For My thoughts are not your thoughts,
>> Nor are your ways My ways," declares the LORD.
> "For *as* the heavens are higher than the earth,
>> So are My ways higher than your ways
>> And My thoughts than your thoughts." (Isaiah 55:8,9)

> "Again what more can David say to You? For You know Your servant,
> O Lord GOD!
> For the sake of Your word, and according to Your own heart, You have
> done all this greatness to let Your servant know.
> For this reason You are great, O Lord GOD; for there is none like
> You, and there is no God besides You, according to all that we have heard
> with our ears." (2 Samuel 7:20-22)

> "To whom then will you liken Me
>> That I would be *his* equal?" says the Holy One. (Isaiah 40:25)

> For thus says the high and exalted One
>> Who lives forever, whose name is Holy,
>> "I dwell *on* a high and holy place,
>> And *also* with the contrite and lowly of spirit
>> In order to revive the spirit of the lowly
>> And to revive the heart of the contrite." (Isaiah 57:15)

"God's transcendence declares that He is the 'high and exalted One' who has no equal in all of creation," expounded Dave. "God is infinitely greater than man in every respect. The chief meaning of God's holiness is that He transcends His creation. The one true God is set apart and utterly unique—completely different from, and infinitely greater than, anything else in existence.

"Unbelievers, especially many philosophers since the eighteenth century, have claimed that God is totally unknowable specifically because He is utterly transcendent. Since God is completely different than man, they reason, then there is no common point of contact through which to communicate information.

"But unbelievers wrongly assume that, in order to know God, man must be the one to find that point of contact. The greatest minds of unbelievers miss the obvious point that the infinite God created finite man, establishing that point of contact from the beginning. Expressly because God is transcendent—infinitely greater than His finite creation—God is able to reveal Himself to man, and to do so however He chooses.

"In the last verses we read from Isaiah, God says that He is transcendent: 'He is high and exalted,' 'His name is Holy,' and 'He dwells on a high and holy place.' But He then says He lives with the contrite and lowly man, and revives his spirit. The infinite, eternal God touches His finite creatures in a very personal way.

"Unbelievers love saying that God is unknowable, simply to escape from God's authority in order to continue in their rebellious lifestyles. But God says in His Word that He is holy—transcendent and pure—*and* that He has revealed Himself through The Word, Jesus Christ. Please read John 1:9, 17 and 18; and Romans 1:18 and 19."

Nick read

There was the true Light which, coming into the world, enlightens every man.

For the Law was given through Moses; grace and truth were realized through Jesus Christ.

No one has seen God at any time; the only begotten God who is in the bosom of the Father, He has explained *Him*. (John 1:9,17,18)

For the wrath of God is revealed from heaven against all ungodliness and unrighteousness of men who suppress the truth in unrighteousness,

because that which is known about God is evident within them; for God made it evident to them. (Romans 1:18,19)

What About the Jungle Native?

"Jesus Christ has revealed the transcendent, holy, invisible God to man," Dave declared. "And God has placed within every man's conscience the fact that He exists, and that He judges all of His creation. Unbelievers must actively suppress that knowledge to continue living in their sin, for which they will be condemned to eternal torture for their rebellion.

"The question is always asked: 'What about the jungle native who has never even heard the name "Jesus"?' That native, and every other human being born of a human father, are all in the same boat.

"God declares that He has given all persons knowledge of Himself within their consciences. But every person actively suppresses that knowledge in order to continue in his or her sin (Romans 1:18,19). Every man, woman and child has stolen this life to serve themselves. Therefore, every man, woman and child is totally guilty of rejecting God and His Son Christ Jesus, creation's only Savior, whether they have heard the gospel or not."

"So, the second meaning of God's holiness is that He is pure, or perfectly good," Nick recounted. "But the main idea of God's holiness is that He is transcendent. This means God is set apart, totally different from anything in creation, and that He exists beyond man's finite experience. Also, God is infinitely greater than creation in all respects, which means He is able to reveal Himself to His creation as He chooses. God places the knowledge of His existence within every person. Mankind is therefore without excuse for not bowing before the one true holy and transcendent God."

"Excellent!" applauded Dave. "Because God is transcendent in His holiness—set apart from and infinitely greater than creation—He has attributes completely unique to Himself. They are His incomprehensibility, indivisibility, immutability, independence and infinity.

Incomprehensibility

"God's *incomprehensibility* does not mean that He cannot be understood, but that the depths of His thoughts are unfathomable. As finite creatures, we cannot, and never will be able to, exhaust the depths of God. The limits of God's thoughts and understanding are inscrutable—incapable of being totally discovered. Please read Isaiah 40:28 and Romans 11:33 and 34."

Nick read:

> Do you not know? Have you not heard?
> > The Everlasting God, the LORD,
> > the Creator of the ends of the earth
> > Does not become weary or tired.
> > His understanding is inscrutable. (Isaiah 40:28)

> Oh, the depth of the riches both of the wisdom and knowledge of
> God! How unsearchable are His judgments and unfathomable His ways!
> > For WHO HAS KNOWN THE MIND OF THE LORD, OR WHO BECAME HIS COUNSELOR?
> > Or WHO HAS FIRST GIVEN TO HIM THAT IT MIGHT BE PAID BACK TO HIM AGAIN?
> > For from Him and through Him and to Him are all things. To Him
> *be* the glory forever. Amen. (Romans 11:33-36)

"Almighty God's wisdom and knowledge, His thoughts and understanding, are infinitely beyond the mind of the creature," Dave articulated. "We oftentimes would not do as God does to bring about His glorious plan. But we—not He—are the finite, sin-marred, short-sighted ones.

"The three aspects of God's incomprehensible thoughts are: they are self-validating, create from nothing, and are immediate. Our thoughts are nothing like that—not even some of the time!

"By *self-validating*, I mean that whatever God thinks **is** the standard of truth. This aspect of Jesus stunned His listeners, because He did not teach as the lawyers and scribes, who always referred to a higher authority such as the Law of Moses. Jesus claimed ultimate authority for His words. During the Sermon on the Mount in Matthew 5, for example, Jesus would declare repeatedly: 'You have heard it said...But I say to you!' Here, read the crowd's reaction in the Gospel of Matthew, chapter 7:

Nick read:

> When Jesus had finished these words, the crowds were amazed at His
> teaching;
> > for He was teaching them as *one* having authority, and not as their
> scribes. (Matthew 7:28,29)

"God's thoughts and God's words are the standard of truth in all of creation," Dave stated. "In this respect, the self-validating aspect of God's incomprehensibility is utterly unique to Himself. Man's thoughts and man's words are never the criterion for truth.

"God's thoughts and words also are able to ***create out of nothing***. Man's words can never create out of nothing. Much of the 'Word-Faith "Name-It-And-Claim-It" heresy' of the late 20th century revolves around man attempting to usurp what belongs solely to God. Incidentally, that is precisely the 'original sin' of the arrogant pride of Adam, as he succumbed to Satan's siren song: 'You will be like God' (Genesis 3:5).

"God and God alone possesses the authority to speak something into existence. Read Romans 4:17."

Nick read:

> ...(as it is written, "A FATHER OF MANY NATIONS HAVE I MADE YOU")
> in the presence of Him whom he believed, *even* God, who gives life to the
> dead and calls into being that which does not exist. (Romans 4:17)

"The idea that we can speak away diseases, or speak into existence a new Cadillac, by the authority of our words, is not only absurd, it is the worst of sins," Dave maintained. "Placing the words of finite creatures on a par with the words of Almighty God is nothing less than idolatry.

"God's word rules every detail of creation. Only if God gives specific authority to man—saved or unsaved—to heal others according to His eternal plan, will healing occur. The power is not in the words spoken by man, but in the authority of the One who alone possesses the power to create out of nothing. This aspect of God's incomprehensibility is utterly unique to God.

"The last aspect of God's incomprehensibility—the unfathomable depths of His thoughts and words—is ***the immediate nature*** of His thoughts and words. God does not gain information by revelation from an outside source, such as the media of television and radio. **God's thoughts and words are the determinant of everything that exists or occurs in creation**. Read Jesus' words in Matthew 10:29 through 31."

Nick read:

> "Are not two sparrows sold for a cent? And *yet* not one of them will fall
> to the ground apart from your Father. But the very hairs of your head are all
> numbered. So do not fear; you are more valuable than many sparrows."
>
> (Matthew 10:29-31)

"For God to know how many hairs are on your head, He does not need to go and count them," Dave averred. "God has determined the exact number of your hairs at every given moment of time in this life, and He ordained those amounts before He created the universe! God's decree of the number of your hairs *is* the number of your hairs. God's thoughts and words are truth, and reality simply obeys and fulfills His decree.

"We, however, are not like God at all in this respect. Everything we know had to be revealed to us by God Himself and through our resulting experiences. So, the immediate aspect of God's thoughts and words is the third aspect of His incomprehensibility."

"Okay, I think I've got it so far," Nick said. "God is holy. The two meanings of His holiness are His transcendence and His goodness (or perfect purity). All of the attributes relating to God's transcendence are unique to Himself, because God's transcendence means He is infinitely beyond man's finite experience.

"The first of the five attributes of God's transcendence is His incomprehensibility, which means the unfathomable depths of His thoughts. The three aspects of God's unique, perfect incomprehensibility are that His thoughts and words are self-validating, can create out of nothing, and are immediate."

"Outstanding!" praised Dave. "You are amazing me with your grasp of these complex aspects of God's eternal character!"

"Well, your outline makes it very easy to keep straight in my mind," answered Nick.

Indivisibility

"Thanks!" Dave responded. "Let's continue with the second of the five unique attributes of God's transcendence—His indivisibility. God's **indivisibility** means there is one and only one God, and He is not a compound of parts. We just studied the scriptures on this when we tackled the mystery of the Trinity (*see Chapter 6*).

"There is only one God, and subsisting under the umbrella of His deity are the three Persons of the Godhead and all of His eternal attributes. The three Persons are each separate and distinct from one another, yet each fully God, being 'under' or 'inside' the one being of the one God. In the finite realm this would be impossible. But in God's infinite realm, this is no problem at all, and contains no illogical contradiction.

"The mystery of the Trinity means that where one Person of the Godhead is at any time, all of the Persons of the Godhead are likewise. And where one attribute of God exists—such as His goodness—all of the other attributes are present as well. God's **simplicity** denotes that He is not a compound of parts. God is always fully God everywhere and at all times. Understanding this fact keeps one from heresy.

"I've known some believers who have told me that they responded to God's gospel of salvation because of His incredible love. But they then say that they cannot believe in hell, because to them, God is so loving. The grievous error they commit here is assuming that God is made up of parts, and we can take the ones we like and discard the rest. After all, we are sometimes loving but not merciful, or just but not gracious.

"The unique attribute of God's indivisibility declares that God is not a compound of parts. He is one being, and whenever and wherever that one God is, the three Persons and all of His attributes are also present. God may not mete out each of His attributes to each person equally, but they are all present in Himself. For example, God is always loving, and He is always just.

Immutability

"The third attribute of God's transcendence is His immutability."

"Oh, I remember that one from Sunday school class," recalled Nick. "God's **immutability** means that God never changes in His character, and never changes His purpose, also known as

His plan which existed eternally in His mind."

"Excellent!" Dave replied. "And we covered the scriptures on God's immutability then as well (*see Chapter 5*).

Independence

"The fourth of the five unique attributes of God's transcendence is God's ***independence***.

"God does not depend on anyone for anything—especially for His existence. God has always existed and will always continue to exist, for He has the power of being within Himself. The first aspect of God's unique eternal attribute of independence is His self-existence. The second aspect is that God and God alone is totally free. Please read the scriptures I have written down about the independence of God."

Nick read:

> Before the mountains were born
>> Or You gave birth to the earth and the world,
>> Even from everlasting to everlasting, You are God. (Psalm 90:2)

> The God who made the world and all things in it, since He is Lord of heaven and earth, does not dwell in temples made with hands;
>> nor is He served by human hands, as though He needed anything, since He Himself gives to all *people* life and breath and all things;
>> for in Him we live and move and exist, as even some of your own poets have said, 'For we also are His children.' (Acts 17:24,25,28)

> "For every beast of the forest is Mine,
>> The cattle on a thousand hills.
> "I know every bird of the mountains,
>> And everything that moves in the field is Mine.
> "If I were hungry I would not tell you,
>> For the world is Mine, and all it contains.
> "These things you have done and I kept silence;
>> You thought that I was just like you;
>> I will reprove you and state *the case* in order before your eyes."
>> (Psalm 50:10-12,21)

"God is God from eternity past through eternity future," Dave elucidated. "The first aspect of God's unique attribute of independence is His ***self-existence***. This means that God exists and continues to exist without depending on anything outside Himself. No law of science or rule of logic forbids the principle of God's self-existence. God depends upon nothing to exist. He has the power of existence within Himself.

"We, however, as creatures, are utterly dependent beings. We depend upon God, not only for the beginning of our existence, but for the sustaining of our existence as well: 'For *in Him* we live and move and exist' (Acts 17:28). If we are deprived of air for ten minutes, water for ten days, or food for ten weeks, our demise is certain!"

"That's true," Nick assented.

"God also depends upon no one to accomplish His plan, or purpose," continued Dave. "God does not need us at all for anything. God reproves the idolatrous Israelites for their heinous error of thinking that God was dependent upon them and their sacrifices. God states that He owns everything in creation, and that He can do anything He pleases with what is His own any time He desires. God does not need us.

"God's scolding of Israel should humble any preacher who feels that he, or his teaching, is indispensable. If we do not proclaim God's truth, He will use the rocks to do it! Read Luke 19:37 through verse 40, please."

Nick read:

> As soon as He was approaching, near the descent of the Mount of
> Olives, the whole crowd of the disciples began to praise God joyfully with a
> loud voice for all the miracles which they had seen,
> > shouting:
> > "BLESSED IS THE KING WHO COMES IN THE NAME OF THE LORD;
> > Peace in heaven and glory in the highest!"
> Some of the Pharisees in the crowd said to Him, "Teacher, rebuke Your
> disciples."
> But Jesus answered, "I tell you, if these become silent, the stones will
> cry out!" (Luke 19:37-40)

"God made creation simply because it was His good pleasure to use it to glorify Himself," Dave asserted. "God made man for the same reason. Those of us whom He chose to become His children were brought into His family because God wanted us, not because He needed us. God was perfectly content with His infinite love among the three Persons of the Trinity in eternity past. We added nothing to His perfection and completeness. Read Ephesians 2:4-7."

Nick read:

> But God, being rich in mercy, because of His great love with which He
> loved us,
> > even when we were dead in our transgressions, made us alive together
> with Christ (by grace you have been saved),
> > and raised us up with Him, and seated us with Him in the heavenly
> *places* in Christ Jesus,
> > so that in the ages to come He might show the surpassing riches of
> His grace in kindness toward us in Christ Jesus. (Ephesians 2:4-7)

"God saved us so that He might display the infinite riches of His eternal love, grace, mercy and kindness," Dave expounded. "God did not save us because He could not accomplish His plan without us. By His grace and kindness, God allows us to participate in His glorious plan. Our holy Father has also ordained for us to receive an inheritance from His generous hand.

"So, the first aspect of God's independence is His self-existence. This means that God is not dependent upon anyone or anything for His existence, or for the completion of His eternal plan. The second aspect of God's independence is that God alone is ***totally free***. The definition of ***free*** used here is to be utterly exempt from external authority or controlling influence.

"There is no authority or law over God, or that authority would be God. God cannot be controlled, influenced or tempted by anything. Read Isaiah 40:13 through 15 and James 1:13, please."

Nick read:

> Who has directed the Spirit of the LORD,
>> Or as His counselor has informed Him?
> With whom did He consult and *who* gave Him understanding?
>> And *who* taught Him in the path of justice and taught Him
>>> knowledge
>> And informed Him of the way of understanding?
> Behold, the nations are like a drop from a bucket,
>> And are regarded as a speck of dust on the scales;
>> Behold, He lifts up the islands like fine dust. (Isaiah 40:13-15)

> Let no one say when he is tempted, "I am being tempted by God";
> for God cannot be tempted by evil, and He Himself does not tempt
> anyone. (James 1:13)

"God is simply not like us," Dave affirmed. "God's knowledge, understanding and power are infinite! So, how could any finite creature possibly control or influence the Almighty? Such a notion is totally absurd."

"I guess that is why the Lord chided Israel in Psalm 50 that I just read," said Nick, "because they thought that God was just like them—dependent and needy."

"Correct," Dave agreed. "God alone is totally free from external authority or controlling influence. We finite men aren't like that at all. Creation is always under the direct rule and authority of God. The will of God is free. The will of man is totally enslaved—the opposite of being free—whether of a believer or unbeliever."

"I constantly hear preachers on 'Christian' radio talking about man's free will, claiming that man is a free moral agent," Nick recalled.

"I will explain 'free will'—the true biblical Christian definition, and the heresy of the concept in the 20th century church—in our next College & Career class," Dave replied. "Suffice it to say, true freedom belongs solely to God. It is the second aspect of God's unique attribute of independence. But, for a taste of what Scripture says about man's will, read Romans 6:16."

Nick read:

> Do you not know that when you present yourselves to someone *as* slaves
> for obedience, you are slaves of the one whom you obey, either of sin
> resulting in death, or of obedience resulting in righteousness?
>> (Romans 6:16)

"The Apostle Paul explains that man was created to be a servant," Dave expounded. "Man is born with a will in slavery to sin. If God sets a man free from his bondage to sin, he becomes a servant of God, and a slave to righteousness. Either way, the will of man is enslaved, and thus cannot be free from all external authority or controlling influence. Only God is totally free.

"Thus, the unique attribute of God's independence involves two aspects: His self-existence—not depending on anything for His existence or for the completion of His plan; and His absolute freedom—being exempt from external authority or controlling influence.

Infinity

"The fifth and final attribute of God's transcendence is His infinity. **Infinity** means limitlessness, boundlessness or endlessness. God's unique attribute of infinity is expressed in three aspects: His omnipotence, omnipresence, and omniscience. Please read the scriptures I have marked for God's infinity and its first aspect, God's omnipotence."

Nick read:

> "But will God indeed dwell on the earth? Behold, heaven and the highest heaven cannot contain You, how much less this house which I have built!" (1 Kings 8:27)

> "Ah Lord GOD! Behold, You have made the heavens and the earth by Your great power and by Your outstretched arm! Nothing is too difficult for You."
> Then the word of the Lord came to Jeremiah, saying,
> "Behold, I am the Lord, the God of all flesh; is anything too difficult for Me?" (Jeremiah 32:17,26,27)

> Mary said to the angel, "How can this be, since I am a virgin?"
> The angel answered and said to her, "The Holy Spirit will come upon you, and the power of the Most High will overshadow you; and for that reason the holy Child shall be called the Son of God.
> "For nothing will be impossible with God." (Luke 1:34,35,37)

"The scripture from First Kings captures the idea of God's infinity," Dave said, "that He is limitless, boundless and endless. The next two passages depict the first aspect of God's infinity, His omnipotence. God alone is all-powerful. To the surprise of many, this does not mean that God can do anything. God's **omnipotence** means God can do anything *that He desires*. God never desires to do anything contrary to His holy nature. Please read 2 Timothy 2:13, and Hebrews 6:17 and 18."

Nick read:

> If we are faithless, He remains faithful, for He cannot deny Himself.
> (2 Timothy 2:13)

In the same way God, desiring even more to show to the heirs of the
promise the unchangeableness of His purpose, interposed with an oath,

so that by two unchangeable things in which it is impossible for God to
lie, we who have taken refuge would have strong encouragement to take hold
of the hope set before us. (Hebrews 6:17,18)

"It is impossible for God to deny Himself, or to lie," Dave repeated. "It is impossible for
God to sin. It is impossible for God to make a rock so big that He cannot move it, for then God
would sin against His omnipotence. God's omnipotence means God is all-powerful and can do
anything that He desires. And The Holy One never desires to sin.

"The second aspect of God's infinity is His *omnipresence*. This means God is 100%
present in His fullness everywhere. God is not spread out like particles throughout the universe.
God is fully present in the most secure vault in Fort Knox, and fully present on the planet Pluto.
God is present in His fullness in heaven and in hell!

"This does not mean that God is in everything, so we can worship trees or rocks, but that
all of creation is visible before Him because He is fully present everywhere. Please read Psalm
139:7 through 10 and Jeremiah 23:23 and 24."

Nick read:

Where can I go from Your Spirit?
Or where can I flee from Your presence?
If I ascend to heaven, You are there;
If I make my bed in Sheol, behold, You are there.
If I take the wings of the dawn,
If I dwell in the remotest part of the sea,
Even there Your hand will lead me,
And Your right hand will lay hold of me. (Psalm 139:7-10)

"Am I a God who is near," declares the LORD,
"And not a God far off?
"Can a man hide himself in hiding places
So I do not see him?" declares the LORD.
"Do I not fill the heavens and the earth?" declares the LORD.
(Jeremiah 23:23,24)

"We already know that God is indivisible, so wherever He is, absolutely all of Him is
present," Dave reminded. "The Psalmist King David and the prophet Jeremiah express the idea
that God is everywhere.

"Incidentally, David says that God is present in Sheol, or hell. Those that desire to go to
hell to escape from God's presence and authority will be sorely disappointed. Precisely because
God is there in His wrath, they will be tormented for eternity as He withholds His grace and
mercy from them for their rebellion. So, God's omnipresence means that He is fully present
everywhere at all times.

"The third aspect of God's unique attribute of infinity is His omniscience. God's **omniscience** means that He knows all things—eternal past, present and eternal future. The immutability of God demands that He can never learn anything, for then He would change. God knows all things because He has ordained all things that exist or happen. And God's **wisdom** is His perfect utilization of His infinite knowledge. Let's read the scriptures on God's omniscience."

They read:

> O Lord, You have searched me and known *me.*
> You know when I sit down and when I rise up;
> > You understand my thought from afar.
> You scrutinize my path and my lying down,
> > And are intimately acquainted with all my ways.
> Even before there is a word on my tongue,
> > Behold, O LORD, You know it all.
> You have enclosed me behind and before,
> > And laid Your hand upon me.
> *Such* knowledge is too wonderful for me;
> > It is *too* high, I cannot attain to it. (Psalm 139:1-6)

> Then the Spirit of the LORD fell upon me, and He said to me, "Say, 'Thus says the LORD, "So you think, house of Israel, for I know your thoughts."'" (Ezekiel 11:5)

> 'SO THAT THE REST OF MANKIND MAY SEEK THE LORD,
> AND ALL THE GENTILES WHO ARE CALLED BY MY NAME,'
> SAYS THE LORD, WHO MAKES THESE THINGS KNOWN FROM LONG
> AGO. (Acts 15:17,18)

> We will know by this that we are of the truth, and will assure our heart before Him
> > in whatever our heart condemns us; for God is greater than our heart and knows all things. (1 John 3:19,20)

"Thus, God's omniscience means that He knows all things from eternity past through eternity future—even our thoughts, and even our words before we speak them," Dave said. "Again, God knows all things because He has ordained all things that exist or happen."

"If God knows our words before we speak them," reasoned Nick, "then why do we pray?"

"We do not pray for God's benefit," answered Dave. "We pray for our benefit. Yes, it is true that God knows all things, and that He knows our needs and our prayers before we ask or pray. Read Jesus' words in Matthew 6:6 through 8 and Matthew 7:7 through 11."

Nick read:

"But you, when you pray, go into your inner room, close your door and pray to your Father who is in secret, and your Father who sees *what is done* in secret will reward you.

"And when you are praying, do not use meaningless repetition as the Gentiles do, for they suppose that they will be heard for their many words.

"So do not be like them; for your Father knows what you need before you ask Him." (Matthew 6:6-8)

"Ask, and it will be given to you; seek, and you will find; knock, and it will be opened to you.

"For everyone who asks receives, and he who seeks finds, and to him who knocks it will be opened.

"Or what man is there among you who, when his son asks for a loaf, will give him a stone?

"Or if he asks for a fish, he will not give him a snake, will he?

"If you then, being evil, know how to give good gifts to your children, how much more will your Father who is in heaven give what is good to those who ask Him!" (Matthew 7:7-11)

"God knows what we need before we ask, but He commands us to keep asking, seeking and knocking!" Nick exclaimed.

"Exactly," Dave replied. "So, obviously God does not command prayer so that He can find out our needs and desires. God commands us to pray continuously so that we develop the practice of getting on His Lap, as well as the practice of depending upon Him for everything.

"Remember, the Father's supreme desire is that we know Him deeply and intimately. The reason is that God Himself is the Source of all life, and Jesus said that knowing God intimately is the very definition of eternal life (John 17:3). Getting on the Father's Lap and staying there, as Jesus told Martha, is the one thing that is necessary to please God. Going to the Father for all of our needs helps us to acknowledge more and more our absolute dependence upon Him."

"I see," Nick said. "Praying is for our benefit. God knows even what my prayers will be tomorrow."

"God knows the future because He has ordained everything that exists or happens in creation," Dave repeated. "Recall that it is blasphemy to say that God needs to look into the future to learn something, because if He learns anything, He changes. Advocating that God learns anything, or changes, denies two of His eternal attributes: His omniscience and His immutability. God's omniscience demands that He knows all things—past, present, and future—because He has appointed all things that occur."

"Yes," Nick agreed, "I remember that from our past lessons."

"So then, the attributes of God are the eternal qualities of His magnificent character," Dave summarized. "God's character is a law unto Himself, and His actions reflect His character. All of God's attributes are enveloped by His holiness.

"The holiness of God involves two parts: His transcendence and His purity, or perfect goodness. The attributes of God's transcendence are unique to God, because His transcendence means that He is in a class by Himself, totally beyond man's finite experience. Would you like to summarize the attributes of God's transcendence?"

"Sure!" answered Nick. "God's transcendence is expressed in five unique attributes: His incomprehensibility, indivisibility, immutability, independence and infinity.

"God's incomprehensibility means that His thoughts are unfathomable. We as finite beings will never be able to reach the depths of God's infinite knowledge.

"The three aspects of God's incomprehensibility are: First, God's thoughts are self-validating, denoting that His thoughts are the criterion for truth. What God thinks, reality obeys and becomes.

"Second, God's thoughts create out of nothing. We cannot bring things to pass simply by thinking, desiring or believing them. But, as God's children, we can go to the Father who alone is able to create out of nothing.

"Third, God's thoughts are immediate. God does not learn by revelation or experience, as we do. What God thinks, is. All knowledge is within Him without any searching required.

"God's indivisibility means that there is one and only one God, and His simplicity indicates that He is not a compound of parts. Wherever God is present, all three Persons of the Trinity, as well as all of His attributes, are present in full measure. God sovereignly may not choose to bestow all of His attributes upon His creatures alike, but they are all present in Him. Remember, the heinous sin of idolatry is committed if we try to keep the attributes of God that we like—His love, for example—while rejecting His justice, wrath and holiness.

"God's immutability entails that God never changes in His character or His purpose, also known as His eternal plan. Since God's attributes are all interdependent and eternally present, God could never learn anything, especially by looking into the future. For if God learns anything, He changes, and then would not be immutable or omniscient.

"God's independence involves the truth that God is not dependent upon anyone or anything for His existence, or the fulfillment of His plan. God and God alone is self-existent and is in need of nothing. Thus, God is totally free—utterly exempt from external authority or controlling influence.

"We as finite, dependent creatures are not purely free. All of creation is under God's authority and rule. Man has a will, but that will is enslaved to sin before being born again. After the new birth, man's will is enslaved to righteousness. Either way, God's holy Word says that man is enslaved.

"Lastly, God's infinity involves the ideas of being limitless, boundless or endless. God's infinity is expressed in three aspects: His omnipotence, omnipresence, and omniscience.

"God's omnipotence means that God can do anything that He desires, and God never desires to sin against His character. As God is eternally and perfectly holy, it is impossible for God to lie or commit any other sin.

"God's omnipresence denotes that God is present in His fullness everywhere at all times. God is not in everything, but all of creation is always in His view.

"God's omniscience entails that God knows all things—past, present and future. God does not look down the corridors of time to discover a future event. This idea is blasphemy, because it denies God's eternal and unique attributes of immutability and omniscience. God knows the future because He has ordained the future—as well as the past and present—down to its most minute detail."

"Outstanding!" praised Dave. "Your grasp of the unique attributes of God's transcendence is excellent!"

"Thanks for the encouragement!" appreciated Nick. "The more you teach me about this awesome God we serve, the more I want to learn! It seems the closer I get to Him, the more marvelous and amazing He is!"

"That is the very effect of God's infinite transcendence upon us as finite creatures," Dave acknowledged. "The more we know about our heavenly Father, the more we realize we don't know, and the more awesome He becomes!"

"Amen!" Nick agreed.

"Well, we've covered the first meaning of God's eternal attribute of holiness—His transcendence," Dave recapped. "Now comes the attributes of His perfect goodness, or purity. We've covered a lot of ground so far. Would you like to continue now, or wait until next week?"

"I want to know all that you can teach me about our heavenly Father," replied Nick. "Knowing Him more and more intimately has become the focus of life for me. If you are willing, let's keep going!"

"Excellent!" Dave answered.

8

God Is Great, God Is Good

"The *holiness* of God has two parts: His *transcendence* and His *goodness*, or *perfect purity*," Dave continued. "Unlike the attributes of God's transcendence, which only He possesses, the attributes of God's perfect goodness He has allowed man to share. Mind you, we employ these attributes imperfectly and intermittently, and know infinitely less about them than does the Almighty God. But God has permitted us to share in them nonetheless, so they are more familiar to us.

"God's purity, or perfect goodness and uprightness, envelops His eternality, love, hatred, truth, justice, wrath, grace, mercy, patience, faithfulness and logic. Remember, these are the eternal and perfect attributes of God's magnificent character which He shares with man. Let's read the scriptures on God's goodness, expressed by His perfect purity and uprightness."

They read:

> For the word of the Lord is upright,
> And all His work is done in faithfulness.
> He loves righteousness and justice;
> The earth is full of the lovingkindness of the Lord.
>
> (Psalm 33:4,5)

> For the Lord is good;
> His lovingkindness is everlasting
> And His faithfulness to all generations. (Psalm 100:5)

The Attributes of God
The eternal, perfect elements of God's magnificent character

HOLINESS

- **TRANSCENDENCE**—*Qualities That God Alone Possesses*
  - ✧ *Incomprehensibility* (Unfathomable Depths)
    - • God's Thoughts are Self-validating
    - • God's Thoughts Create from Nothing
    - • God's Thoughts are Immediate
  - ✧ *Indivisibility*
    - • One God in Unity and Diversity
    - • Simplicity—Not A Compound of Parts
  - ✧ *Immutability*
    - • Eternal Character
    - • Eternal Purpose (or Plan)
  - ✧ *Independence*
    - • Self-existence
    - • God Alone is Free
  - ✧ *Infinity*
    - • Omnipotence
    - • Omnipresence
    - • Omniscience

- **GOODNESS**—*Qualities God Shares With His Creatures*
  - ✧ *Purity and Uprightness*
    - • Eternality
    - • Love
    - • Hatred
    - • Truth
    - • Justice/Righteousness
    - • Wrath
    - • Grace
    - • Mercy/Lovingkindness
    - • Patience
    - • Faithfulness
    - • Logic/Reason

You are good and do good;
   Teach me Your statutes. (Psalm 119:68)

The way of the righteous is smooth;
   O Upright One, make the path of the righteous level.
Indeed, *while following* the way of Your judgments, O LORD,
   We have waited for You eagerly;
   Your name, even Your memory, is the desire of *our* souls.
At night my soul longs for You,
   Indeed, my spirit within me seeks You diligently;
   For when the earth experiences Your judgments
   The inhabitants of the world learn righteousness. (Isaiah 26:7-9)

"God's Word manifests the purity of God's holiness with words like 'good' and 'upright,'" Dave expounded. "These very passages demonstrate that God's excellent purity—or perfect goodness and uprightness—envelops His faithfulness, justice and lovingkindness (or mercy), along with His ways, acts and judgments! God's goodness is perfect, infinite and eternal.

Eternality, Love and Hatred

"The **eternality** of God means that He is without beginning or end, and transcends time. God lives from eternity past through eternity future, if one may put it that way. All of God's holy attributes are eternal because God Himself is eternal.

"A second meaning of **eternality** conveys the idea of lasting forever, or never ending. We thus include the eternalness of God with the attributes that God shares with His creation. Though man has a definite beginning at conception, he is made in the image of God, which partially means that man is created to be an everlasting being. The only question is where man will spend eternity—in heaven with God's eternal blessings, or in hell under God's eternal wrath.

"Let's read the scriptures involving the eternal God and His everlasting attributes."
They read:
   Before the mountains were born
      Or You gave birth to the earth and the world,
      Even from everlasting to everlasting, You are God. (Psalm 90:2)

For thus says the high and exalted One
   Who lives forever, whose name is Holy,
   "I dwell *on* a high and holy place,
      And *also* with the contrite and lowly of spirit
      In order to revive the spirit of the lowly
   "And to revive the heart of the contrite." (Isaiah 57:15)

"My sheep hear My voice, and I know them, and they follow Me; and I give eternal life to them, and they will never perish; and no one will snatch them out of My hand." (John 10:27,28)

Now to the King eternal, immortal, invisible, the only God, *be* honor and glory forever and ever. Amen. (1 Timothy 1:17)

"God's commandment to mankind is to 'be holy, for I the LORD your God am holy' (Leviticus 19:1,2). The eternal God the Son, Jesus Christ, quotes this law as God's standard for going to heaven: "'Therefore you are to be perfect, as your heavenly Father is perfect'" (Matthew 5:48). The Lord Jesus equates God's holiness with God's perfection—His perfect goodness or purity—which is an utterly impossible standard for man to achieve.

"But Christ Jesus gives eternal life to those whom God has loved and thus had chosen to be in His family before the world began. And, by definition, eternal life can never end, or it is not eternal life!

"This love of God is eternal, and is wrapped in His purity and perfect goodness. God's *love* is His everlasting commitment to His children to remake them into the image of God the Son, ultimately bringing them home to Love Himself! Let's read the scriptures pertaining to God's holy love."

They read:

The LORD appeared to him from afar, *saying,*

"I have loved you (My chosen people) with an everlasting love; Therefore I have drawn you with lovingkindness."

(Jeremiah 31:3; *parenthesis mine*)

"Just as the Father has loved Me, I have also loved you; abide in My love.

"If you keep My commandments, you will abide in My love; just as I have kept My Father's commandments, and abide in His love.

"These things I have spoken to you so that My joy may be in you, and *that* your joy may be made full.

"This is My commandment, that you love one another, just as I have loved you.

"Greater love has no one than this, that one lay down his life for his friends.

"You are My friends if you do what I command you."

(John 15:9-14)

"The glory which You have given Me I have given to them, that they may be one, just as We are one;

"I in them and You in Me, that they may be perfected in unity, so that the world may know that You sent Me, and loved them, even as You have loved Me.

"Father, I desire that they also, whom You have given Me, be with
Me where I am, so that they may see My glory which You have given Me,
for You loved Me before the foundation of the world.

"O righteous Father, although the world has not known You, yet I
have known You; and these have known that You sent Me;

and I have made Your name known to them, and will make it known,
so that the love with which You loved Me may be in them, and I in
them." (John 17:22-26)

But God, being rich in mercy, because of His great love with which
He loved us,

even when we were dead in our transgressions, made us alive together
with Christ (by grace you have been saved),

and raised us up with Him, and seated us with Him in the heavenly
places in Christ Jesus,

so that in the ages to come He might show the surpassing riches of
His grace in kindness toward us in Christ Jesus. (Ephesians 2:4-7)

The one who does not love does not know God, for God is love.

We have come to know and have believed the love which God has for
us. God is love, and the one who abides in love abides in God, and God
abides in him.

By this, love is perfected with us, so that we may have confidence in
the day of judgment; because as He is, so also are we in this world.

There is no fear in love; but perfect love casts out fear, because fear
involves punishment, and the one who fears is not perfected in love.

We love, because He first loved us. (1 John 4:8,16-19)

"Those whom the Father has set His love upon from all eternity," Dave explained,
"experience an eternal love. Jesus says that this love is the very same love with which God the
Father loved God the Son from all eternity. God invites His children to abide in His love, which
casts out all fear. When we share the Father's love with others, this True Love is a commitment
to draw them to the Source of love—God Himself.

"As we have seen during the College & Career Sunday school class," Dave reminded, "God
also hates. God's ***hatred*** of sin, and those who love sinning, is a holy hatred, expressed in
righteous anger and meted out with severe wrath. Let's read the scriptures on God's hatred."

They read:

For You are not a God who takes pleasure in wickedness;
No evil dwells with You.
The boastful shall not stand before Your eyes;
You hate all who do iniquity.

> You destroy those who speak falsehood;
>> The LORD abhors the man of bloodshed and deceit.
>>> (Psalm 5:4-6)

> The LORD tests the righteous and the wicked,
>> And the one who loves violence His soul hates. (Psalm 11:5)

And not only this, but there was Rebekah also, when she had conceived *twins* by one man, our father Isaac;
> for though *the twins* were not yet born and had not done anything good or bad, so that God's purpose according to *His* choice would stand, not because of works but because of Him who calls,
>> it was said to her, "THE OLDER WILL SERVE THE YOUNGER."
> Just as it is written, "JACOB I LOVED, BUT ESAU I HATED."
>>> (Romans 9:10-13)

> "To the angel of the church in Ephesus write:
The One who holds the seven stars in His right hand, the One who walks among the seven golden lampstands, says this:
>> "I know your deeds and your toil and perseverance, and that you cannot tolerate evil men, and you put to the test those who call themselves apostles, and they are not, and you found them *to be* false;
>> and you have perseverance and have endured for My name's sake, and have not grown weary.
>> "Yet this you do have, that you hate the deeds of the Nicolaitans, which I also hate." (Revelation 2:1-3,6)

"God says that He hates all who 'do iniquity,' 'speak falsehood,' or 'love violence.' God 'abhors the man of bloodshed and deceit,'" Dave recounted. "God says He chose the family of Jacob to bear His Name, while hating Esau and his descendants, before either were even born! God says He hates the deeds of 'the Nicolaitans'—false Christians who wielded power and authority as 'God's anointed mouthpieces' over the laity in the church. This ungodly position directly disobeyed the Lord Jesus' commands in Mark 10:
> Calling them to Himself, Jesus said to them, "You know that those who are recognized as rulers of the Gentiles lord it over them; and their great men exercise authority over them.
> "But it is not this way among you, but whoever wishes to become great among you shall be your servant;
> and whoever wishes to be first among you shall be slave of all.
> "For even the Son of Man did not come to be served, but to serve, and to give His life a ransom for many." (Mark 10:42-45)

Truth, Justice and Wrath

"God's holy hatred is toward anyone and anything contrary to His holy, good and pure character," Dave explained. "God abhors those who speak falsehood, because God is eternally truthful, and always speaks the truth. *Truth*—reality as perceived by God—is another expression of God's goodness, or purity. God is perfectly truthful, conveying the idea of being honorable in principles, intentions and actions; putting forth the traits of honesty, integrity and incorruptibility. Let's read the scriptures on the truth of God."

They read:

"This is eternal life, that they may know You, the only true God, and Jesus Christ whom You have sent.

"Sanctify them in the truth; Your word is truth." (John 17:3,17)

Jesus said to him, "I am the way, and the truth, and the life; no one comes to the Father but through Me.

"I will ask the Father, and He will give you another Helper, that He may be with you forever;

that is the Spirit of truth, whom the world cannot receive, because it does not see Him or know Him, *but* you know Him because He abides with you and will be in you." (John 14:6,16,17)

"But when He, the Spirit of truth, comes, He will guide you into all the truth; for He will not speak on His own initiative, but whatever He hears, He will speak; and He will disclose to you what is to come.

"He will glorify Me, for He will take of Mine and will disclose *it* to you.

"All things that the Father has are Mine; therefore I said, that He takes of Mine, and will disclose *it* to you." (John 16:13-15)

So Jesus was saying to those Jews who had believed Him, "If you continue in My word, *then* you are truly disciples of Mine;

and you will know the truth, and the truth will make you free."

(John 8:31,32)

What then? If some did not believe, their unbelief will not nullify the faithfulness of God, will it?

May it never be! Rather, let God be found true, though every man *be found* a liar, as it is written,

"THAT YOU MAY BE JUSTIFIED IN YOUR WORDS,

AND PREVAIL WHEN YOU ARE JUDGED." (Romans 3:3,4)

And I heard the altar saying, "Yes, O Lord God, the Almighty, true and righteous are Your judgments." (Revelation 16:7)

"And to the angel of the church in Philadelphia write:
He who is holy, who is true, who has the key of David, who opens and no
one will shut, and who shuts and no one opens, says this.

"To the angel of the church in Laodicea write:
The Amen, the faithful and true Witness, the Beginning of the creation of
God, says this." (Revelation 3:7,14)

"Wow! Talk about the indivisibility of The Trinity!" Nick exclaimed. "God the Father is called 'the only true God.' Jesus calls Himself 'the truth,' and calls the Holy Spirit 'the Spirit of truth.' The Word of the Father is truth. Jesus says His Word is truth, and sets the obedient disciple free. And Jesus says the Holy Spirit will disclose God's Word and lead His children into all truth!"

"Amen!" Dave agreed. "And not only that—in heaven, God's judgments are praised as 'true and righteous.' God's purity, or goodness, is additionally expressed through His justice, which the Bible also calls His righteousness. *Justice* means perfect adherence to a righteous standard. This includes the perfect dispensing of deserved punishment that 'fits the crime' for failure to adhere, or promised reward for perfect obedience.

"For entering heaven, that standard is absolute perfection—which is, by definition, the holy character of Almighty God. Since God appointed Himself as the true Judge of all creation, the one and only attribute that God owes to His creation is justice. Let's read the scriptures of God's justice, otherwise called His righteousness."

They read:

"For I proclaim the name of the LORD;
    Ascribe greatness to our God!
"The Rock! His work is perfect,
    For all His ways are just;
    A God of faithfulness and without injustice,
    Righteous and upright is He." (Deuteronomy 32:3,4)

"The God of Abraham, Isaac and Jacob, the God of our fathers, has
glorified His servant Jesus, *the one* whom you delivered and disowned in the
presence of Pilate, when he had decided to release Him.

"But you disowned the Holy and Righteous One and asked for a
murderer to be granted to you,

but put to death the Prince of life, *the one* whom God raised from the
dead, *a fact* to which we are witnesses." (Acts 3:13-15)

And they sang the song of Moses, the bond-servant of God, and the
song of the Lamb, saying,

"Great and marvelous are Your works,
    O Lord God, the Almighty;
    Righteous and true are Your ways,

King of the nations!

"Who will not fear, O Lord, and glorify Your name?

For You alone are holy;

For ALL THE NATIONS WILL COME AND WORSHIP BEFORE YOU,

For YOUR RIGHTEOUS ACTS HAVE BEEN REVEALED."

(Revelation 15:3,4)

"God's justice entails that His acts are perfectly aligned with His character. Both are perfect and good—or, in a word, holy," Dave expounded. "The righteousness, or justice, of God means perfect adherence to the standard of perfection.

"In dealing with man, Jesus commands perfect justice, or righteousness, in order to enter heaven: '"Therefore you are to be perfect, as your heavenly Father is perfect"' (Matthew 5:48). Perfect righteousness is God's standard for living with Him in His eternal heavenly paradise. God, as Supreme Judge of the universe, guarantees perfect justice will be meted out to everyone according to what they have done, or deserved. Thus, justice is merited—or earned—by man, and owed by God as the Self-appointed Righteous Judge."

"Thank God for sending His Son to die on the cross and pay the penalty of God's perfect justice," Nick praised. "Because Jesus paid for our sins, we are justified in God's sight—free from the guilt and penalty for our heinous crimes! Because Christ's perfect life is credited to our accounts, we are as perfect as God is perfect!"

"Amen!" Dave agreed. "All of us born of a human male deserve eternal torture for our sin and rebellion against God and His eternal holiness. But God's wrath has been appeased toward His children because His justice has been satisfied. God accepted the death of Jesus Christ on the cross as a *propitiation*—or substitute payment in full—for the sins of only those whom He has chosen to be in His family. Let's read the scriptures where God's true children are no longer subject to His **wrath**—God's righteous anger, indignation and punishment."

They read:

And you were dead in your trespasses and sins,

in which you formerly walked according to the course of this world, according to the prince of the power of the air, of the spirit that is now working in the sons of disobedience.

Among them we too all formerly lived in the lusts of our flesh, indulging the desires of the flesh and of the mind, and were by nature children of wrath, even as the rest.

But God, being rich in mercy, because of His great love with which He loved us,

even when we were dead in our transgressions, made us alive together with Christ (by grace you have been saved). (Ephesians 2:1-5)

For God has not destined us for wrath, but for obtaining salvation through our Lord Jesus Christ,

who died for us, so that whether we are awake or asleep, we will live together with Him. (1 Thessalonians 5:9,10)

My little children, I am writing these things to you so that you may
not sin. And if anyone sins, we have an Advocate with the Father, Jesus
Christ the righteous;

and He Himself is the propitiation for our sins; and not for ours only,
but also for *those of* the whole world. (1 John 2:1,2)

"God has not destined His children for wrath, even though we were born with a sinful
nature deserving of His wrath," Dave explained. "Because God loved us as His own, He rescued
us from our spiritual death and rebellion, and made us alive in Christ Jesus. Like unrepentant
sinners, we—God's true children—also received His justice. But, God poured out our
punishment upon His own Son on the cross. We have escaped the righteous anger, indignation
and punishment of God only because God Himself loved us and wanted us in His family."

"Thank You, Jesus!" exclaimed Nick.

"Amen!" Dave returned. "We now approach the somber attribute of God's holy wrath
toward sinners. God's perfect justice demands that sin be punished to the exact degree of its
offense against God and His holiness. God's holiness is eternal. His eternal holiness is offended
by man's sin and rebellion. Therefore, the just punishment for sin is eternal conscious torture
in hell.

"Many idolaters in the modern church preach that there is no hell, for such torture by God
would be unloving. They prefer to believe that God annihilates the sinner, so that he ceases to
exist. Thus, these false preachers exchange the One True God—whom they despise—for an idol,
a god of their own depraved imaginations.

"What these unbelievers fail to see is that if God does not punish sin, then by definition,
God Himself is not just. And that is blasphemy against the One True God. God's holy Word
speaks of hell far more than it speaks of heaven. Let's read the scriptures about God's holy wrath
toward the rebellious unbeliever."

They read:

> Therefore the LORD heard and was full of wrath;
>> And a fire was kindled against Jacob
>> And anger also mounted against Israel,
> Because they did not believe in God
>> And did not trust in His salvation.
> For they provoked Him with their high places
>> And aroused His jealousy with their graven images.
> When God heard, He was filled with wrath
>> And greatly abhorred Israel. (Psalm 78:21,22,58,59)

"The Father loves the Son and has given all things into His hand.

"He who believes in the Son has eternal life; but he who does not
obey the Son will not see life, but the wrath of God abides on him."

(John 3:35,36)

But because of your stubbornness and unrepentant heart you are storing up wrath for yourself in the day of wrath and revelation of the righteous judgment of God,

who WILL RENDER TO EACH PERSON ACCORDING TO HIS DEEDS.

But if our unrighteousness demonstrates the righteousness of God, what shall we say? The God who inflicts wrath is not unrighteous, is He? (I am speaking in human terms.)

May it never be! For otherwise, how will God judge the world?

What then? Are we better than they? Not at all; for we have already charged that both Jews and Greeks are all under sin;

as it is written,

"THERE IS NONE RIGHTEOUS, NOT EVEN ONE;

   THERE IS NONE WHO UNDERSTANDS,

   THERE IS NONE WHO SEEKS FOR GOD;

    ALL HAVE TURNED ASIDE, TOGETHER THEY HAVE BECOME USELESS;

"THERE IS NONE WHO DOES GOOD,

"THERE IS NOT EVEN ONE." (Romans 2:5,6; 3:5,6,9-12)

"But when the Son of Man comes in His glory, and all the angels with Him, then He will sit on His glorious throne.

"All the nations will be gathered before Him; and He will separate them from one another, as the shepherd separates the sheep from the goats;

and He will put the sheep on His right, and the goats on the left.

"Then He will also say to those on His left, 'Depart from Me, accursed ones, into the eternal fire which has been prepared for the devil and his angels;

"These will go away into eternal punishment, but the righteous into eternal life." (Matthew 25:31-33,41,46)

Then I saw a great white throne and Him who sat upon it, from whose presence earth and heaven fled away, and no place was found for them.

And I saw the dead, the great and the small, standing before the throne, and books were opened; and another book was opened, which is *the book* of life; and the dead were judged from the things which were written in the books, according to their deeds.

And the sea gave up the dead which were in it, and death and Hades gave up the dead which were in them; and they were judged, every one *of them* according to their deeds.

Then death and Hades were thrown into the lake of fire. This is the second death, the lake of fire.

And if anyone's name was not found written in the book of life, he was thrown into the lake of fire. (Revelation 20:11-15)

"God must be perfectly righteous—in other words, perfectly just—in judging the world," Dave expounded. "Because if He were unjust, He could not be a judge of the unjust. How could a thief condemn one who steals? That person is a hypocrite—a most unworthy judge!

"Since God is perfectly just, He will condemn anyone who is not perfectly righteous, whether a Jew or Gentile. The sentence for sinners who have rejected Christ's salvation will be eternal conscious torture in hell's lake of fire. To deny God's justice calls Jesus Christ a liar, for He taught that 'these will go away into eternal punishment' (Matthew 25:46). Obviously, eternal punishment and annihilation are opposites, totally exclusive of one another."

"No doubt, our God's justice and wrath are holy and righteous," Nick replied somberly. "I am so glad that He pulled me out of my spiritual death march into hell, and raised me up in Christ Jesus my Savior."

Grace, Mercy, Patience and Faithfulness

"God did it by His grace," Dave continued, "which is the next attribute of God's holy goodness. God's grace is conferred only upon His children. I've heard it said that the word stands for **G**od's **R**iches **A**t **C**hrist's **E**xpense.

"**Grace** depicts unearned, positive favor given to one who has despised and rejected the giver of such favor. Donating one of your kidneys to your loving brother does not complete the idea of God's saving grace towards sinners. Donating your kidney to a robber who beat you, your wife and your kids, while stealing everything you own—and while the thief screams after saving his life that he will rob you again and again—is closer to the expression of God's grace."

"That is intense," Nick pondered.

"Yes. **Grace** must be unearned, or it is not grace," Dave continued. "Favor given to someone in return for doing something is earned, or merited. It is a wage paid to a worker.

"The worker performs a task, by an agreement with an employer, and earns a paycheck. This cannot, by definition, be grace. That which is earned by man is justice, and God as Judge will perfectly dispense reward and punishment according to His righteous standard of perfection. Again, **grace** is unearned, positive favor given to one who actually deserves retribution. Let's read the scriptures on God's amazing grace."

They read:

> And the Word became flesh, and dwelt among us, and we saw His glory, glory as of the only begotten from the Father, full of grace and truth.
>
> John testified about Him and cried out, saying, "This was He of whom I said, 'He who comes after me has a higher rank than I, for He existed before me.'"
>
> For of His fullness we have all received, and grace upon grace.
>
> For the Law was given through Moses; grace and truth were realized through Jesus Christ. (John 1:14-17)

> "And God, who knows the heart, testified to them giving them the Holy Spirit, just as He also did to us;
>
> and He made no distinction between us and them, cleansing their hearts by faith.

"Now therefore why do you put God to the test by placing upon the neck of the disciples a yoke which neither our fathers nor we have been able to bear?

"But we believe that we are saved through the grace of the Lord Jesus, in the same way as they also are." (Acts 15:8-11)

For if Abraham was justified by works, he has something to boast about, but not before God.

For what does the Scripture say? "ABRAHAM BELIEVED GOD, AND IT WAS CREDITED TO HIM AS RIGHTEOUSNESS."

Now to the one who works, his wage is not credited as a favor, but as what is due.

But to the one who does not work, but believes in Him who justifies the ungodly, his faith is credited as righteousness,

just as David also speaks of the blessing on the man to whom God credits righteousness apart from works:

"BLESSED ARE THOSE WHOSE LAWLESS DEEDS HAVE BEEN FORGIVEN,
AND WHOSE SINS HAVE BEEN COVERED.

"BLESSED IS THE MAN WHOSE SIN THE LORD WILL NOT TAKE INTO ACCOUNT." (Romans 4:2-8)

God has not rejected His people whom He foreknew. Or do you not know what the Scripture says in *the passage about* Elijah, how he pleads with God against Israel?

"Lord, THEY HAVE KILLED YOUR PROPHETS, THEY HAVE TORN DOWN YOUR ALTARS, AND I ALONE AM LEFT, AND THEY ARE SEEKING MY LIFE."

But what is the divine response to him? "I HAVE KEPT for Myself SEVEN THOUSAND MEN WHO HAVE NOT BOWED THE KNEE TO BAAL."

In the same way then, there has also come to be at the present time a remnant according to *God's* gracious choice.

But if it is by grace, it is no longer on the basis of works, otherwise grace is no longer grace.

What then? What Israel is seeking, it has not obtained, but those who were chosen obtained it, and the rest were hardened. (Romans 11:2-7)

But God, being rich in mercy, because of His great love with which He loved us,

even when we were dead in our transgressions, made us alive together with Christ (by grace you have been saved),

and raised us up with Him, and seated us with Him in the heavenly *places* in Christ Jesus,

so that in the ages to come He might show the surpassing riches of His grace in kindness toward us in Christ Jesus.

For by grace you have been saved through faith; and that not of yourselves, *it is* the gift of God;

not as a result of works, so that no one may boast. (Ephesians 2:4-9)

Because of the surpassing greatness of the revelations, for this reason, to keep me from exalting myself, there was given me a thorn in the flesh, a messenger of Satan to torment me—to keep me from exalting myself!

Concerning this I implored the Lord three times that it might leave me.

And He has said to me, "My grace is sufficient for you, for power is perfected in weakness." Most gladly, therefore, I will rather boast about my weaknesses, so that the power of Christ may dwell in me.

Therefore I am well content with weaknesses, with insults, with distresses, with persecutions, with difficulties, for Christ's sake; for when I am weak, then I am strong. (2 Corinthians 12:7-10)

"Jesus Christ completed the grace of God in creation, and enabled its implementation by satisfying the justice of God through His death on the cross," Dave explained. "God could never sin against His justice by bestowing positive favor upon criminals who deserved punishment. Before His grace could be given to His children, Someone must have taken upon Himself that just punishment. Christ suffered and died for the sins of God's children, and the Father accepted Christ's sacrifice as payment in full.

"Thus, God can grant the totally unearned favor of eternal life upon wretches whom He chose to be in His family. With God's justice now satisfied, those wretches are given perfectly clean slates and eternal salvation. Those wretches—now God's children—are given God's holy grace. And, as the Apostle Paul discovered, God's grace also keeps us in His family by ensuring our perseverance through the trials and sufferings of this present life."

"I am speechless," Nick said in awe. "I have no idea what to say to God for His amazing, awesome grace."

"Just say, 'thank You, Lord,'" Dave replied. "There simply is nothing left to say.

"God's mercy—sometimes called His lovingkindness in Scripture—is the next attribute of God's purity, or goodness. Unlike God's grace, which is given only to His children, God's mercy is bestowed on the saved and unsaved alike.

"God's *mercy* is His compassion, and kindly forbearance, shown to both His enemies and His children. Like God's grace, mercy is never owed by God to anyone. The only perfection God owes to His creation is, by definition, justice. Let's read the scriptures on God's mercy, His compassionate lovingkindness."

They read:

The LORD's lovingkindnesses indeed never cease,

For His compassions never fail.

They are new every morning;

Great is Your faithfulness. (Lamentations 3:22,23)

> Be gracious to me, O God, according to Your lovingkindness;
>> According to the greatness of Your compassion blot out my
>> transgressions.
> Wash me thoroughly from my iniquity
>> And cleanse me from my sin. (Psalm 51:1,2)

> Blessed *be* the God and Father of our Lord Jesus Christ, the Father of
> mercies and God of all comfort,
>> who comforts us in all our affliction so that we will be able to comfort
> those who are in any affliction with the comfort with which we ourselves
> are comforted by God. (2 Corinthians 1:3,4)

> But you, beloved, building yourselves up on your most holy faith,
> praying in the Holy Spirit,
>> keep yourselves in the love of God, waiting anxiously for the mercy of
> our Lord Jesus Christ to eternal life.
> And have mercy on some, who are doubting;
>> save others, snatching them out of the fire; and on some have mercy
> with fear, hating even the garment polluted by the flesh. (Jude 20-23)

> "You have heard that it was said, 'YOU SHALL LOVE YOUR NEIGHBOR
> and hate your enemy.'
> "But I say to you, love your enemies and pray for those who persecute
> you,
>> so that you may be sons of your Father who is in heaven; for He
> causes His sun to rise on *the* evil and *the* good, and sends rain on *the*
> righteous and *the* unrighteous." (Matthew 5:43-45)

"For His children," Dave taught, "God grants mercy in that He does not severely beat us when we are disobedient, but corrects us in love. God also answers our prayers with His compassion, even when we fail Him during our growth as Christians. God's lovingkindness enables us to be merciful to others—believers and unbelievers.

"For His enemies as well as His children, God provides a 'common mercy'—sometimes mislabeled 'common grace'—where He gives rain for crops to provide food to eat, and sunshine for those crops to grow. God is compassionate toward the needs of even those who despise Him."

"It sounds like God's mercy works closely with His patience," Nick commented.

"Excellent observation," Dave agreed. "God's *patience* involves His slowness to anger, bearing with human imperfections as He works out His perfect, eternal plan. Let's read the scriptures on God's patience, sometimes called His longsuffering."

They read:

Then the LORD passed by in front of him and proclaimed, "The LORD, the LORD God, compassionate and gracious, slow to anger, and abounding in lovingkindness and truth;

who keeps lovingkindness for thousands, who forgives iniquity, transgression and sin; yet He will by no means leave *the guilty* unpunished, visiting the iniquity of fathers on the children and on the grandchildren to the third and fourth generations." (Exodus 34:6,7)

Or does not the potter have a right over the clay, to make from the same lump one vessel for honorable use and another for common use?

What if God, although willing to demonstrate His wrath and to make His power known, endured with much patience vessels of wrath prepared for destruction?

And *He did so* to make known the riches of His glory upon vessels of mercy, which He prepared beforehand for glory. (Romans 9:21-23)

Or do you think lightly of the riches of His kindness and tolerance and patience, not knowing that the kindness of God leads you to repentance? (Romans 2:4)

But do not let this one *fact* escape your notice, beloved, that with the Lord one day is like a thousand years, and a thousand years like one day.

The Lord is not slow about His promise, as some count slowness, but is patient toward you, not wishing for any to perish but for all to come to repentance.

Therefore, beloved, since you look for these things, be diligent to be found by Him in peace, spotless and blameless,

and regard the patience of our Lord *as* salvation; just as also our beloved brother Paul, according to the wisdom given him, wrote to you.

(2 Peter 3:8,9,14,15)

"Towards the vessels of mercy that God prepared before creation—His true children—God's patience waits for His appointed time of conversion of every child belonging to Him," Dave stated. "God is not willing that any of His 'beloved' children should perish.

"Towards the vessels of wrath that God prepared for destruction—His enemies—God endures their heinous crimes, and does not instantly consume them, awaiting the coming final day of judgment."

"I thank God that He is patient with me," Nick said, "and that He is faithful to keep His promises to me even when I fail Him."

"Amen!" Dave agreed. "God's **faithfulness**, the next attribute of His perfect character, works closely with His patience and immutability. God is eternally faithful, meaning that He is true to His word—trustworthy—and can be totally relied upon to fulfill His promises. Let's look at the scriptures on God's faithfulness, sometimes called His steadfastness."

They read:

"Know therefore that the LORD your God, He is God, the faithful God, who keeps His covenant and His lovingkindness to a thousandth generation with those who love Him and keep His commandments;

but repays those who hate Him to their faces, to destroy them; He will not delay with him who hates Him, He will repay him to his face."

(Deuteronomy 7:9,10)

"God is not a man, that He should lie,

Nor a son of man, that He should repent;

Has He said, and will He not do it?

Or has He spoken, and will He not make it good?"

(Numbers 23:19)

I will sing of the lovingkindness of the LORD forever;

To all generations I will make known Your faithfulness with my mouth.

For I have said, "Lovingkindness will be built up forever;

In the heavens You will establish Your faithfulness."

O LORD God of hosts, who is like You, O mighty LORD?

Your faithfulness also surrounds You.

"But I will not break off My lovingkindness from him,

Nor deal falsely in My faithfulness.

"My covenant I will not violate,

Nor will I alter the utterance of My lips.

"Once I have sworn by My holiness;

I will not lie to David." (Psalm 89:1,2,8,33-35)

Your lovingkindness, O LORD, extends to the heavens,

Your faithfulness *reaches* to the skies. (Psalm 36:5)

It is a trustworthy statement:

For if we died with Him, we will also live with Him;

If we endure, we will also reign with Him;

If we deny Him, He also will deny us;

If we are faithless, He remains faithful, for He cannot deny Himself. (2 Timothy 2:11-13)

If we confess our sins, He is faithful and righteous to forgive us our sins and to cleanse us from all unrighteousness. (1 John 1:9)

"God keeps His covenant promises to His true children. He will bring us home to His heavenly kingdom, despite our unfaithfulness to Him," Dave averred. "To 'confess our sins' means to go to our heavenly Father and agree with Him that we have rebelled against His holy commands. God is faithful to forgive our sins because Christ our Savior has paid for them.

"God is also faithful to keep His promises to His enemies. He will judge them for their heinous crimes of rebellion against His eternal holiness, and throw them into hell to be tortured forever."

"Thank You, God, for Your faithfulness," replied Nick. "And thank You, Jesus—God in the flesh—for Your holy sacrifice!"

Logic/Reason

"Yes!" Dave agreed. "We come to the final, eternal, holy attribute of God's goodness: **logic**, or **reason**, the use of logic. The Lord Jesus Himself is the manifestation of God's eternal logic to mankind. God's ways—His eternal purpose, or the reasons for His actions—are explained in His Word.

"The Apostle John interestingly calls Jesus Christ 'the Word' in his writings, and he does so for three very important reasons. First: God the Son became a man to communicate to man the Personhood of God and the ways of God. Obviously, a 'word' is the element of communication. Let's read the scriptures where John calls Christ Jesus 'the Word.'"

They read:

> In the beginning was the Word, and the Word was with God,
>   and the Word was God.
> He was in the beginning with God.
> All things came into being through Him, and apart from Him
> nothing came into being that has come into being.
> And the Word became flesh, and dwelt among us, and we saw His
> glory, glory as of the only begotten from the Father, full of grace and
> truth. (John 1:1-3,14)

> What was from the beginning, what we have heard, what we have
> seen with our eyes, what we have looked at and touched with our hands,
> concerning the Word of Life—
>   and the life was manifested, and we have seen and testify and proclaim
> to you the eternal life, which was with the Father and was manifested to us—
>   what we have seen and heard we proclaim to you also, so that you too
> may have fellowship with us; and indeed our fellowship is with the Father,
> and with His Son Jesus Christ. (1 John 1:1-3)

> And I saw heaven opened, and behold, a white horse, and He who sat
> on it *is* called Faithful and True, and in righteousness He judges and wages
> war.
>   His eyes *are* a flame of fire, and on His head *are* many diadems; and He

has a name written *on Him* which no one knows except Himself.

He is clothed with a robe dipped in blood, and His name is called
The Word of God (Revelation 19:11-13)

And Jesus cried out and said, "He who believes in Me, does not
believe in Me but in Him who sent Me.

"He who sees Me sees the One who sent Me.

"For I did not speak on My own initiative, but the Father Himself
who sent Me has given Me a commandment *as to* what to say and what to
speak." (John 12:44,45,49)

"God, through the Apostle John, conveyed the idea that God the Son was sent by God the Father to communicate His ways to His people," Dave expounded. "The second reason Jesus Christ is called 'The Word' reveals the true identity of the Person of Christ, and has an interesting history.

"The Greek term here—translated as 'Word' in English—is *logos*. We get our English word 'logic' from the Greek term 'logos.' The full meaning of ***logos*** is the embodiment of an idea, or the embodiment of reason. Now, a 'word' is certainly the embodiment of an idea—thus the translation to English as 'word.' However, the Apostle John calls Jesus Christ the 'Logos' because He is the embodiment of reason, or logic.

"The ancient Greeks believed that God—whatever that was to them—was utterly transcendent from the world, and absolutely nothing could be known about Him or It. Anytime sinful humanity cannot know God, or does not like the revealed One True God, mankind always responds in the same way. Depraved man rejects the true God, and creates an idol in man's own image that he likes. This happens today in the cults, and in the pews and pulpits of churches.

"So the Greeks, since they could know nothing about God, made up all kinds of myths about all kinds of fictitious gods."

"Sure," recalled Nick. "I remember studying about Zeus, Hercules, Hermes and Poseidon during middle school in the eighth grade."

"Exactly," Dave said. "The Apostle Paul witnessed this first hand on his missionary trip through Athens. Read Acts 17:16, 22 and 23."

Nick read:

Now while Paul was waiting for them at Athens, his spirit was being
provoked within him as he was observing the city full of idols.

So Paul stood in the midst of the Areopagus and said, "Men of
Athens, I observe that you are very religious in all respects.

"For while I was passing through and examining the objects of your
worship, I also found an altar with this inscription, 'TO AN
UNKNOWN GOD.' Therefore what you worship in ignorance, this I
proclaim to you." (Acts 17:16,22,23)

"The Greeks called the force or principle that develops and governs the universe the '*Logos*,' Dave continued. "The Apostle John was very familiar with Greek culture, as he ministered for many years in Ephesus, where he wrote his Gospel and his Letters. The second century church father Justyn Martyr, who also lived in Ephesus and probably knew John's students, wrote of John's reason for calling Christ the 'Logos.'

"The Apostle John takes the Greek concept of the Logos—the impersonal force that develops and governs the universe—and applies it to the *Person* of God the Son, Jesus Christ! The Greeks did not invent this concept. God from eternity through eternity created and sustains everything that exists. John simply connects the idea of the Logos to the Person of Christ, stating emphatically from verse one of his Gospel that the Lord Jesus is the very One who created and governs the universe!

"Just as 'God is love' (1 John 4:8,16), 'God is light' (1 John 1:5), and 'God is spirit' (John 4:24), God the Son is also **the Logos**—the physical embodiment of reason, or logic—who created and sustains all of reality!

"Logic, or reason, is as much a part of the holy eternal character of God as love and truth," Dave continued. "The third reason the Apostle John calls Christ the 'Logos' is that Christ came to show God's ways by demonstrating His attributes, one of which is logic. Again, we get our English word 'logic' from the Greek term 'logos.'

"*Logic* is the science of laws which regulate correct thinking. Just as any game has rules to determine a winner, thinking also has rules for sound conclusions. When a player violates the rules of a game, he is disqualified. Likewise, violating the laws of logic results in unsound, and oftentimes false conclusions.

"Many churches rebuff this concept, thinking that it elevates logic to the level of God. This error is actually a result of illogical thinking!

"Logic is not God, just like love is not God, and light is not God. But God is love, and God is light, as we just cited from Scripture. Just because all apples are fruit does not mean that all fruit are apples! The reverse is not true, because that reasoning violates the laws of logic, committing a **logical fallacy**. But God is logic, love and light, meaning that logic, love, truth, and all the other attributes of God are eternal elements of His holy character.

"Many churches commit the opposite error of disdaining knowledge and the understanding of the laws of logic, preferring to forgo correct thinking in favor of ecstatic experience. Since logic, love and truth are part of Christ's eternal attributes, renouncing logic is just as sinful as renouncing love or truth. Since God communicates to us through His Word—which requires logic to understand any of it—renouncing logic always leads to aberrant and heretical teaching."

"It seems to me that nothing would make sense without logic," mused Nick.

"Correct," Dave responded. "We can know absolutely nothing without logic—not even our own names! As we contemplate His teachings with their many truths, the Lord Jesus Christ expects man to be able to reason correctly.

"It is critical for our logic to conform to God's inherent attribute of logic. Once again, we can know absolutely nothing without logic. More than that, our logic must be the same as God's logic, or His Word would make no sense whatsoever.

"Many cult systems accept illogical contradictions in their beliefs, saying that God simply goes by a different system of logic than man. If this were the case, for all we know, evil could be good and good could be evil. But, throughout all of His teachings and parables, Christ confirmed that man is responsible to use the same logic inherent in God's holy character.

"Thus, even God cannot reconcile illogical contradictions—for two reasons: by definition, illogical contradictions are nonsensical, or without any sense to reconcile. Also, to even attempt to reconcile an illogical contradiction would sin against His own holy character—which, as we know from studying God's omnipotence, God would never desire to do.

"Therefore, God's holy Word cannot contain contradictions, for it is impossible for the eternally holy God to lie, or sin against Himself. Logic is an eternal attribute of God's holy goodness, or purity—and He has graciously allowed man to use reason as a tool to learn about Him and His creation.

"You did such a great job summarizing the unique attributes of God's transcendence. Would you like to try to recap the attributes of God's goodness that He shares with us?"

"I'll give it a try," said Nick. "All of the attributes of God's character are enveloped by His holiness.

"The holiness of God has two parts: His transcendence and His goodness, or purity.

"Unlike the attributes of God's transcendence, which only He possesses, the eternal and perfect attributes of God's goodness He has allowed man to share.

"We employ these attributes imperfectly and intermittently, and know infinitely less about them than does the Almighty God.

"God's goodness, or purity and uprightness, envelops His eternality, love, hatred, truth, justice, wrath, grace, mercy, patience, faithfulness and reason.

"The eternality of God means that He is without beginning or end, and transcends time. God lives from eternity past through eternity future. All of God's holy attributes are eternal because God Himself is eternal.

"A second meaning of eternality conveys the idea of lasting forever, or never ending. We thus include the eternalness of God with the attributes that God shares with His creation.

"Though man has a definite beginning at conception, he is made in the image of God, which partially means that man is everlasting. The only question is where man will spend eternity—in heaven with God's eternal blessings, or in hell under God's eternal wrath.

"God's love is His commitment to His children to protect and care for them, ultimately bringing them to Love Himself!

"God's children are to abide in His love—the very same love with which God the Father loved God the Son from all eternity—which casts out all fear.

"When we share the Father's love with others, we have a commitment to draw them to the Source of love—God Himself.

"God also hates. God's holy hatred is toward anyone and anything contrary to His holy, good and pure character.

"God's hatred of sin, and those who love sinning, is a holy hatred, expressed in righteous anger and meted out with severe wrath.

"God abhors those who speak falsehood, because God is eternally truthful, and always speaks the truth—another expression of the goodness of God's magnificent character.

"God is eternally truthful, conveying the idea of being honorable in principles, intentions and actions; putting forth the traits of honesty, integrity and incorruptibility.

"God the Father is called 'the only true God.' Jesus calls Himself 'the truth,' and calls the Holy Spirit 'the Spirit of truth.'

"The Holy Spirit reveals God's Word—which is truth—and it is the truth which sets the obedient disciple free.

"God's purity, or goodness, is also expressed through His justice, which the Bible also calls His righteousness.

"Justice means perfect adherence to the standard of perfection. The standard of perfection is, of course, the holy character of Almighty God.

"God's justice entails that His acts are perfectly aligned with His character—both being good, perfect and holy.

"In dealing with man, Jesus commands perfect justice, or righteousness, in order to enter heaven: '"Therefore you are to be perfect, as your heavenly Father is perfect (Matthew 5:48)."'

"All of us born of a human male deserve eternal torture for our sin and rebellion against God and His eternal holiness.

"But God's wrath—His righteous anger, indignation and punishment—has been appeased toward His children because His justice has been satisfied.

"God accepted the death of Jesus Christ on the cross as a propitiation—or substitute payment in full—for the sins of only those whom He has chosen to be in His family.

"God's perfect justice demands that sin be punished to the exact degree of its offense against God and His holiness.

"Since God's infinite and eternal holiness is infinitely offended by man's sin and rebellion, the just punishment for sin is eternal conscious torture in hell.

"Many idolaters in the modern church preach that there is no hell, for such torture by God would be unloving.

"These idolaters prefer to believe that God annihilates the sinner, so that he ceases to exist. God is sort of a kinder, gentler Judge, just like these unbelieving idolaters would be.

"These false preachers exchange the One True God, whom they despise, for an idol, a god of their own depraved imaginations.

"It is blasphemy against God's holy character to say He would compromise His holy justice, which would then actually be injustice.

"God's holy Word speaks of hell far more than it speaks of heaven.

"God must be perfectly righteous—in other words, perfectly just—in judging the world, because if He were unjust, He could not be a judge of the unjust. How could a thief condemn one who steals?

"Since God is perfectly just, He will condemn anyone who is not perfectly righteous, whether a Jew or Gentile.

"The sentence for sinners who have rejected Christ's salvation will be eternal, conscious torture in hell's lake of fire. To deny God's justice calls Jesus Christ a liar, for He taught that 'these will go away into eternal punishment.'

"God pulled those whom He chose to be in His eternal family before creation out of their spiritual death march to hell, and saved them by His holy grace.

"God's grace is conferred only upon His children.

"Grace means unearned, positive favor given to one who has despised and rejected the giver of such favor.

"An analogy, as weak as finite analogies are in explaining the infinite grace of Almighty God, might be donating your kidney to a robber who beat you, your wife and your kids—while stealing everything you own—and while the thief screams he will rob you again and again after recovery!

"Grace must be unearned, or it is not grace.

"Favor given to someone in return for doing something is earned, or merited. It is a wage paid to a worker.

"God could never sin against His justice by bestowing positive favor upon criminals who deserved punishment. Before His grace could be given to His children, Someone must have taken upon Himself that just punishment.

"Jesus Christ suffered and died for the sins of God's children, and the Father accepted Christ's sacrifice as payment in full, satisfying the demands of His justice.

"Thus, God can grant the totally unearned favor of eternal life—His holy grace—upon wretches whom He chose to be in His family.

"Not only this, but amazingly God's grace also keeps us in His family through the trials and sufferings of this present life. God does it all.

"Whereas God's grace is given only to His children, God's mercy is bestowed on the saved and unsaved alike.

"God's mercy is His compassion and kindly forbearance shown to His enemies and His children.

"For His children, God grants mercy in that He does not severely beat us when we are disobedient, but corrects us in love, and answers our prayers with His compassion even when we fail Him during our growth as Christians.

"God's lovingkindness, or mercy, enables us to be merciful to others—believers and unbelievers.

"For His enemies as well as His children, God provides a 'common mercy'—sometimes mislabeled 'common grace'—where He gives rain for crops to provide food to eat, and sunshine for those crops to grow. God is compassionate toward the needs of even those who despise Him.

"God's mercy works closely with His patience, as well as with all of His other holy and eternal attributes—they are all present in Him.

"God's patience involves His slowness to anger, bearing with human imperfections as He works out His perfect, eternal plan.

"Towards the vessels of mercy that God prepared before creation—His children—God's patience waits for the conversion of every child belonging to Him," Dave stated, "because He is not willing that any of His 'beloved' children should perish.

"Towards the vessels of wrath that God prepared for destruction—His enemies—God endures their heinous crimes and does not instantly consume them, awaiting the coming final day of judgment.

"God's eternal faithfulness means that He is true to His word—trustworthy—and can be totally relied upon to fulfill His promises.

"God keeps His covenant promises to His children, to bring them home to His heavenly kingdom, despite our unfaithfulness to Him!

"God is faithful and just to forgive the sins of His children because Christ our Savior has paid for them. God does require us, however, to get on His Lap and agree that we have rebelled against Him.

"God is also faithful to keep His promises to His enemies, to judge them for their heinous crimes of rebellion against His eternal holiness, and to throw them into hell to be tortured forever.

"Finally, Jesus Christ is called 'The Word' by the Apostle John.

"John had three important reasons for calling Christ 'The Word,' the first being that Christ communicates God's Personhood and ways to creation.

"The Greek term translated 'Word' is logos, which means the embodiment of an idea or the embodiment of reason. We get our word 'logic' from 'logos.'

"The ancient Greeks defined 'The Logos' as the force or principle that develops and governs the universe.

"The ancient Greeks believed that God was utterly transcendent from the world—absolutely nothing could be known about Him or It. So, they made up all kinds of myths about all kinds of gods.

"Anytime sinful humanity cannot know God or does not like the revealed One True God, depraved man creates an idol in man's own image that he does like. This happens today in the cults, and in the pews and pulpits of churches.

"Both Apostles John and Paul taught the Greeks that 'The Logos' is a Person—Jesus Christ, God the Son! Christ is the embodiment of logic, and He created and governs the universe with reason, and that He can be known intimately by men!

"Logic, or reason, is as much a part of the holy eternal character of God as love and truth.

"We can know absolutely nothing without logic. More than that, our logic must be the same as God's logic, or His Word would make no sense whatsoever.

"Even God cannot reconcile illogical contradictions, because illogical contradictions are nonsensical, or without any sense to reconcile. Also, to even attempt to reconcile an illogical contradiction would sin against His own holy character—which, as we know from studying God's omnipotence, God would never desire to do.

"Therefore, God's holy Word cannot contain contradictions, for it is impossible for the eternally holy God to lie or sin against Himself.

"Logic is an eternal attribute of God's holy goodness, and He has graciously allowed man to use reason as a tool to learn about Him and His creation!"

"Outstanding summary!" recognized Dave. "I hope that this intense and in-depth study of God's holy and magnificent character will help you to know Him more intimately and to understand His ways."

"This was an awesome experience learning about our Lord and just how incredible and beautiful He is!" exclaimed Nick.

"Would you like to close our Bible study in prayer?" asked Dave.

"I'd be honored." said Nick as he took Dave's hands. "Dear heavenly Father, You truly are holy, holy, holy! You are infinitely beyond any other being, and Your ways and Your thoughts are infinitely higher than ours. Yet, loving Father, You have set apart a people for Yourself that You have loved with an everlasting love! We thank You so much for choosing us out of the world, totally deserving of Your holy wrath, but saving us by Your grace through the blood sacrifice of Your Son. Words fail to express our gratitude for Your salvation.

"Most holy Lord, we long to know You more intimately and to become better acquainted with Your ways. The holy attributes of Your most magnificent character are awe-inspiring. Help us to avoid remaking You into our image, and to bow before You and who You say You are in Your holy Word. You are a great mystery, and yet You allow us to get on Your Lap as Your children and love You as our Father. All I can say is thank You. In Jesus' Name we pray, amen!"

"Praise God!" Dave augmented. "Keep worshiping our gracious Lord, and I'll meet you here to go to College & Career class at church on Sunday!"

"Thanks again for your time and effort," Nick said as he opened the door. "And I'll keep praying that the Lord blesses you mightily for teaching me to love Him!"

"Thanks!" Dave replied as they embraced. "Call me with any questions on your Bible reading."

"Will do," answered Nick as he walked down the hall, seemingly without touching the ground. "Our God is awesome!"

"Yes, He is!"

9

Dead Men Walking

"Let the dead bury their own dead."

The College & Career Sunday school class quieted down with Dave's strange announcement.

Dave began reading aloud:

As they were going along the road, someone said to Him, "I will follow You wherever You go."

And Jesus said to him, "The foxes have holes and the birds of the air *have* nests, but the Son of Man has nowhere to lay His head."

And He said to another, "Follow Me." But he said, "Lord, permit me first to go and bury my father."

But He said to him, "Allow the dead to bury their own dead; but as for you, go and proclaim everywhere the kingdom of God."

(Luke 9:57-60)

"Matt, would you please open our Bible study with prayer?"

"Yes," Matt replied, as the class prepared to reverence the Holy Father. "Dear Lord God, we praise You and worship Your Holy Name. We honor You as Your children, and we adore You for the awesome love that You have given to us through Jesus Christ Your Son.

"Pour out Your love upon us through Your Holy Spirit, and guide us into Your truth, that we may know You more and more intimately. I ask that You would bless our teacher Dave, and give him wisdom and knowledge straight from Your throne. And I ask that You give us, Your children, ears to hear Your Word, minds to understand it, and hearts to embrace Your truth. Continue to make us into the image of Your Son. In Jesus' Name we pray, amen."

"Thank you, Matt," acknowledged Dave. "The goal of our Bible study—and of our Christian lives—is to know God intimately, and enjoy Him forever as our Father. As Jesus prayed in His 'High Priestly Prayer' in the Gospel of John: 'This is eternal life, that they may know You, the only true God, and Jesus Christ whom You have sent' (John 17:3).

"We have spent several weeks studying God Himself, since knowing Him more intimately requires knowing more and more about Him. We focused on what God says about Himself in His Word, not what man-made tradition is saying in the modern church. No doubt, as we learn more about God, you may be changing some of your answers to the questions on the Pop Quiz. We will revisit that quiz for more answers and explanations as we move along.

"We have studied God—by far the greatest of endeavors—by looking at His eternal purpose for creation, His holy character, His eternal attributes and His triune nature.

"Now we turn our attention to man and his relationship to God. Let's go around the room, beginning with Ed here, and read the scriptures that I have written on the chalkboard."

The class read:

> The LORD God commanded the man, saying, "From any tree of the garden you may eat freely;
>
> but from the tree of the knowledge of good and evil you shall not eat, for in the day that you eat from it you will surely die." (Genesis 2:16,17)

> Then to Adam He said, "Because you have listened to the voice of your wife, and have eaten from the tree about which I commanded you, saying, 'You shall not eat from it'":
>
> therefore the LORD God sent him out from the garden of Eden, to cultivate the ground from which he was taken.
>
> So He drove the man out; and at the east of the garden of Eden He stationed the cherubim and the flaming sword which turned every direction to guard the way to the tree of life. (Genesis 3:17,23,24)

> For since by a man *came* death, by a man also *came* the resurrection of the dead.
>
> For as in Adam all die, so also in Christ all will be made alive.
>
> (1 Corinthians 15:21,22)

> Another of the disciples said to Him, "Lord, permit me first to go and bury my father."
>
> But Jesus said to him, "Follow Me, and allow the dead to bury their own dead." (Matthew 8:21,22)

> "Woe to you, scribes and Pharisees, hypocrites! For you are like whitewashed tombs which on the outside appear beautiful, but inside they are full of dead men's bones and all uncleanness." (Matthew 23:27)

And you were dead in your trespasses and sins,

in which you formerly walked according to the course of this world, according to the prince of the power of the air, of the spirit that is now working in the sons of disobedience.

Among them we too all formerly lived in the lusts of our flesh, indulging the desires of the flesh and of the mind, and were by nature children of wrath, even as the rest.

But God, being rich in mercy, because of His great love with which He loved us,

even when we were dead in our transgressions, made us alive together with Christ (by grace you have been saved). (Ephesians 2:1-5)

Do not participate in the unfruitful deeds of darkness, but instead even expose them;

for it is disgraceful even to speak of the things which are done by them in secret.

But all things become visible when they are exposed by the light, for everything that becomes visible is light.

For this reason it says,

"Awake, sleeper,

And arise from the dead,

And Christ will shine on you." (Ephesians 5:11-14)

When you were dead in your transgressions and the uncircumcision of your flesh, He made you alive together with Him, having forgiven us all our transgressions. (Colossians 2:13)

But she who gives herself to wanton pleasure is dead even while she lives. (1 Timothy 5:6)

For certain persons have crept in unnoticed, those who were long beforehand marked out for this condemnation, ungodly persons who turn the grace of our God into licentiousness and deny our only Master and Lord, Jesus Christ.

These are the men who are hidden reefs in your love feasts when they feast with you without fear, caring for themselves; clouds without water, carried along by winds; autumn trees without fruit, doubly dead, uprooted;

wild waves of the sea, casting up their own shame like foam; wandering stars, for whom the black darkness has been reserved forever.

(Jude 4,12,13)

"Thank you, class," Dave said. "Can anyone summarize what God has to say in His holy Word about unregenerate man?"

"What does 'unregenerate man' mean?" asked Nick.

"An unregenerate man is a person who has not been born again," answered Paul.

"Very good," Dave commended. "As we have studied, every person born of a human male is spiritually dead because of the 'original sin' of Adam imputed, or credited, to his account. We call that person **unregenerate**, meaning that God has not placed the Holy Spirit inside that person and made them spiritually alive. The term '**unregenerate man**' applies to anyone who may never be born again; or to anyone that God has chosen to be born again, but has not yet, as of this point in time, been made spiritually alive by Him.

"Let's hear a summary of God's Word on unregenerate man. Anna?"

"Adam disobeyed God's commandment, and, true to God's warning, that day he died," began Anna. "This was obviously not physical death—though that would come later—but spiritual death. God drove Adam and Eve out of the garden because of their sin. God's requirement to live with Him in paradise is to be as perfect as He is perfect. Their disobedience terminated the intimate relationship that they had with their Creator, the only Source of Life, resulting in spiritual death.

"The Bible makes it very clear that everyone 'in Adam'—persons born of Adam or any male descendant of Adam—are born spiritually dead. Our Lord Jesus calls them 'dead.' The Apostle Paul calls unbelievers 'dead,' and calls believers before they were born again 'dead.' The Apostle Jude calls 'ungodly persons' in the church 'doubly dead.'"

"Excellent recap, Anna," recognized Dave. "Everyone born of a human male is born spiritually dead in sin. So, what does that mean—'dead,' or 'spiritually dead?'

"Well," reasoned Nick, "I imagine Webster would say that '**dead**' means utterly devoid of life."

"Very good, Nick. That is a great working definition," praised Dave. "A physically-dead person cannot do anything involving the physical world. He cannot think, breath, choose, not choose, accept, receive...anything! He is dead.

"A spiritually-dead person can do nothing towards fixing the terminated relationship with God his Creator. Man, a spiritual corpse, is dead to the only Source of life. A spiritually-dead sinner cannot desire God, seek God, reconcile with God, reach out for God, accept God or choose God. He is dead to God and the things of God.

"The term '**spiritually dead**' does not imply that an unregenerate man does not have a spirit. Being spiritually dead means man has no desire for God to rule the life he lives. That spirit is dead to the things of God, and desires only evil continually—even when giving to charity or going to church.

"God created all life, and therefore owns all life. God gave man life in order to love and serve God, his Creator. But, spiritually-dead man stole this life to love and serve himself, rebelling against God and His right to rule. Thus, everything natural man does is evil, because he is doing it with a stolen life. Unregenerate man, being dead in sin, is unable and unwilling to come to Christ to be saved from God's wrath."

"But I've heard evangelists and preachers on the radio say differently," commented Chelsea.

"Just the other day, someone said, and I quote, 'A sinner is never "so dead" that he cannot accept Jesus Christ as his personal Savior.'"

"How silly is that!" replied Jennifer. "Being somewhat dead is like being somewhat pregnant! I mean, you are either dead or you are not!"

"And that is exactly what our Lord Jesus and the Apostle Paul meant by the word 'dead,'" Dave agreed. "In their time and in the context in which they spoke, death in this world was real and permanent. A miraculous intervention by God Himself was the only way a dead person could be brought back to life. Today, we have respirators, drugs and other technology to prolong life, but not then. That is why, whenever Jesus raised a person from the dead—like Lazarus (John 11), or Jairus' daughter (Luke 8)—the people were utterly astonished.

"When the Lord Jesus and the Apostle Paul used the word '***dead***' as a metaphor to describe a living person, they were integrating the same ideas towards spiritual death. We are born spiritually-dead sinners—spiritual corpses—and only a miraculous intervention from God Himself could bring us to spiritual life."

"I don't understand," Matt interjected. "All I hear these days from preachers is that a person has to choose Jesus Christ as His personal Savior, or that man is doomed to hell. I can't tell you how many times I've heard evangelists give the following scenario:

> A sinner is like a man who is lying on his death bed with a grave disease.
> A cure is found, and the medicine is brought to the man. A nurse can bring
> the medicine that would save him to his mouth. But, unless the man chooses
> to open his mouth and take the medicine, he will surely perish.
>
> Salvation is like that—God has done all He could do. It's now up to you
> to accept the gift that God is holding out to you. Choose Jesus! Accept Jesus
> Christ as your personal Savior, and you accept God's gift of eternal life in
> heaven!

"Oh, yes, Matt," Chelsea assented. "I've heard that all my Christian life. There's also the one about the drowning man going down for the last time. God can throw a life preserver right to his very hand, but unless he chooses to grab hold of it, he will perish."

"But the scriptures that we just read make it very clear that unregenerate man is dead to the things of God," Anna recounted. "Being spiritually dead, a sinner cannot choose God, reach out and accept a gift from God, or open his mouth and take the cure, or anything—he's dead!"

"There seems to be direct contradictions being presented here," Ed observed.

"Well, remember that this Bible study is solely dedicated to God, and what He says in His Word, because that is the only standard of truth we have in this universe," Dave answered. "Man-made traditions are being taught in the modern church as biblical truth. If we recall a few weeks back, the Lord Jesus really hates this sin, and condemned the Pharisees for committing this hypocritical crime against God. Paul, please read Mark 7:5-9 for us."

Paul read:

> The Pharisees and the scribes asked Him, "Why do Your disciples not
> walk according to the tradition of the elders, but eat their bread with impure
> hands?"

And He said to them, "Rightly did Isaiah prophesy of you hypocrites,
as it is written:

    'THIS PEOPLE HONORS ME WITH THEIR LIPS,
      BUT THEIR HEART IS FAR AWAY FROM ME.
    'BUT IN VAIN DO THEY WORSHIP ME,
      TEACHING AS DOCTRINES THE PRECEPTS OF MEN.'

"Neglecting the commandment of God, you hold to the tradition of men."

He was also saying to them, "You are experts at setting aside the commandment of God in order to keep your tradition." (Mark 7:5-9)

"Thank you, Paul," Dave acknowledged. "Holding to man-made tradition when God's holy Word specifically rejects it—and continuing to teach the tradition as God's truth—is the ultimate in hypocrisy. A *hypocrite* is a phony, pretending to be a true Christian on the outside, but not having the Holy Spirit on the inside. He is the lowest of unbelievers. At least devil worshipers admit their true allegiance.

"The Lord Jesus declares: 'Heaven and earth will pass away, but My words will not pass away' (Mark 13:31); and, 'He who rejects Me and does not receive My sayings, has one who judges him; the word I spoke is what will judge him at the last day' (John 12:48). God's Word is eternal and unchanging. It will judge us on Judgment Day.

"Have we, as professing Christians, so totally deceived ourselves as to think that God will relent concerning His eternal Word on the day of judgment? Do we live in utter denial of the truth, thinking God will say: 'O child, you rejected My holy Word and lived according to your own ideas of truth, but that's okay'? Or will we hear, '"Why do you call me 'Lord, Lord,' and not do what I say? DEPART FROM ME, YOU WHO PRACTICE LAWLESSNESS"' (MATTHEW 7:23)!

"The true believer should be teachable, and have an attitude of humility before God. If a truth can be proven with the whole counsel of Scripture—the continuous testimony throughout the different books of the Bible—then the true disciple has a responsibility to abandon man-made tradition and hold to God's Word. Remember, man can be wrong, and often is wrong. But God is never wrong!"

"Well, we sure have a continuous testimony from Genesis to Jude here," Anna noted. "The Bible definitely says that unregenerate man is dead in sin. And, if God's Word is the eternal standard of truth and judgment, man-made traditions are utterly worthless."

"Especially if the tradition contradicts God's truth!" Ed added. "But, if the Bible has been around for all these centuries, and it has not changed, where did all these man-made traditions come from?"

"Great question!" Dave applauded. "The Apostle Jude just warned us that unbelievers crept into the church in the first century, and the same is true throughout history. There is the visible church—everyone you see in the pulpits and pews—which is made up of true believers and unbelievers. But *God's true church* is the 'invisible' church made up only of all true believers around the world. Only persons having the Holy Spirit in them, all of those having been truly born again, are members of the universal, true church of God.

"The Lord Jesus tells several parables—such as 'The Wheat and the Tares' (Matthew 13) and 'The Ten Virgins' (Matthew 25)—warning His true followers that the visible church will have believers and unbelievers mixed together until He returns at the end of the age. The Apostle Paul says the same thing, comparing the visible church to a house. Nick, please read 2 Timothy 2:19-21 for us."

Nick read:

> Nevertheless, the firm foundation of God stands, having this seal, "The Lord knows those who are His," and, "Everyone who names the name of the Lord is to abstain from wickedness."
>
> Now in a large house there are not only gold and silver vessels, but also vessels of wood and of earthenware, and some to honor and some to dishonor.
>
> Therefore, if anyone cleanses himself from these *things*, he will be a vessel for honor, sanctified, useful to the Master, prepared for every good work. (2 Timothy 2:19-21)

"Thank you, Nick," Dave said. "God knows the ones who are His true children in the visible church because He chose them! But we can only guess by the spiritual fruit in a person's life. And we finite humans can guess wrongly. We humans can never be absolutely certain that another person is a true believer, no matter who the person is. Galatians

"But a true believer can be absolutely certain that he *himself* is a true child of God, because God gives him that knowledge through the Holy Spirit (Romans 8:16). Between God and His child, salvation is assured. But horizontally—among men—we can only judge by the fruit the Holy Spirit produces, or the lack of it, as the Apostle Paul discusses in the Letter to the Galatians, chapter 5."

"So true," assented Grant. "I heard on the radio the other day a pastor and his wife telling their story. They had been leading a church for more than two decades, and then received true salvation. They were giving their testimony about trying to be Christians by their own works to merit salvation. When Jesus Christ opened their eyes to salvation by grace through faith in Him and His work alone, they were astounded. They claimed God really changed their lives!"

Humanism Invades the Visible Church

"Awesome testimony, Grant!" Dave replied. "Down through the history of the visible church, unbelievers became leaders with power to create and enforce doctrine. Since they did not have the Holy Spirit, their decisions could only result in man-made traditions, just like the Pharisees in first-century Judaism whom the Lord Jesus condemned as hypocrites.

"In the 1800s, humanism became the dominant system of belief in the world among unbelievers, many of whom by then ran the churches."

"What is humanism?" asked Matt.

"**Humanism** is the belief system emphasizing human potential and fulfillment using logical reasoning, positive thinking, and science in the natural world—often denying the existence of God, and thus rejecting man's dependence upon God," Dave explained.

"It is the ultimate expression of human sinful pride, and it has existed since Adam first sinned. This system says that man can build his own heaven here on earth. Humanism is the antithesis of God's truth. Humanism is a heinous, arrogant rejection of God and His holy Word; an ungodly system inspired by the devil himself.

"In the 19th and 20th centuries, humanism invaded the Christian churches, and made huge in-roads in replacing God's Word with man-made traditions. With the newly-invented mass communications of radio and television, hundreds of parachurch ministries sprang up, and teaching moved farther and farther away from God's Word."

"I can see how this could happen," Anna added. "If I hear something taught over and over again, I could easily come to believe that the teaching is true—unless, of course, I checked it out against God's Word!"

"So true, Anna," Dave agreed. "The Word of God commended the people of Berea when the Apostle Paul preached to them, because they did not blindly take his word as God's truth, but checked what he said against Scripture (Acts 17). The church of the 20th century should have rejected the humanistic teachings by diligently comparing them to God's Word.

"Since humanism and God's truth are opposites, the difference is easy to spot. Teaching that glorifies man is humanism. Teaching from God's Word that glorifies God is true. It's just that simple.

"As strange as it may seem, there are true Christians who hold to these humanistic lies, and even teach them. One's doctrine does not necessarily make a person saved or unsaved. A person is truly saved if God places His Holy Spirit within that person and regenerates him. All true believers are then commanded by God to diligently study His holy Word in order to know His ways and teach them correctly (2 Timothy 2:15).

"The Lord Jesus considers His truth—correct doctrine—to be critically important, and will hold teachers strictly accountable for what they teach His flock (James 3:1). Any true believer who teaches humanism under the guise of Christianity has committed the heinous sin of glorifying man-made tradition over the holy Word of God.

"Many church leaders, and even well-meaning believers who blindly accepted the humanistic teachings, adopted the 20th century attitude of trying to simplify the Bible's message. They set about reducing God's Word to simple sayings or positive confessions for wider appeal and acceptance. In the process, they eliminated crucial but 'offensive' essentials like 'repentance,' and redefined critical terms like 'belief in Christ' and even 'faith.'

"'God, I see what You are trying to do here,' they would reason, 'so I'll take it from here. I'll give Your message a modern spin and go with it!'" Dave continued.

"Meanwhile, the Lord Jesus says:

"Abide in Me, and I in you. As the branch cannot bear fruit of itself, unless it abides in the vine, so neither *can* you unless you abide in Me.

"I am the vine, you are the branches; he who abides in Me and I in him, he bears much fruit, for apart from Me you can do nothing.

"If anyone does not abide in Me, he is thrown away as a branch and dries up; and they gather them, and cast them into the fire and they are burned." (John 15:4-6)

"Sounds like exact opposites!" appraised Ed. "Jesus says to stay with Him, and He will make this life fruitful. Running off and doing my own will in His Name will result in drying up."

"Excellent observation, Ed," acknowledged Dave. "Also, those who purposefully reject God's Word to promote their humanistic agendas show their true identities: unbelievers whom the Lord Jesus said are destined for the fires of hell.

"So, much of today's church is a bad mixture of humanistic, man-made traditions with snippets of God's holy Word thrown in to sound good. Ed noticed the obvious contradictions between the evangelist's preaching and the Scripture right away, because the difference is obvious. Again, teaching that glorifies man is humanism. Teaching from God's Word that glorifies God is true.

"Salvation, according to God's Word, is not like a sick man on his death bed, who must accept the medicine of the gospel. Salvation is not like a man drowning who must grab hold of the life preserver of the gospel. Man is born spiritually *dead!* Salvation only occurs when God places His Holy Spirit inside of a corpse, born dead in sin, and brings it to life."

"So, why do preachers and evangelists teach that salvation is man's choice to make, when the Lord Jesus, His Apostles, and the rest of the Bible repeatedly assert that unbelievers are spiritually dead and cannot choose God?" Matt asked.

"Critical question, Matt," Dave responded. "Many true believers, and all unbelievers, simply do not know—or even worse, refuse to accept—what God says in His holy Word about man and his sinful condition.

"They read the repeated testimony of Scripture: man is spiritually dead and morally bankrupt. Since they cannot understand how God's truth fits into His total plan, or since the truth does not fit into their preconceived lies, they deny the truth. They claim to believe the Bible, yet they reject what the Bible teaches. Then they commit the heinous crime of holding to humanistic tradition instead of submitting to God's holy Word, which cannot lie.

"But Almighty God has a response for those refusing to bow to His Word. 'The Lord scoffs at them. Then He will speak to them in His anger' (Psalm 2:4,5). God's Word is the only standard of truth in the universe. The Eternal Truth, the Lord Jesus Christ, will declare to the unbelieving: "*I am...the truth*" (John 14:6). I do not change for you or your blind, sin-marred, finite ideas. Either you conform your ideas of truth to Me, or you pay the dire consequences.'

Whose Choice Is Salvation—Man's or God's?

"Correct understanding of the teaching of the Bible, concerning man and his relationship to God, stands on the correct answer to **The Pivotal Question: 'Whose choice is salvation—man's or God's?'**"

"Maybe it is both?" offered Chelsea.

"Well, what does God's holy Word declare?" Dave probed. "Let's take a look. We have already found that the Bible teaches that people who have not been born again by the Holy Spirit are spiritually dead. By 'spiritually dead,' God's Word affirms the idea that unregenerate man can do nothing towards pleasing God. Sinners are not able to begin a relationship with God, or even desire God, because they are dead in sin, running away from God as quickly as possible.

"Let's take a closer look at what being 'dead in sin' entails. Grant, would you read the next four scriptures on the board, please?"

Grant read:

> For the wrath of God is revealed from heaven against all ungodliness and unrighteousness of men who suppress the truth in unrighteousness,
>
> because that which is known about God is evident within them; for God made it evident to them.
>
> For even though they knew God, they did not honor Him as God or give thanks, but they became futile in their speculations, and their foolish heart was darkened.
>
> Professing to be wise, they became fools. (Romans 1:18,19,21,22)

> The Lord's bond-servant must not be quarrelsome, but be kind to all, able to teach, patient when wronged,
>
> with gentleness correcting those who are in opposition, if perhaps God may grant them repentance leading to the knowledge of the truth,
>
> and they may come to their senses *and escape* from the snare of the devil, having been held captive by him to do his will.
>
> (2 Timothy 2:24-26)

> And even if our gospel is veiled, it is veiled to those who are perishing,
>
> in whose case the god of this world has blinded the minds of the unbelieving so that they might not see the light of the gospel of the glory of Christ, who is the image of God. (2 Corinthians 4:3,4)

> Now we have received, not the spirit of the world, but the Spirit who is from God, so that we may know the things freely given to us by God,
>
> which things we also speak, not in words taught by human wisdom, but in those taught by the Spirit, combining spiritual *thoughts* with spiritual *words*.
>
> But a natural man does not accept the things of the Spirit of God, for they are foolishness to him; and he cannot understand them, because they are spiritually appraised. (1 Corinthians 2:12-14)

"Thank you, Grant," recognized Dave. "God declares that, although He placed within man the knowledge that He exists, unregenerate man actively suppresses that knowledge in order to continue in his sin. The sinner has resolved, in his rebellion, to run away from God as fast as his legs can carry him.

"God also declares in His Word that unregenerate man is 'held captive by Satan to do the devil's will.' Satan has also 'blinded man's mind' so that he cannot see the truth of God's gospel. The sinner 'cannot accept' God's truth because his blinded mind 'cannot understand' God's truth—it is even 'foolishness to him!' Unless God grants 'repentance leading to the knowledge of the truth,' unregenerate man remains ensnared in sin. Again, Holy Scripture declares that unregenerate man is held captive by the devil, and can only do Satan's will, which is only evil continuously.

"If you want a complete synopsis of God's Word on every person who is not born again—the condition of every one of us at conception—here it is:

> What then? Are we better than they? Not at all; for we have already
> charged that both Jews and Greeks are all under sin;
> as it is written,
> "THERE IS NONE RIGHTEOUS, NOT EVEN ONE;
> THERE IS NONE WHO UNDERSTANDS,
> "THERE IS NONE WHO SEEKS FOR GOD;
> ALL HAVE TURNED ASIDE, TOGETHER THEY HAVE BECOME
> USELESS;
> "THERE IS NONE WHO DOES GOOD,
> "THERE IS NOT EVEN ONE."
> "THEIR THROAT IS AN OPEN GRAVE,
> WITH THEIR TONGUES THEY KEEP DECEIVING,"
> "THE POISON OF ASPS IS UNDER THEIR LIPS";
> "WHOSE MOUTH IS FULL OF CURSING AND BITTERNESS";
> "THEIR FEET ARE SWIFT TO SHED BLOOD,
> DESTRUCTION AND MISERY ARE IN THEIR PATHS,
> AND THE PATH OF PEACE THEY HAVE NOT KNOWN."
> "THERE IS NO FEAR OF GOD BEFORE THEIR EYES." (Romans 3:9-18)

"Wow," Nick mused, "now that is ominous. No fear of God. A mouth full of cursing and bitterness. Not even one who does good or understands. None righteous. None who seeks for God. Yep—that was me in a nutshell before God got a hold of me."

"Notice," Dave added, "that 'none seeks for God.' Many people want God's ***benefits***: blessings, eternal life in paradise, and escape from hell. But not one unregenerate soul seeks God Himself to rule over this life, even though God owns this life because He created and sustains this life.

"Notice that 'there is none who does good.' Giving to charity or going to church may be 'good' in man's eyes. But in God's eyes, they are heinous crimes of rebellion by the unregenerate. These actions are heinous crimes against God because all persons born of a human male have stolen this life to serve themselves. Thus, anything an unregenerate person does is rebellion. Again, if any thought or action has not been preceded by being born again through faith in Jesus Christ, 'whatever is not from faith is sin' (Romans 14:23)."

"Why would an unregenerate sinner even want to go to church?" asked Pam.

"Great question," Dave replied. "People have many reasons for going to church. Though sinners are dead in sin, they do know that there is a spiritual vacuum in their hearts that needs filling.

"Some people go to church to try to assuage their guilt. Some think that by going, God is obligated to let them into heaven. Some go simply by habit, or to feel like part of a group. Others go to make business or social contacts. But only a truly born-again believer goes to church to worship his Master, Almighty God—by far and wide the most important reason for being there.

"So, what have we discovered about unregenerate man according to God's holy Word?"

"Well, the Bible says that every person born of a human male is born dead in sin—spiritually dead—and cannot do anything towards God, because he is dead," Anna stated.

"Unregenerate man, according to God's very words, does not fear God or desire God," furthered Paul. "Not one person born of a human male is righteous, seeks for God, or does good."

"Everyone who is not born again is held captive by Satan to do the devil's will," Jennifer contributed. "Satan blinds their minds so they are not able to understand or accept the Word of God."

"Therefore, a spiritually-dead sinner cannot desire God, seek God, reconcile with God, reach out for God, accept God or choose God," Matt added. "In fact, unregenerate man actively suppresses the knowledge of God in order to continue in his sin. He runs away from God as fast as he can."

"Excellent recap," Dave praised. "Thus, Pop Quiz question 7 is false. The statement is, 'Salvation is a gift of God, but, like any gift, we must reach out and take it.' We, as dead sinners, can't reach out for God's gift of salvation, because we are dead."

"Wait a minute!" Ed interrupted. "If all these things are true—and God's Word declares them to be true all over the place—then it is absolutely impossible for man to choose God! Salvation, then, could not possibly depend on man, or no man would ever be saved—because no unregenerate man desires or even seeks after God. In fact, he's running away from God!"

"Bingo!" Dave shouted. "Ladies and gentlemen, the light has been turned on! Excellent conclusion, Ed! Remember The Pivotal Question: 'Whose choice is salvation—man's or God's?' Scripture declares that it is impossible for man to choose salvation in God, because man is unable to do so. Unregenerate man does not desire to choose God, and indeed he cannot, because he is spiritually dead in sin."

"Are you saying that God commands something that is impossible for man to do?" asked Chelsea.

"Bingo again!" Dave applauded. "Excellent observation, Chelsea! Do you remember God's standard for getting into heaven? God commanded it in the Law of Moses, in Leviticus 19:2; and the Lord Jesus repeated the command in His Sermon on the Mount. Read Matthew 5:48 for us, Chelsea."

"'"Therefore you are to be perfect, as your heavenly Father is perfect."'"

"God's standard for living with Him is impossible for man to achieve from the get-go," Dave explained. "The entire reason for our need of a Savior is that we cannot do what God commands of us in order to live in heaven. Salvation is based upon God requiring perfection, man unable to meet God's standard, and God sending the Lord Jesus to obtain guaranteed perfection for His children.

"So, in answer to your question, God absolutely commands what is impossible for man to do. And that command is to be as perfect as God is perfect. Only God can be perfect as God is perfect!

"Remember, there are only two ways for a man to be as perfect as God is perfect. One is to be God Himself, whom we are not! The second is if God bestows the gift of His perfection upon a man by crediting that person's account with the perfect life of God the Son, Jesus Christ!"

"Okay," Ed remarked, "if it is impossible for man to choose salvation, then how do we become saved?"

"Superior question!" Dave acknowledged. "Let me show you from God's holy Word. God gave us the record of the Old Testament as a physical example of events that occur in the spiritual realm. God uses *types* and *foreshadows*, which are visible examples of how the invisible God is working His eternal plan for creation, so man can learn His ways.

"For example, God chose a people, the nation of Israel, to demonstrate His power and presence to the world. In the Old Testament, Israel was a foreshadow of the 'invisible' true church, made up only of spiritually born-again believers around the world. This true church is to demonstrate God's power and presence to the New Testament world.

"In the book of the prophet Ezekiel, God dramatically shows His prophet exactly how He brings about salvation in spiritually-dead people. Grant, would you please read Ezekiel 37, verses 1 through 14 for us?"

Grant read:

Vision of the Valley of Dry Bones

The hand of the LORD was upon me, and He brought me out by the Spirit of the LORD and set me down in the middle of the valley; and it was full of bones.

He caused me to pass among them round about, and behold, *there were* very many on the surface of the valley; and lo, *they were* very dry.

He said to me, "Son of man, can these bones live?" And I answered, "O Lord GOD, You know."

Again He said to me, "Prophesy over these bones and say to them, 'O dry bones, hear the word of the LORD.'

"Thus says the Lord GOD to these bones, 'Behold, I will cause breath to enter you that you may come to life.

"'I will put sinews on you, make flesh grow back on you, cover you with skin and put breath in you that you may come alive; and you will know that I am the LORD.'"

So I prophesied as I was commanded; and as I prophesied, there was a noise, and behold, a rattling; and the bones came together, bone to its bone.

And I looked, and behold, sinews were on them, and flesh grew and skin covered them; but there was no breath in them.

Then He said to me, "Prophesy to the breath, prophesy, son of man, and say to the breath, 'Thus says the Lord GOD, "Come from the four winds, O breath, and breathe on these slain, that they come to life."'"

So I prophesied as He commanded me, and the breath came into them, and they came to life and stood on their feet, an exceedingly great army.

The Vision Explained

Then He said to me, "Son of man, these bones are the whole house of Israel; behold, they say, 'Our bones are dried up and our hope has perished. We are completely cut off.'

Therefore prophesy and say to them, 'Thus says the Lord GOD, "Behold, I will open your graves and cause you to come up out of your graves, My people; and I will bring you into the land of Israel.

"Then you will know that I am the LORD, when I have opened your graves and caused you to come up out of your graves, My people.

"I will put My Spirit within you and you will come to life, and I will place you on your own land. Then you will know that I, the LORD, have spoken and done it," declares the LORD.'" (Ezekiel 37:1-14)

"Thank you, Grant," said Dave. "There is God's perfect example of how spiritually-dead sinners are brought to spiritual life. Again, the Old Testament is a physical picture of reality in the spiritual realm. What exactly did those dead, dry bones do to effect their coming to life again?"

"Nothing," Ed answered. "They couldn't do anything...they were long dead."

"...an exact picture of souls born into this world spiritually dead," Dave added. "The Apostle Paul means just that when he declares: 'And you were dead in your trespasses and sins' (Ephesians 2:1). God's holy Word emphatically declares over and over again that man is born spiritually dead, and simply can do nothing towards salvation.

"The Apostle explicitly details that it is while we are dead in sin that God raises us from spiritual death to new life in Christ:

And you were dead in your trespasses and sins.

But God, being rich in mercy, because of His great love with which He loved us,

even when we were dead in our transgressions, made us alive together with Christ (by grace you have been saved). (Ephesians 2:1,4,5)

"The bones in Ezekiel's prophecy were long dead. They did not choose to live again. God, by His sovereign choice, chose to make this great army alive again. God and God alone put flesh onto, and life into, these dead, dry bones.

"Likewise, God and God alone takes a spiritually-dead sinner and puts His Holy Spirit into him so that he becomes spiritually alive. The sinner only then realizes that he is guilty of offending the holiness of his Creator with every breath he breathes, every thought he thinks, and every act he does. Only the indwelling Holy Spirit frees the sinner from enslavement to the devil, gives the sinner the power to repent, and gives him the faith to believe in Christ's perfect work for salvation.

"Remember The Pivotal Question: 'Whose choice is salvation—man's or God's?' **The correct answer to this critical question is the foundation upon which all correct biblical teaching rests concerning man and his relationship to God**. The only correct answer to The Pivotal Question is that the choice of salvation is God's and God's alone.

"Thus, the humanistic preacher's idea that man's eternal destiny is determined by man's choice is a lie. This falsehood is a man-made, man-glorifying tradition that God's holy Word specifically rejects.

"The humanistic evangelist's plea for man to choose God is also a lie. God's life-giving medicine is not given to a dying man, but it is given to a corpse. God's life-preserving salvation is not thrown to a man who is drowning, but is thrust upon a corpse long dead at the bottom of the sea. The modern church saying is a lie: **Unregenerate man is not a free, moral agent. Unregenerate man is an enslaved, immoral spiritual corpse!**

The Predestination of the Elect

"God alone sovereignly places His Holy Spirit in spiritually-dead corpses—those whom He has already chosen to be in His family from before the foundation of the world—and raises them to new life in Christ.

"Jennifer, please read the passages on the chalkboard declaring that God alone chooses who gets the gift of His perfection."

Jennifer read:

> Blessed is the nation whose God is the LORD,
> The people whom He has chosen for His own inheritance.
>
> (Psalm 33:12)

> At that time Jesus said, "I praise You, Father, Lord of heaven and earth, that You have hidden these things from *the* wise and intelligent and have revealed them to infants.
>
> "Yes, Father, for this way was well-pleasing in Your sight.
>
> "All things have been handed over to Me by My Father; and no one knows the Son except the Father; nor does anyone know the Father except the Son, and anyone to whom the Son wills to reveal *Him*."
>
> (Matthew 11:25-27)

> "For those days will be a *time of* tribulation such as has not occurred since the beginning of the creation which God created until now, and never will.
>
> "Unless the Lord had shortened *those* days, no life would have been saved; but for the sake of the elect, whom He chose, He shortened the days." (Mark 13:19,20)

And He was saying, "For this reason I have said to you, that no one can come to Me unless it has been granted him from the Father."

(John 6:65)

So, as those who have been chosen of God, holy and beloved, put on a heart of compassion, kindness, humility, gentleness and patience;
bearing with one another, and forgiving each other, whoever has a complaint against anyone; just as the Lord forgave you, so also should you.

(Colossians 3:12,13)

We give thanks to God always for all of you, making mention *of you* in our prayers;
constantly bearing in mind your work of faith and labor of love and steadfastness of hope in our Lord Jesus Christ in the presence of our God and Father,
knowing, brethren beloved by God, *His* choice of you.

(1 Thessalonians 1:4,5)

For God has not destined us for wrath, but for obtaining salvation through our Lord Jesus Christ. (1 Thessalonians 5:9)

Blessed be the God and Father of our Lord Jesus Christ, who according to His great mercy has caused us to be born again to a living hope through the resurrection of Jesus Christ from the dead.

(1 Peter 1:3)

But as many as received Him, to them He gave the right to become children of God, *even* to those who believe in His name,
who were born, not of blood nor of the will of the flesh nor of the will of man, but of God. (John 1:12,13)

So then it does not depend on the man who wills or the man who runs, but on God who has mercy (Romans 9:16)

"Thank you, Jennifer," Dave acknowledged. "This small sampling of the many scriptures we could read emphatically declares that God chooses who receives salvation. The Apostle Peter says that God is the one who 'causes us to be born again.' The Apostle Paul writes that God 'destines' true believers for salvation—sinners 'who have been chosen by God' to be regenerated.

"Finally, the Lord Jesus puts the matter to rest plainly and succinctly. Christ Jesus simply states that 'no one' is able to 'come to Him' unless God the Father grants it. Then Jesus declares that 'no one knows' Himself or the Father unless 'the Son wills to reveal Them' to a sinner.

"Please notice that man's choice or man's will is nowhere to be found in God's answer to

The Pivotal Question. In fact, God specifically says that man's will or actions are not involved in salvation. Thus, to teach that salvation is man's choice is to directly deny God's holy Word.

"God declares in His holy Word that *He* chooses whom He wants in His family, and God the Son is the one who wills to reveal salvation. And God sovereignly made His choices when He formed His perfect plan for His creation before the foundation of the world!

"Anna, would you please read the next four passages on the chalkboard for us, please?"

Anna read:

> Blessed *be* the God and Father of our Lord Jesus Christ, who has blessed
> us with every spiritual blessing in the heavenly *places* in Christ,
>   just as He chose us in Him before the foundation of the world, that we
> would be holy and blameless before Him. In love
> He predestined us to adoption as sons through Jesus Christ to Himself,
> according to the kind intention of His will,
>   to the praise of the glory of His grace, which He freely bestowed on
> us in the Beloved. (Ephesians 1:3-6)

> But we should always give thanks to God for you, brethren beloved
> by the Lord, because God has chosen you from the beginning for salvation
> through sanctification by the Spirit and faith in the truth.
>   It was for this He called you through our gospel, that you may gain
> the glory of our Lord Jesus Christ. (2 Thessalonians 2:13,14)

> Therefore do not be ashamed of the testimony of our Lord or of me
> His prisoner, but join with *me* in suffering for the gospel according to the
> power of God,
>   who has saved us and called us with a holy calling, not according to
> our works, but according to His own purpose and grace which was
> granted us in Christ Jesus from all eternity. (2 Timothy 1:8,9)

> All who dwell on the earth will worship him (the Beast), *everyone*
> whose name has not been written from the foundation of the world in the
> book of life of the Lamb who has been slain.
>   (Revelation 13:8; *parenthesis mine*)

"Thank you, Anna," recognized Dave. "God's holy Word declares that God chose those who would be saved, and He made His choices before the foundation of the world. God's sovereign choice of those He wanted in His family was eternally in His mind, in His eternal plan for creation. The Apostle Paul calls this 'predestination.'

"**Predestination** means that God chose before creation the spiritually-dead sinners He would make spiritually alive, by His Holy Spirit, in order to become members of His family. These ones chosen by God for salvation are called **the elect**. Scripture calls God's chosen ones **the elect** because God elected them to salvation, not because they elected to be saved. As the scriptures we just read testify, God repeatedly declares that He simply chose sovereignly, according to His own good pleasure and purpose, and for no other reasons.

"God could not have made His choice based upon what He foresaw in man, for there is nothing good to see in spiritually-dead sinners. We are all born dead in sin, and live filthy lives of rebellion against God (Ephesians 2:3).

"If God chose us instead of our neighbors—based upon something good in us, or that He foresaw that we would choose Jesus as our Savior—then we earned salvation. If we earned salvation by our goodness, or our good choices, then salvation cannot be by grace. By definition, *grace* means unearned favor. But God's Word declares the exact opposite of all of these fabrications of man. Pam, please read for us the next four scriptures on the board."

Pam read:

> Then the LORD saw that the wickedness of man was great on the earth,
> and that every intent of the thoughts of his heart was only evil continually.
>
> (Genesis 6:5)

> For I know that nothing good dwells in me, that is, in my flesh.
>
> (Romans 7:18a)

> For by grace you have been saved through faith; and that not of
> yourselves, *it is* the gift of God;
> not as a result of works, so that no one may boast. (Ephesians 2:8,9)

> He saved us, not on the basis of deeds which we have done in
> righteousness, but according to His mercy, by the washing of regeneration
> and renewing by the Holy Spirit,
> whom He poured out upon us richly through Jesus Christ our Savior,
> so that being justified by His grace we would be made heirs according
> to *the* hope of eternal life. (Titus 3:5-7)

"Remember from past classes that it is blasphemy to say that God looks down the corridors of time and makes choices according to what He learns. This teaching is heresy, for it maintains that God is not omniscient, and not immutable.

"If God must look into the future to see what you would choose, then He does not eternally know this action, and He learns something. If God learns anything, He changes in His character; because he would then no longer be omniscient, and then would not be immutable.

"We have read many scriptures declaring that God knows the future expressly because He has ordained everything that exists or happens in creation according to His perfect plan. We also have read where God proclaims that He never changes in His character and His purpose, or plan. Therefore, if anyone teaches that God predestines people to salvation based upon what He sees they would choose in the future, that teacher has blasphemed our holy God and has committed heresy.

"Not to mention, that teacher has committed great error. For God's Word says over and over that spiritually-dead sinners can't choose God. Sinners can't come to Jesus to be saved, because they are dead in sin. Unregenerate man is running away from God as fast as he can run. He will not choose God, because he does not desire God."

The Foreknowledge of God

"What about the scriptures that speak of God's foreknowledge?" Ed questioned.

"Excellent question," Dave replied. "Ed, please read for us the next six passages on the chalkboard concerning God's foreknowledge."

Ed read:

> Peter, an apostle of Jesus Christ,
> To those who reside as aliens, scattered throughout Pontus, Galatia, Cappadocia, Asia, and Bithynia,
> who are chosen according to the foreknowledge of God the Father, by the sanctifying work of the Spirit, to obey Jesus Christ and be sprinkled with His blood: May grace and peace be yours in the fullest measure.
>
> (1 Peter 1:1,2)

> God has not rejected His people whom He foreknew. Or do you not know what the Scripture says in *the passage about* Elijah, how he pleads with God against Israel?
> "Lord, THEY HAVE KILLED YOUR PROPHETS, THEY HAVE TORN DOWN YOUR ALTARS, AND I ALONE AM LEFT, AND THEY ARE SEEKING MY LIFE."
> But what is the divine response to him? "I HAVE KEPT for Myself SEVEN THOUSAND MEN WHO HAVE NOT BOWED THE KNEE TO BAAL."
> In the same way then, there has also come to be at the present time a remnant according to *God's* gracious choice.
> But if it is by grace, it is no longer on the basis of works, otherwise grace is no longer grace. (Romans 11:2-6)

> Now the word of the LORD came to me saying,
> "Before I formed you in the womb I knew you,
> And before you were born I consecrated you;
> I have appointed you a prophet to the nations." (Jeremiah 1:4,5)

> "At that time," declares the LORD, "I will be the God of all the families of Israel, and they shall be My people."
> The LORD appeared to him from afar, *saying,*
> "I have loved you with an everlasting love;
> Therefore I have drawn you with lovingkindness.
>
> (Jeremiah 31:1,3)

...just as He chose us in Him before the foundation of the world, that we would be holy and blameless before Him. In love

He predestined us to adoption as sons through Jesus Christ to Himself, according to the kind intention of His will,

to the praise of the glory of His grace, which He freely bestowed on us in the Beloved. (Ephesians 1:4-6)

And we know that God causes all things to work together for good to those who love God, to those who are called according to *His* purpose.

For those whom He foreknew, He also predestined *to become* conformed to the image of His Son, so that He would be the firstborn among many brethren;

and these whom He predestined, He also called; and these whom He called, He also justified; and these whom He justified, He also glorified.

(Romans 8:28-30)

"Thank you, Ed," said Dave. "The ungodly humanist claims that the meaning of God's *foreknowledge*—the meaning that God *foreknew*—is that God knows beforehand about individuals and what they will do in the future. Although God certainly knows all things, the humanist's definition of 'foreknew' is impossible, as I will easily demonstrate using 'The Golden Chain' of Romans 8:28-30.

"Here the Apostle Paul gives an unbreakable chain of events caused by God:

Those He foreknew, He predestined;

Those He predestined, He called;

Those He called, He justified;

Those He justified, He glorified.

"The logical conclusion of 'The Golden Chain' is that those God foreknew, He has justified and glorified. The omniscient God certainly knows beforehand all about believers and unbelievers alike. But Paul says that those God foreknew, He justified and glorified. Unbelievers, from God's eternal perspective, are *never* justified and glorified. The Lord Jesus emphatically declared to unbelievers: '"you will die in your sins"' (John 8:24).

"So, God's meaning of *foreknew* cannot be the humanist's definition, which is: 'knew beforehand about individuals and their future actions.' If the humanist was correct, individuals who die in their sins would still have to be justified and glorified!

"God's meaning of *foreknew* is 'loved with a special, caring love beforehand.' The Apostle Paul writes to the Ephesians: '*In love* He predestined us to adoption as sons.' God has loved His special, chosen children 'with an everlasting love.'

"It is similar to the use of the word 'knew' in the King James Bible: 'And Adam knew Eve his wife; and she conceived, and bare Cain, and said, I have gotten a man from the LORD' (Genesis 4:1). The intimate affection that a man has for his wife is a type—a foreshadow, or example—of the intimate, eternal love God has for His chosen family members.

"God uses the terms 'foreknew' and 'foreknowledge,' not about knowing beforehand what individuals would *do*, but about loving beforehand the individuals *themselves*. God told Jeremiah that he would be God's future prophet. But God says to him, "'Before I formed you in the womb I knew you'" (Jeremiah 1:5). God eternally loved Jeremiah, like all of His chosen children, with a special, caring, saving love before birth!

"So, the meaning of *foreknowledge* cannot be that God knows about individuals and what they would do in the future. Though God does know these things, that is not the meaning of this term. God's *foreknowledge* is the special, caring, saving love that God reserved beforehand only for His children—specifically defined by God as 'those who are called according to His purpose' (Romans 8:28).

"Therefore, God does not predestine individuals to become His children based upon what He sees them do in the future. Such teaching is blasphemy. God predestines individuals to salvation based on His eternal love that He set upon certain ones by His own good pleasure and sovereign choice."

Free Will

"What about man's free will?" asked Paul.

"The ungodly humanist defines *free will* as man having the ability to choose God or not choose God," Dave answered. "One must always clarify definitions of theological terms like 'free will.' The ungodly humanist's definition glorifies man as the final determiner of his fate. This directly contradicts all of the scriptures we have read today.

"The true believer, however, defines *free will* as the ability of man to choose *what he desires*. The problem, as we have just read, is that the desires of anyone born of a human male are only evil continually (Genesis 6:5)! The unregenerate sinner actively suppresses the knowledge of God so he can continue to fulfill the desires of his own sin. He is held captive by Satan to do the devil's will. He is dead in sin, and he cannot choose God because he does not even desire or seek for God!

"The concept of free will being taught in the modern church, however, aligns with the heresy of the humanist, blaspheming the sovereign Almighty God and His holy Word. This is quite embarrassing, for it shows a serious misunderstanding of the different parts which make up a human being, and the specific functions of those parts.

"God created human beings in the following manner," Dave said as he drew a diagram on the chalkboard.

The Composition of Man

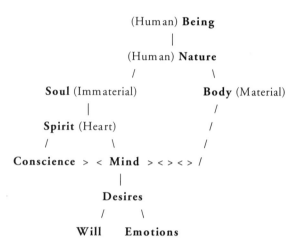

"Man is a ***being*** with a ***nature*** that God has created explicitly for humans," Dave explained. "God 'programs' all of His creatures with a nature specific to its kind. It is a cat's nature to chase mice, but it is not an elephant's nature to do so. The nature controls the entire being.

"God gave the human being a nature with two major parts: a ***soul***, which is immaterial, and a ***body***, which is material, or physical. The immaterial part—the soul—is controlled by the ***spirit***, which is why the two terms are often interchangeable in God's Word. The spirit of man, often symbolically called the '***heart***' in Scripture, can be dead to the things of God, or made alive to God by the regeneration of the Holy Spirit.

"The human spirit has two parts—the ***mind*** and the ***conscience***. The mind sends and receives information to and from the body. From the dictation of the human nature, the mind also generates ***desires*** that control the ***will*** and the ***emotions***.

"Regardless of whether the spirit has or has not been regenerated, God placed the conscience in man's spirit to perform two important functions: first, to inform the man that God exists; and second, to inform the man of God's standard of righteousness, which requires that God will judge him for his thoughts and actions that fail to meet His standard. It is this knowledge of God that sinful man actively suppresses, and from which he runs away, in order to continue in his rebellion against his Creator by doing his own thing (Romans 1:18-32).

"When God first made man, He made Adam good and upright, but with the ability to do good or evil—the ability to obey God's law and serve Him, or disobey God's law and serve himself. God easily communicated His law to Adam through his conscience, because Adam's conscience was not mired in a sinful nature. Once Adam chose evil, he and his posterity fell from the life-giving, intimate communion with God into the death of sin and enslavement to the devil (2 Timothy 2:24-26).

"The Fall affected every area of the human being, including the conscience, so man could no longer hear God's law clearly. As we have seen, The Fall totally affected the spirit. Adam originally had the ability to desire good (obedience to God) or evil (disobedience to God), and thus the ability to choose good or evil with his will. **Since The Fall, Adam, and every person born of a human male, only have the ability to desire evil, and thus only have the ability to choose evil.**

"We just read God's announcement of the true state of fallen man. Nick, please read again for us Romans 3:9-12, as well as Romans 8:5-9 and Romans 14:23b."

Nick read:

> What then? Are we better than they? Not at all; for we have already charged that both Jews and Greeks are all under sin;
>> as it is written,
>> "THERE IS NONE RIGHTEOUS, NOT EVEN ONE;
>>> THERE IS NONE WHO UNDERSTANDS,
>> "THERE IS NONE WHO SEEKS FOR GOD;
>>> ALL HAVE TURNED ASIDE, TOGETHER THEY HAVE BECOME USELESS;
>> "THERE IS NONE WHO DOES GOOD,
>> "THERE IS NOT EVEN ONE." (Romans 3:9-12)

> For those who are according to the flesh set their minds on the things of the flesh, but those who are according to the Spirit, the things of the Spirit.
> For the mind set on the flesh is death, but the mind set on the Spirit is life and peace,
> because the mind set on the flesh is hostile toward God; for it does not subject itself to the law of God, for it is not even able *to do so*,
> and those who are in the flesh cannot please God.
> However, you are not in the flesh but in the Spirit, if indeed the Spirit of God dwells in you. But if anyone does not have the Spirit of Christ, he does not belong to Him. (Romans 8:5-9)

> And whatever is not from faith is sin. (Romans 14:23b)

"Thank you, Nick," recognized Dave. "God declares in His holy Word: 'There is none who does good.' By 'good,' God means perfect obedience to His law—His perfect standard of righteousness. Anything less is a heinous rebellion against God's right to rule His own creation.

"'Those who are according to the flesh' are the unregenerate people—those who have not been born again. God says that anyone born of a human male who has not been born again is not able to obey the law of God, and is hostile toward Him. God declares that it is impossible for the unregenerate man to please Him, because everything he does is sin—he has no faith in God.

"The ungodly humanist would argue with the Bible, saying that man can do good. But his definition of 'good' is relative to man: giving to charity is 'good,' but robbing a bank is not 'good.'

"But God clearly declares that every person stealing this life to serve himself is living in utter rebellion. When any unregenerate person who was born of a human male is choosing which church to attend, or what to have for dinner, he is choosing between the wicked and the sinister. Everything he does is only evil continually. God, the Judge of the universe, defines 'good' as perfect obedience to His law. Since God is the Judge, He wins, and the ungodly humanist will be condemned."

"So, exactly how did The Fall affect man's free will?" asked Ed.

"Again," Dave reiterated, "since The Fall, Adam and every person born of a human male only have the ability to desire evil, and thus only have the ability to choose evil.

"Remember," Dave replied, "the ungodly humanist defines *free will* as the ability of man to choose good or evil; to choose God or not choose God; to choose Jesus as his Savior, or not choose Jesus as his Savior. The humanist avers that man is the determiner of his own fate, and his choice is king. This directly contradicts God's Word. God says that unregenerate man's will is enslaved to the devil, and every choice he makes is evil. The ungodly humanist proves this when he wickedly equates man's free will with autonomy."

"What is autonomy?" queried Nick.

"*Autonomy* means total independence—utterly exempt from external authority or controlling influence," Dave answered. "To be autonomous is to be utterly free. If you remember from our class on God's unique attributes, God and God alone is independent, or utterly free. As we have seen, man is utterly dependent upon God for his next breath, not to mention his very existence! God alone is autonomous.

"The ungodly humanist is simply replaying the original sin of Adam—inspired by Satan—to be like God Almighty. It is the humanist's cause to usurp for man what only belongs to the infinite Creator, and steal the glory that belongs to God alone. The sad part is that the modern church not only does not stand up for the truth of God, but rolls out the red carpet for this satanic teaching.

"God, however, defines *free will* as the ability of man to choose what he desires. The confusion rests in the use of the word 'free.' A better name for this concept would be '*able will*.' God gave man a *will*, which is the capacity to make choices. These are real choices for which the person is responsible, and these choices have real consequences. We can choose to eat, or not to eat, the chocolate mousse cheesecake, and our waistlines will show the consequences of our decisions.

"The will is called 'free,' or better yet 'able,' because the will that God gave to man always has the ability to choose what the mind desires. This is the key to understanding 'free will.' Whatever the man's mind desires, he is able to choose—he is not a robot. In fact, we must choose whatever we desire *the most* at the moment of any decision, or the will is not free. If there are no desires at all, then by definition there is no choice, and the will is not involved.

"The problem with fallen man is that the human nature—that which controls the whole being—is enslaved to Satan to do the devil's will. Therefore, as we have seen from the diagram, the spirit is dead to the things of God, and the mind is darkened. Since the nature, the spirit and the mind are imprisoned in sin by the devil, the desires which the mind generates are only evil and selfish continually.

"**The will is totally dependent on desires**. By definition, the will chooses what we desire the most at the moment of decision. Thus, if our desires are only evil continually, our will is still making choices. But, we are choosing between the bad and the worse; between the wicked and the sinister. So, the will is free, or able, to choose according to our desires, but all of our desires are only evil continually.

"Left to ourselves, we would never choose God. We would never choose Jesus as our Savior, because our sinful desires do not want God to rule in our lives. True believers did not just 'get smart' one day and decide for Jesus.

"Anyone who is truly born again is spiritually alive because God alone, in His love and mercy, put His Holy Spirit inside the person and freed his captured nature, mind and desires from the devil. Only then could that person see the heinous crimes he has committed against God and His holiness by stealing this life. Only then does God grant the sinner the holy desire and the ability to repent; and only then does God give him the faith to believe in Jesus Christ.

"Before he is made spiritually alive by God, unregenerate man can only choose evil because all of his desires are evil. After regeneration, the man is freed from slavery to the devil, and is given a new heart by God, so that the man actually desires to come to Jesus Christ in repentance and faith. Only after being born again by the Holy Spirit are we able, for the first time, to choose between good (obedience to God) and evil (disobedience to God). As the prophet Ezekiel portends God's very words:

> "And I will give them one heart, and put a new spirit within them. And I will take the heart of stone out of their flesh and give them a heart of flesh,
>
> that they may walk in My statutes and keep My ordinances and do them. Then they will be My people, and I shall be their God.
>
> "But as for those whose hearts go after their detestable things and abominations, I will bring their conduct down on their heads," declares the Lord GOD. (Ezekiel 11:19-21)

"Please understand this critical truth," Dave pleaded. "We make many choices with our wills: which brand of toothpaste to use, where to go to school, etc. **We make many choices with our wills, but salvation is not and has never been our choice**.

"Being rebellious from birth, our desires are only evil, and thus our wills choose only evil. We are blind to our depravity in our total rebellion against God. Choosing between brands of toothpaste, and any other choice we make as unbelievers, is a choice between the wicked and the sinister. Unregenerate people live every moment of life, regardless of what they are doing, in rebellion against and hatred toward God. Therefore, if anyone is going to be saved, salvation must be the choice of God and God alone!

"This is the biblical concept that humanism denies, and of which the modern church blindly rejects. The humanist claims man is free to do what he wishes, good or evil. Almighty God declares that man is born enslaved to the evil one; and should God set a man free, he is free to obey and serve his new Master, God.

"Why do almost eighty percent of modern American churchgoers believe that man is basically good? This is a direct rejection of the eternal words of the Lord Jesus Christ, who loudly and clearly proclaims: "'No one is good except God alone'" (Luke 18:19).

"Why do almost none of modern American churchgoers know God's standard for getting into heaven? The Lord Jesus openly declares it in the Bibles they supposedly read: "'Therefore you are to be perfect, as your heavenly Father is perfect'" (Matthew 5:48). The sad reasons are because the modern church has succumbed to the man-made traditions of unbelievers, and the true teachings of God's holy Word are virtually nowhere to be found."

"Wasn't the 20th century the bloodiest in history—with wars, crime, and the heinous murder of abortion killing more people than ever before?" asked Paul. "How could anyone think man is basically good—especially churchgoers, who should have the testimony of God's Word?"

"The evil pride of man simply refuses to believe that man is as wicked as God's Word declares," Dave replied. "Consider this next heresy widely taught in the church today. Chelsea, please read Pop Quiz question 8 for us."

"'God would never violate man's "free will" to accept or reject Christ, for that would be unloving,'" quoted Chelsea.

"Here, the ungodly humanist calls God's love into question if He does not give man the choice to determine his own destiny," Dave examined. "Could man possibly devise a more wicked position than to call into question the love of God, in order to justify man's own depraved desires to dethrone God by stealing this life? The answer to this quiz question is false because it is completely unbiblical. Ponder the following parable.

> Two neighbors, standing in a driveway leading to a very busy street, were talking as their sons played in the yard. The small boys decided to have a race, and they lined up by the house and took off running toward the street.
>
> Both fathers realized the danger as the boys ran toward the traffic. The one father said, "Let them go. Boys should be allowed to make their own choices. Interfering would be unloving."
>
> But the other father ran and grabbed his son just as the two went into the street, but he was unable to grab the other boy. His son kicked and screamed in his father's arms: "You made me lose the race!"
>
> But the other boy was hit by a car, and suffered injuries that would last the rest of his life.
>
> Which father truly loved his son?

"The father who saved his son, despite his son's rebellion, truly loved his son," Chelsea commented. "The other father, in claiming to be loving, caused his son to live in suffering."

"Exactly," Dave replied. "As rebellious humans born with a sinful nature, we hate God and run from Him. God, in His love and mercy, chose to save His true children from eternal torment which they truly deserved. God did not ask them if they wanted to be saved, for they, in their rebellion, would have shown their revulsion by kicking and screaming at Him.

"God—*without man's consent and against man's wishes*—sovereignly placed His Holy Spirit into the rebellious sons He had chosen to save, and gave them a new heart. God raised them from spiritual death, allowed them to see their own filthiness, and gave them the power to repent and believe in Christ Jesus their Savior. With their new hearts, God's true children now desire God and value Him above everything and anything.

"Jennifer, please read for us Ephesians 2:1-9."

Jennifer read:

> And you were dead in your trespasses and sins,
>
> in which you formerly walked according to the course of this world, according to the prince of the power of the air, of the spirit that is now working in the sons of disobedience.
>
> Among them we too all formerly lived in the lusts of our flesh, indulging the desires of the flesh and of the mind, and were by nature children of wrath, even as the rest.
>
> But God, being rich in mercy, because of His great love with which He loved us,
>
> even when we were dead in our transgressions, made us alive together with Christ (by grace you have been saved),
>
> and raised us up with Him, and seated us with Him in the heavenly *places* in Christ Jesus,
>
> so that in the ages to come He might show the surpassing riches of His grace in kindness toward us in Christ Jesus.
>
> For by grace you have been saved through faith; and that not of yourselves, *it is* the gift of God;
>
> not as a result of works, so that no one may boast. (Ephesians 2:1-9)

"Thank you, Jennifer," Dave said. "God's Word sums it up perfectly. Without God moving sovereignly to change a spiritually-dead person's heart, each and every person would die in his sins and be tormented forever. It is precisely God's love for those He chose to be His children that brings them eternal life in paradise.

"The ungodly humanist, who insists that God would be unloving not to give man the choice of salvation, shows his depraved hypocrisy. His heresy guarantees eternal suffering for man, for rebellious man would never choose Christ as his Savior.

"Man's mind is deceitful, depraved and enslaved to a sinful nature—and *that very mind* tells him he really is not all that bad! But God asserts quite the opposite—loudly and clearly—in His holy Word. Here are but a few scriptures on the effects of The Fall on man. Grant, would you read for us the next seven passages on the board?"

Grant read:

> "The heart is more deceitful than all else
>   And is desperately sick;
>   Who can understand it?" (Jeremiah 17:9)

> "This is the judgment, that the Light has come into the world, and men loved (desired) the darkness rather than the Light, for their deeds were evil." (John 3:19; *parenthesis mine*)

"For from within, out of the heart of men, proceed the evil thoughts, fornications, thefts, murders, adulteries,

deeds of coveting *and* wickedness, *as well as* deceit, sensuality, envy, slander, pride *and* foolishness.

"All these evil things proceed from within and defile the man."

(Mark 7:21-23)

For even though they knew God, they did not honor Him as God or give thanks, but they became futile in their speculations, and their foolish heart was darkened.

And just as they did not see fit to acknowledge God any longer, God gave them over to a depraved mind, to do those things which are not proper. (Romans 1:21,28)

Because the mind set on the flesh is hostile toward God; for it does not subject itself to the law of God, for it is not even able *to do so*.

(Romans 8:7)

Among them we too all formerly lived in the lusts of our flesh, indulging the desires of the flesh and of the mind, and were by nature children of wrath, even as the rest. (Ephesians 2:3)

To the pure, all things are pure; but to those who are defiled and unbelieving, nothing is pure, but both their mind and their conscience are defiled. (Titus 1:15)

"Need I say more?" Dave asked. "Scripture over and over again speaks for itself. And Scripture gives us the answers to Pop Quiz questions 9, 10 and 11. Would you read them again?"

"Okay," Nick assented. "Question 9: 'Man is born with a "free will," which means he has the ability to accept or reject Christ as his Savior.' Question 10: 'Predestination means that God, before creation, looked down the corridors of time to see who would choose Jesus as Savior, and God then chose those ones to be saved.' And Question 11: 'Salvation is a decision each person is responsible to make.'"

"As we have read in Scripture today," Dave recounted, "all of those statements are false.

"The humanistic meaning of 'free will' is rejected by Scripture, which repeatedly states that unregenerate man's desires are only evil continually, enslaved to the devil, and utterly unable to accept Christ as his Savior.

"God's true meaning of 'free will' is that man is able to choose what he desires. Since unregenerate man's desires are only evil, man is freely choosing between the wicked and the sinister. The only way a man desires God is after God has regenerated that man by His Holy

Spirit, setting him free from slavery to the devil, giving him the ability to repent, and giving him the faith to trust in Christ as his Savior.

"Predestination means that God, before creation, sovereignly chose those He desired for His family to be destined for salvation. If God chose after seeing what man would choose, it would have to be called *post*-destination, not *pre*destination.

"Scripture repudiates that heresy for two reasons. First, it blasphemes the omniscient and immutable God, requiring God to look and learn something before acting. Second, it makes salvation something that is earned by man, and not a gift of God's grace.

"Lastly, salvation is a decision that only God makes, as man is dead to God, unable and unwilling to desire Him."

Draw or Drag?

"If salvation is decided by God alone, why does Jesus say that the Father 'draws' us?" asked Ed. "It sounds as if Jesus is saying that God woos us, enticing us to change our minds about Him, and accept Jesus as our Savior."

"Superb question, Ed," Dave commended. "Recall that God's Word is only God's originally intended meaning of His words, not our assumptions of their meanings. Remember when we first took the Pop Quiz, we discussed how the meaning of the word 'bad' has changed from its original intention to a modern teenager's use, which is the exact opposite?

"Indeed, you have correctly presented the modern church's take on the Lord Jesus' words. But, is the modern church's assumption correct? Let's obey God and diligently study His Word. Ed, would you read for us John 6:44 please."

Ed read: "'"No one can come to Me unless the Father who sent Me draws him; and I will raise him up on the last day"' (John 6:44)."

"Thank you, Ed," Dave said. "Ed has related modern teaching that we have all heard. The idea is that God does not violate our wills in our rebellion against Christ. Instead, God 'woos' us to come to Christ, much like a mother woos her stubborn child into going along with her plans. Is this the originally intended meaning of God's Word?

"Let's read the scriptures where the same Greek verb *helko* is used in order to determine the reason God would use it here in John 6:44. When studying the Bible to find God's originally intended meaning, it is always a good idea to locate all of the uses of a term, getting the whole counsel of God. I will write the English translation of the Greek verb in bold on the board."

The class read:

"No one can come to Me unless the Father who sent Me **draws** him; and I will raise him up on the last day." (John 6:44; *emphasis mine*)

And He said to them, "Cast the net on the right-hand side of the boat and you will find *a catch*." So they cast, and then they were not able **to haul** it in because of the great number of fish.

Simon Peter went up, and **drew** the net to land, full of large fish, a hundred and fifty-three; and although there were so many, the net was not torn. (John 21:5,6,11; emphases mine)

> Simon Peter then, having a sword, **drew** it and struck the high priest's slave, and cut off his right ear; and the slave's name was Malchus.
>
> > (John 18:10; *emphasis mine*)

> So Jesus said to them, "Children, you do not have any fish, do you?" They answered Him, "No."
>
> It happened that as we were going to the place of prayer, a slave-girl having a spirit of divination met us, who was bringing her masters much profit by fortune-telling.
>
> Following after Paul and us, she kept crying out, saying, "These men are bond-servants of the Most High God, who are proclaiming to you the way of salvation."
>
> She continued doing this for many days. But Paul was greatly annoyed, and turned and said to the spirit, "I command you in the name of Jesus Christ to come out of her!" And it came out at that very moment.
>
> But when her masters saw that their hope of profit was gone, they seized Paul and Silas and **dragged** them into the market place before the authorities. (Acts 16:16-19; *emphasis mine*)

> When the seven days were almost over, the Jews from Asia, upon seeing him in the temple, *began* to stir up all the crowd and laid hands on him,
>
> crying out, "Men of Israel, come to our aid! This is the man who preaches to all men everywhere against our people and the Law and this place; and besides he has even brought Greeks into the temple and has defiled this holy place."
>
> Then all the city was provoked, and the people rushed together, and taking hold of Paul they **dragged** him out of the temple, and immediately the doors were shut. (Acts 21:27,28,30; *emphasis mine*)

> Listen, my beloved brethren: did not God choose the poor of this world *to be* rich in faith and heirs of the kingdom which He promised to those who love Him?
>
> But you have dishonored the poor man. Is it not the rich who oppress you and personally **drag** you into court? (James 2:5,6; *emphasis mine*)

"God's many uses of the same Greek term demonstrate a clear indication of God's intended meaning," Dave counseled. "Peter yanks his sword from its sheath to attack the approaching Jews. The disciples were unable to drag the net full of fish to shore until Peter returned to help them pull it.

"When the masters of the demon-possessed slave-girl saw the Apostle Paul cast the demon out, they attacked him and Silas as an irate mob, dragging them to the authorities. The Asian Jews despised Paul and caused another mob scene, dragging Paul out of the Temple in Jerusalem.

"The Apostle James decries discriminating on the basis of wealth or appearance, observing that it is 'the rich who...drag you into court.' So, having the whole counsel of God, what can we infer about God's originally intended meaning of the Greek term *helko*?"

"Well," Anna replied, "the meaning definitely conveys dragging, requiring force against something or someone that is greatly resisting the force."

"Excellent synopsis, Anna," Dave applauded. "Lexicons employing the finest scholars on early Greek literature agree on the use of this verb. **Helko** involves the use of force to move an object that cannot move itself, or to affect a person against that person's will. God's originally intended meaning of John 6:44 is: '"No one can come to Me unless the Father who sent Me **drags him against his will**; and I will raise him up on the last day."' God seizes a rebellious sinner and gives him a new heart with the Holy Spirit, and then with that new heart the man—for the first time—desires the things of God."

"Then, why do the translators use the word 'draw' in that passage?" asked Nick.

"Some Greek scholars have defended that translation, citing secular Greek literature. They say these works use *helko* for 'drawing' water from a well. Even the Bible uses *helko* when Peter 'draws' his sword from its sheath.

"The translation as 'draw' is not wrong, as long as God's original intent is kept. One may 'draw' water from a well, but according to physics, the water's state is to remain at rest in the well. A force greater than gravity must be thrust upon the water, and the water must then be dragged from its place of rest toward the person wielding the force. A sword may be 'drawn' from its sheath, but a force must be exerted upon the sword to rip it from its resting place.

"The error in modern church teaching comes when God's original meaning of the word 'draw' is changed to convey 'wooing.' God never brought this idea into His Word. Man sinfully altered God's meaning to promote man-made tradition, which became the exact opposite of God's truth.

"No man has the right to bring his own interpretation to God's holy Word. The Bible is God's Word, not man's word. God's Word is eternal and perfect, and it does not change according to man's desires or circumstances. God states exactly what He means, and man is commanded by God to study in order to know God's originally intended meaning of His Word.

"So, to answer your question, Ed," Dave concluded, "the Lord Jesus does say: '"No one can come to Me unless the Father who sent Me **draws** him."' But, Christ's meaning is that the Father must wield a force upon a rebellious sinner, against the man's will, in order to change the sinner's heart and bring him to salvation in Christ. This original intent of God lines up with the myriad of passages we have read that emphatically deny that man's will plays an active role in salvation.

"Thus, the answer to Pop Quiz question 12, 'No one can come to Jesus unless the Father draws, or woos, him,' is false. God never intended the false idea of 'wooing' to be part of His original meaning in His Word.

"We've covered a lot of ground today, so let's do a quick review of what we have learned.

"The goal of our Bible study—and our Christian lives—is to know God intimately, and enjoy Him forever as our Father.

"An unregenerate man is a person who has not been born again. He is spiritually dead because of the 'original sin' of Adam imputed, or credited, to his account.

"Adam and Eve disobeyed God's commandment, and, true to God's warning, that day they died.

"Their disobedience terminated the intimate relationship that they had with their Creator—the Source of Life—resulting in spiritual death.

"'Dead' means utterly devoid of life.

"A physically-dead person cannot do anything involving the physical world. He cannot think, breath, choose, not choose, accept, receive...anything! He is dead.

"A spiritually-dead person can do nothing towards fixing the terminated relationship with God his Creator. He, the spiritual corpse, is dead to the only Source of Life.

"A spiritually-dead sinner cannot desire God, seek God, reconcile with God, reach out for God, accept God or choose God. He is dead to God.

"The term 'spiritually dead' does not imply that an unregenerate man has no spirit, but that a man has no desire for God to rule the life he lives.

"The spirit of an unregenerate man is dead to the things of God, and desires only evil continually—even when giving to charity or going to church. Everything he does is evil, because 'whatever is not from faith is sin' (Romans 14:23).

"The 'Silliest Statement of the Century' goes to: 'A sinner is never "so dead" that he cannot accept Jesus Christ as his personal Savior.'

"Being somewhat dead is like being somewhat pregnant! You are either dead or you are not!

"Any person born of a human male is born a spiritually-dead sinner—a spiritual corpse—and only a miraculous intervention from God Himself could bring him to spiritual life.

"The Lord Jesus really hates the sin of setting aside the Word of God in favor of man-made tradition—and condemned the Pharisees for committing this hypocritical crime against God.

"If a truth can be proven in Scripture by the continuous testimony throughout the different books of the Bible, then the true disciple of Christ has a responsibility to abandon man-made tradition and hold to God's Word.

"If a person abandons God's Word in favor of man-made tradition, he is a hypocrite—a phony, and the lowest of unbelievers.

"The Apostle Jude warned us that unbelievers crept into the church in the first century, and the same is true throughout history.

"There is the visible church—everyone you see in the pulpits and pews—made up of true believers and unbelievers.

"But God's true church is the universal, invisible church made up only of all true believers—those that have the Holy Spirit in them, and who have truly been born again.

"A true believer can be absolutely certain that he himself is a true child of God, because God gives him that knowledge through the Holy Spirit. Between God and His child, salvation is assured.

"Horizontally, among men, we can never be absolutely certain that another person is a true believer. We can only judge by the fruit the Holy Spirit produces, or the lack thereof.

"Down through the history of the visible church, unbelievers became leaders with power to create and enforce doctrine. Since they did not have the Holy Spirit, their decisions could only result in man-made traditions, just like the Pharisees in first-century Judaism whom Jesus condemned as hypocrites.

"In the 1800s, humanism became the dominant system of belief in the world among unbelievers, many of whom by then ran the churches.

"Humanism is the belief system emphasizing human potential and fulfillment using logical reasoning, positive thinking, and science in the natural world—rejecting man's dependence upon God, and often even denying the existence of God.

"Humanism is the ultimate expression of human sinful pride—a heinous, arrogant rejection of God, inspired by the devil himself—and it has existed since Adam first sinned.

"In the nineteenth and twentieth centuries, humanism invaded the Christian churches, and made huge in-roads in replacing God's Word with man-made traditions.

"One of the most effective ways to get people to believe lies is to repeat them over and over—in all forms of media—for generations. Since they have heard the lies repeated so often, they reason that they must be true.

"The only way to discern if a statement is truth or a lie is to check it against God's holy Word—the only standard of truth we have in this universe.

"Teaching that glorifies man is humanism.

"Teaching from God's Word that glorifies God is true.

"In the process of trying to reduce God's Word to small bites for wider consumption, religious leaders and teachers eliminated crucial but 'offensive' essentials like 'repentance,' and redefined critical terms like 'belief in Christ.'

"The Lord Jesus says to abide in Him—stay on the Lap of God—and He will make us fruitful. Running around doing our wills in God's Name will only result in drying up, for apart from Christ we can accomplish nothing!

"Sadly, today's church is a bad mixture of humanistic man-made traditions with snippets of God's holy Word thrown in to sound good.

"Salvation, according to God's Word, is not like a man on his death bed, who must accept the medicine of the gospel. Nor is salvation like a man drowning, who must grab hold of God's life preserver of the gospel.

"Salvation is God alone placing His Holy Spirit inside of a corpse born dead in sin and raising it to life.

"Unregenerate man is not a free, moral agent. Unregenerate man is an enslaved, immoral spiritual corpse!

"Many true believers, and all unbelievers, simply do not know, or refuse to accept, what God says in His holy Word about man and his sinful condition.

"They claim to believe the Bible, yet they reject what the Bible teaches. Then they commit the heinous crime of holding to humanistic tradition instead of bowing to God's holy Word, which cannot lie.

"Correct understanding of the teaching of the Bible concerning man and his relationship to God stands on the correct answer to The Pivotal Question: 'Whose choice is salvation—man's or God's?'

"God declares that, although He placed within man the knowledge that He exists, unregenerate man actively suppresses that knowledge in order to continue in his sin. The sinner has resolved, in his rebellion, to run away from God as fast as his legs can carry him.

"Holy Scripture declares that unregenerate man is held captive by the devil, and can only do Satan's will, which is only evil continuously.

"Satan has also blinded man's mind so that he cannot see the truth of God's gospel. The sinner cannot understand God's truth, because his blinded mind cannot accept God's truth—it is even foolishness to him!

"Unless God grants 'repentance leading to the knowledge of the truth,' unregenerate man remains ensnared in sin.

"Romans 3:11 states that 'none seeks for God.' Many people want God's benefits—blessings, eternal paradise, escape from hell—but not one unregenerate soul seeks God Himself to rule over this life.

"Romans 3:12 says that 'there is none who does good.' Giving to charity or going to church may be 'good' in man's eyes, but in God's eyes, they are heinous crimes of rebellion by the unregenerate.

"If any thought or action is not preceded by being born again through faith in Jesus Christ, 'whatever is not from faith is sin' (Romans 14:23).

"Unbelievers have many reasons for going to church. Though sinners are dead in sin, they do know that there is a spiritual vacuum in their hearts that needs filling.

"Some people go to church to assuage their guilt. Some think that by going, God is obligated to let them into heaven. Some go simply by habit, and others to make business or social contacts.

"Only a truly born-again believer goes to church to worship his Master, Almighty God—by far and wide the most important reason for being there.

"It is impossible for man to choose salvation in God, because man is unable to do so. Unregenerate man does not desire to choose God, and indeed he cannot, because he is spiritually dead in sin.

"God absolutely commands what is impossible for man to do. And that command is to be as perfect as God is perfect.

"There are only two ways to be as perfect as God is perfect. One is to be God Himself, whom we are not! The second is if God bestows the gift of His perfection upon a man by crediting that person's account with the perfect life of God the Son, Jesus Christ!

"The entire Bible declares how God saves sinners. God gave us the record of the Old Testament as a physical example of events that occur in the spiritual realm.

"The bones in Ezekiel's prophecy were long dead—they did not choose to live again. God, by His sovereign choice, chose to make this great army alive again. God and God alone put flesh unto, and life into, these dead, dry bones.

"Likewise, God and God alone takes a spiritually-dead sinner and puts His Holy Spirit into him so that he becomes spiritually alive.

"The sinner only then realizes that he is guilty of offending the holiness of his Creator with every breath he breathes, every thought he thinks, and every act he does.

"Only the indwelling Holy Spirit frees the sinner from enslavement to the devil, gives the sinner the power to repent, and gives him the faith to believe in Christ's perfect work for salvation.

"The only correct answer to The Pivotal Question is that the choice of salvation is God's and God's alone.

"The humanistic preacher's idea that man's eternal destiny is determined by man's choice is a lie. This falsehood is a man-made, man-glorifying tradition that God's holy Word specifically rejects.

"The humanistic evangelist's plea for man to choose God is also a lie. God's life-giving medicine is not given to a dying man, but it is given to a corpse.

"God alone places His Holy Spirit in spiritually-dead corpses—those whom He has already chosen to be in His family from before the foundation of the world.

"Predestination means that God chose before creation the spiritually-dead sinners He would make spiritually alive, by His Holy Spirit, in order to become members of His family.

"These ones chosen by God for salvation are called the elect. Scripture calls God's chosen ones the elect because God elected them to salvation, not because they elected to be saved.

"God simply chose sovereignly, according to His own good pleasure and purpose, and for no other reasons.

"God could not have made His choice based upon what He foresaw in man—for there is nothing good to see in spiritually-dead sinners. We are all born dead in sin, and live filthy lives of rebellion against God (Ephesians 2:3).

"If God chose us instead of our neighbors—based upon something good in us, or that we would choose Jesus as our Savior—then we earned salvation.

"If we earned salvation by our goodness or good choices, then, by definition, it cannot be by grace. But God's Word declares that salvation is by grace, and based on nothing in ourselves.

"It is blasphemy to say that God looks down the corridors of time and makes choices according to what He learns. This teaching is heresy, for it maintains that God is not omniscient and not immutable.

"If God must look into the future to see what you would choose, then He does not eternally know this action, and He learns something. If God learns anything, He changes in His character—because he then would not longer be omniscient—and then would not be immutable.

"The meaning of foreknowledge cannot be that God knows about individuals and what they would do in the future. Though God does know these things, this is not the meaning of this term.

"God's foreknowledge is the special love that God eternally has only for His children—'those who are called according to His purpose.'

"The ungodly humanist defines free will as man having the ability to choose God or not choose God—to choose Jesus as his Savior or not choose Jesus. The ungodly humanist's definition glorifies man as the final determiner of his fate.

"The ungodly humanist wickedly errs when he equates man's free will with autonomy.

"Autonomy means total independence—utterly exempt from external authority or controlling influence. To be autonomous is to be utterly free. God alone is autonomous.

"Man, however, is utterly dependent upon God for his next breath, not to mention his very existence!

"One must always clarify definitions of theological terms like 'free will,' because cultists and unbelievers like using the same terms as Christians, but apply to them different and heretical meanings.

"The true believer defines free will as the ability of man to choose what he desires.

"Man is a being with a nature that God has created explicitly for humans, and the nature controls the entire being.

"God gave humans a nature with two major parts: a soul, which is immaterial, and a body, which is material, or physical.

"The soul is controlled by the spirit, which is why the two terms are often interchangeable in God's Word.

"The spirit of man, often symbolically called 'the heart' in Scripture, can be dead to the things of God, or made alive to God by the regeneration of the Holy Spirit.

"The human spirit has two parts—the mind and the conscience.

"The mind sends and receives information to and from the body, as well as generating—from the dictation of the human nature—desires that control the will and the emotions.

"Regardless of whether the spirit has or has not been regenerated, God placed the conscience in man's spirit to perform two important functions: first, to inform the man that God exists; and second, to inform the man of God's standard of righteousness, which requires that God will judge him for his thoughts and actions that fail to meet His standard.

"When God first made man, He made Adam good and upright, but with the ability to do good or evil—the ability to obey God's law and serve Him, or disobey God's law and serve himself.

"God easily communicated His law to Adam through his conscience, because Adam's conscience was not mired in a sinful nature.

"Once Adam chose evil, he and his posterity fell from the life-giving, intimate communion with God into the death of sin and enslavement to the devil.

"The Fall affected every area of the human being, including the conscience, so man could no longer hear God's law clearly.

"The Fall totally affected the spirit. Adam originally had the ability to desire good (obedience to God) or evil (disobedience to God), and thus the ability to choose good or evil with his will.

"Since The Fall, Adam, and every person born of a human male, only have the ability to desire evil, and thus only have the ability to choose evil.

"A better name for the concept of 'free will' would be 'able will.'

"God gave man a will, which is the capacity to make choices. These are real choices for which the person is responsible, and these choices have real consequences.

"The reason why the will is called 'free,' or better yet, 'able,' is that the will that God gave to man always has the ability to choose what the mind desires. This is the key to understanding free will.

"Whatever the man's mind desires, he is able to choose—he is not a robot.

"We must choose whatever we desire the most at the moment of any choice, or the will is not free.

"If there are no desires at all, then by definition there is no choice, and the will is not involved.

"The problem with fallen man is that the human nature—that which controls the whole being—is enslaved to Satan to do the devil's will.

"The spirit is dead to the things of God, and the mind is darkened. Since the nature and the spirit and the mind are imprisoned in sin, the desires which the mind generates are only evil and selfish continually.

"The will is totally dependent on desires. By definition, the will chooses what we desire the most at the moment of choice.

"If our desires are only evil continually, the will is choosing between the bad and the worse—between the wicked and the sinister.

"So, the will is free, or able, to choose according to our desires, but all of our desires are only evil continually.

"Left to ourselves, we would never choose God—we would never choose Jesus as our Savior—because our sinful desires do not want God to rule in our lives.

"True believers did not just 'get smart' one day, and decide for Jesus.

"Anyone who is truly born again is spiritually alive because God alone, in His love and mercy, put His Holy Spirit inside the person and freed his captured nature, mind and desires from the devil.

"Only then could that person see the heinous crimes he has committed against God and His holiness.

"Only then does God grant him the ability and desire to repent; and only then does God give him the faith to believe in Jesus Christ.

"In conclusion, we make many choices with our wills, but salvation is not and has never been our choice. Salvation is the choice of God and God alone!

"The Lord Jesus does say: "'No one can come to Me unless the Father who sent Me draws him.'" Christ's meaning is that the Father must wield a force upon a rebellious sinner, against the man's will, in order to change the sinner's heart and bring him to salvation in Christ.

"No man has the right to bring his own interpretation to God's holy Word. The Bible is God's Word, not man's word. God's Word is eternal and perfect, and it does not change according to man's desires or circumstances. God states exactly what He means, and man is commanded by God to study in order to know God's originally intended meaning of His Word.

"The Bible emphatically declares that before he is made spiritually alive by God, unregenerate man can only choose evil because all of his desires are evil.

"After regeneration, the man is freed from slavery to the devil, and is given a new heart by God, so that he desires to come to Jesus Christ in repentance and faith. As a born-again

Christian, we are able for the first time to choose between good (obedience to God) and evil (disobedience to God)," Dave finished.

"Praise God for freeing us from slavery to the devil!" Nick exclaimed. "I hope I always love God enough to choose to obey Him!"

"Amen!" Dave assented. "Nick, would you like to close our Bible study class with prayer?"

"I would love to!" Nick replied. "I'm going home this week for Thanksgiving break, as most of you guys are also going to see your families. So, the next time I see you all will be here next Sunday. I'd like to pray for safety in traveling, and that God would bless us to be witnesses of His love to our families.

"Dear heavenly Father, we love You and praise You for choosing us to be in Your family. Thank You for breaking the chains of the devil and setting us free in Your Son, Jesus Christ. Continue to fill us with Your Holy Spirit, and give us Your love to love You first and foremost, so that we may choose to obey You always.

"Fill us with Your love, so that we may show You to our families at Thanksgiving. Bring salvation to those who do not know You, and draw those who are Your children into a closer relationship with Yourself. Keep us safe in our travels, and bring us back to learn more of You, so we may love You more and more!

"Thank You for our teacher, Dave, and bless him with knowledge of Your ways, and the wisdom to teach them to us. In Jesus' holy Name we pray, amen!"

"Amen!" the class resounded.

"So, I won't see you Tuesday, but we'll come together here next Sunday?" Dave asked.

"Right!" Nick clarified. "I'll stop by the dorm room next Sunday morning as usual. Now let's go worship our awesome Father together in the service!"

"Yes!" Dave agreed. "Let's go praise God!"

10

God Saves Sinners!

"Welcome back!" Dave called over the din of excited students who have just returned from Thanksgiving break. The College & Career Bible study quickly came to order. "Ed, would you open our study in prayer?"

"Dear heavenly Father, thank You so much for the great Thanksgiving we had with family and friends. Thank You for bringing us back safely to study Your holy Word. Seeing some family members and friends that do not know You has given us a deeper appreciation of Your Son Jesus, and the salvation He secured for us on the cross.

"Fill us now with Your precious Holy Spirit, and help us to understand Your ways, so that we may love You more intimately, and enjoy You as our Father. Fill our teacher Dave with Your Holy Spirit, and use him mightily to explain Your Word. In Jesus' Name we pray, amen!"

"Thank you, Ed," Dave responded. "Our Bible study began with that very goal of knowing God intimately and enjoying Him forever as our Father. We spent several weeks studying God as He defines Himself in His Word, and contrasting His truth with man-made tradition.

"Last week we began studying man and his relationship to God. We found that God created His universe for the expressed purpose of bringing all honor and glory to God the Son, Jesus Christ. To guarantee Christ's supremacy, God, in His infinite wisdom, subjected His entire creation to slavery to evil. All glory would then go to Christ Jesus as the only way out of that slavery.

"God made man upright, with the ability to obey or not obey his Creator. But man chose to sin against God, fulfilling God's eternal plan to create the need for a Savior. Instead of humbly submitting to his Creator, man desired to be as God, just as man does today. As a result, man died spiritually. The Fall affected every part of man's being. Also, every being that would be conceived by a human male would be born with a nature enslaved to sin.

"Thus, unregenerate man is dead to God, and cannot choose God because he never desires God. The sinner runs away from God, continuing in his rebellion against his holy Creator, doing only evil continually. God, the Creator and rightful owner of all life, gave life to man for man to glorify and serve God with it. But, man has stolen this life to serve himself. Thus, the sinner could never live with God in His paradise, because the standard for going to heaven is to be as perfect as God is perfect.

"God, in His great mercy and love, sovereignly chose a remnant of these heinous criminals to save, and to bring into His family. As His plan for creation eternally existed in His mind, God chose His 'elect' before the foundation of the world. God did not choose certain people because of any good in them, or anything they would do. God ordained that everyone born of a human male would be utterly sinful and spiritually dead, doing only evil continuously.

"God sovereignly predestines the ones He wants to be in His family, making His choice based upon His own will and good pleasure. God owns everything in His creation, and can do whatever He desires with what is His own.

"The only reason the elect come to Christ for salvation is that God alone placed His Holy Spirit in them to raise them from spiritual death, and to release them from enslavement to the devil. Only then does a sinner realize he has offended the holiness of his Creator. God then grants him the desire to come to Him and the ability to repent. God then gives him His gift of faith, the power to trust in Christ and His perfect work for salvation," Dave concluded.

Federal Representation

"I know we've read scriptures that say that Adam's original sin is credited to everyone born from him through a human male," Matt interjected. "But why am *I* credited with *Adam's* sin? Why does Adam have to represent me before God? I don't think that is fair."

"Great questions, Matt," Dave responded. "You've brought up two extremely important issues: federal representation and fairness. I'll address them one at a time.

"Most definitely, as a Christian, you want Adam to be the representative, or federal head, of the human race. Yes, he fell; and yes, his imputed sin causes everyone born of a human male to be born with a sinful nature. But, if you want God's system of representation eliminated, then Christ would not be your representative before God—and you really do not want that to happen! Let's read the passages in God's holy Word regarding the federal representation of Adam for his people, and Christ for His people."

The class read:

> But now Christ has been raised from the dead, the first fruits of those who are asleep.
>
> For since by a man *came* death, by a man also *came* the resurrection of the dead.
>
> For as in Adam all die, so also in Christ all will be made alive.
>
> So also it is written, "The first MAN, Adam, BECAME A LIVING SOUL."
>
> The last Adam *became* a life-giving spirit. (1 Corinthians 15:20-22,45)

Therefore, just as through one man sin entered into the world, and death through sin, and so death spread to all men, because all sinned—

For if by the transgression of the one, death reigned through the one, much more those who receive the abundance of grace and of the gift of righteousness will reign in life through the One, Jesus Christ.

So then as through one transgression there resulted condemnation to all men, even so through one act of righteousness there resulted justification of life to all men. (Romans 5:12,17,18)

For the anxious longing of the creation waits eagerly for the revealing of the sons of God.

For the creation was subjected to futility, not willingly, but because of Him who subjected it, in hope

that the creation itself also will be set free from its slavery to corruption into the freedom of the glory of the children of God.

For we know that the whole creation groans and suffers the pains of childbirth together until now. (Romans 8:19-22)

"For just as the Father raises the dead and gives them life, even so the Son also gives life to whom He wishes.

"For not even the Father judges anyone, but He has given all judgment to the Son,

so that all will honor the Son even as they honor the Father. He who does not honor the Son does not honor the Father who sent Him."

(John 5:21-23)

"We still have God's decree that to live in heaven one must be as perfect as God is perfect (Matthew 5:48)," Dave warned. "As finite, created beings, we can never be as perfect as God is perfect. God subjected all of creation to slavery to evil—utter 'futility'—and every person born from a human male is conceived with a sinful nature. But God's awesome, eternal plan, which includes federal representation, succeeds in every one of its goals!

"Remember, God's primary reason for creation is to bring total honor and glory to God! By subjecting all of creation to slavery to the devil, Christ becomes the only salvation from this evil condition! Thus, God the Son Jesus Christ—the Supreme Judge and the only Savior of the universe—gets all of the honor and glory as the only way out of that slavery!

"All persons represented by Adam—all those born of a human male—are born dead in sin and rebel against God continuously. Unless they are born again by the Spirit of God, they will be judged by the Supreme Judge of the universe for being imperfect, and will perish in hell for their sins.

"All persons represented by Christ—all those sinners whom God has chosen to save and bring into His family—have been born again, or will be born again during this life, by the work of the Holy Spirit. Christ is their Savior, who took the wrath of God for their sins on the cross, and credited to their accounts His perfect life. Since Christ is God, they are then as perfect as God is perfect!

"So, as the Apostle Paul declares, all men 'in Adam' die in their sins and suffer the perfectly just, eternal wrath of God. All men 'in Christ' are saved from the wrath of God, and live in heaven with Him for eternity! Your representative before God makes all the difference for eternity!" Dave concluded.

Justice vs. Fairness

"Okay, I want representation," Matt assented, "because salvation only comes by being in Christ. But it still does not seem fair that God doesn't save everybody."

"Oh, it most definitely is *not* fair," Dave answered to the surprise of most of the students. **"God never said He was fair.** God says that He is just. And the two can be incompatible."

"I thought justice and fairness were the same," Chelsea said. "What's the difference?"

"Justice and fairness are not the same," Dave replied. "They can co-exist in some situations but not in others. The best way to demonstrate this is to examine the condition of sinful man."

Dave turned and drew a diagram on the chalkboard.

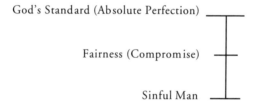

"Sinful man," explained Dave, "would say to God: 'God, You are way up there and I am way down here. Your standard is absolute perfection, and I am a sinner. Let's be fair about this, and meet in the middle. You lower Your standard, and I'll try harder to do better and reach it.'

"God replies from His holy Word: 'I am perfectly just, and will never compromise My holy standard for anyone or anything. Meet it or pay the consequences. You are a sinner, and because you are not represented by My Son, everything you do, think and say is an abomination to Me and My holiness. Therefore, you can never rise above your depth of depravity by your own efforts, no matter how hard you try!'

"That is the difference between justice and fairness. *Justice* means absolute adherence to a standard, and punishment that perfectly 'fits the crime' for failure to do so. Almighty God is eternally perfect and perfectly just, and His standard is to be as perfect as He is perfect.

"*Fairness* can mean treating everything the same, or it can mean compromising. God never compromises the attributes of His holy character. In doing so, He would sin against Himself, and that is impossible for an eternally perfect, holy Being.

"Sometimes God is fair in treating everyone the same because it aligns with His justice.

Paul, please read Romans 3:19 and 20, and Acts 10:34 and 35."

Paul read:

> Now we know that whatever the Law says, it speaks to those who are under the Law, so that every mouth may be closed and all the world may become accountable to God;
>
> because by the works of the Law no flesh will be justified in His sight; for through the Law *comes* the knowledge of sin. (Romans 3:19,20)

> Opening his mouth, Peter said:
>
> "I most certainly understand *now* that God is not one to show partiality, but in every nation the man who fears Him and does what is right is welcome to Him." (Acts 10:34,35)

"Thank you, Paul," recognized Dave. "The entire world is under the law of God, and is accountable to the Supreme Judge of the universe for not keeping God's law perfectly. In this respect, God is fair in treating every person the same. Also, God shows no partiality to ethnic origin or nationality with regards to whom He chooses to be in His family. There will be people of every tongue, tribe and nation represented in the kingdom of God (Revelation 5:9). In these cases, God can be said to be fair.

"But God never said He must be fair at all times. **Fairness is not one of God's eternal attributes**. Consider the people in the Bible. God made Abraham and Job very wealthy men in their times. Does He bestow wealth on all of His children? God enabled Moses to see a portion of His glory. Does He allow that to everyone? God enabled the prophets Isaiah, Ezekiel, Daniel and the Apostle Paul to see a vision of God's throne in heaven. Do all Christians get to see this?

"Obviously, no. If God were eternally and perfectly fair, everyone would have to be made physically the same and have the same experiences. But this is definitely not the case. God grants some to have perfect eyesight, where I must wear eyeglasses. God makes some extremely intelligent, where I must struggle to understand complex ideas. Some people have even walked on the moon!

"Get the idea? Rarely is God fair, except when fairness in treating everyone the same just happens to coincide with His perfect justice. God is always perfectly just, which means absolute adherence to His standard. Again, God's standard for going to heaven is to be as perfect as God is perfect. Meet it or pay the consequences.

Why Does God Not Save Everyone?

"Many people mistakenly think that if God saves one person, He should save all people. Since no one is perfect, all people are on the same level, and should be treated the same in order to be fair. But the answer to Pop Quiz question 13 is false. God is not always fair, and never claimed to be always fair. God says He is eternally just.

"God is under absolutely no obligation to save anyone! The question is not, 'why does God not save everyone?' but, 'why should God save anyone at all?' For the Scripture makes it very clear that everyone born of a human male is born with a rebellious, sinful nature that desires only selfish evil continuously. Why would God want any of us?

"But God definitely gives us a specific reason why He chooses not to save everyone. Jennifer, please read for us the next four scriptures on the board."

Jennifer read:

> But God, being rich in mercy, because of His great love with which He loved us,
>
> even when we were dead in our transgressions, made us alive together with Christ (by grace you have been saved),
>
> and raised us up with Him, and seated us with Him in the heavenly *places* in Christ Jesus,
>
> so that in the ages to come He might show the surpassing riches of His grace in kindness toward us in Christ Jesus. (Ephesians 2:4-7)

> "Enter through the narrow gate; for the gate is wide and the way is broad that leads to destruction, and there are many who enter through it.
>
> "For the gate is small and the way is narrow that leads to life, and there are few who find it." (Matthew 7:13,14)

> The LORD has made everything for its own purpose,
>> Even the wicked for the day of evil. (Proverbs 16:4)

> Or does not the potter have a right over the clay, to make from the same lump one vessel for honorable use and another for common use?
>
> What if God, although willing to demonstrate His wrath and to make His power known, endured with much patience vessels of wrath prepared for destruction?
>
> And *He did so* to make known the riches of His glory upon vessels of mercy, which He prepared beforehand for glory,
>
> *even* us, whom He also called, not from among Jews only, but also from among Gentiles. (Romans 9:21-24)

"Thank you, Jennifer," acknowledged Dave. "Honoring and glorifying God the Son, Jesus Christ, was God's primary reason for creation. **The infinite worth of the sacrifice of Christ**—His leaving His glorious throne, taking on the limits of human flesh, being crucified and dying at the hands of those He created, and bearing the wrath of God for the sins of His elect—**is *never* to be even slightly dishonored**.

"If everyone received salvation automatically, Christ's sacrifice would be cheapened in the eyes of man, eventually having little or no value. Look at the difference between a diamond and gravel. One can find gravel almost anywhere, and no one cares if you have even a large quantity of these stones. Its value is almost non-existent—practically worthless.

"But one perfect, white diamond will cost tens of thousands of dollars. Why is there a difference? Everyone can find gravel, but very few can find that perfect, white diamond, making it extremely precious in the eyes of man.

"To absolutely insure the infinite worth of Christ's precious sacrifice, God chose to bestow His awesome saving benefits upon a very few. These few children will then see the incredible gift of eternal life as extremely precious, never taking it for granted. They will always highly esteem Christ, along with His perfect work and sacrifice, far more than the finest diamond in the universe! The glory of God the Son is God's primary reason for saving only the few.

"The Lord Jesus just verified that only the few will be saved. God says that He chose to save some from His wrath so that He will be totally glorified when these elect see 'the surpassing riches of His grace in kindness...in Christ Jesus' (Ephesians 2:7).

"God says that another reason He chose not to save the vast majority was to use them to demonstrate His power and wrath against sin. The elect would see the masses' descent into depravity, knowing the eternal sentence of torment coming upon them. God's few chosen children would then be extremely grateful for being rescued from the eternal torture which they truly deserved. Thus, Christ's precious sacrifice would always be highly honored, and God would be totally glorified."

"Are you saying that God predestined people to go to hell?" Nick asked.

"What does God say in His holy Word?" Dave responded. "God created and sustains everything, and therefore everything belongs to Him to do with as He pleases. God is The Potter (Romans 9:21). The Potter molds the clay for *His* purposes, not for the clay's benefit.

"In giving a very clear answer to this question, the Apostle Paul states that from the very same clay God makes vessels for His wrath and vessels for His salvation. God did this for His glory, that He would be highly honored when the vessels of salvation realize the eternal torment from which they were spared.

"**God's primary purpose for creation is not the happiness and comfort of man, or man's salvation, or for blessing man's life**. The depraved, selfish, sinful mind of the ungodly humanist insists that man's comfort, happiness, health and wealth must be the ultimate concern of a loving God. If God's primary concern is not the comfort of man, then God's love is in question. This blasphemy now reigns in the modern church.

"I cannot state this enough: God's primary purpose for creation is for the glory of God Himself, because God—not man—is the reason anything exists or continues to exist. God achieves His glory by insuring the supremacy of God the Son, Christ Jesus, as the only Savior and Judge of the universe. God guarantees His Son the highest honor for His infinite sacrifice, and His true children value Him beyond all of creation added together.

Did Christ Die for Every Person?

"Another heinous blasphemy is being taught in the modern church concerning Christ's precious sacrifice," Dave continued. "This heresy says that Jesus Christ died for every human being, so that every person is saved; man just has to exercise his faith in God by choosing Jesus Christ as his Savior. This subversive teaching is straight from hell-inspired humanism, glorifying man while seeking to steal the honor and glory that belongs only to God.

"This shady heresy is extremely insidious for two reasons. It denies God's holy Word, that man is born dead in sin, and thus cannot and never will choose God. It makes man, instead of God, the final determiner of his fate. But, even more abhorrent, it denigrates the infinite worth of the precious sacrifice of Christ. It maintains that His death actually *never saved anyone*, but only made salvation *possible*, and allows man to make the final decision in choosing his own destiny.

"Could any teaching be more blasphemous to the Lord Jesus Christ? Did Christ actually leave His glorious throne, take on human flesh, suffer the torture of sinful man, and die on the brutal cross just to make salvation *possible*—to leave His glory in the hands of spiritually-dead sinners?"

"But I've heard this taught and preached everywhere during my Christian life," Pam said. "They even cite scriptures to prove their point."

"In our last class, we read passage after passage in the Bible declaring that man is born dead in sin and desires only evil continually," Dave reviewed. "Rebellious man is running away from God by actively suppressing the knowledge of God within his conscience. Man is spiritually dead. He cannot even understand the things of God, and thus he never chooses God because he never desires God.

"We also read passage after passage stating that salvation is the choice of God and God alone. This was the biblical answer to The Pivotal Question: 'Whose choice is salvation—man's or God's?' This must be so if any are saved, because Scripture repeatedly declares that unregenerate man will never exercise his will to choose God.

"Remember, the Apostles John and Paul state that the will of man, or the actions of man, are not involved in being born again! Anna, please reread for us these two passages."

Anna read:

> But as many as received Him, to them He gave the right to become children of God, *even* to those who believe in His name,
>
> who were born not of blood, nor of the will of the flesh, nor of the will of man, but of God. (John 1:12,13)

> So then it (God's mercy for salvation) *does* not *depend* on the man who wills or the man who runs, but on God who has mercy.
>
> (Romans 9:16; *parenthesis mine*)

"Thank you, Anna," said Dave. "God's holy Word specifically dictates that those who are born again into God's family were not born again by the will of man. They were born again by the will of God alone. Scripture cannot be more clear on this point: the choice of salvation has nothing to do with man; the choice belongs to God and God alone. To say that man has the right to choose or not choose salvation directly rebels against God, and contradicts His Word.

"We also read passage after passage that God sovereignly chose which sinners He willed to be in His family. God chose according to His own good pleasure, having nothing to do with the persons themselves, for there is nothing good in rebellious sinners. We also saw that God chose His elect before anyone existed, as God eternally knew His eternal plan for creation before the foundation of the world."

"I guess that pretty much destroys the first argument for the heresy that Christ died for everyone," Paul surmised. "God's Word repeatedly declares that sinful man can never and will never choose Jesus Christ as his Savior. So he will certainly never put faith in Christ's sacrifice for his sins."

"Exactly," acknowledged Dave. "Humanism's teaching that Christ's death on the cross paid for the sins of every human being glorifies man by rejecting Scripture's repeated decree that man is dead in sin. 'Man is not spiritually dead,' the heretic claims, 'but is just sick, and can choose God in his frail condition.'

"This is blasphemy because it attempts to steal the glory that belongs to God alone. God says He chose whom He wanted in His family before creation. God says He chose sovereignly, because everything is His, and He can do with it whatever He desires. God clearly declares through the Apostles John and Paul that those who are born again are regenerated, not by man's will or choice, but by the will of God and God alone. This is God's Word on the subject, and His truth brings total honor and glory to God and God alone!

"But the second argument of the ungodly humanist is even more heinous, if that were possible! The humanistic heresy that 'Christ died for every human being' denigrates the precious worth of Christ's sacrifice by claiming that Christ's death *never actually saved anyone!* Christ's death on the cross only made salvation *possible*, the heretic claims. Man must then determine his own fate by choosing or not choosing Christ as his Savior."

"I would certainly not want to appear on my judgment day before the exalted Judge of the universe, Jesus Christ, and say that His awesome sacrifice on the cross never actually saved anyone!" Chelsea said. "You know, listening to the heresy by itself, it sounds so good. I think that the many people who believe this teaching never actually took this lie to its logical conclusion to see how it blasphemes the Lord Jesus."

"Precisely, Chelsea," Dave agreed. "The modern church should have behaved like the noble Bereans (Acts 17), and compared this man-glorifying teaching against Scripture. Instead, the modern church lazily accepts any teaching as long as it sounds good. But, let's act like the noble Bereans, and read what God's holy Word says about Christ's sacrifice on the cross. We need to answer the critical question: 'Did Christ come and die to save sinners, or did Christ come merely to make salvation possible?'"

The class read:

> But when he had considered this, behold, an angel of the Lord appeared to him in a dream, saying, "Joseph, son of David, do not be afraid to take Mary as your wife; for the Child who has been conceived in her is of the Holy Spirit.
>
> "She will bear a Son; and you shall call His name Jesus, for He will save His people from their sins." (Matthew 1:20,21)

> And Jesus said to him, "Today salvation has come to this house, because he, too, is a son of Abraham.
>
> "For the Son of Man has come to seek and to save that which was lost."
> (Luke 19:9,10)

It is a trustworthy statement, deserving full acceptance, that Christ Jesus came into the world to save sinners, among whom I am foremost *of all.*

(1 Timothy 1:15)

He saved us, not on the basis of deeds which we have done in righteousness, but according to His mercy, by the washing of regeneration and renewing by the Holy Spirit,

whom He poured out upon us richly through Jesus Christ our Savior.

(Titus 3:5,6)

"Well," Kelly reflected, "Scripture definitely says that Christ Jesus came to save sinners. The Lord Jesus Himself says that He came to seek and to save, not to seek out possibilities and make their salvation possible."

"Absolutely," commended Dave. "God's holy Word repeatedly declares that God saves sinners. God does not rely on man for anything, let alone depend on man to 'do his part' by trusting Christ for salvation. God did not send His Son into the world to make salvation merely possible for man to save himself. The glorious sacrifice of Christ *secured* salvation for those God chose for His family before creation.

"Now, God does not save all sinners. In fact, the Lord Jesus Himself declared that only 'the few' will be saved, as we read earlier (Matthew 7:13,14). Christ Jesus condemned entire cities to hell! So, if all people are not saved, for whom did Christ die? Let's hear the answer from the Lord's own words."

The class read:

"Woe to you, Chorazin! Woe to you, Bethsaida! For if the miracles had been performed in Tyre and Sidon which occurred in you, they would have repented long ago, sitting in sackcloth and ashes.

"But it will be more tolerable for Tyre and Sidon in the judgment than for you.

"And you, Capernaum, will not be exalted to heaven, will you? You will be brought down to Hades!" (Luke 10:13-15)

And the disciples came and said to Him, "Why do You speak to them in parables?"

Jesus answered them, "To you it has been granted to know the mysteries of the kingdom of heaven, but to them it has not been granted.

"For whoever has, to him *more* shall be given, and he will have an abundance; but whoever does not have, even what he has shall be taken away from him.

"Therefore I speak to them in parables; because while seeing they do not see, and while hearing they do not hear, nor do they understand.

"But blessed are your eyes, because they see; and your ears, because they hear." (Matthew 13:10-13,16)

He said to them, "But who do you say that I am?"

Simon Peter answered, "You are the Christ, the Son of the living God."

And Jesus said to him, "Blessed are you, Simon Barjona, because flesh and blood did not reveal *this* to you, but My Father who is in heaven."

(Matthew 16:15-17)

The Jews then gathered around Him, and were saying to Him, "How long will You keep us in suspense? If You are the Christ, tell us plainly."

Jesus answered them, "I told you, and you do not believe; the works that I do in My Father's name, these testify of Me.

"But you do not believe because you are not of My sheep.

"My sheep hear My voice, and I know them, and they follow Me;

and I give eternal life to them, and they will never perish; and no one will snatch them out of My hand.

"My Father, who has given *them* to Me, is greater than all; and no one is able to snatch *them* out of the Father's hand.

"I and the Father are one." (John 10:24-30)

Jesus spoke these things; and lifting up His eyes to heaven, He said, "Father, the hour has come; glorify Your Son, that the Son may glorify You,

even as You gave Him authority over all flesh, that to all whom You have given Him, He may give eternal life.

"This is eternal life, that they may know You, the only true God, and Jesus Christ whom You have sent.

"I glorified You on the earth, having accomplished the work which You have given Me to do.

"Now, Father, glorify Me together with Yourself, with the glory which I had with You before the world was.

"I have manifested Your name to the men whom You gave Me out of the world; they were Yours and You gave them to Me, and they have kept Your word.

"I ask on their behalf; I do not ask on behalf of the world, but of those whom You have given Me; for they are Yours;

"I am no longer in the world; and *yet* they themselves are in the world, and I come to You. Holy Father, keep them in Your name, *the name* which You have given Me, that they may be one even as We *are*.

"Father, I desire that they also, whom You have given Me, be with Me where I am, so that they may see My glory which You have given Me, for You loved Me before the foundation of the world."

(John 17:1-6,9,11,24)

Jesus said to them, "I am the bread of life; he who comes to Me will not hunger, and he who believes in Me will never thirst.

"But I said to you that you have seen Me, and yet do not believe.

"All that the Father gives Me will come to Me, and the one who comes to Me I will certainly not cast out.

"For I have come down from heaven, not to do My own will, but the will of Him who sent Me.

"This is the will of Him who sent Me, that of all that He has given Me I lose nothing, but raise it up on the last day.

"For this is the will of My Father, that everyone who beholds the Son and believes in Him will have eternal life, and I Myself will raise him up on the last day."

And He was saying, "For this reason I have said to you, that no one can come to Me unless it has been granted him from the Father."

(John 6:35-40,65)

"I am the good shepherd, and I know My own and My own know Me, even as the Father knows Me and I know the Father; and I lay down My life for the sheep." (John 10:14,15)

"Christ Jesus' very words destroy the ungodly humanist's blasphemous heresy that Christ died for every human being," Dave pronounced. "Christ spoke to the multitudes in parables because '"to them it has not been granted to know the mysteries of the kingdom of heaven."' But, to '"all that the Father gives Me,"' Jesus explains everything, because '"to you it has been granted."'

"Christ Jesus says that those who have eyes to behold Him—to understand that He is God the Son, the Savior—are blessed. And the reason why they are blessed, Christ tells Peter, is because God the Father Himself revealed Jesus' true identity to His chosen ones. It is not because they, in their own flesh and blood wills, chose Christ. Jesus flatly declares, '"no one can come to Me unless it has been granted him from the Father."'

"As we read last week, God chose before the foundation of the world which sinners He wanted in His family (Ephesians 1:3-6; 2 Timothy 1:8,9). Therefore, Christ speaks of these specific elect persons as belonging to the Father, and of the Father giving them to Christ to save.

"Christ calls these specific chosen ones 'His sheep,' and says, '"I lay down My life for the sheep."' Jesus ends all debate by declaring that His sacrifice on the cross is specifically for His sheep! Christ tells the Jews gathered there, '"you do not believe because you are not of My sheep."'

"Please notice that Jesus does not say that they are not of His sheep because they do not believe! The reverse is not true. The Lord says that they do not believe because they are not His! The issue is not the unbelievers' lack of faith, but their identity. They have not been chosen by God to be in His family. Because they are not chosen to be in His family, God has not given them the faith to believe, and thus they do not believe in Him. If they were chosen by God to be in His fold, 'the Father would grant them the faith to know the mysteries of the kingdom of heaven!'

"The final nail in the coffin of the humanist's heresy—that Christ died for every human being—comes in the Lord's 'High Priestly Prayer,' where He prays to the Father for the salvation of the elect. Jesus prays:

> "I have manifested Your name to the men whom You gave Me out of the world; they were Yours and You gave them to Me, and they have kept Your word.
>
> "I ask on their behalf; I do not ask on behalf of the world, but of those whom You have given Me; for they are Yours." (John 17:6,9)

"The Lord Jesus specifically does '"not ask on behalf of the world"' for salvation, but only for '"the men whom You gave Me out of the world,"' because the saved elect belonged to the Father who chose them before the world was made.

"Thus, holy Scripture retains for God alone the full honor and glory of the infinite worth of Christ's sacrifice on the cross," Dave concluded. "God never made salvation only possible, so that men could choose for themselves and steal part of His glory. If that were true, the ungodly humanist would then be forced to admit that man deserves *at least part of the credit* for his salvation—because he chose Jesus whereas his neighbor did not. This heinous lie steals the glory that belongs to God alone, and cheapens Christ's sacrifice by concluding that His death never actually saved anyone.

"But the Almighty God declares:

> "I am the LORD, that is My name;
>
> I will not give My glory to another,
>
> Nor My praise to idols." (Isaiah 42:8)

"God himself will deal with and punish the idolaters, who attempt to usurp the glory that belongs solely to Him, for their own selfish, evil pride.

"The Bible declares that God and God alone saves sinners. God chose the specific ones He wanted in His family, and gave them to His Son to secure their salvation through His glorious sacrifice on the cross.

"Thus, we come to Pop Quiz question 14. The statement says: 'By dying on the cross for man's sins, Jesus only made salvation possible.' The answer is now obviously false.

"The humanist's teaching that Christ's death paid for all the sins of all people is not even logically possible. There are only four options." Dave turned and began writing on the chalkboard.

> The Death of Christ paid for:
> 1. All of the sins of all people
> 2. Some of the sins of all people
> 3. Some of the sins of some people
> 4. All of the sins of some people

"The humanist supports position one, saying that everyone is saved, they just must place their faith in Christ as their Savior. Well, if I am saved, but do not believe in Christ as my Savior, is not my unbelief a sin? Since unbelief is a sin, and Christ's death paid for *all* of the sins of all people, then why does His death not also pay for my sin of unbelief?

"The humanist's position becomes illogical when he says that not believing in Christ will result in eternal torment in hell. If not believing in Christ is a sin, and Christ's death paid for all sins, then the heretic has an irreconcilable problem. The ungodly humanist must revert to position two, saying that Christ's death paid for all sins except unbelief in Christ.

"Holding positions two or three guarantees that no one is saved and going to heaven, but that all people are going to hell. Why? God's standard for going to heaven is to be as perfect as God is perfect (Matthew 5:48). If Christ's sacrifice did not pay for absolutely every sin, then any candidate for heaven could never possibly meet God's standard for living with Him. Every person conceived from a human male is born with the sin of unbelief, and must be born again in order to see the kingdom of heaven (John 3:3).

"The only possible position is position four, and this is the clear teaching of Scripture. Christ's sacrifice on the cross paid for absolutely every sin committed *by the elect*. Christ Himself says that He laid down His life *for His sheep only*, not for every person.

"Every sin of every person that God the Father chose out of the world before creation, and gave to Christ, is paid in full. God legally transfers the elect's sin to Christ on the cross. Christ's sacrifice wipes the elect's slate completely clean. Then the Father imputes God the Son's perfect life to the elect's account, making that elect person now legally as perfect as God is perfect.

"The few to whom salvation is granted are guaranteed eternal life in heaven, for, as Christ declares, 'Truly, truly, I say to you, he who hears My word, and believes Him who sent Me, has eternal life, and does not come into judgment, but has passed out of death into life' (John 5:24). The only ones that can hear Christ's word and believe in the Father are those to whom salvation is granted by the Father (Matthew 13:10-13; John 6:65). Christ states that this elect one chosen by the Father *has* (present tense) eternal life, will never be judged and condemned, and '"has passed out of death into life!"'"

"But the value of Christ's sacrifice is infinite," Paul mused. "So, if God had so desired, Christ's sacrifice would have been enough to pay for the sins of every human being. That would be an awful lot of sins, but it would still be a finite number."

"That is absolutely true," Dave agreed. "But, in review, to absolutely insure the infinite worth of Christ's precious sacrifice in man's eyes, God chose to bestow His awesome saving benefits upon a very few. Saving everyone would cheapen the sacrifice of Christ like diamonds to gravel, because sinful man would take the Lord's suffering totally for granted.

"Honoring and glorifying God the Son, Jesus Christ, was God's first and foremost reason for creation. The infinite worth of the sacrifice of Christ is never to be even slightly dishonored.

"God's second reason for not saving the vast majority was to demonstrate His power and wrath against sin, and that the elect would be extremely grateful for being rescued from the eternal torture which they deserved. Thus, Christ's precious sacrifice would always be highly honored, and God would be totally glorified.

"And that brings us to Pop Quiz question 15: 'Jesus' death on the cross paid for all of the sins of all of mankind.' The answer is false. The Lord's death could have paid for all of the sins of every man who ever lived. But God chose to use Christ's sacrifice for the very few He elected to salvation, in order to ensure the glory of God."

Is God Not Willing that Any Should Perish?

"But doesn't the Bible say that 'God is not willing that any should perish, but for all to come to repentance?" asked Anna.

"Congratulations!" Dave applauded.

"What for?" Anna replied, completely befuddled.

"You have just alluded to the 'all-time, number one most misquoted and misused passage' on salvation in all of Scripture!" Dave answered with a smile. "Please do not be offended. Many Christians in the modern church—pastors, teachers and laypersons—have been heard incorrectly quoting, and thus incorrectly understanding, this passage.

"I'm going to write the scripture on the chalkboard as Anna, along with almost every teacher on today's Christian radio and television, quotes it." Dave turned and wrote Anna's exact words on the board. "Now, let's turn to the third chapter of the Apostle Peter's Second Epistle, and read verses 1 through 4 to get the context, and then verses 7 through 9."

The class read:

1   This is now, **beloved**, the second letter I am writing **to you** in which I am stirring up **your** sincere mind by way of reminder,

2   that **you** should remember the words spoken beforehand by the holy prophets and the commandment of the Lord and Savior *spoken* by **your apostles**.

3   Know this first of all, that in the last days mockers will come with *their* mocking, following after their own lusts,

4   and saying, "Where is the promise of His coming? For *ever* since the fathers fell asleep, all continues just as it was from the beginning of creation."

7   But by His word the present heavens and earth are being reserved for fire, kept for the day of judgment and destruction of ungodly men.

8   But do not let this one *fact* escape **your** notice, **beloved**, that with the Lord one day is like a thousand years, and a thousand years like one day.

9   The Lord is not slow about His promise, as some count slowness, but is patient **toward you**, not wishing for **any** to perish but for **all** to come to repentance. (2 Peter 3:1-4,7-9; *emphasis mine*)

"Now, in the first two verses," Dave expounded, "the Apostle Peter directs his words to the 'beloved.' These must be the true Christians whom God chose for salvation, for Peter says the 'beloved' are under 'the commandment of the Lord and Savior spoken by your apostles.' In contrast to the 'ungodly men' in verse 7, Peter again addresses his following words to the 'beloved' true Christians in verse 8.

"Then comes the 'all-time, number one most misquoted and misused verse' in the entire Bible on salvation. Out of God's 30 words in verse 9, most Christians completely eliminate the 14 middle words from 'not slow' through 'patient toward you,' sinfully changing the Word of God and its meaning.

"'The Lord is not slow about His promise, as some count slowness.' What promise? In verse 4, we find unbelievers—here referred to as 'some'—mocking 'the promise of His coming' again in judgment of them for their sin.

"'*But* is patient toward *you*'—Peter contrasts the unbelieving 'some' with 'you,' the 'beloved' true children of God toward whom the Lord is patient. 'You' must refer to the 'beloved' to whom Peter is writing. The Lord is 'not wishing for *any* to perish.' 'Any' what? Monkeys? Bananas? What?

"'Any' must refer back to 'you,' the beloved. "'All' must also refer to 'you,' the beloved true Christians. If one wanted to amplify the Greek text here, verse 9 must read:

> 9   The Lord is not slow about His promise to come again in judgment, as
> some mockers count slowness, but is patient toward you the beloved ones,
> not wishing for any of you beloved ones to perish, but for all of you beloved
> ones to come to repentance.

"The only reason Peter does not write all of this out," Dave avers, "is because his language in this chapter's context is quite clear. The true meaning of this verse is that the Lord wills that all of His beloved—every person He has chosen to be in His family from before creation—come to repentance leading to salvation, and that none of His beloved perish in hell.

"Peter's true meaning aligns perfectly with Christ's own words:

> "All that the Father gives Me will come to Me, and the one who comes
> to Me I will certainly not cast out.
>
> "For I have come down from heaven, not to do My own will, but the
> will of Him who sent Me.
>
> "This is the will of Him who sent Me, that of all that He has given Me
> I lose nothing, but raise it up on the last day."
>
> And He was saying, "For this reason I have said to you, that no one can
> come to Me unless it has been granted him from the Father."
>
> (John 6:37-39,64)

> "But you do not believe because you are not of My sheep.
>
> "My sheep hear My voice, and I know them, and they follow Me;
>
> and I give eternal life to them, and they will never perish; and no one
> will snatch them out of My hand.
>
> "My Father, who has given *them* to Me, is greater than all; and no one
> is able to snatch *them* out of the Father's hand." (John 10:26-29)

"The Lord Jesus specifically says that the only ones that can come to Him must have been chosen by the Father," Dave continued. "Christ also says that he will lose none of these elect whom the Father has given Him. The Lord gives 'eternal life to them, and they will never perish.'

"This is exactly Peter's message. All of the elect, whom the Father chose for salvation before the foundation of the earth, will come in time to repentance, because this is the patient Lord's will. The Lord will not return in judgment until He has brought to repentance and salvation, in His predetermined timing, every one whom the Father has given Him before the foundation of the world to save."

"Wow!" Nick exclaimed. "When the entire verse is read in its context, God's original meaning is totally different from its usage in the modern church."

"Exactly!" commended Dave. "God's holy Word is the only standard of truth in the universe. Only God's intended, original meaning is God's holy Word, and all of His essential doctrines are supported throughout the Bible as a whole.

"All other interpretations are mere speculation; or worse, man-made tradition; or even worse yet, the teaching of satanic humanism. Many such heresies come from three common errors: quoting Scripture out of its original context; eliminating words, or, as in the case above, entire phrases from God's holy Word; and assigning man-glorifying meanings to terms instead of determining God's intended definitions.

Only God's Original Meaning Matters

"Words like 'all' or 'any' or 'the world' must be carefully examined in their contexts to determine God's intended meanings. A great example is the small excerpt we read from John 17 (*see pages 207-208*). In His prayer, the Lord Jesus uses the term 'the world' five times—with three completely different meanings! He uses 'the world' to mean the physical earth (vv.5,11,24), the entire human race (v.6), and the entire class of sinners predestined for hell (v.9).

"The word 'all' is especially complicated. **All** can mean 'all without exception' or 'all without distinction.' Suppose we went down to Al's Grocery Store and looked at the bananas, and I said, 'All the bananas are ripe.' Do I intend to mean all of the bananas in the entire world *without exception* are ripe? Obviously not. I mean all of the bananas within the context of Al's Grocery Store—*without distinction*—are ripe.

"Rarely in Scripture do we find the usage as 'all without exception,' except in cases where God and the infinite attributes of His holy character are addressed. For two examples:

> The LORD has established His throne in the heavens,
> And His sovereignty rules over all. (Psalm 103:19)

> The LORD is righteous in all His ways
> And kind in all His deeds. (Psalm 145:17)

"A classic example where 'all' cannot mean 'all without exception' is found in Paul's Letter to the Romans. Pam, please read Romans 3:23 for us."

Pam read, "'...for all have sinned and fall short of the glory of God' (Romans 3:23)."

"Thanks, Pam," Dave replied. "'All' who? All humans? The Lord Jesus was fully human, 'yet without sin' (Hebrews 4:15). Thus, the Apostle's use of 'all' here was meant to be restricted to 'all humans born of a human father.' *Within that one class* of human beings—those fathered by human males—all are included without distinction. God's intended meaning of 'all' will be unrestricted ('all without exception') or restricted ('all without distinction') depending upon the context," Dave concluded.

"First John 2:2 is another passage that ungodly humanists have twisted for their own agenda," Paul added. "Here the Apostle uses the term 'the whole world.'"

"Excellent example," commended Dave. "Paul, would you please read the first two verses of 1 John 2 for us? Also read 1 John 5:18 and 19 as well as the Gospel of John 3:36."

Paul read:

> **My little children**, I am writing these things **to you** so that **you** may not sin. And if **anyone** sins, **we** have an Advocate with the Father, Jesus Christ the righteous;
>
> and He Himself is the propitiation for **our** sins; and not for **ours** only, but also for those of **the whole world**. (1 John 2:1,2; *emphasis mine*)

> We know that no one who is born of God sins; but He who was born of God keeps him, and the evil one does not touch him.
>
> We know that we are of God, and that **the whole world** lies in the power of the evil one. (1 John 5:18,19; *emphasis mine*)

> "He who believes in the Son has eternal life; but he who does not obey the Son will not see life, but the wrath of God abides on him."
>
> (John 3:36)

"Thank you, Paul," Dave said. "The humanist would stand and proudly announce at the reading of 1 John 2:2 that he is right—Christ's death paid for the sins of every person in 'the whole world.' Humanism teaches that the meaning of the phrase '*the whole world*' must be: 'every person who has lived on earth.' Is this the Apostle's intended meaning?

"If it is, then the Apostle—writing God's Word superintended by the Holy Spirit—contradicts himself in his own letter! For, a few chapters later, John uses the exact same phrase. The Apostle declares that the evil one 'does not touch' a truly born-again believer, and 'that the whole world lies in the power of the evil one!'

"It is impossible for the words 'the whole world' here to have the meaning that the humanist assigns to the phrase. If 'every person who has lived on earth' is in the power of the evil one, how can the Apostle just declare that the evil one 'does not touch' a truly born-again believer—one who obviously lives on earth?

"The Apostle in chapter 5 is clearly setting the true children of God against the rest of humanity destined to perish. God's intended meaning of 'the whole world' here is exclusively the entire class of unbelievers, whom are held captive by Satan to do the devil's will (2 Timothy 2:26). The context determines the meaning of the words.

"In chapter 2, the Apostle is directly addressing his 'little children'—the specific ones to whom he is writing who became believers under his ministry. John pens, 'I am writing these things to *you.*' He goes on to say that Christ is the propitiation, the payment in full, for *our* sins—the sins of we true believers. Not just for those in our little group here, but Christ's payment is in full for all of God's true children throughout *the whole world.*

"The Apostle here certainly would not be claiming a pardon for sin resulting in eternal life for unbelievers. John wrote about the Lord's condemnation of unbelievers in his Gospel, quoting Christ's words that they abide (present tense) under the fierce wrath of God.

"There is only one Author of God's holy Word—Almighty God the Holy Spirit. Since He sovereignly superintended the original writings through human vessels, then all of God's Word must agree perfectly. None of it may contradict. Because God is perfect—and as it is impossible for God to lie (Hebrews 6:18)—His Word must be *inerrant*, or without error. Personal interpretations must give way to the original meaning intended by God in the original writings, as the Apostle Peter says:

> But know this first of all, that no prophecy of Scripture is *a matter* of one's own interpretation,
>
> for no prophecy was ever made by an act of human will, but men moved by the Holy Spirit spoke from God. (2 Peter 1:20,21)

"Thus," Dave concluded, "we come to Pop Quiz questions 16, 17 and 18. Would you read them for us, Ed?"

"Sure," Ed replied. "'Question 16: 'God is not willing for anyone to perish, but for everyone to come to repentance.' Question 17: 'In the Bible, the word "all" always means "all without exception."' Lastly, Question 18: 'In the Bible, the phrase "the whole world" always means "everyone living on the face of the earth."'"

"Thank you, Ed," Dave replied. "We find all of these statements to be false. God is not willing that any of His chosen children perish, but that they all come to repentance before the day of judgment. 'All' rarely means 'all without exception,' but usually means 'all without distinction,' and is restricted in the context in which the word is used. Lastly, phrases like 'the whole world' can have several different meanings, as our Lord Jesus demonstrated in His prayer in John 17.

"Therefore, all of the doctrines in the Word of God line up perfectly and logically. If the modern church claims that it is God's will that not one human being should perish, and yet God the Son condemns entire cities to perish, something is wrong. The meanings the modern church assigns to misquoted and misused verses in order to advance ungodly, humanistic teachings must be condemned.

"The church must return to God's Word and His original meaning! As the Apostle Peter warns: 'For *it is* time for judgment to begin with the household of God; and if *it begins* with us first, what *will be* the outcome for those who do not obey the gospel of God (1 Peter 4:17)?' We true believers must abandon and condemn man-made, man-glorifying traditions. True Christians are only made perfect as God is perfect by what Christ has done period—not by our decisions, actions, or anything else we do!

Do the Children of God Become Gods?

"Since we as true believers are now as perfect as God is perfect, does that mean we now become gods?" asked Ed. "I've heard some cults teach that we can achieve godhood. They even quote the Lord Jesus saying that 'we are gods.'"

"Excellent question, Ed," Dave responded. "This is another heinous lie of humanism. Once again, the humanist attempts to usurp the glory belonging to God alone, foolishly trying to glorify man.

"This heresy fails for three reasons. First, God declares repeatedly in His Word that there is one and only one God—and He is it! Second, in the alluded passage, the Lord Jesus is quoting Psalm 82 and condemning the religious rulers to death! Third, true believers are *legally* as perfect as God is perfect in God's eyes, but *practically* we continue to stumble daily. We do not become gods!

"We have read passage after passage where God specifically states there is only one God—one, not many! Pam, would you please read for us the last three scriptures on the board?"

Pam read:

> "I am the LORD, and there is no other;
>
> Besides Me there is no God.
>
> I will gird you, though you have not known Me;
>
> "That men may know from the rising to the setting of the sun
>
> That there is no one besides Me.
>
> I am the LORD, and there is no other,
>
> "The One forming light and creating darkness,
>
> Causing well-being and creating calamity;
>
> I am the LORD who does all these." (Isaiah 45:5-7)

> "Remember the former things long past,
>
> For I am God, and there is no other;
>
> *I am* God, and there is no one like Me." (Isaiah 46:9)

> Jesus answered, "The foremost is, 'HEAR, O ISRAEL! THE LORD OUR GOD IS ONE LORD.'" (Mark 12:29)

"Thank you, Pam," Dave acknowledged. "Almighty God cannot state the facts any more clearly than these passages. 'Besides Me there is no God.' If any other kind of god—capital 'G' or small 'g'—actually exists outside of man's imagination, then God lies. Since God obviously remembers 'the former things long past'—as He is omniscient—God could not be mistaken. Since 'it is impossible for God to lie' (Hebrews 6:18), then no other God can exist. Period.

"In the passage to which Ed alluded, the Lord Jesus is being bitingly facetious as He condemns the unbelieving Jews to certain death. Let's read the passage in the Gospel of John."

They read:

> "I and the Father are one."
>
> The Jews picked up stones again to stone Him.

Jesus answered them, "I showed you many good works from the Father; for which of them are you stoning Me?"

The Jews answered Him, "For a good work we do not stone You, but for blasphemy; and because You, being a man, make Yourself out *to be* God."

Jesus answered them, "Has it not been written in your Law, 'I SAID, YOU ARE GODS'?

"If he called them gods, to whom the word of God came (and the Scripture cannot be broken),

do you say of Him, whom the Father sanctified and sent into the world, 'You are blaspheming,' because I said, 'I am the Son of God'?

"If I do not do the works of My Father, do not believe Me;

but if I do them, though you do not believe Me, believe the works, so that you may know and understand that the Father is in Me, and I in the Father."

Therefore they were seeking again to seize Him, and He eluded their grasp. (John 10:30-39)

"The Lord Jesus is quoting Psalm 82 here. Though most modern Christians have no idea what that Psalm says, the Jews here knew the passage very well, as evidenced by their reaction of rage. Psalm 82 says:

God takes His stand in His own congregation;
He judges in the midst of the rulers.
How long will you judge unjustly
And show partiality to the wicked? Selah.
I said, "You are gods,
And all of you are sons of the Most High.
"Nevertheless you will die like men
And fall like *any* one of the princes." (Psalm 82:1,2,6,7)

"God chastises the judges He had placed over His people as His representatives to execute justice and righteousness," Dave expounded. "These wicked judges became filled with their own sense of power, acting as if they were 'little gods' over the people. Though God placed them there to rule according to His holiness, God condemns them to death for their wickedness.

"The Lord Jesus is saying the same thing to the ruling Jews who are questioning His claim to be God Himself—and they knew it! Christ condemns the Jews to death for their unbelief despite His many miracles, and the Jews try to seize Him. Jesus is not saying they are gods, or can become gods. The Lord is condemning them to death for acting like gods, but using their power for evil."

"Wow!" Nick exclaimed. "Knowing the context and the reference being quoted makes all the difference in understanding the passage!"

"So true!" Dave agreed. "Lastly, the ungodly humanist's heresy that man can become a god is foolish because of a fundamental misunderstanding of true Christians 'being made perfect as

God is perfect.' This perfection is a ***foreign perfection***, or ***foreign righteousness***."

"What does that mean?" Jennifer asked.

"It means that God's perfection is not inherent *within us*," Dave answered. "God's perfection is not infused into our being so that we become gods with God's perfect attributes. If that were true, a truly regenerated Christian could never sin. Sinning would never even be a possibility!

"But the Apostle John, in writing to true believers, says God has made provision for when we do sin. He writes: 'My little children, I am writing these things to you so that you may not sin. And if anyone sins, we have an Advocate with the Father, Jesus Christ the righteous' (1 John 2:1).

"We are granted a righteousness that has nothing to do with ourselves. Our accounts are credited with a ***foreign righteousness***—Christ's perfection. Thus, true Christians are *legally* in perfect standing before God, but *practically* they continue to struggle with the sinful nature. We do not become gods.

"To illustrate, imagine a judge's son stealing a $50 watch from a store. Another judge imposes a fine for the crime, and the first judge pays the fine for his son. *Legally*, the son is free because the judgment has been satisfied. But the son does not automatically become a judge simply because he has been exonerated by a judge. The son does not qualify for the position—many more qualifications are required to become a judge. But the son stands in a *legal position* as being completely free from wrong.

"True Christians are legally considered by God to be as perfect as He is perfect, because God the Son's perfection has been credited to their accounts. But we ourselves are still finite, dependent beings. God's ways, thoughts and Being are infinitely beyond those of mere humans (Isaiah 55:8,9).

"Therefore, humanism attempts to steal the glory that belongs only to God in order to glorify man. One way he attempts this is through the heresy that men can become gods.

"But, this heresy fails miserably on three counts. First, God declares that there is no god except Himself. Second, the Lord Jesus condemns men to death who use God-given power and authority for evil purposes. Third, true Christians are made legally perfect as God is perfect, but we do not become gods. Mortal man simply does not qualify to be the infinitely, eternally perfect God. Man is born spiritually dead with a sinful nature—he has absolutely no righteousness of his own. If God grants a man His perfect righteousness, it is Christ's perfection that is applied to the sinner's account!

"Am I ever grateful to God for choosing to give me His Son's righteousness!" exclaimed Nick. "What a plan! We've covered a lot of ground today. Would you do a quick review?"

"Okay," answered Dave. "We still have God's decree that to live in heaven one must be as perfect as God is perfect (Matthew 5:48).

"God subjected creation to slavery, evil, and imperfection in order to guarantee all honor and glory to God the Son, Jesus Christ, the only Savior and Judge of the universe.

"In His plan of redemption, God set up a system of representation: Adam being the federal head of his people, and Christ being the federal head of His people.

"All persons represented by Adam—those born of a human male—are born dead in sin and rebel against God continuously. Unless they are born again by the Spirit of God, they will be judged by the Supreme Judge of the universe for being imperfect. These will perish in hell for their sins, being burned alive in the lake of fire, experiencing agony that will never end.

"All persons represented by Christ—those sinners whom God has chosen to save and bring into His family—have been born again, or will be born again during their lives by the Holy Spirit. Christ is their Savior, who took the wrath of God for their sins on the cross, and credited to their accounts His perfect life. Since Christ is God, they are then as perfect as God is perfect!

"It most definitely is not fair that God does not save every person.

"God never said He was fair. God says that He is just.

"Justice and fairness are not the same. They can co-exist in some situations but not in others.

"Justice means absolute adherence to a standard, and punishment that perfectly 'fits the crime' for failure to do so. Almighty God is eternally and perfectly just, and His standard is to be as perfect as He is perfect.

"Fairness can mean treating everything the same, or it can mean compromising. God never compromises the attributes of His holy character. In doing so, He would sin against Himself, and that is impossible for an eternally and perfectly holy Being.

"But God never said He must be fair at all times. Fairness is not one of God's eternal attributes.

"God is under absolutely no obligation to save anyone! The question is not, 'why does God not save everyone?' but 'why should God save anyone at all?'

"God's primary purpose for creation is not the happiness of man, or man's salvation, or for blessing man's life, as the ungodly humanist would assert.

"Honoring and glorifying God the Son, Jesus Christ, was God's primary reason for creation.

"The infinite worth of the sacrifice of Christ—His leaving His glorious throne, taking on the limits of human flesh, being crucified and dying at the hands of those He created, and bearing the wrath of God for the sins of His elect—is never to be even slightly dishonored.

"To absolutely insure the infinite worth of Christ's precious sacrifice in man's eyes—God's primary concern—God chose to bestow His awesome saving benefits upon a very few. These few children will always highly esteem Christ and His perfect work and sacrifice more than the finest diamond in the universe!

"God says that another reason He chose not to save the vast majority was to demonstrate His power and wrath against sin, and that the elect would be extremely grateful for being rescued from the eternal torture which they deserved. Thus, Christ's precious sacrifice would always be highly honored, and God would be totally glorified.

"God created and sustains everything, and therefore everything belongs to Him to do with as He pleases. God is The Potter, and He molds the clay for His purposes, not the other way around.

"In the modern church, a heinous blasphemy is being taught which says that Jesus Christ died for every human being, so that every person is saved—they just have to exercise their faith in God by choosing Jesus Christ as their Savior.

"This shady heresy is extremely insidious for two reasons. It denies God's holy Word, that man is born dead in sin, and thus cannot and never will choose God. It makes man, instead of God, the final determiner of his fate.

"But, even more abhorrent, it denigrates the infinite worth of the precious sacrifice of Christ by saying His death never saved anyone. This heresy claims that Christ's death only made salvation possible, and allows man to choose his own destiny.

"The Apostle John states that the will of man is not involved in being born again, but only the will of God is involved (John 1:12,13).

"God's holy Word repeatedly declares that God saves sinners. The glorious sacrifice of Christ secured salvation for those God chose for His family.

"God does not rely on man for anything, let alone depend on man to 'do his part' by trusting Christ for salvation. God did not send His Son into the world to make salvation merely possible for man to save himself.

"God does not save all sinners. The Lord Jesus Himself declared that only 'the few' will be saved (Matthew 7:13,14).

"Christ spoke to the multitudes in parables, because 'to them it has not been granted to know the mysteries of the kingdom of heaven.' But, to 'all that the Father gives Me,' Jesus explains everything, because 'to you it has been granted.'

"Christ Jesus says that they are blessed who have eyes to behold Him; to understand that He is God the Son, the Savior. And the reason why they are blessed, Christ tells Peter, is because God the Father Himself gave them eyes to see.

"God Himself revealed Jesus' true identity to His chosen ones by His own sovereign choice, not because they, in their own flesh and blood wills, desired Christ.

"Jesus flatly declares, '"no one can come to Me unless it has been granted him from the Father."'

"Christ calls these specific chosen ones 'His sheep,' and says, '"I lay down My life for the sheep."' Jesus ends all debate by declaring that His sacrifice on the cross is specifically for His sheep! Christ tells the Jews gathered there, '"you do not believe because you are not of My sheep."'

"In His 'High-Priestly Prayer,' the Lord Jesus specifically does '"not ask on behalf of the world"' for salvation, but only for '"the men whom You gave Me out of the world,"' because the saved elect belonged to the Father who chose them before the world was made.

"The value of Christ's sacrifice is infinite. If God had so desired, Christ's sacrifice would have been enough to pay for the sins of every human being. That would be many, many sins, but it would still be a finite number.

"The 'all-time, number one most misquoted and misused passage' in all of Scripture on salvation is 2 Peter 3:9, which says: 'The Lord is not slow about His promise, as some count slowness, but is patient toward you, not wishing for any to perish but for all to come to repentance.'

"Out of the 30 words in verse 9, most Christians completely eliminate the 14 middle words from 'not slow' through 'patient toward you,' sinfully changing the Word of God and its meaning.

"The true meaning of this verse is that the Lord wills that all of His beloved—every person

He has chosen to be in His family from before creation—come to repentance leading to salvation, and that none of His beloved perish in hell.

"God's holy Word is the only standard of truth in the universe. Only the original meaning intended by God is God's holy Word. All other interpretations are mere speculation; or worse, man-made tradition; or even worse yet, the teaching of ungodly humanists.

"Words like 'all' or 'any' or 'the world' must be carefully examined in their contexts to determine God's intended meanings.

"For example, looking at John 17 alone, the Lord Jesus in His prayer uses the term 'the world' five times, with three completely different meanings!

"There is only one Author of God's holy Word: Almighty God the Holy Spirit.

"Since the Holy Spirit superintended the original writings through human vessels, resulting in utter inerrancy—and it is impossible for God to lie (Hebrews 6:18)—all of God's Word must agree. None of it may contradict.

"Personal interpretations must give way to the original meaning intended by God.

"The meanings the modern church assigns to misquoted and misused verses in order to advance ungodly humanistic teachings must be condemned.

"The church must return to God's Word and its original teachings, 'For it is time for judgment to begin with the household of God; and if it begins with us first, what will be the outcome for those who do not obey the gospel of God (1 Peter 4:17)?'

"The ungodly humanist's teaching that Christ's death paid for all the sins of all people is not even logically possible.

"God sent His Son into the world to save sinners, not just to make salvation possible for ungodly men to choose.

"Every sin of every person that God the Father chose out of the world before creation and gave to Christ is paid for by Christ's death on the cross.

"Christ's sacrifice wipes the elect's slate completely clean, and the elect becomes as perfect as God is perfect because the Father imputes God the Son's perfect life to the elect's account!

"The ungodly humanist attempts to steal the glory that belongs only to God in order to glorify man in another way—through the heresy that men can become gods.

"But, this heresy fails miserably on three counts. First, God declares that there is no god except Himself.

"Second, the Lord Jesus condemns men to death who use God-given power and authority for evil purposes.

"Third, true Christians are legally perfect as God is perfect, be we do not become gods. Mortal man simply does not qualify to be the infinitely, eternally perfect God. Man is born spiritually dead with a sinful nature—he has absolutely no righteousness of his own. If God grants a man His perfect righteousness, it is Christ's perfection that is applied to his account!

"Matt, would you please close our Bible study with prayer?" asked Dave.

"Heavenly Father, thank You for Your awesome plan of salvation! We cannot thank You enough for choosing us before creation as Your children. May we never cheapen the precious sacrifice of Christ our Savior on the cross, but cherish it beyond anything this sinful world has to offer.

"Thank You, Lord Jesus, for taking our sins, and nailing them to the brutal cross in Your body. Thank You for giving us Your perfect life, so that we may stand in the presence of our holy God on the day of judgment. Thank You, Holy Spirit, for raising us from the dead, empowering us to glorify You during this life on earth.

"Thank You, Father, for our teacher Dave, and we ask that You continue to bless Him by showing him Your ways. Fill us with Your Holy Spirit, and prepare our hearts to worship You. You deserve all of the praise, honor and glory, for You are the holy Almighty God. In Jesus' Name we pray, amen!"

11

Have Faith In GOD

Nick greeted his brother-in-Christ with his usual ear-to-ear grin as he reached the open doorway in the middle of the dormitory hall.

"Hey, bro! How are you?"

"Excellent, my man! Come on in!" Dave answered.

"I tell you, I am learning so much about God, and man, and the relationship between the two, and how it all affects me," Nick said excitedly. "I am so grateful for this time that you spend with me, and for the great lessons in Sunday school. There is nothing else in all of the world like learning about the awesome God that created it all."

"Amen!" agreed Dave. "Would you like to open our study today with prayer?"

"Absolutely! Holy Father, we praise You and worship You with every ounce of our beings. You deserve all honor and all glory, because You are the Creator and Sustainer of all that is! We thank You so much for Your precious Son, whom You sent to redeem us from our sins and to bring us into Your family. Thank You, Lord Jesus, for the perfect life You lived and the precious sacrifice of your death upon the brutal cross.

"Father, fill us now with the power of Your glorious Holy Spirit, that we may have minds to know Your ways in order to love You more intimately than ever. I ask You to bless Dave's teaching, and I ask that You bless him mightily for doing Your will. Thank You for the awesome promise of Your presence here with us. In Jesus' Name we pray, amen."

"Amen! Let it be so," Dave echoed.

"Let it be so?" asked Nick.

"Let it be so. That is what 'amen' means," Dave replied.

"Aaah...very good. I learn something neat like that every day now, it seems," said Nick.

"Well, we have covered a lot of ground since that Friday night when God saved you," Dave began. "We've discussed many deep and critical issues, both here and in Sunday school. Do you have any questions that you would like to ask, or anything I can make more clear?"

The Brotherhood of Man?

"As a matter of fact, I have a couple of questions." Nick appeared grateful for the opportunity to get a better grasp of some concepts. "First off, are all of the members of the human race my brothers? I mean, these days you hear a lot on television about 'the Fatherhood of God and the brotherhood of man.' Is this a Christian concept?"

"No," Dave answered, "this is not a Christian concept. This is a teaching of humanism, not from God's holy Word. Let's read some passages concerning God—who is Creator of all and Father to some—and man, and his relationship to other human beings."

They read:

> For by Him all things were created, *both* in the heavens and on earth, visible and invisible, whether thrones or dominions or rulers or authorities—all things have been created through Him and for Him.
>
> He is before all things, and in Him all things hold together.
>
> (Colossians 1:16,17)

> "I speak the things which I have seen with *My* Father; therefore you also do the things which you heard from *your* father.
>
> "You are doing the deeds of your father." They said to Him, "We were not born of fornication; we have one Father: God."
>
> Jesus said to them, "If God were your Father, you would love Me, for I proceeded forth and have come from God, for I have not even come on My own initiative, but He sent Me.
>
> "You are of *your* father the devil, and you want to do the desires of your father. He was a murderer from the beginning, and does not stand in the truth because there is no truth in him. Whenever he speaks a lie, he speaks from his own *nature,* for he is a liar and the father of lies.
>
> "But because I speak the truth, you do not believe Me.
>
> "He who is of God hears the words of God; for this reason you do not hear *them,* because you are not of God." (John 8:38,41,42,44,45,47)

> By this we know that we abide in Him and He in us, because He has given us of His Spirit.
>
> We have seen and testify that the Father has sent the Son *to be* the Savior of the world.
>
> Whoever confesses that Jesus is the Son of God, God abides in him, and he in God.
>
> We have come to know and have believed the love which God has for

us. God is love, and the one who abides in love abides in God, and God abides in him.

If someone says, "I love God," and hates his brother, he is a liar; for the one who does not love his brother whom he has seen, cannot love God whom he has not seen.

And this commandment we have from Him, that the one who loves God should love his brother also. (1 John 4:13-16,20,21)

For those who are according to the flesh set their minds on the things of the flesh, but those who are according to the Spirit, the things of the Spirit.

However, you are not in the flesh but in the Spirit, if indeed the Spirit of God dwells in you. But if anyone does not have the Spirit of Christ, he does not belong to Him.

For all who are being led by the Spirit of God, these are sons of God.

For you have not received a spirit of slavery leading to fear again, but you have received a spirit of adoption as sons by which we cry out, "Abba! Father!"

The Spirit Himself testifies with our spirit that we are children of God. (Romans 8:5,9,14-16)

And a lawyer stood up and put Him to the test, saying, "Teacher, what shall I do to inherit eternal life?"

And He said to him, "What is written in the Law? How does it read to you?"

And he answered, "YOU SHALL LOVE THE LORD YOUR GOD WITH ALL YOUR HEART, AND WITH ALL YOUR SOUL, AND WITH ALL YOUR STRENGTH, AND WITH ALL YOUR MIND; AND YOUR NEIGHBOR AS YOURSELF."

And He said to him, "You have answered correctly; DO THIS AND YOU WILL LIVE."

But wishing to justify himself, he said to Jesus, "And who is my neighbor?"

The Good Samaritan

Jesus replied and said, "A man was going down from Jerusalem to Jericho, and fell among robbers, and they stripped him and beat him, and went away leaving him half dead.

"And by chance a priest was going down on that road, and when he saw him, he passed by on the other side.

"Likewise a Levite also, when he came to the place and saw him, passed by on the other side.

"But a Samaritan, who was on a journey, came upon him; and when he saw him, he felt compassion,

and came to him and bandaged up his wounds, pouring oil and wine on *them*; and he put him on his own beast, and brought him to an inn and took care of him.

"On the next day he took out two denarii and gave them to the innkeeper and said, 'Take care of him; and whatever more you spend, when I return I will repay you.'

"Which of these three do you think proved to be a neighbor to the man who fell into the robbers' *hands?*"

And he said, "The one who showed mercy toward him." Then Jesus said to him, "Go and do the same." (Luke 10:25-37)

"God's holy Word emphatically declares that God is the Creator and Sustainer of everything, including all of mankind," Dave expounded. "But the Lord Jesus makes a definite distinction between those whose father is the devil, and those whose Father is Almighty God. The elect—those to whom God gave His Holy Spirit and raised to eternal life—are in God's family, and can call God 'Abba, Father!' In God's true family, the elect are brothers and sisters to each other.

"However, in the world, we are neighbors, not brothers. We are to love our neighbors as ourselves. Even if they are our enemies, we are to show them mercy and kindness. But, as the Lord Jesus Himself declared, the majority of the people in the world will never become our brothers or sisters in Christ (Matthew 7:13ff).

"Thus, Quiz question 19—'All people are children of God and are part of His family'—is false, because it expressly contradicts the Word of God.

"So," Dave concluded, "the biblical concept is that God is the Creator, Sustainer and Judge of every person. God is only the Father of those He has chosen to come into His family. Those in God's family are brothers and sisters to each other. Outside of God's family, we are all neighbors."

"Thanks," responded Nick. "That really clears that up. Could we go back to the humanist's assertion that Christ died for every person?"

"Okay," Dave agreed. "What can I clarify?"

"I saw that the main problem with the humanist's position," recalled Nick, "was his assumption that faith is inherent within every person. In this unbiblical view, all persons' sins were paid for by Christ's sacrifice, but they are responsible to put their faith in Christ as their Savior in order for their forgiveness to become effective. Am I getting this right?"

"Well," Dave reviewed, "by far the most serious crime in the humanistic position—that Christ died for everyone—is that it blasphemes Christ by saying that His sacrifice never actually saved anyone. According to this heresy, Christ's sacrifice only made salvation possible for man to save himself. Man, then, determines his own eternal destiny by choosing to place or not to place his faith in Christ as his Savior.

"This is a blatant lie, of course, because we have read Scripture passage after passage declaring that God saves sinners. He doesn't just make salvation possible. We also read God's

Word stating directly that man's will is not even involved in becoming born again (John 1:12,13; Romans 9:16), but that God's will alone determines who will be saved.

"We also found that the ungodly humanist's position is not even logically possible. His heresy is based on the lie that Christ died for every sin of every person—each person must then believe in Christ to make God's forgiveness effective. But we are all born committing the sin of unbelief. If Christ died for every sin, then he died for the sin of unbelief also. By the ungodly humanist's own absurd position, I can remain in my unbelief and still be saved!

"Of course, the ungodly humanist must then revert to saying that Christ's death paid for all sins except unbelief—in which case not one person could possibly be saved. If Christ's death did not pay for the sin of unbelief—which every person born of a human male commits from conception—then no one could be as perfect as God is perfect, God's standard for going to heaven and avoiding hell.

Simple Faith vs. Faith In Christ

"The first problem we covered with the ungodly humanist's heresy—that Christ died for everyone—relates to your present question regarding faith. 'Faith' and 'faith in Christ' are not the same, and this is where much of the confusion lies.

"*Faith* is simple trust that an object can perform that for which one hopes. Every person exercises *simple faith*. We trust that a chair will hold us up as we sit down, for example. We believe that gravity will bring us back down to the ground after we jump up, or hold our books on our desks where we set them down. Every person uses simple faith every moment of his conscious existence.

"But only the elect are granted 'faith in Christ'—or 'saving faith'—by God. *Believing in Christ*, or *faith in Christ*, means to place total trust in Christ's two-part perfect work for salvation from the wrath of God for sin. In the legal transfer, the sins of God's people—the elect—were placed on Christ as He suffered on the cross, and were completely paid for in His death. God the Son's perfect life was then credited to the accounts of the elect, making them as perfect as God is perfect. This legal swap did not just make it possible for man to save himself. This legal transfer secured the salvation of God's true children.

"**'Faith in Christ' is not man's gift to God**, as the ungodly humanist would assert. **'Faith in Christ' is God's gift to those He has chosen to be in His family**.

"Only true 'faith in Christ' can save a sinner from the wrath of God, because faith is only as good as the object in which it is placed. One can have faith in a doorknob, or a block of wood, and believe with all his heart, with complete sincerity, that it will save him from destruction. But, unless the object of the faith is able to perform that for which one hopes, his faith—though utterly sincere—is in vain, and totally worthless.

"The Old Testament gives us many, many examples of the nation of Israel abandoning God for the idolatrous practices of the surrounding pagan nations. They worshiped idols made by the hands of men. These idols were not alive, and could not speak, hear or walk! God chided them for their stupidity. In response to their heinous sin of idolatry, God ripped them out of their promised land and sold them into slavery to those very pagans!

"Nick, please read the next four scriptures I have written down regarding *worthless faith*, which is placing faith in anything or anyone except God for the miraculous."

Nick read:

> *As for* the idol, a craftsman casts it,
>> A goldsmith plates it with gold,
>> And a silversmith *fashions* chains of silver.
>
> He who is too impoverished for *such* an offering
>> Selects a tree that does not rot;
>> He seeks out for himself a skillful craftsman
>> To prepare an idol that will not totter. (Isaiah 40:19,20)

> They will be turned back *and* be utterly put to shame,
>> Who trust in idols,
>> Who say to molten images,
>> "You are our gods." (Isaiah 42:17)

> "For the customs of the peoples are delusion;
>> Because it is wood cut from the forest,
>> The work of the hands of a craftsman with a cutting tool.
> "They decorate *it* with silver and with gold;
>> They fasten it with nails and with hammers
>> So that it will not totter.
> "Like a scarecrow in a cucumber field are they,
>> And they cannot speak;
>> They must be carried,
>> Because they cannot walk!
>> Do not fear them,
>> For they can do no harm,
>> Nor can they do any good." (Jeremiah 10:3-5)

> Every man is stupid, devoid of knowledge;
>> Every goldsmith is put to shame by his idols;
>> For his molten images are deceitful,
>> And there is no breath in them.
> They are worthless, a work of mockery;
>> In the time of their punishment they will perish.
>>   (Jeremiah 10:14,15)

"Only faith in the One True God—'faith in Christ'—can save one from perishing," Dave averred. "Idolatrous Israel exercised faith all right—in blocks of wood—and God called them 'stupid' and 'devoid of knowledge!'

"'Faith' and 'faith in Christ' are as different as man using his will to choose, and man using his will to choose Christ. We make many choices with our wills, such as which brand of toothpaste to use, or where to go to school. We also exercise simple faith in chairs and gravity.

"But we can only choose Christ, and desire His salvation, after we are regenerated by the Holy Spirit. He first must raise us from spiritual death and release us from captivity by the devil. We can only exercise 'faith in Christ' after God the Holy Spirit grants us the power to repent, and gives us His gift of 'saving faith' to believe in Christ.

"Now please read the next scriptures on true 'faith in Christ'—the only faith that can save."
Nick read:

> And Jesus answered saying to them, "Have faith in God."
>
> (Mark 11:22)

> Now faith is the assurance of *things* hoped for, the conviction of things not seen. (Hebrews 11:1)

> For by grace you have been saved through faith; and that not of yourselves, *it is* the gift of God;
> not as a result of works, so that no one may boast.
>
> (Ephesians 2:8,9)

> For to you it has been granted for Christ's sake, not only to believe in Him, but also to suffer for His sake. (Philippians 1:29)

> Finally, brethren, pray for us that the word of the Lord will spread rapidly and be glorified, just as *it did* also with you;
> and that we will be rescued from perverse and evil men; for not all have faith. (2 Thessalonians 3:1,2)

"'Not all have faith!'" Dave echoed the passage. "Man does not have 'faith to believe in Christ' inherent within his being, or the Apostle Paul could not make that statement. If the ungodly humanist's position on faith was correct, the Apostle could only say something like, 'for not all have chosen to exercise the faith they have.' But he does not say that!

"To 'believe in Christ' must be granted by God (Philippians 1:29). Unregenerate man has no 'faith in Christ' to exercise or not exercise. Again, and this point is critical: 'Faith in Christ' is not man's gift to God, as the ungodly humanist would assert. 'Faith in Christ' is God's gift to those He has chosen to be in His family.

"One last crucial point on 'faith in Christ' must be made. As the idolatrous Israelites learned, the only spiritual faith that is true faith must be centered in God Himself alone! True *spiritual faith* is trusting God Himself alone to perform the miraculous. A sinner becoming born again is a miraculous intervention by God, raising the spiritually-dead to life. Real healings are miraculous. Correct teaching of the spiritual principles from God's holy Word is a miraculous gift from the Holy Spirit Himself, without which we would be left in the mire of finite, sin-marred human opinion.

"The Lord Jesus' command is: '"Have faith in GOD"' (Mark 11:22; *caps mine*). God and

God alone is able to answer prayers of faith because He created and sustains everything that exists or happens.

"The modern church commits the same heinous, idolatrous blasphemies that Israel committed when saying, 'I have faith for my healing' or 'I have faith for my new Cadillac.' The object of true spiritual faith cannot be healing, cars or anything else! The only object of true spiritual faith is God Himself alone! All other uses of spiritual faith are heinous, ungodly, humanistic, blasphemous idolatry!

"True spiritual faith says this: 'I have faith in God alone, and entrust everything to Him. God will give me His desires for this life which I have given totally to Him for His use.' As God's children, we can and should ask of Him any and all needs or desires—and ask repeatedly! But we, as true believers, ask in total submission to the Father, for this is now His life! God will only grant that which is according to His will, which is set in His eternal purpose for His creation. The focus of true spiritual faith is God and His will, for this is His life! Let's read what God says in His holy Word regarding true spiritual faith."

They read:

> This is the confidence which we have before Him, that, if we ask anything according to His will, He hears us.
>
> And if we know that He hears us *in* whatever we ask, we know that we have the requests which we have asked from Him. (1 John 5:14,15)

> Now when John, while imprisoned, heard of the works of Christ, he sent *word* by his disciples
>
> and said to Him, "Are You the Expected One, or shall we look for someone else?"
>
> Jesus answered and said to them, "Go and report to John what you hear and see:
>
> *the* BLIND RECEIVE SIGHT and *the* lame walk, *the* lepers are cleansed and *the* deaf hear, *the* dead are raised up, and *the* POOR HAVE THE GOSPEL PREACHED TO THEM." (Matthew 11:2-5)

> "I and the Father are one."
>
> The Jews picked up stones again to stone Him.
>
> Jesus answered them, "I showed you many good works from the Father; for which of them are you stoning Me?"
>
> The Jews answered Him, "For a good work we do not stone You, but for blasphemy; and because You, being a man, make Yourself out *to be* God."
>
> "If I do not do the works of My Father, do not believe Me;
> but if I do them, though you do not believe Me, believe the works, so that you may know and understand that the Father is in Me, and I in the Father." (John 10:30-33,37,38)

For He grew up before Him like a tender shoot,
>> And like a root out of parched ground;
>>> He has no *stately* form or majesty
>>> That we should look upon Him,
>>> Nor appearance that we should be attracted to Him.
> He was despised and forsaken of men,
>> A man of sorrows and acquainted with grief;
>>> And like one from whom men hide their face
>>> He was despised, and we did not esteem Him.
Surely our griefs (*margin*: Or, *sickness*) He Himself bore,
>> And our sorrows He carried;
>>> Yet we ourselves esteemed Him stricken,
>>> Smitten of God, and afflicted.
> But He was pierced through for our transgressions,
>> He was crushed for our iniquities;
>>> The chastening for our well-being *fell* upon Him,
>>> And by His scourging we are healed.
All of us like sheep have gone astray,
>> Each of us has turned to his own way;
>>> But the LORD has caused the iniquity of us all
>>> To fall on Him. (Isaiah 53:2-6)

When evening came, they brought to Him many who were demon-possessed; and He cast out the spirits with a word, and healed all who were ill.

This was to fulfill what was spoken through Isaiah the prophet: "HE HIMSELF TOOK OUR INFIRMITIES AND CARRIED AWAY OUR DISEASES."
(Matthew 8:16,17)

For you have been called for this purpose, since Christ also suffered for you, leaving you an example for you to follow in His steps,

WHO COMMITTED NO SIN, NOR WAS ANY DECEIT FOUND IN HIS MOUTH;

and while being reviled, He did not revile in return; while suffering, He uttered no threats, but kept entrusting *Himself* to Him who judges righteously;

and He Himself bore our sins in His body on the cross, so that we might die to sin and live to righteousness; for by His wounds you were healed. (1 Peter 2:21-24)

Therefore, those also who suffer according to the will of God shall entrust their souls to a faithful Creator in doing what is right. (1 Peter 4:19)

The Spirit Himself testifies with our spirit that we are children of God,

and if children, heirs also, heirs of God and fellow heirs with Christ,

if indeed we suffer with *Him* so that we may also be glorified with *Him*.

(Romans 8:16,17)

"By His stripes we are Healed!"

"Both Apostles Peter and Paul declare in God's Word that true Christians are called for the purpose of suffering, since our Savior suffered for us as an example," Dave confirmed. "The ungodly, humanistic notion that God wants to—or worse, must—heal every believer, or alleviate all suffering, or make believers materially prosperous—directly contradicts these Bible passages.

"God may desire to heal, or may desire to bless materially. But it is according to His will, not our wills. God is under no obligation to anyone at any time for any reason outside of His own good pleasure and purpose. To say that God is obligated to His creation outside of His own will is to commit the greatest of blasphemies, because this error makes the Almighty Creator subject to His creation!

"But, many humanistic preachers attempt to comfort the sick and the suffering by giving them a false hope through false teachings. One of the most misquoted and misused passages is Isaiah 53 when pulled out of its context. The humanist boldly claims that Matthew verifies this passage as meaning that Jesus came to heal all diseases.

"One might come to such a travesty if one ignores God's original intended meaning of the text. Isaiah 53 gives a chronological picture of the Messiah when He comes in the flesh. Isaiah moves from Christ's birth—'He grew up before Him like a tender shoot'—to His death—'He was crushed for our iniquities.'

"Matthew tells us that Jesus healed all who were sick *at that time* in order to fulfill the prophecies God gave concerning His Messiah. The Lord answers John the Baptist's disciples by saying that the proof of His Messiahship rests in fulfilling the miracles God gave Him to accomplish during His earthly ministry. The Apostle John quotes Jesus as saying that His miracles, both of healing and casting out demons, were specifically done to prove that He was the Christ by fulfilling the prophecies about the Messiah.

"The Lord's fulfillment of the Messianic prophecies during His incarnation in no way obligate Him to heal everyone throughout history. Christ did not even heal everyone during His earthly ministry! In John 5, Jesus healed *one man* out of the multitude of sick people by the pool at Bethesda!

"Thus, Isaiah's prophecy concerned the works the Messiah would accomplish during His earthly ministry. The Christ's earthly work would culminate in His death on the cross, which would pay for all of the sins of all of God's true children. The Apostle Peter quotes Isaiah 53:5 to explain God's true meaning of the words, 'by His scourging (stripes, KJV) we are healed.' It is 'our sins,' which 'He Himself bore in His body on the cross,' that His wounds healed.

"Over and over in Scripture, the death of Christ is said to pay for the sins of God's chosen children," Dave concluded. "Nowhere does this justification for sin obligate God for physical healing. The Sovereign God may heal anyone at any time He so desires, but it is according to His eternal will and sovereign plan, not our wills and desires."

"Why would our heavenly Father, who loves us greatly, not want to heal every one of His children?" asked Nick.

"Excellent question," applauded Dave. "What is love?"

"Well...'*God* is love!'" quoted Nick.

"Exactly," Dave said. "And to love another is a commitment to bring that person closer to the Source of true Love—God Himself! We humans oftentimes get so involved in this worldly life that we ignore or even forget our heavenly Father. God uses suffering to get us out of ourselves and this perishing world, which is taking us away from Love. God brings us back to the only true Love that will eternally matter, God Himself!

"Sometimes God has His saints suffer to fulfill His plan of bringing the testimony of His holiness and judgment to the wicked (Matthew 10:17ff). God also uses the suffering of His children to fill up the sins of those destined for hell (1 Thessalonians 2:14ff). This is God's life to use as He pleases. But rest assured that the deaths of His children are precious in the Father's sight (Psalm 116:15), and the reward that the heavenly Father gives will be immense! We rejoice greatly in these brutal times, as the Lord Jesus said:

> "Blessed *are* you who hunger now, for you shall be satisfied. Blessed *are* you who weep now, for you shall laugh.
>
> "Blessed are you when men hate you, and ostracize you, and insult you, and scorn your name as evil, for the sake of the Son of Man.
>
> "Be glad in that day and leap *for joy,* for behold, your reward is great in heaven. For in the same way their fathers used to treat the prophets."
>
> (Luke 6:21-23)

"In getting on our loving heavenly Father's Lap, God comforts us and gives us His grace in times of need. We would fail miserably to endure godly suffering in our own strength. We must totally rely on the true love and true grace that God gives to those He has chosen as His children. God loved these elect from before the foundation of the world, and gave them the faith to trust everything to Christ. God's gift of 'faith in Christ' secured our salvation so that we may live eternally in absolute paradise with Love Himself—our heavenly Father!

"So," Dave summarized, "'faith' and 'faith in Christ' are not the same. The ungodly humanist errs greatly when he assumes that 'faith to trust God for salvation'—or 'saving faith'—is inherent in every person, and that each person must choose to exercise or not exercise it. Everyone has simple faith, such as trusting that a chair will hold us up. But God must grant 'faith in Christ,' and He gives this gift only to those He has chosen to be in His family.

"Finally, the only true spiritual faith is faith in God Himself alone. Faith in anything or anyone else for the miraculous is heinous, ungodly, blasphemous, humanistic idolatry."

"You are right," commended Nick. "There is confusion in thinking that 'faith' and 'faith in Christ' are similar. This is just like the confusion humanism has brought with 'free will.' Being able to choose brands of toothpaste does not mean we are able to choose Christ as Savior. The ability to choose God only comes after we are made alive from spiritual death by the Holy Spirit. The faith to trust Christ for salvation is a specific gift given to us from God. It is not something with which we are born, and can conjure up."

"You've got it!" Dave exclaimed.

If God Is Sovereign, Why Evangelize?

"Thanks!" Nick replied. "So, if God chose before creation which sinners would be in His family, and Christ's sacrifice secured their salvation...why evangelize? Since God predestined His elect to come to Christ, why preach the gospel throughout the world?"

"Great question!" Dave replied. "A few weeks back, we read passage after passage from God's holy Word, regarding God Himself, that we humans always forget. In answer to the question of why Christians should evangelize, let's review some scriptures. Please read the next six passages I have marked down."

Nick read:

> The LORD has established His throne in the heavens,
>   And His sovereignty rules over all. (Psalm 103:19)

> "Who then is he that can stand before Me?
> "Who has given to Me that I should repay *him?*
>   *Whatever* is under the whole heaven is Mine." (Job 41:10b,11)

> For I know that the LORD is great
>   And that our Lord is above all gods.
> Whatever the LORD pleases, He does,
>   In heaven and in earth, in the seas and in all deeps.
>   (Psalm 135:5,6)

> "Remember the former things long past,
>   For I am God, and there is no other;
>   *I am* God, and there is no one like Me,
> "Declaring the end from the beginning,
>   And from ancient times things which have not been done,
>   Saying, 'My purpose will be established,
>   And I will accomplish all My good pleasure.'"
>   (Isaiah 46:9,10)

> And Jesus came up and spoke to them, saying, "All authority has been given to Me in heaven and on earth.
>   "Go therefore and make disciples of all the nations, baptizing them in the name of the Father and the Son and the Holy Spirit,
>   teaching them to observe all that I commanded you; and lo, I am with you always, even to the end of the age." (Matthew 28:18-20)

"Almighty God is sovereign," Dave expounded, "which means that He has ordained absolutely everything that exists or happens in all of creation at all times. God owns everything, and He does whatever pleases Him.

"Our God 'is the blessed and only Sovereign, the King of kings and Lord of lords' (1 Timothy 6:15). God established His plan before the foundation of the world, and He will accomplish all of it perfectly, for no one can stop Him. Every sinner that becomes a true Christian will be born again at the exact moment, and in the exact manner, that Almighty God had ordained it without fail.

"As we have learned, God is absolutely independent. God does not depend on anyone for anything. God *causes* absolutely everything that occurs in creation to happen according to His perfect plan—especially salvation. God initiates salvation, causes all spiritual growth within the Christian, and brings the process to glorious completion in His heavenly kingdom!

"Since God explicitly declares that man's will is not even involved in salvation (John 1:12,13; Romans 9:16), God is certainly not waiting for man to 'decide for Jesus,' as the ungodly humanist would claim. God sovereignly begins and completes the process of salvation in those whom He specifically chose out of the world for His own pleasure (John 17). Again, God has ordained absolutely everything that occurs in time and space; and everything Almighty God has ordained will occur without fail—especially salvation! Nick, please read these next three passages."

Nick read:

> *For I am* confident of this very thing, that He who began a good work
> in you will perfect it until the day of Christ Jesus. (Philippians 1:6)

> Then Job answered the LORD and said,
> "I know that You can do all things,
> And that no purpose of Yours can be thwarted." (Job 42:2)

> In Him also we have obtained an inheritance, having been predestined
> according to His purpose who works all things after the counsel of His will.
> (Ephesians 10b,11)

"The first and most important reason why God's children should go to all the nations and preach the gospel, making disciples, is that God commands it. If our loving Father commands anything—whether we understand His reasons or not—we must do it. The only proper way to ask God 'why' is after we have submitted to His command, humbly knowing that the eternal, all-wise, good Father never has to explain Himself—and rarely does.

"The second reason to evangelize should be obvious from the scriptures we have read. If God ordains everything, and 'works all things after the counsel of His will,' then God ordains every step involved in salvation as well. **God ordains *the ends* as well as *the means*.** He starts the process, works every detail in the process, and brings His perfect result at the specific second which He had planned it before creation to occur.

"The third reason God commands us to evangelize is that He has ordained for each child an inheritance based upon the works He has prepared. God has allowed man to share in the completion of His eternal plan. As the true Christian obeys God and fulfills the work God prepared, the believer will receive a reward for his eternal inheritance.

"Last but certainly not least, the final reason to evangelize is that we do not know whom God has chosen to come into His family. We cannot see into another person's heart, regardless of what he looks like on the outside, or regardless of his past. Our task is to proclaim God's message of the true gospel. Those whom God has enabled to understand His truth will respond—by the Holy Spirit's power—with remorse, repentance and belief.

The Foolishness of the Gospel

"I mean, when you think about it—looking at it from man's point of view—preaching the gospel is totally foolish!"

"What?" Nick looked at Dave with amazement at that statement.

"Absolutely," Dave replied, "and the Apostle Paul says exactly that in God's Word! Nick, please read the next passages I have written down."

Nick read:

> For the word of the cross is foolishness to those who are perishing, but to us who are being saved it is the power of God.
>
> Where is the wise man? Where is the scribe? Where is the debater of this age? Has not God made foolish the wisdom of the world?
>
> For since in the wisdom of God the world through its wisdom did not *come to* know God, God was well-pleased through the foolishness of the message preached to save those who believe.
>
> For indeed Jews ask for signs and Greeks search for wisdom;
>
> but we preach Christ crucified, to Jews a stumbling block and to Gentiles foolishness,
>
> but to those who are the called, both Jews and Greeks, Christ the power of God and the wisdom of God.
>
> Because the foolishness of God is wiser than men, and the weakness of God is stronger than men.
>
> For consider your calling, brethren, that there were not many wise according to the flesh, not many mighty, not many noble;
>
> but God has chosen the foolish things of the world to shame the wise, and God has chosen the weak things of the world to shame the things which are strong.
>
> But by His doing you are in Christ Jesus, who became to us wisdom from God, and righteousness and sanctification, and redemption.
>
> (1 Corinthians 1:18,20-27,30)

"The Apostle Paul is speaking here, arguably the greatest preacher of all time. He writes that God has sent us to unbelievers with a message that they absolutely will not understand, but will certainly think is total foolishness! Is that a recipe for disaster, or what?" asked Dave.

"You and the Apostle both have a point there," answered Nick.

"The Apostle says that God set it up this way on purpose," Dave explained. "Paul ends his discussion on the wisdom of God, and the foolishness of man, saying: 'by *His* doing you are in Christ Jesus.'

"Paul makes it absolutely clear that the Almighty uses something that could never succeed—preaching to 'brick walls'—to show that God Himself is the only cause of salvation. It is not the preaching, or the eloquence of words, or the logic of the argument, or the passionate speech that opens blind eyes and deaf ears to receive Christ as Savior. Salvation itself is God's work and God's work alone! Thus, God gets all of the glory!

"Get in on It!"

"God also says that He has predestined not only our salvation, but an inheritance for each of His chosen ones according to His purpose, or plan. In a word, God wants His children to '**get in on it!**' God wants His children to participate in His great plan which He formed before creation, and He will give them a reward for their obedience. Instead of zapping us up to heaven the moment He gave us salvation, it was His good pleasure to keep us here and use us to display God's love and mercy to a dying world.

"Yes, Almighty God could accomplish His entire plan with just the proverbial snap of His fingers. Again, God does not need anyone for anything! On His way to Jerusalem, the Lord Jesus said that if the children of God did not praise Him, God would cause the rocks to cry out (Luke 19:40)!

"But, even though salvation itself is only God's work, He has chosen to use us in bringing the rest of His eternal plan to fruition. Also, to demonstrate His unending love and generosity toward His children, He prepared for us an awesome inheritance. The reward is for doing specifically what God wants done, not what we wish to do in His Name.

"God reveals to His children His desires for them when they give up this life, put aside this world, get on His Lap and learn of His ways. Then the Holy Spirit opens His holy Word to us as we study the Bible, attend worship services, and fellowship with committed Christians.

"God is to be revered infinitely more than this world's gold and treasures. God's treasures are everlasting. But they are extremely precious, and God only gives His gems to the one willing to give up everything for them. God rewards the one who insists on seeking Him with all of his heart.

"Let's read about the value that our Lord Jesus places on God's kingdom, and how we are to be devoted to it. Please read the next two scriptures, Nick."

Nick read:

Hidden Treasure

"The kingdom of heaven is like a treasure hidden in the field, which a
man found and hid *again*; and from joy over it he goes and sells all that he
has and buys that field.

A Costly Pearl

"Again, the kingdom of heaven is like a merchant seeking fine pearls,
and upon finding one pearl of great value, he went and sold all that he had
and bought it." (Matthew 13:44-46)

"As we have already learned," Dave recalled, "*the will of God* for every real Christian is to get on the Lap of the Father, seeking to love Him and know Him more intimately. God then reveals His plan for each child—to each child—as he seeks Him.

"The Lord Jesus makes it very clear that when a seeker finds the treasure—when God reveals Himself to His child—the Christian must give up everything for Him. To the degree the child obeys this command is the extent that God reveals His deep treasures, and blesses His child with the real riches of knowing Him intimately.

Sharing the True Gospel

"Sharing the *gospel*—God's good news of salvation—is one of the deep treasures and blessed privileges that God gives to His children. People who regularly share the gospel know of the exhilarating blessing they receive from God as they do His will.

"We are not to go and save sinners. *God* saves sinners. We are commanded to go and '"make disciples"' (Matthew 28:19). We are to go and share the marvelous things God has done for us.

"It all begins with the indispensable first step: getting on the Lap of the Father, and asking Him to bring opportunities to share with the people He wants to hear His Word. Sharing the gospel without prayer is a most frustrating experience, because God alone is the one who brings the results!

"Then we share God's standard for going to heaven—to be perfect as God is perfect—and the horrible alternative of paying for our imperfections in hell. We explain the impossible predicament in which we were imprisoned, and how God set us free!

"Yes, sharing God's good news requires correct understanding of God's plan for mankind as found in His holy Word. But slamming people who are not interested is not necessary. God commands us to relate our own experiences with God, according to His Word, to people who are interested.

"In sharing the gospel correctly, according to God's Word, we are not to plead unceasingly with sinners who show no interest, and even spurn God's precious sacrifice. The Lord Jesus commanded His disciples: '"Do not give what is holy to dogs, and do not throw your pearls before swine, or they will trample them under their feet, and turn and tear you to pieces"' (Matthew 7:6).

"It is absolutely futile to run around trying to save everyone, for the Lord Jesus explicitly declared that only the few will be saved (Matthew 7:13,14). You are to share '"what great things the Lord has done for you, and how He had mercy on you"' (Mark 5:19). Then, to the ones who show interest, you can explain the gospel in greater detail and answer any questions.

"The ones God has chosen to be in His family will be moved by the Holy Spirit to ask how they can be saved from eternal torture, and become as perfect as God is perfect. The ones God has chosen will truly desire to come to Christ, repent by giving up their lives to Him, and trust in Christ's work alone for salvation. The rest will never be convinced through argument or reason, because God's truth is total foolishness to the sinner whom God has not regenerated by His Holy Spirit.

"Again, Christ never commanded us to go save sinners, but to go and make disciples.

Sharing the gospel means making known God's standard for entering heaven, and the awesome way He has accomplished this for us. The elect—those God has chosen to be in His family—will respond at exactly the moment when the Holy Spirit has ordained and enabled them to respond.

"Please read our Lord Jesus' words on how to share the gospel correctly."

Nick read:

The Rich Young Ruler

A ruler questioned Him, saying, "Good Teacher, what shall I do to inherit eternal life?"

And Jesus said to him, "Why do you call Me good? No one is good except God alone.

"You know the commandments, 'DO NOT COMMIT ADULTERY, DO NOT MURDER, DO NOT STEAL, DO NOT BEAR FALSE WITNESS, HONOR YOUR FATHER AND MOTHER.' "

And he said, "All these things I have kept from *my* youth."

When Jesus heard *this,* He said to him, "One thing you still lack; sell all that you possess and distribute it to the poor, and you shall have treasure in heaven; and come, follow Me."

But when he had heard these things, he became very sad, for he was extremely rich.

And Jesus looked at him and said, "How hard it is for those who are wealthy to enter the kingdom of God!

"For it is easier for a camel to go through the eye of a needle than for a rich man to enter the kingdom of God."

They who heard it said, "Then who can be saved?"

But He said, "The things that are impossible with people are possible with God."

Peter said, "Behold, we have left our own *homes* and followed You."

And He said to them, "Truly I say to you, there is no one who has left house or wife or brothers or parents or children, for the sake of the kingdom of God,

who will not receive many times as much at this time and in the age to come, eternal life." (Luke 18:18-30)

"The Lord Jesus demonstrates in this passage the perfect way to preach the gospel," Dave expounded. "A person asks the most important question one could ever ask in this world: 'What must I do to be saved?' Here is a man who is obviously interested in the things of God, but he has no knowledge or understanding.

"In answer to his question, the Lord immediately quotes the Law of Moses. In our study next week I will explain the Law of God, the Law of Christ and the Law of Moses in full detail, with their correct relation to the Christian. Suffice it to say, the Law of Moses—which begins with the Ten Commandments—was given by God for two reasons: to show God's standard of righteousness, and the absolute impossibility for man to obey God's commands.

"The Law of Moses is a list of over 600 specific commands from God with one huge, insurmountable stumbling block: one must keep all of God's commands perfectly at all times; for if a person breaks one command just once, he is guilty of breaking the entire Law (Leviticus 19:37; James 2:10). Thus, in the Lord Jesus' words: '"Therefore you are to be perfect, as your heavenly Father is perfect"' (Matthew 5:48, quoting Leviticus 19:2 in the Law of Moses).

"In this encounter with the rich ruler, the Lord was using the Law of Moses—which the man knew very well, obviously—to show the man how far short he was of God's perfection. The Lord Jesus declared that keeping the Law perfectly would give the man eternal life. However, he prefaced that fact by saying, '"No one is good except God alone."' Since no man conceived by a human father could be as perfect as God is perfect, then it is absolutely impossible for anyone with a sin nature to keep the Mosaic Law.

"Being God, Jesus knew the man's greed, and that he had set up his riches as his god. This violated the first commandment of having no other gods but God Himself (Exodus 20:1-3). In taking away the rich man's idol, his money, the Lord put him in a saving position of having to depend upon God for everything.

"The ruler had remorse. But it was not a remorse for his sinful, idolatrous rebellion against God and His holiness. That holy remorse only comes from the Holy Spirit's regeneration. The rich man was sad because he loved his money more than anything, even eternal life, and he could not have both!

"The rich, young ruler, as with any true believer, had to give up everything he had for eternal life with the One True God. This is repentance, the first of the two absolutely necessary responses to God's salvation. **Repentance** means changing one's mind about who is master of this life, and totally giving back this life to Christ, its rightful owner, for whatever He wishes to do with it.

"The second, absolutely necessary response to God's salvation—at which the rich, young ruler never even arrived—is to believe. **Believing** means to totally trust in Christ and only the merits of His two-part perfect work for salvation: His death on the cross to pay for sins, and His perfect life credited to the believer's account. These are the two required *responses* (Mark 1:15) by a regenerated person in whom God has already placed His Holy Spirit.

"To inherit eternal life, Jesus commanded the man to give up all he had—to repent—and to follow Him—to believe. This is the perfect pattern for correctly preaching the gospel:

1. Ascertain a person's interest
2. Give him God's standard for going to heaven (Matthew 5:48)
3. Explain the alternative of eternal torture in hell for not meeting the standard (Matthew 25; Mark 9:43-48)
4. If the person still wants to know how to meet God's standard and go to heaven:
   ✧ Explain the command to *repent* (Mark 1:15; Mark 8:34,35)
   ✧ Explain the command to *believe* (Mark 1:15; John 5:24; Romans 5:8-10)
   ✧ Explain how to "*come to Christ*" (Matthew 11:28-30)

"That seems like a simple plan," observed Nick.

"Yes," Dave agreed. "Imagine we were eating lunch in the dorm cafeteria before the Lord saved you. Let's do a role-play, and I'll show you how simple the gospel is to share."

"Great!"

"Hey, Nick!" greeted Dave. "Did you hear about that famous race car driver that died during the race this weekend?"

"Oh yeah," recalled Nick. "I saw the crash on the news."

"Wasn't that something?" Dave continued. "One second he's driving near 200 miles per hour, and the next moment he is before the throne of God for judgment!"

"What?" asked Nick, somewhat surprised at the comment. "How do you know that?"

"Every single person, including you, knows that," Dave responded. "God placed in every person's conscience the knowledge that He exists, and that He will judge every person's life immediately after the moment of death. God says in His Word that 'it is appointed for men to die once and after this comes judgment' (Hebrews 9:27).

"Tell me, Nick. If you were to die unexpectedly today—like that race car driver—would God send you to heaven for an eternity in paradise, or hell for an eternity in torment?"

"Well," pondered Nick, "I'm a good guy. I've never murdered anybody, and I treat people pretty much like I want to be treated. So, I guess God would say my good deeds outweigh my bad ones, and He would let me into heaven."

"It's great that your good deeds outweigh your bad deeds," Dave replied, "but that is not God's standard for getting into heaven. God's standard for getting into heaven is that '"you are to be perfect, as your heavenly Father is perfect"' (Matthew 5:48)."

"Perfect as God is perfect?!" exclaimed Nick. "No one is as perfect as that! Heaven must be an empty place!"

"No, there are many, many people in heaven," Dave responded, "but there are many times more people burning in hell. They died and went before God in judgment, and were not perfect as God is perfect. God condemned them to eternal torture in hell, being burned alive, feeling all of the agony, and never being consumed. The torture will never, ever end. One might guess that the German dictator Adolph Hitler has been burning in hell for over fifty years now—with an eternity to go."

"Wow," lamented Nick.

"Even worse, every human being born by a human father inherits the original sin of Adam, and a totally sinful nature. Adam, the first human, rebelled against God's command. As part of his punishment, all of his descendants born of a human male inherit his guilt and sinful nature.

"We are sinners from birth. God gave us this life to serve Him with it. But every person born from a human father has selfishly stolen this life to serve himself, continuously fulfilling his own selfish, sinful desires. We have all rebelled and sinned against God, the holy Creator."

"There is no hope!" Nick bemoaned.

"But there are actually two ways to be as perfect as God is perfect," answered Dave. "One is to be God Himself."

"That does me no good. From going to church as a kid, and learning what little I've heard about God, I am certainly not God. My grades alone this semester will prove that I don't know everything!"

"Good point—neither do I," Dave said. "But the second way to 'be as perfect as God is perfect' is the most amazing truth you will ever hear.

"The sober fact is that 'all have sinned and fall short of the glory of God' (Romans 3:23). God is perfectly just, meaning that someone has to pay for your sins against Him—either you by burning in hell, or someone willing to take your place."

"Who would be willing to take my torture?" asked Nick.

"Well, you would have to find someone that is perfect as God is perfect. Anyone who is not perfect as God is perfect has his own sins for which to pay."

"There is no one like that," concluded Nick.

"God knew that there was no human being able to be your substitute. So, He did an amazing thing! He sent His Son, Almighty God Jesus Christ, to take on human flesh in order to pay for your sins.

"Since God the Son Jesus Christ *is* God, He lived a perfectly sinless life as a man. Then, in agreement with God the Father, Christ died on the cross. He took the full wrath of God for all of the sins committed by the people God would choose to come into His heaven.

"God the Holy Spirit will convict those chosen ones of their rebellion and sin against God. They will feel remorse for offending God by stealing this life for their own selfish purposes instead of serving God."

"Yeah, I kind of know what you mean," said Nick. "As you have been speaking, I feel bad for the life I've lived. I want to make it right before God so I don't burn in hell forever."

"Remember, to avoid burning in hell, you must be perfect as God is perfect. That is God's standard for getting into His heaven," Dave repeated. "God Himself has made the only way for this to happen where we were utterly hopeless. God the Father sacrificed His only Son to pay for the sins of those He had chosen to be in His family. Rejecting such an incredible sacrifice will be met with God's extreme wrath.

"If you have been chosen by God to come to His heaven, then Jesus Christ's death on the cross paid for all of your sins, wiping your slate clean. God then credits your account with the sinless, perfect life that God the Son lived on earth! It's a legal transfer. God transfers your sin to Christ on the cross, and He pays your penalty by taking the wrath of God as your substitute. God then transfers His Son's perfect life to your account, making you perfect as God is perfect, because Jesus Christ is God!"

"Wow, that's almost unbelievable that God would do that," Nick contemplated. "So, how do I know if I have been chosen by God to come into His heaven?"

"Every person conceived by a human father is born spiritually dead," Dave began. "The sinner is dead to the things of God, and lives only to serve himself, always rebelling against God. Again, the sinner has stolen this life from God, the Creator and rightful owner of all life.

"True remorse for offending God is only experienced after God places His Holy Spirit inside of a sinner, and makes him spiritually alive. If then the Holy Spirit has convicted you of your rebellion and sin against the holy God, and you have remorse for specifically offending God and His holiness, then you are most likely chosen. Those not chosen by God will simply go on living this life for themselves—just as you have done since you were born—and will never even experience true remorse for offending God."

"I do feel that remorse for sinning against God. What do I do now?" asked Nick.

"Christ Jesus gives two specific commands: "'repent and believe in the gospel'" (Mark 1:15).

"To **repent** means changing your mind about who owns this life, giving back this life totally to Christ, its rightful owner, for whatever He wants to do with it. God gave us life to serve Him with it, but we stole it to serve ourselves. God commands us to relinquish our rebellious hold on this life, and give it totally back to Him. All of it. Without repentance—totally giving up this life to God—Christ's substitute sacrifice does not apply (Luke 13:1-9).

"To **believe** means trusting totally in Christ and His two-part work for salvation. We place absolutely no trust in ourselves, our 'goodness' and our deeds. Again, Christ died on the cross, paying God's just penalty for your sin, which wiped your slate clean. Then, God transfers Christ's perfect life to your account, making you legally as perfect as God is perfect!

"Thus, you are not only able to go to heaven, but are sealed and secured by the Holy Spirit! Since God had chosen you before creation to be in His kingdom, you are guaranteed eternal life. You have passed out of any judgment, because Christ took your judgment for you (John 5:24)!"

"What an incredible plan!" Nick exclaimed. "How do I get this deal with God?"

"Well, if the Holy Spirit has given you the desire, then God's command is to **come to Christ** and follow His direction. Jesus says:

"Come to Me, all who are weary and heavy-laden, and I will give you rest.

"Take My yoke upon you and learn from Me, for I am gentle and humble in heart, and YOU WILL FIND REST FOR YOUR SOULS.

"For My yoke is easy and My burden is light." (Matthew 11:28-30)

"Since God is everywhere and sees everything, you can go to Him in prayer right now," Dave explained. "If God has placed His Holy Spirit in you and has given you new life in Christ, God requires you to respond to His miracle. Ask Him to forgive you of your rebellion and sin against Him. You can ask to enter His deal for eternal life, and agree to give this life back to Him for whatever He wants to do with it. Then you can agree to trust only in Christ and His work for your salvation. Would you like to pray to God and enter His deal?"

"You bet! I don't want to wait another moment!" Nick played his role perfectly.

"Then you would lead your friend in a prayer to God much like I did that Friday night with you," Dave continued. "The prayer should include five steps:

1. Remorse—true sorrow for leading a rebellious, sinful life against God
2. Repentance—totally giving back this life to God, its rightful owner
3. Believing in Christ's work alone for perfection and salvation
4. Resting in the security of God's promise of eternal life
5. Thankfulness to God for rescue from deserved eternal torture

"You make witnessing for Christ seem so easy!" Nick exclaimed.

"Oh, you will run into many objections and hateful responses," Dave warned. "But remember: it is not our mission to save the world. God saves sinners, the few He has chosen to be in His family. We are simply to share what great things God has done for us. If a person is interested, then we can explain the gospel in more detail.

"The ones that God has chosen to come to heaven will experience remorse brought on by the conviction of sin by the Holy Spirit. They will ask the critical question: 'What must I do to be saved?'

"The ones not chosen by God to be rescued from their deserved punishment will fight against God's message in order to continue in their rebellion and sin. We are commanded by Christ not to pummel these people with God's message, for they will never understand or receive the truth. They will only trample God's Word and attack you (Matthew 7:6)."

"Thanks for doing that role-play with me," said Nick. "It took out the fear of the unknown in sharing the gospel with others. I don't have to have all the answers to all of the objections out there. I can just share what God has done for me in giving me eternal life. If they are not interested, fine. If they are, I have a solid biblical understanding now of how to explain my faith!"

Four Major Errors of the Modern Gospel

"Excellent!" Dave applauded. "There are four major errors that should be avoided in sharing God's true gospel, because they are not supported by Scripture.

"The first error is telling someone that God loves him, or that God loves everyone. God emphatically states in many places in His Word that He does not love everyone (*see Chapter 8*). God 'abhorred' the unbelievers in Old Testament Israel, and most of the Book of Revelation chronicles God's severe wrath upon New Testament unbelievers. Nick, please read the verses I wrote down from Psalm 78, Hebrews 10, Revelation 14 and 20, and lastly John 3."

Nick read:

> Therefore the LORD heard and was full of wrath;
>> And a fire was kindled against Jacob
>> And anger also mounted against Israel,
> Because they did not believe in God
>> And did not trust in His salvation.
> For they provoked Him with their high places
>> And aroused His jealousy with their graven images.
> When God heard, He was filled with wrath
>> And greatly abhorred Israel. (Psalm 78:21,22,58,59)

> For if we go on sinning willfully after receiving the knowledge of the
> truth, there no longer remains a sacrifice for sins,
>> but a terrifying expectation of judgment and THE FURY OF A FIRE WHICH
> WILL CONSUME THE ADVERSARIES.
> Anyone who has set aside the Law of Moses dies without mercy on *the
> testimony of* two or three witnesses.
> How much severer punishment do you think he will deserve who has
> trampled under foot the Son of God, and has regarded as unclean the
> blood of the covenant by which he was sanctified, and has insulted the
> Spirit of grace? (Hebrews 10:26-29)

Then another angel, a third one, followed them, saying with a loud voice, "If anyone worships the beast and his image, and receives a mark on his forehead or on his hand,

he also will drink of the wine of the wrath of God, which is mixed in full strength in the cup of His anger; and he will be tormented with fire and brimstone in the presence of the holy angels and in the presence of the Lamb.

"And the smoke of their torment goes up forever and ever; they have no rest day and night, those who worship the beast and his image, and whoever receives the mark of his name." (Revelation 14:9-11)

Then I saw a great white throne and Him who sat upon it, from whose presence earth and heaven fled away, and no place was found for them.

And if anyone's name was not found written in the book of life, he was thrown into the lake of fire. (Revelation 20:11,15)

"For God so loved the world, that He gave His only begotten Son, that whoever believes in Him shall not perish, but have eternal life.

"He who believes in Him is not judged; he who does not believe has been judged already, because he has not believed in the name of the only begotten Son of God.

"He who believes in the Son has eternal life; but he who does not obey the Son will not see life, but the wrath of God abides on him."

(John 3:16,18,36)

"The ungodly humanist will immediately point to John 3:16 and declare that God loves every person in the world," Dave commented. "Once again, the humanist falsely assumes that the definition of Christ's term '*the world*' is 'every person on earth.' How can God love someone while 'the wrath of God abides on him?' God does not have a split personality.

"If we were to attend a general session of the United Nations in New York City, we would see one person from practically every nation on the earth. I can correctly say that 'the whole world' is in this room. But 'every single person in the world' is not in the room—the room could not hold six billion people!

"'The world' is there, however, because every nation is represented. Every nation will also be represented in heaven before God's throne! The chosen ones that God eternally loves and saved from His wrath will be there worshiping Him. This is the Lord's meaning in John 3:16, just as that same Apostle John wrote in the Book of Revelation. Nick, please read this passage."

Nick read:

After these things I looked, and behold, a great multitude which no one could count, from every nation and *all* tribes and peoples and tongues, standing before the throne and before the Lamb, clothed in white robes, and palm branches *were* in their hands;

and they cry out with a loud voice, saying,

"Salvation to our God who sits on the throne, and to the Lamb."

(Revelation 7:9,10)

"God eternally loves those He chose, giving them saving faith to believe in Christ, and saving them from deserved eternal wrath. But, God also abhors the sinners who love their rebellion, and spurn the sacred sacrifice of His Son. These sinners have already been judged (John 3:18), and their future is the lake of fire. Since we finite humans do not know in advance if a certain sinner has been chosen, we cannot definitely tell him that God loves him.

"We can say that God loves sinners He has chosen to come into His family. Committing the error of telling an unrepentant sinner that God loves him gives the sinner the mistaken impression that he has escaped God's wrath even in his rebellion. The Lord Jesus emphatically denied this (John 3:36).

"The second error commonly found in sharing God's true gospel with sinners is quoting a passage of Scripture: Romans 10:9 and 10."

"How could quoting God's Word be a mistake?" Nick asked, puzzled.

"Read the passage, and I'll show you."

Nick read:

> ...that if you confess with your mouth Jesus *as* Lord, and believe in your
> heart that God raised Him from the dead, you will be saved;
>
> for with the heart a person believes, resulting in righteousness, and with
> the mouth he confesses, resulting in salvation. (Romans 10:9,10)

"Let's say that one day you get a long letter from an old friend in the mail," Dave explained. "Do you turn to page 10, read one sentence, and then think that you have caught up with all of the details of your pal's life?"

"Of course not," answered Nick. "That would be silly. I would need to read the whole letter."

"Exactly," Dave responded. "Many Christians pull this sentence out of chapter 10 of the Apostle Paul's Letter to the Romans and quote it to someone who has no idea what the first nine chapters have to say! This promise in chapter 10 is totally dependent upon understanding all of the deep, theological issues discussed in the nine chapters before it.

"Telling an unrepentant sinner that if you just 'confess with your mouth Jesus as Lord, and believe in your heart that God raised Him from the dead, you will be saved' is not just silly, it is downright irresponsible—if not reprehensibly sinful! The sinner has no idea of the true meanings of 'confess,' 'Lord,' 'believe,' 'raised Him from the dead,' or, for that matter, 'saved.' If a person does not understand that he is a sinner who has offended God the Eternal Judge, then, in his mind, from what does he need to be saved??

"I actually have had members of cults—people with no idea of the identity of the One True God, or of their sinful condition—tell me that they were already saved because a Christian told them all they had to do is what verses 9 and 10 say. Could anything be more irresponsible?

"Committing this grave error causes spiritual abortions. It creates in the minds of sinners, living just as rebelliously as before, that they are in good standing with God just because they 'plugged into this formula for salvation.' Could anything be more heinous, or more blasphemous against our holy God?"

"I see what you mean," said Nick. "Unless we are willing to explain the context of certain scriptures, using them irresponsibly actually causes more harm than good."

"Correct," Dave acknowledged. "God's true gospel must be shared in the manner God wants it explained, because it is *God's* good news to sinners! Thus, Pop Quiz question 20 is false. The statement is, 'All that is necessary to be saved is to confess with your mouth Jesus as Lord and believe in your heart that God raised Him from the dead.' The Apostle makes this conclusion only after nine chapters of deep theology explaining God and His plan for His universe. If a sinner does not understand these concepts, then the promise does not apply.

"The third mistake of modern evangelism involves the misuse and abuse of another passage of Scripture," Dave continued. "I'll bet you have heard this one: 'Jesus stands at the door of the sinner's heart, just waiting for him to invite Him in.'"

"Oh, I've heard that a hundred times from preachers and evangelists," Nick agreed. "I've also read it on the Pop Quiz at question 21. Isn't that a quote from a passage in the Book of Revelation?"

"Let's read the scripture," Dave answered.

Nick read:

> "To the angel of the church in Laodicea write:
> The Amen, the faithful and true Witness, the Beginning of the creation of God, says this:
>
> "I know your deeds, that you are neither cold nor hot; I wish that you were cold or hot.
>
> "...you say, 'I am rich, and have become wealthy, and have need of nothing,' and you do not know that you are wretched and miserable and poor and blind and naked.
>
> "Those whom I love, I reprove and discipline; therefore be zealous and repent.
>
> "Behold, I stand at the door and knock; if anyone hears My voice and opens the door, I will come in to him and will dine with him, and he with Me.
>
> "He who has an ear, let him hear what the Spirit says to the churches." (Revelation 3:14,15,17,19,20,22)

"The first thing we notice," Dave expounded, "is that Jesus is talking to '*the church!*'

"The Lord is reproving the church at Laodicea for going through religious motions without their hearts being totally in it. They became fat and happy from material wealth, and relied upon their riches instead of Christ Himself.

"Christ says He is standing outside of the church door, instead of being in their midst. If any of His children inside care to return to seeking Him, instead of being complacent with mere religious ritual, Christ will show them the real experience of God's awesome, intimate love.

'Anyone' refers directly back to 'those whom I love,' which can only refer to God's true children.

"This passage does not involve unbelievers at all. Christ is addressing believers who have become lazy in their religion instead of fervently seeking Him for abundant life. Thus, Pop Quiz question 21 is false. The Lord God Almighty does not wait upon humans to decide anything concerning salvation. And since salvation is not the choice of man at all, misusing this passage for evangelism blasphemes the sovereignty of God.

"The fourth mistake is by far the most common, and this one is not even found anywhere in the Bible! Telling a sinner, 'Just accept Jesus Christ as your personal Lord and Savior, and you will be saved!' is nowhere to be found in God's holy Word!"

"What? But I hear that all the time from evangelists and preachers!" exclaimed Nick.

"No kidding!" answered Dave. "This is an ungodly, humanistic, simplified attempt at putting God's eternal gospel into a 30-second 'TV commercial' slogan. Again, a sinner has no idea of the meanings of 'Lord,' 'Savior,' and 'saved.' Worse yet, it heinously lies by contradicting God's Word, giving man the decision 'to accept' salvation.

"The Scripture cannot be more clear on this point: man's will or choice has absolutely nothing to do with salvation. As we read earlier today, it is 'by His (God's) doing you are in Christ Jesus' (1 Corinthians 1:30). Please read John 1:12 and 13, Romans 9:16 and Ephesians 2:4 and 5 again."

Nick read:

> But as many as received Him, to them He gave the right to become children of God, *even* to those who believe in His name,
>
> who were born, not of blood nor of the will of the flesh nor of the will of man, but of God. (John 1:12,13)

> So then it (salvation) *does* not *depend* on the man who wills or the man who runs, but on God who has mercy.
>
> (Romans 9:16; *parenthesis mine*)

> But God, being rich in mercy, because of His great love with which He loved us,
>
> even when we were dead in our transgressions, made us alive together with Christ (by grace you have been saved). (Ephesians 2:4,5)

"God's Word declares emphatically that we sinners were 'dead in our transgressions,'" Dave expounded. "Dead people cannot accept, or reach out, or choose, or anything. They are dead!

"God's Word also states that those who are born again as children of God were not born again by the will of man. Scripture plainly asserts that salvation does not depend on the man who wills (man's choices) or the man who runs (man's actions).

"All scriptures on salvation clearly affirm that becoming born again depends solely upon God Almighty alone. To reject this obvious fact is to deny God's Word, and side with humanism, which desires to usurp God's glory for sinful man.

"When we were sinners, we could not accept any truth regarding God, for it was total foolishness to us. Read God's truth on this matter in 1 Corinthians 1:18 and 2:14."

Nick read:

> For the word of the cross is foolishness to those who are perishing, but to us who are being saved it is the power of God. (1 Corinthians 1:18)

> But a natural man does not accept the things of the Spirit of God, for they are foolishness to him; and he cannot understand them, because they are spiritually appraised. (1 Corinthians 2:14)

"Asking a sinner to 'accept Jesus Christ as your personal Lord and Savior' is like asking an actual corpse to stand and sing a song. It is ridiculous," Dave contended. "I will explain the differences between 'accepting' something and 'receiving' something this Sunday in the College & Career class. Telling a sinner to accept Christ as his Savior is not the gospel. That denies, and directly contradicts, the clear teaching of Scripture.

"God's Word gives the only effective way to share God's true gospel. The Lord Jesus demonstrated assessing a person's interest, giving him God's standard for going to heaven, and explaining the alternative of eternal torture for not meeting the standard.

"If that person becomes convicted of his sin by the Holy Spirit, and expresses remorse specifically for offending God and His holiness, then most likely he is chosen by God for eternal life. Those not chosen by God will simply reject God's Word as foolishness, and continue their lives of rebellion.

"To the person who is genuinely interested and remorseful, we explain the Lord's command to repent, and then to believe only in Christ and His work for salvation (Mark 1:15). If the Holy Spirit has given him the faith to desire Christ, we explain how to come to Christ and thank God for His salvation in prayer."

"God's Word seems much more effective than today's trite attempts at sharing God's gospel," Nick agreed.

"So true," Dave added. "To be sure, God—in His infinite mercy—has truly saved people even through false gospels. Ungodly humanism has totally invaded the Christian gospel in an attempt to water it down, steal God's glory, and deceive many. But, we must reject the errors of humanism and submit to God's way of sharing His true gospel. Well, let's review what we have covered today.

"'Amen' means 'let it be so!'

"'The Fatherhood of God and the Brotherhood of Man' is not a Christian concept in relating to the entire human race. This is a teaching of the ungodly humanist.

"God is Creator and Sustainer of all, but only Father to those sinners He has chosen to make perfect in Christ and bring into His family.

"Once in God's family, truly born-again believers are brothers and sisters to each other.

"Those outside of God's family are the Christian's neighbors, and we are to love them with the love of God, showing them mercy and kindness.

"The modern church has succumbed to other humanistic lies, such as the heresy that Christ's death paid for the sins of everyone.

"The most serious crime in the ungodly humanist's position, that Christ died for everyone, is that it blasphemes Christ by saying that His sacrifice never actually saved anyone. It only made salvation possible for man to save himself.

"Man, then, determines his own eternal destiny by choosing to place or not to place his faith in Christ as his Savior.

"But Scripture repeatedly and emphatically declares that God saves sinners—He doesn't just make salvation possible.

"God's Word also states directly that man's will is not even involved in becoming born again (John 1:12,13; Romans 9:16), but that God's will alone determines who will be saved.

"The ungodly humanist's position is not even logically possible. His heresy is based on the lie that Christ died for every sin of every person, and that each person must exercise his faith in Christ to make God's forgiveness effective.

"But we are all born committing the sin of unbelief. If Christ died for every sin, then he died for the sin of unbelief also. By the ungodly humanist's own absurd position, I can remain in my unbelief and still be saved!

"Of course, the ungodly humanist must then revert to saying that Christ's death paid for all sins except unbelief—in which case not one person could possibly be saved. If Christ's death did not pay for the sin of unbelief—which every person born of a human male commits from conception—then no one could be as perfect as God is perfect, God's standard for going to heaven and avoiding hell.

"'Faith' and 'faith in Christ' are not the same.

"Faith is simple trust that an object can perform that for which one hopes. Every person exercises 'simple faith' every moment of conscious existence. We trust that a chair will hold us up as we sit down, or gravity will bring us back down to earth after we jump up.

"But only the elect are granted 'faith in Christ'—or 'saving faith'—by God. Believing in Christ, or 'faith in Christ,' means to place total trust in Christ's two-part perfect work for salvation from the wrath of God for sin.

"'Faith in Christ' is not man's gift to God, as the ungodly humanist would assert. 'Faith in Christ' is God's gift to those He has chosen to be in His family.

"Only true 'faith in Christ' can save a sinner from the wrath of God, because faith is only as good as the object in which it is placed.

"One can have faith in a doorknob or a block of wood, and believe with all his heart with complete sincerity that it will save him from destruction. But, unless the object of the faith is able to perform that for which one hopes, his faith—though utterly sincere—is in vain and totally worthless.

"Man can only desire Christ and His salvation after he is regenerated by the Holy Spirit, who raises him from spiritual death and releases him from captivity by the devil.

"We can only exercise 'faith in Christ' after God the Holy Spirit grants us the power to repent and gives us His gift of 'saving faith' to believe in Christ.

"Man does not have 'faith to believe in Christ' inherent within his being.

"If the ungodly humanist's position on faith was correct, the Apostle Paul could only say something like, 'for not all have chosen to exercise the faith they have'—but he does not say that!

"The Apostle declares, 'Not all have faith' (2 Thessalonians 3:1,2).

"To 'believe in Christ' must be granted by God (Philippians 1:29). Unregenerate man has no 'faith in Christ' to exercise or not exercise.

"True spiritual faith is trusting God Himself alone to perform the miraculous.

"The Lord Jesus' command is: '"Have faith in GOD"' (Mark 11:22; caps mine).

"God and God alone is able to answer prayers of faith because He created and sustains everything that exists or happens.

"The modern church commits the same heinous, idolatrous blasphemies that Israel committed when saying, 'I have faith for my healing' or 'I have faith for my new Cadillac.' The object of true spiritual faith cannot be healing, cars, or anything else!

"The only object of true spiritual faith is God Himself alone! All other uses of spiritual faith are heinous, ungodly, humanistic, blasphemous idolatry!

"True spiritual faith says this: 'I have faith in God, and entrust everything to Him. God will give me His desires for this life which I have given totally to Him for His use.'

"We, as God's children, can and should ask of Him any and all needs or desires—and ask repeatedly! But God will only grant that which is according to His will, which is set in His eternal purpose—or plan—for His creation.

"The focus of true spiritual faith is God and His will—for this is His life!

"The ungodly, humanistic notion that God wants to—or worse, must—heal every believer, or alleviate all suffering, or make believers materially prosperous, directly contradicts repeated Bible passages.

"God may desire to heal, or may desire to bless materially. But it is according to His will, not our wills.

"God is under no obligation to anyone at any time for any reason outside of His own good pleasure and purpose.

"To say that God is obligated to His creation outside of His own will is to commit the greatest of blasphemies, because this error makes the Almighty Creator subject to His creation!

"Almighty God is sovereign (1 Timothy 6:15). He has ordained absolutely everything that exists or happens in all of creation at all times. God owns everything, and He does whatever pleases Him, especially in regards to salvation.

"God is absolutely independent. God does not depend on anyone for anything.

"Every sinner that becomes a true Christian will be born again at the exact moment and in the exact manner that Almighty God had ordained it without fail.

"Since God explicitly declares that man's will is not even involved in salvation (John 1:12,13; Romans 9:16), God is certainly not waiting for man to decide, as the ungodly humanist would claim.

"God sovereignly begins and completes the process of salvation in those He specifically chose out of the world for His own pleasure (John 17; Philippians 1:6).

"The first and most important reason why God's children should go to all the nations and preach the gospel, making disciples, is that God commands it. If our loving Father commands anything—whether we understand His reasons or not—we must do it.

"The second reason to evangelize is that God ordains the ends as well as the means. He starts the process, works every detail in every step of the process, and brings His perfect result at the specific second which He had planned it before creation to occur.

"The third reason God commands us to evangelize is that He has ordained for each child an inheritance. God has allowed man to share in completing His eternal plan. As the true Christian obeys God and fulfills the work God prepared, the believer will receive a reward for his eternal inheritance.

"The fourth and final reason to evangelize is that we do not know whom God has chosen to come into His family. We cannot see into another person's heart, regardless of what he looks like on the outside or his past.

"Our task is to proclaim God's message of the true gospel. Those whom God has enabled to understand His truth will respond—by the Holy Spirit's power—with remorse, repentance and belief.

"The very idea of preaching is foolish. The Apostle Paul writes that God has sent us to unbelievers with a message that they absolutely will not understand, but will certainly think is total foolishness! That is a recipe for guaranteed failure.

"Almighty God set it up this way on purpose, so that 'by His doing you are in Christ Jesus' (1 Corinthians 1:30).

"It is not the preaching, or the eloquence of words, or the logic of the argument, or the passionate speech that opens blind eyes and deaf ears to receive Christ as Savior.

"The Almighty uses something that could never succeed—preaching—to show that God Himself is the only cause of salvation. Salvation itself is God's work and God's work alone! Thus, God gets all of the glory!

"God also says that He has predestined not only our salvation, but an inheritance for each of His chosen ones according to His plan. This demonstrates His unending love and generosity toward His children, preparing for us an awesome inheritance for doing specifically what God wants done—not what we wish to do in His Name.

"God wants His children to 'get in on it!' Though salvation itself is only God's work, He has chosen to use us in bringing the rest of His eternal plan to fruition, and He will give us a reward for our obedience.

"Instead of zapping us up to heaven the moment He gave us salvation, it was His good pleasure to keep us here and use us to display God's love and mercy to a dying world.

"The will of God for every real Christian is to get on the Lap of the Father, seeking to love Him and know Him more intimately. God then reveals His plan for each child—to each child—as he seeks Him.

"God reveals to His children His desires for them when they put aside this world and get on His Lap, learning of His ways. Then the Holy Spirit opens His holy Word to us, and God only gives His gems to the one willing to give up everything for them, and to seek Him with all of one's heart.

"Sharing the gospel—God's good news of salvation—is one of the deep treasures and blessed privileges that God gives to His children. People who regularly share the gospel know of the exhilarating blessing they receive from God as they do His will.

"We are not to go and save sinners. God saves sinners. We are commanded to go and '"make disciples"' (Matthew 28:19). We are to go and share the marvelous things God has done for us.

"It all begins with the indispensable first step: getting on the Lap of the Father, and asking Him to bring opportunities to share with the people He wants to hear His Word. Sharing the gospel without prayer is a most frustrating experience, because God alone is the one who brings the results!

"A great plan for sharing the gospel is as follows:

1. Ascertain a person's interest
2. Give him God's standard for going to heaven (Matthew 5:48)
3. Explain the alternative of eternal torture in hell for not meeting the standard (Matthew 25; Mark 9:43-48)
4. If the person still wants to know how to meet God's standard and go to heaven:
   ✧ Explain the command to *repent* (Mark 1:15; Mark 8:34,35)
   ✧ Explain the command to *believe* (Mark 1:15; John 5:24; Romans 5:8-10)
   ✧ Explain how to *"come to Christ"* (Matthew 11:28-30)

"The ones God has chosen to be in His family will be moved by the Holy Spirit to ask how they can be saved from eternal torture, and become as perfect as God is perfect. The ones God has chosen will truly desire to come to Christ, repent by giving up their lives to Him, and trust in Christ's work alone for salvation.

"The rest will never be convinced through argument or reason, because God's truth is total foolishness to the sinner whom God has not regenerated by His Holy Spirit.

"When a person desires to come to Christ for salvation, a good outline for leading him in prayer is:

1. Remorse—true sorrow for leading a rebellious, sinful life against God
2. Repentance—totally giving up this life to God
3. Believing in Christ's work alone for perfection and salvation
4. Resting in the security of God's promise of eternal life
5. Thankfulness to God for rescue from deserved eternal torture

"The four errors of today's feeble attempts at sharing the gospel are to be avoided, because they cause great harm and lead to spiritual abortions.

"The first grave error is telling a sinner that God loves him, or loves everyone, when we do not know for sure.

"The second heinous error is using scriptures like Romans 10:9-10 to give trite salvation 'formulas' without understanding the terms or their contexts.

"The third error is misusing passages that involve only believers, and misapplying them out of context to unbelievers. Revelation 3:20, where Jesus says He stands at the door and knocks, is a prime example.

"The fourth and most commonly used error is not even in the Bible! It is telling a sinner to just 'accept Jesus Christ as your personal Lord and Savior and you will be saved.' This denies

God's Word on salvation, and sides with the ungodly humanist who desires to steal God's glory for himself.

"Have we been through enough material for you today?" concluded Dave.

"Oh, yes!" Nick answered. "But I love it! The more I learn about our awesome God and His great plan of salvation, the more I love and adore Him!"

"Excellent!" Dave replied. "Would you like to close our study in prayer?"

"Yes! Dear heavenly Father, we love You and adore You! We worship You as the Lord God Almighty, the Creator and Sustainer of the universe! We praise You for Your awesome plan of salvation, and thank You so much for choosing us to be in Your family—even when we were rebelling against You!

"Thank You for Your Son, who came and died for our sins and took upon Himself the wrath that we should have received. Fill us now with Your blessed Holy Spirit. Empower us, as mere humans, to please You in everything we do, say and think. Bring us opportunities to share Your great gospel with those who You want to hear it.

"I thank You once again for bringing my brother Dave into my life, for our great fellowship, and for the effort he puts forth to teach me to be like Christ. Bless him mightily, and bless me to put into practice what I have learned. In Jesus' holy Name we pray, amen!"

"Let it be so!"

12

Once Saved, Always Saved?

"Good morning!" Dave greeted the College & Career Sunday school class, and they began taking their seats.

"Once saved, always saved...true or false?" Dave asked. Several murmurs could be heard throughout the room, with an occasional "absolutely true!" or a dissenting "no such animal!" ringing out loud.

"The subject of *eternal security*—or, 'once saved, always saved'—never ceases to amaze me!" Dave said. "A friend of mine, a pastor, once hosted a gathering of his denomination's area pastors, and he posed that very question to them. As astounding as it may seem, the entire room became as divided as this room on this critical subject. Even more incredibly, they didn't suspend all other activity in order to discover God's definitive answer to this imperative issue! As far as I know, they are still divided to this day! And these are pastors teaching God's Word to congregations!

"When I received salvation way back in the olden days," Dave continued as the class snickered, "the very first question I had after understanding the basics was: 'Can I lose my salvation?' My relationship with God became my reason for living. If there was anything I could do to lose that relationship, I wanted to know about it so I could avoid it at all costs. And, to my utter amazement, professing Christians could not definitively tell me yes or no!

"Today, we will leave knowing God's definite answer to my question. Paul, would you open our Bible study with prayer?"

"Dear heavenly Father, we praise You for being the awesome Creator and Sustainer of all that exists! We, as Your children, worship You, adoring You with all of our hearts! Thank You for Your great salvation, and thank You for sending Your holy Son Jesus to pay the price for our sins.

"Thank You for Your glorious Word, and for gifting Dave to teach us Your deep truths. Fill us now, we pray, with Your mighty Holy Spirit, and enable us to understand Your ways. Allow us to know You more closely, so that we may love You more intimately than ever. In Jesus' Name we ask these things, amen!"

"Thank you, Paul. Once saved, always saved...true or false?" Dave repeated. "As I've said, after learning the basics of the Christian faith, this was my most critical question. I'm sure many of you, as well as many millions of people throughout history, have wondered about God's truth on this issue.

Many vs. Few

"Let's begin by looking at the Lord Jesus' statements as to who will be saved from the wrath of God. Pam, would you please read for us the first passage of Scripture I have written on the chalkboard?"

Pam read:

"Enter through the narrow gate; for the gate is wide and the way is broad that leads to destruction, and there are **many** who enter through it.

"For the gate is small and the way is narrow that leads to life, and there are **few** who find it." (Matthew 7:13,14; *emphasis mine*)

"Thank you, Pam," Dave acknowledged. "I have in my hand ten pencils. Now, if I were to give Ed here five of these ten pencils, would you say that Ed now has *many* of the pencils?"

"No," Matt offered, "I'd say he has half of them."

"Okay, so half—or five pencils out of ten—would not qualify as having *many* of the ten pencils," Dave agreed. "What if I gave Ed one more, so that now he has six pencils, and I have four? Does Ed now have *many* of the ten pencils?"

"No, he has just a bit more than half," Paul answered. "I don't think that six of ten qualifies as *many* either."

"All right," Dave agreed, "so six out of ten is not *many* of the pencils. What if I gave Ed another pencil? Now Ed has seven, and I now have three pencils. Can it be accurately said that Ed has *many*, and I have *few*, of the ten pencils?"

"Uhhh, maybe," Nick replied. "But if Ed had eight and you have only two, then definitely it can be said that Ed has *many* and you have *few* of the ten pencils."

"So, maybe seven, but definitely eight out of ten qualifies as ***many***; and definitely two out of ten qualifies as ***few***," Dave summarized. "Apply these accurate definitions to the Lord Jesus' words we just heard.

"The Lord Jesus stated that there are 'few' who find the way to life, and 'many' who go the way of destruction. Thus, about two out of every ten people that have lived on earth will find eternal life, according to the Lord. About eight out of every ten people will burn in hell forever for their deliberate, rebellious sin against God, their holy Creator.

"These are sobering words, but the Lord goes on to give even more solemn details concerning who will be saved. Jennifer, would you please read for us the next two passages on the board?"

Jennifer read:

> "I am the good shepherd; the good shepherd lays down His life for the sheep.
>
> "I am the good shepherd, and I know My own and My own know Me, even as the Father knows Me and I know the Father; and I lay down My life for the sheep." (John 10:11,14,15)

> "Beware of the false prophets, who come to you in sheep's clothing, but inwardly are ravenous wolves.
>
> "Not everyone who says to Me, 'Lord, Lord,' will enter the kingdom of heaven, but he who does the will of My Father who is in heaven *will enter*.
>
> "**Many** will say to Me on that day, 'Lord, Lord, did we not prophesy in Your name, and in Your name cast out demons, and in Your name perform many miracles?'
>
> "And then I will declare to them, 'I **never** knew you; DEPART FROM ME, YOU WHO PRACTICE LAWLESSNESS.'"
>
> (Matthew 7:15,21-23; *emphasis mine*)

"Thank you, Jennifer," recognized Dave. "The Lord Jesus also declares that 'many' people who claim Jesus as their 'Lord' will be rejected by the Lord Himself for entrance into the kingdom of heaven on the day of judgment.

"Now, Muslims and Buddhists do not claim Jesus as their Lord and Master. Jesus is talking about people who claim to be Christians, who claim to be His 'sheep,' but '"inwardly are ravenous wolves."'

"So, not only will 'many' of the people that have ever lived on earth burn in hell forever, but also 'many' of the people who claim Jesus as their 'Lord' will burn in hell. Not only will about eight out of ten people who ever lived on earth go to hell, but the Lord declares that just as many of the people who claim Jesus as their 'Lord' will go to hell.

"Chelsea, please read the next passage on the board."

Chelsea read:

> Do not be deceived, God is not mocked; for whatever a man sows, this he will also reap.
>
> For the one who sows to his own flesh will from the flesh reap corruption, but the one who sows to the Spirit will from the Spirit reap eternal life. (Galatians 6:7,8)

"Thank you, Chelsea," Dave said. "'Do not be deceived, God is not mocked!' Absolutely no one will 'pull the wool over God's eyes' on the judgment day. As people looking at other people, it may be difficult—actually, it is impossible—to tell definitively who is a true Christian and who is a false Christian. 'Nevertheless, the firm foundation of God stands, having this seal, "The Lord *knows* those who are His"' (2 Timothy 2:19).

"The Lord Jesus affirms: '"I know My own and My own know Me."' But to the 'many' false Christians, He pronounces: '"I *never* knew you; DEPART FROM ME!"' God knows intimately those whom He chose to be His children—those whom He gave, or will give, His Holy Spirit with the faith to become followers of Christ. But, to the false Christians, the Lord declares: 'I *never* knew you.' These false believers were not saved and then lost—God never saved them at all.

False Brethren in the Church

"Not everyone who calls himself a Christian will go to heaven. In fact, as the Lord Himself said, many of the people naming themselves as Christians will go to hell. The Bible is very explicit that false brothers and false sisters sit in the pews and preach in the pulpits. Nick, please read the next five passages on the board."

Nick read:

> I wrote you in my letter not to associate with immoral people;
>
> I *did* not at all *mean* with the immoral people of this world, or with the covetous and swindlers, or with idolaters, for then you would have to go out of the world.
>
> But actually, I wrote to you not to associate with any so-called brother if he is an immoral person, or covetous, or an idolater, or a reviler, or a drunkard, or a swindler—not even to eat with such a one.
>
> For what have I to do with judging outsiders? Do you not judge those who are within *the church*? (1 Corinthians 5:9-12)

> For such men are false apostles, deceitful workers, disguising themselves as apostles of Christ.
>
> No wonder, for even Satan disguises himself as an angel of light.
>
> Therefore it is not surprising if his servants also disguise themselves as servants of righteousness, whose end will be according to their deeds.
>
> *I have been* on frequent journeys, in dangers from rivers, dangers from robbers, dangers from *my* countrymen, dangers from the Gentiles, dangers in the city, dangers in the wilderness, dangers on the sea, dangers among false brethren. (2 Corinthians 11:13-15,26)

> But *it was* because of the false brethren secretly brought in, who had sneaked in to spy out our liberty which we have in Christ Jesus, in order to bring us into bondage.
>
> But we did not yield in subjection to them for even an hour, so that the truth of the gospel would remain with you. (Galatians 2:4,5)

Beware of the dogs, beware of the evil workers, beware of the false circumcision;

for we are the *true* circumcision, who worship in the Spirit of God and glory in Christ Jesus and put no confidence in the flesh.

(Philippians 3:2,3)

But false prophets also arose among the people, just as there will also be false teachers among you, who will secretly introduce destructive heresies, even denying the Master who bought them, bringing swift destruction upon themselves.

Many will follow their sensuality, and because of them the way of the truth will be maligned;

and in *their* greed they will exploit you with false words; their judgment from long ago is not idle, and their destruction is not asleep.

(2 Peter 2:1-3)

"Thank you, Nick," appreciated Dave. "Scripture definitely warns us that false brothers and sisters are in the church—even ones who teach 'destructive heresies.' **But we are not to 'yield in subjection to them for even an hour, so that the truth of the gospel would remain.'**

"The true gospel of true, biblical Christianity gives birth to true Christians. All false gospels—and there are many of them out there, especially in the churches—give birth to false Christians. Ed, please read the next four scriptures on the board."

Ed read:

You foolish Galatians, who has bewitched you, before whose eyes Jesus Christ was publicly portrayed *as* crucified?

This is the only thing I want to find out from you: did you receive the Spirit by the works of the Law, or by hearing with faith?

Are you so foolish? Having begun by the Spirit, are you now being perfected by the flesh? (Galatians 3:1-3)

You have been severed from Christ, you who are seeking to be justified by law; you have fallen from grace.

For we through the Spirit, by faith, are waiting for the hope of righteousness. (Galatians 5:4,5)

Children, it is the last hour; and just as you heard that antichrist is coming, even now many antichrists have appeared; from this we know that it is the last hour.

They went out from us, but they were not *really* of us; for if they had been of us, they would have remained with us; but *they went out,* so that it would be shown that they all are not of us. (1 John 2:18,19)

I am amazed that you are so quickly deserting Him who called you by
the grace of Christ, for a different gospel;

which is *really* not another; only there are some who are disturbing
you and want to distort the gospel of Christ.

But even if we, or an angel from heaven, should preach to you a
gospel contrary to what we have preached to you, he is to be accursed!

As we have said before, so I say again now, if any man is preaching to
you a gospel contrary to what you received, he is to be accursed!

(Galatians 1:6-9)

True Christianity vs. Humanism

"Thank you, Ed," Dave remarked. "Throughout all of history and to the end of time, only
two faiths exist in the universe: true Christianity and humanism. **True Christianity** preaches
the true gospel of the One True God, who alone is able to save a person from the wrath due to
him for his rebellion against the One True God.

"Every other religion or belief system preaches the false gospel of humanism, and leads to
guaranteed eternal torture in hell. This is so because following **humanism** is rebellion against
the One True God, and Christ's perfect work is not applied, leaving the rebels infinitely short
of God's required perfection to enter heaven.

"Look at this list." Dave turned and drew a table on the chalkboard.

TRUE FAITHS (GUARANTEE SALVATION)	**FALSE FAITHS** (GUARANTEE HELL)
True Christianity	*Humanism*
	=False Christianity
	=All Cults
	=Atheism
	=Everything else

"The fundamental difference between the two categories is simple—but critical," Dave
explained. "**Any faith teaching that man actively participates in his salvation in any
way—whether in obtaining or keeping salvation—is the false faith of *humanism*.**

"Again, there are only two faiths in the world throughout history, one true—true
Christianity—and one false—humanism. There are also only two methods of salvation, one
true—*salvation by God's grace*—and one false—*salvation by man's works*. 'Grace' and
'works' are mutually exclusive methods. By definition, if one is true, the other is utterly
impossible.

"The reason is that *grace* means totally unearned or undeserved favor. Not only is this
favored treatment undeserved, but the recipient actually deserves torment instead of favor. If
favor is given as a result of *work*—such as a paycheck for a job done—then the favor is earned
and deserved. This kind of benefit, then, is not by grace.

"God's holy Word specifically states that salvation is by God's grace, and thus absolutely
cannot be earned or kept by 'good works.' There are many scriptures on this matter, so let's read

the passages that make this statement abundantly clear."

The class read:

> For by grace you have been saved through faith; and that not of
> yourselves, *it is* the gift of God;
>
> not as a result of works, so that no one may boast. (Ephesians 2:8,9)

> God has not rejected His people whom He foreknew. Or do you not
> know what the Scripture says in *the passage about* Elijah, how he pleads with
> God against Israel?
>
> "Lord, THEY HAVE KILLED YOUR PROPHETS, THEY HAVE TORN DOWN
> YOUR ALTARS, AND I ALONE AM LEFT, AND THEY ARE SEEKING MY LIFE."
>
> But what is the divine response to him? "I HAVE KEPT for Myself SEVEN
> THOUSAND MEN WHO HAVE NOT BOWED THE KNEE TO BAAL."
>
> In the same way then, there has also come to be at the present time a
> remnant according to *God's* gracious choice.
>
> But if it is by grace, it is no longer on the basis of works, otherwise
> grace is no longer grace. (Romans 11:2-6)

> Now we know that whatever the Law says, it speaks to those who are
> under the Law, so that every mouth may be closed and all the world may
> become accountable to God;
>
> because by the works of the Law no flesh will be justified in His sight;
> for through the Law *comes* the knowledge of sin.
>
> But now apart from the Law *the* righteousness of God has been
> manifested, being witnessed by the Law and the Prophets,
>
> even *the* righteousness of God through faith in Jesus Christ for all
> those who believe; for there is no distinction.
>
> Where then is boasting? It is excluded. By what kind of law? Of
> works? No, but by a law of faith.
>
> For we maintain that a man is justified by faith apart from works of
> the Law. (Romans 3:19-22,27,28)

> For if Abraham was justified by works, he has something to boast
> about, but not before God.
>
> For what does the Scripture say? "ABRAHAM BELIEVED GOD, AND IT
> WAS CREDITED TO HIM AS RIGHTEOUSNESS."
>
> Now to the one who works, his wage is not credited as a favor, but as
> what is due.
>
> But to the one who does not work, but believes in Him who justifies
> the ungodly, his faith is credited as righteousness. (Romans 4:2-5)

"Again, any faith teaching that man actively participates in his salvation in any way—whether in obtaining or keeping salvation—is the false faith of ***humanism***. I realize that this is an astounding statement to an entire generation of churchgoers who may have never heard the true gospel.

"The ***true gospel*** is the good news that God Himself—before creation—chose a remnant of rebellious sinners to save from due wrath in order to bring them into His eternal family! Though all persons born of a human male deserved eternal punishment for their rebellion against God, He graciously chose an elect few to legally declare as perfect as God is perfect. God satisfied His perfect justice by pouring out the chosen sinners' due wrath upon His own holy Son, and transferred God the Son's infinite perfection to the accounts of His elect.

"In true Christianity, these elect sinners 'were dead in their trespasses and sins' (Ephesians 2:1,5). Dead people do not actively participate in anything—they are dead. Spiritually-dead people cannot accept, reach out for, believe in, desire, understand, or think according to God's truth—they are spiritually dead. We have read many scriptures confirming God's Word that man is born dead in sin (*see chapter 9*).

"True Christianity therefore demands that God alone must then initiate and complete every detail of salvation into the spiritually-dead corpses He chose to come into His family. The corpses do not help in any way—they are dead. The dead sinner is being operated upon by the Divine Doctor, and He alone infuses spiritual life into the corpse. The corpse only *passively receives* the changes wrought by the Divine Hand. Upon becoming alive with a new heart, he desires for the first time the things of God. Grant, please read Ezekiel 36:25 through 27 for us."

Grant read:

"Then I will sprinkle clean water on you, and you will be clean; I will cleanse you from all your filthiness and from all your idols.

"Moreover, I will give you a new heart and put a new spirit within you; and I will remove the heart of stone from your flesh and give you a heart of flesh.

"I will put My Spirit within you and cause you to walk in My statutes, and you will be careful to observe My ordinances."

(Ezekiel 36:25-27)

"Thank you, Grant," said Dave. "*God* is speaking here. *God* will cleanse the filthy sinner. *God* will remove the dead heart of stone in the spiritual corpse, and *God* will replace it with a new heart. *God* will place His Holy Spirit in the corpse, making it spiritually alive, and *God* will cause the new man to obey Him.

"**There is a universe of difference between 'accepting' and 'receiving' something—especially in regards to salvation!**

Accepting vs. Receiving

"In order to ***accept*** something, I must actively, willfully choose it. If I willfully choose to 'accept' something, then I get the credit for making the decision. This is required in the heresy, 'Just accept the Lord Jesus Christ as your personal Savor, and you will be saved.' This humanistic teaching is false precisely because it requires a spiritually-dead person to *do* something for salvation. Thus, this false method of salvation cannot be by God's grace—as true salvation is—because it rests on human works! Even worse, it gives at least part of the credit to sinful man!

"Every Sunday, somewhere in the modern church, the following illogical, contradicting message is preached: 'In Christianity, there is absolutely nothing you can do to be saved. In order to be saved, you must do this: accept Jesus Christ as your personal Savior.' Does anyone here see the obvious logical problems with this teaching?"

"Sure," Ed replied. "One minute, there is nothing I can do for salvation. The next minute, you are requiring me to do something for salvation."

"Exactly!" Dave agreed. "It is no wonder the world has no clue what modern Christianity teaches. Humanistic false Christianity is inherently illogical—it makes no sense! The reason humanism is nonsense is because it blatantly contradicts God's holy Word, the only standard of truth in the universe! Nick, please read for us the next three passages."

Nick read:

> For the word of the cross is foolishness to those who are perishing, but to us who are being saved it is the power of God. (1 Corinthians 1:18)

> But a natural man does not accept the things of the Spirit of God, for they are foolishness to him; and he cannot understand them, because they are spiritually appraised. (1 Corinthians 2:14)

> And even if our gospel is veiled, it is veiled to those who are perishing, in whose case the god of this world has blinded the minds of the unbelieving so that they might not see the light of the gospel of the glory of Christ, who is the image of God. (2 Corinthians 4:3,4)

"Thank you, Nick," Dave said. "God's holy Word specifically states that 'a natural man *does not accept* the things of the Spirit of God, for they are foolishness to him; and he cannot understand them!' So, how is it that the modern church says that in order to become a believer, a non-believer must 'accept' Jesus Christ as his personal Savior? Do the teachers in the modern church not read the Word of God—the very standard they claim to uphold?

"But how does the Word of God answer the question, 'What must I do to be saved?' Matt, please read the next passages."

Matt read:

> But about midnight Paul and Silas were praying and singing hymns of praise to God, and the prisoners were listening to them;
> and suddenly there came a great earthquake, so that the foundations of the prison house were shaken; and immediately all the doors were opened and everyone's chains were unfastened.
> When the jailer awoke and saw the prison doors opened, he drew his sword and was about to kill himself, supposing that the prisoners had escaped.

But Paul cried out with a loud voice, saying, "Do not harm yourself, for we are all here!"

And he called for lights and rushed in, and trembling with fear he fell down before Paul and Silas,

and after he brought them out, he said, "Sirs, what must I do to be saved?"

They said, "Believe in the Lord Jesus, and you will be saved, you and your household." (Acts 16:25-31)

For to you it has been granted for Christ's sake, not only to believe in Him, but also to suffer for His sake. (Philippians 1:29)

Therefore do not be ashamed of the testimony of our Lord or of me His prisoner, but join with *me* in suffering for the gospel according to the power of God,

who has saved us and called us with a holy calling, not according to our works, but according to His own purpose and grace which was granted us in Christ Jesus from all eternity. (2 Timothy 1:8,9)

"Thank you, Matt," stated Dave. "The apostle's answer to the question, 'What must I do to be saved?' is to 'Believe in the Lord Jesus.' The modern humanistic church would define 'believing in Christ' as something a person must bring up within himself; a decision a person must make based on the facts; choosing to exercise this faith that every person inherently possesses; or something each person must *do*. Nothing could be further from God's truth!

"The Apostle Paul labors in his letters to hammer home the major doctrine that believing in Christ must be granted by God! 'Faith in Christ' is a gift from God the Holy Spirit when He enters a sinner and regenerates him. God gives the spiritual corpse a new heart, making him spiritually alive, so he can—for the first time—desire the things of God!

"Believing in Christ is not something a man *does*, but is something a regenerated man *is*—a state of being that the man *receives!* Ask a mathematician why a square has four equal sides, and he will say, 'that defines its very being!' Having four sides is not what it *does*, but what it *is!*

"Likewise, believing in Christ is not something a true Christian does or does not do, depending on his mood. Believing in Christ defines the true believer's very being! He cannot help but believe in Christ, for a believer believes in Christ or he is not a believer at all!

"The Apostle Paul's answer to the jailer's urgent question is: 'if you believe, then you will be saved; because if you believe in Christ, then God has already made you a believer.' That faith in Christ is a power that comes from outside of the person. It must be granted by God to an unbeliever. Faith in Christ becomes the new believer's state of being—infused throughout his soul—and it comes only with the Holy Spirit when He makes a sinner 'a new creation' (Galatians 6:15)!

"True, biblical salvation is received only by God's grace—I cannot do anything to be saved! To **receive** salvation, my will and desires are not even involved. It is something that happens *to* me, like a car seemingly coming out of nowhere and crashing into my car. I am utterly passive.

I have no choice in the matter. If anything, I do not desire it.

"This is an accurate picture of the difference between true Christianity and all false faiths. We, as spiritually-dead corpses, passively receive God's work of salvation. We are running away from God as fast as we can run.

"'There is none who seeks for God (Romans 3:11),' until God grabs a man of His choice, takes out the dead heart of stone, and gives His chosen child a new heart filled with His Holy Spirit. The Holy Spirit infuses in the man's soul the faith to trust Christ and His two-part perfect work for his salvation. The man now believes in Christ as the essence of his very being, because God has made him a believer. God does everything in salvation, because we are dead in rebellion and can do absolutely nothing!

"Thus," Dave concluded, "Quiz questions 22, 23 and 24 are false because they are unbiblical. Chelsea, would you please read them for us?"

"Okay," answered Chelsea. "Question 22: 'The essence of the gospel is to accept Jesus Christ as your personal Lord and Savior in order to be saved from your sins.' Question 23: 'In the process of salvation, faith is man's part—to believe the gospel of Jesus Christ.' Question 24: 'Jesus did all He could do on the cross in paying for man's sins—now it's up to man.'"

"Thank you, Chelsea," Dave replied. "God's Word states that 'a natural man does not accept the things of the Spirit of God, for they are foolishness to him; and he cannot understand them' (1 Corinthians 2:14). So, telling a person in his natural state of sinful rebellion to 'accept Jesus Christ as his personal Savior' is ridiculous. This is not the essence of God's true gospel, and it directly contradicts the Bible.

"Sinners cannot accept anything having to do with God; all they do is reject Him. This is the reason salvation cannot be up to man, and that faith cannot possibly be man's part. Unsaved man has no saving faith to contribute to the process. If salvation was up to man, no one would ever be saved, because man is dead in sin and rebellion against God.

"The only reason some people have been born again is because God chose them to be in His family from before creation, and He made them alive by His Holy Spirit. Christ's first commands, that He expects His new servant to obey, is *not* to 'accept' Him, but to 'repent and believe' (Mark 1:15)! The true Christian's response to God's salvation is to give this life back totally to Christ, its rightful owner; and to trust in Christ's perfect work to be made perfect and stand before the holy God on Judgment Day.

Only True Salvation Brings God-Glorifying Works

"Only after we are regenerated and made spiritually alive, then we get on the Father's Lap and learn to love Him intimately," Dave continued. "Then God reveals His purposes to His child, in God's time, as the child forsakes this world and seeks Him. The Apostle Paul declares: 'For we are His workmanship, created in Christ Jesus for good works, which God prepared beforehand so that we would walk in them' (Ephesians 2:10).

"We can do these good works God has prepared only after God has given us eternal life. **These deeds have absolutely nothing to do with gaining or keeping salvation**, for we already have eternal life at this point! Ed, please read the next two passages on the board for us."

Ed read:

"Truly, truly, I say to you, he who hears My word, and believes Him who sent Me, has eternal life, and does not come into judgment, but has passed out of death into life." (John 5:24)

For no man can lay a foundation other than the one which is laid, which is Jesus Christ.

Now if any man builds on the foundation with gold, silver, precious stones, wood, hay, straw,

each man's work will become evident; for the day will show it because it is *to be* revealed with fire, and the fire itself will test the quality of each man's work.

If any man's work which he has built on it remains, he will receive a reward.

If any man's work is burned up, he will suffer loss; but he himself will be saved, yet so as through fire. (1 Corinthians 3:11-14)

"Thank you, Ed," Dave replied. "True Christians will undergo a judgment, but this judgment has nothing to do with salvation. That has already been decided by God before creation began. The Lord Jesus specifically states that His child 'has'—present tense—'eternal life, and does not come into judgment' anymore regarding salvation, 'but has passed out of death into life.' Salvation is a 'done deal.'

"But the true Christian will have his works as a believer tested for rewards. If he gave up this world's passing lusts to get on the Father's Lap and seek His will, God showed His child what works God had prepared for him to do. Insomuch as the child obeyed in accomplishing the works God prepared beforehand, the believer will receive a reward. If he spent his time doing his own thing in God's name, he will suffer loss with no reward.

"But notice! Though a true believer's earthly work may be burned up with no reward, still 'he himself will be saved!' The true Christian always was, and always will be God's child.

"This scripture absolutely destroys any attempts by ungodly humanists to say that true Christians must keep doing their ideas of 'good works' in order to keep their salvation. This error of humanism glorifies man by rejecting God's decree that He chooses to save whomever He desires, that His choice is eternal and unchanging, and that God Himself ordains every good work that a true believer completes.

"Good works and their resulting rewards have absolutely nothing to do with obtaining or keeping salvation. That being said, **true faith *always* produces the good works which God has prepared**. Those claiming to be Christians, but living in rebellion against God and not producing godly fruit, are deceiving themselves. They are false believers who were *never* saved.

"Any rewards received by true believers are totally from the grace of God, because He prepared all of the works we are to do before creation (Ephesians 2:10). God prepares the works, gives us life, and sustains every moment of our existence. God does it all, so He gets all of the glory.

"This is precisely why the Lord Jesus commands His followers: '"So you too, when you do all the things which are commanded you, say, 'We are unworthy slaves; we have done *only* that which we ought to have done''' (Luke 17:10). God makes it all happen, so He gets all of the glory.

"In humanistic false faiths, humans are said to play at least some role in salvation, in order to steal some of the glory that belongs to God alone for this miracle. Revisiting our example, in false Christianity, we are told to 'accept Jesus Christ as your Lord and Savior and you will be saved.' This heinously places salvation in the hands of spiritual corpses who cannot and do not accept anything having to do with God (1 Corinthians 1:18, 2:14; 2 Corinthians 4:3,4).

"This false gospel gives birth to false Christians, who falsely assume they can 'make an altar call' or 'pray a sinner's prayer' and avoid the wrath of God—while never being truly regenerated! The result of this false gospel is spiritual abortions—unregenerate people living their rebellious, ungodly, unchanged lives while thinking they are saved. It is a travesty.

"Therefore, as Christ Himself declared, only 'the few' of the people who call themselves Christians actually are true Christians. All of the rest, 'the many' false Christians, will spend eternity in hell with their father the devil (John 8:44). These *so-called brothers* sometimes look and act like the real thing—even for decades—but 'their judgment from long ago is not idle, and their destruction is not asleep' (2 Peter 2:3).

Made Perfect by Christ's Work

"All true Christians will spend eternity in heaven with God their Father, because they have been legally declared perfect by God the Son's perfect work on their behalf. This was ordained by God's decree in eternity past (Ephesians 3:11), and effectually completed during this world's existence. The Lord Jesus paid for their sins on the cross, and God transferred Christ's perfect life to their accounts. God started the process of salvation, and God brings it to completion.

"This process of justification satisfies God's standard for going to heaven: '"Therefore you are to be perfect, as your heavenly Father is perfect"' (Matthew 5:48). Anna, please read the next four scriptures stating that true Christians are legally made perfect in order to live in heaven."

Anna read:

> I press on toward the goal for the prize of the upward call of God in Christ Jesus.
> Let us therefore, as many as are perfect, have this attitude; and if in anything you have a different attitude, God will reveal that also to you; however, let us keep living by that same *standard* to which we have attained. (Philippians 3:14-16)

> Epaphras, who is one of your number, a bondslave of Jesus Christ, sends you his greetings, always laboring earnestly for you in his prayers, that you may stand perfect and fully assured in all the will of God.
> (Colossians 4:12)

> For by one offering He has perfected for all time those who are sanctified. (Hebrews 10:14)

> But you have come to Mount Zion and to the city of the living God, the heavenly Jerusalem, and to myriads of angels,
>
> to the general assembly and church of the firstborn who are enrolled in heaven, and to God, the Judge of all, and to the spirits of *the* righteous made perfect,
>
> and to Jesus, the mediator of a new covenant, and to the sprinkled blood, which speaks better than *the blood* of Abel. (Hebrews 12:22-24)

"Thank you, Anna," recognized Dave. "Right now, in this perishing fleshly body, we live lives far, far, far from being perfect. But, we are in a legal standing of absolute perfection in God's eyes, because the perfect life of God the Son has been credited to our accounts!

"The true believer's salvation depends upon absolutely nothing that the believer does, but solely upon the perfect work that Christ alone has already done! This perfecting has already occurred in the true Christian, and will last for eternity, because 'by one offering He has perfected for all time those who are sanctified' (Hebrews 10:14). Paul, please read the next passage on the board for us."

Paul read:

> See how great a love the Father has bestowed on us, that we would be called children of God; and *such* we are. For this reason the world does not know us, because it did not know Him.
>
> Beloved, now we are children of God, and it has not appeared as yet what we will be. We know that when He appears, we will be like Him, because we will see Him just as He is. (1 John 3:1,2)

Eternal Life Can Never End

"Thank you, Paul," Dave replied. "We, as true Christians, are—present tense—children of God now. God gives us eternal life now—present tense—beginning at regeneration! 'Eternal life' is a critical term that we bounce around without thinking much about it. Can anyone tell me the definition of 'eternal'?"

"I would say that '*eternal*' means lasting forever, without end," proposed Matt.

"And Webster would agree with you, Matt. 'Lasting forever, without end,'" Dave repeated. "So, if God promises His child eternal life, and God says that this eternal life begins now—at the moment of regeneration—how could it be lost, and then end?"

A 'light bulb' seemed to turn on in the faces of many of the students in the classroom.

"The Lord Jesus contrasts eternal punishment with eternal life," Dave explained. "In recounting the deeds that make a false Christian differ from one who is already a true Christian, Jesus concludes: '"These will go away into eternal punishment, but the righteous into eternal life"' (Matthew 25:46).

"Every human will exist forever, because that is part of the meaning of being created in the image of God (Genesis 1:26,27). The only question is *where* a man will spend eternity. Sinners not chosen by God 'will go away into eternal punishment' to pay for their rebellion, burning alive forever in the lake of fire. Sinners chosen by God to come into His family are promised eternal life in God's glorious kingdom paradise, and that eternal life begins *now!*

"Let's read God's promises in His holy Word regarding His gift of eternal life." The class read:

"As Moses lifted up the serpent in the wilderness, even so must the Son of Man be lifted up;

so that whoever believes will in Him have eternal life.

"For God so loved the world, that He gave His only begotten Son, that whoever believes in Him shall not perish, but have eternal life."

(John 3:14-16)

"For this is the will of My Father, that everyone who beholds the Son and believes in Him will have eternal life, and I Myself will raise him up on the last day.

"Truly, truly, I say to you, he who believes has eternal life.

"But there are some of you who do not believe." For Jesus knew from the beginning who they were who did not believe, and who it was that would betray Him.

And He was saying, "For this reason I have said to you, that no one can come to Me unless it has been granted him from the Father."

(John 6:40,47,64,65)

"My sheep hear My voice, and I know them, and they follow Me; and I give eternal life to them, and they will never perish; and no one will snatch them out of My hand.

"My Father, who has given *them* to Me, is greater than all; and no one is able to snatch *them* out of the Father's hand." (John 10:27-29)

And not through the blood of goats and calves, but through His own blood, He entered the holy place once for all, having obtained eternal redemption.

For this reason He is the mediator of a new covenant, so that, since a death has taken place for the redemption of the transgressions that were *committed* under the first covenant, those who have been called may receive the promise of the eternal inheritance. (Hebrews 9:12,15)

And the testimony is this, that God has given us eternal life, and this life is in His Son.

He who has the Son has the life; he who does not have the Son of God does not have the life.

These things I have written to you who believe in the name of the Son of God, so that you may know that you have eternal life.

(1 John 5:11-13)

This is the promise which He Himself made to us: eternal life.

(1 John 2:25)

"It's very, very simple," Dave expounded. "**Life that can be lost, or ended, cannot truthfully be called 'eternal' life!** The Lord Jesus guarantees that the sheep that the Father gave to Him 'will never perish.' If just ONE true Christian loses his salvation, then Almighty God the Son lies! Or, at best, He would be seriously mistaken—with grave consequences! Being that either option is impossible (Hebrews 6:18; John 6:64), then God's *eternal life* is exactly what He declares that it means: everlasting life, without end, beginning at regeneration.

"Let's read the scriptures declaring that true Christians can never and will never perish." The class read:

"What do you think? If any man has a hundred sheep, and one of them has gone astray, does he not leave the ninety-nine on the mountains and go and search for the one that is straying?

"If it turns out that he finds it, truly I say to you, he rejoices over it more than over the ninety-nine which have not gone astray.

"So it is not *the* will of your Father who is in heaven that one of these little ones perish." (Matthew 18:12-14)

Therefore there is now no condemnation for those who are in Christ Jesus. (Romans 8:1)

For you have died and your life is hidden with Christ in God.

When Christ, who is our life, is revealed, then you also will be revealed with Him in glory. (Colossians 3:3,4)

Therefore, since we receive a kingdom which cannot be shaken, let us show gratitude, by which we may offer to God an acceptable service with reverence and awe. (Hebrews 12:28)

"The reason true Christians can never and will never perish is that they are sealed by God Himself, and kept by God for the day of redemption," Dave continued. "Let's read God's Word declaring that God is the one who, without fail, brings every child home to His heavenly kingdom."

The class read:

"All that the Father gives Me will come to Me, and the one who comes to Me I will certainly not cast out.

"For I have come down from heaven, not to do My own will, but the will of Him who sent Me.

"This is the will of Him who sent Me, that of all that He has given Me I lose nothing, but raise it up on the last day." (John 6:37-39)

"I am no longer in the world; and *yet* they themselves are in the world, and I come to You. Holy Father, keep them in Your name, *the name* which You have given Me, that they may be one even as We *are.*

"While I was with them, I was keeping them in Your name which You have given Me; and I guarded them and not one of them perished but the son of perdition, so that the Scripture would be fulfilled.

"I do not ask You to take them out of the world, but to keep them from the evil *one.*" (John 17:11,12,15)

...the testimony concerning Christ was confirmed in you,
so that you are not lacking in any gift, awaiting eagerly the revelation of our Lord Jesus Christ,
who will also confirm you to the end, blameless in the day of our Lord Jesus Christ.
God is faithful, through whom you were called into fellowship with His Son, Jesus Christ our Lord. (1 Corinthians 1:6-9)

In Him, you also, after listening to the message of truth, the gospel of your salvation—having also believed, you were sealed in Him with the Holy Spirit of promise,
who is given as a pledge of our inheritance, with a view to the redemption of *God's own* possession, to the praise of His glory.
(Ephesians 1:13,14)

Do not grieve the Holy Spirit of God, by whom you were sealed for the day of redemption. (Ephesians 4:30)

For I am confident of this very thing, that He who began a good work in you will perfect it until the day of Christ Jesus. (Philippians 1:6)

Now may the God of peace Himself sanctify you entirely; and may your spirit and soul and body be preserved complete, without blame at the coming of our Lord Jesus Christ.
Faithful is He who calls you, and He also will bring it to pass.
(1 Thessalonians 5:23,24)

The Lord will rescue me from every evil deed, and will bring me safely to His heavenly kingdom; to Him *be* the glory forever and ever. Amen. (2 Timothy 4:18)

We know that no one who is born of God sins; but He who was born of God keeps him, and the evil one does not touch him. (1 John 5:18)

Blessed be the God and Father of our Lord Jesus Christ, who according to His great mercy has caused us to be born again to a living hope through the resurrection of Jesus Christ from the dead,

to *obtain* an inheritance *which is* imperishable and undefiled and will not fade away, reserved in heaven for you,

who are protected by the power of God through faith for a salvation ready to be revealed in the last time. (1 Peter 1:3-5)

Jude, a bond-servant of Jesus Christ, and brother of James, To those who are the called, beloved in God the Father, and kept for Jesus Christ:

Now to Him who is able to keep you from stumbling, and to make you stand in the presence of His glory blameless with great joy,

to the only God our Savior, through Jesus Christ our Lord, *be* glory, majesty, dominion and authority, before all time and now and forever. Amen. (Jude 1,24,25)

"The Apostle Paul ends all debate on eternal security by declaring that true believers 'were sealed in Him with the Holy Spirit of promise, who is given as a pledge of our inheritance' (Ephesians 1:13,14). The Greek word he uses for 'a pledge' is *arabon*. This word means an earnest guarantee. For example, Webster's Dictionary tells us that **earnest money** is money given to bind a contract.

"God gave His Holy Spirit to seal His child for eternal life, and to bind His covenant with that child. The Apostle was clearly communicating to his readers that whoever was given the Holy Spirit by God was guaranteed eternal life.

"Scripture repeatedly confirms that God chooses whom He will save; God gives His elect eternal life beginning at regeneration; God will never allow His children to perish; and God seals, protects and keeps His children for the day of redemption.

"Therefore, salvation is entirely the work of God and God alone. Once God chose His elect before the foundation of the world, and saved these sinners during their earthly lives, these children of God are eternally saved and can never be lost," Dave summarized.

"How could anyone miss all of these scriptures?" Chelsea asked.

The Heinous Heresy of Keeping Oneself Saved

"The reason the ungodly humanist holds that a person can lose his salvation," Dave answered, "is that, in his heretical belief system, salvation depends on man and what man does. Ignoring the clear scriptures that declare that man's will is not even involved in salvation (John 1:12,13; Romans 9:16), the false Christian depends on man's decision to be saved.

"Bringing that heresy to its logical conclusion, the ungodly humanist holds that man must also keep himself saved as well. This vicious circle never ends, because living 'as perfect as God is perfect' is an impossible task for finite man to accomplish. We fall short of that commandment every moment of our existence here on earth. For just one of many examples,

God is perfect in His omnipotence. Can any Christian be as perfect as God is perfect in absolute power, 'who gives life to the dead and calls into being that which does not exist' (Romans 4:17)? The mere thought is completely absurd, not to mention unbiblical.

"Salvation, then, must be initiated and completed by God Himself. Only resting—not working and striving—resting in the work that *Christ alone* accomplished for salvation is man's only hope for avoiding the wrath of God. True Christians rest in God's faithfulness, knowing that we ourselves fall far short, but that God has legally declared us perfect with Christ's perfection. But most humans live in utter denial of the extent of their own filthiness."

"I've actually heard sermons teaching that salvation is like God giving us mountain-climbing gear," Paul recalled. "But it is totally up to us to use that gift to reach the top and be saved."

"That is a classic example of humanistic false Christianity," Dave replied. "This heresy claims that God gives 'the gift' of salvation, but it is totally up to man to actually keep himself saved. This flatly denies the Lord Jesus' standard for entering heaven: '"Therefore you are to be perfect, as your heavenly Father is perfect"' (Matthew 5:48). It is absolutely impossible for any man to fulfill that commandment by his own efforts to keep himself saved.

"In order to propose something so foolish, the ungodly humanist has to redefine God. The false Christian rejects the perfection God ascribes to Himself in His holy Word, and invents a god of his own imagination—an **idol** made in his own depraved image. Since the humanistic false god is just like the sinful human, the false Christian believes he can live up to this heinous idol's 'relative perfections.' In his utter denial of the truth, depraved man thinks he 'isn't so bad.' This is abject blasphemy.

"This heresy also denies all of the scriptures we just read where God declares that *He* keeps, guards and protects His children; *He* confirms His child blameless until the end; *He* seals His child for the day of redemption; *He* begins the good work of salvation and perfects it; *He* will bring to pass our complete preservation; *He* will bring us safely to His heavenly kingdom; and *He* will raise us up on that day and lose not one of His children!

"I guess that preacher missed those passages. He also missed the scores of passages promising eternal life, which, by definition, can never end. And he missed the verses that say eternal life begins now—at the moment of regeneration. And he missed the scriptures that demand that true salvation is by God's grace alone, which then excludes all human works.

"As a result of being cursed with a sinful nature, all human beings—as well as true Christians—have a propensity to try to be holy and acceptable to God by what we can do. This is a fatal trap, and must be avoided at all costs. It openly denies God's standard for His acceptance, to be perfect as He is perfect. This is simply and categorically impossible to achieve by finite man.

"Even if a true Christian mistakenly, or rebelliously, teaches the errors and blasphemies of humanistic false Christianity, this does not make the false teachings true. The only standard of truth in the universe is God's holy Word. God's meaning is truth, not the human messenger.

"False Christians who demand to play a part in their salvation only guarantee their eternal punishment, because 'all our righteous deeds are like a filthy garment' (Isaiah 64:6). The 'good works' or 'obedience' they claim to keep themselves saved only pollute the perfectly pure righteousness of Christ, ensuring their future in the lake of fire for their arrogant rebellion against God's only provision for perfection.

"True Christians are only made perfect as God is perfect by the payment of our sins by Christ on the cross, and the transfer of God the Son's perfect life to our accounts. **WARNING: We cannot add anything of our own to God's perfection, or we only taint it—and then we would *not* be as perfect as God is perfect!**

"Thus, Quiz question 25 must be false. It reads: 'Salvation is like God giving a man mountain-climbing gear, but it is up to the man to climb to the top to be finally saved.' If salvation is up to our deeds to remain as perfect as God is perfect, any honest man would admit that he is doomed.

"The Apostle Paul and the writer of the Letter to the Hebrews state it very succinctly. Nick, would you please read the next passage on the board for us?"

Nick read:

> Beware of the dogs, beware of the evil workers, beware of the false circumcision;
>
> for we are the *true* circumcision, who worship in the Spirit of God and glory in Christ Jesus and put no confidence in the flesh. (Philippians 3:2,3)

> Therefore, let us fear if, while a promise remains of entering His rest, any one of you may seem to have come short of it.
>
> For indeed we have had good news preached to us, just as they also; but the word they heard did not profit them, because it was not united by faith in those who heard.
>
> So there remains a Sabbath rest for the people of God.
>
> For the one who has entered His rest has himself also rested from his works, as God did from His.
>
> Therefore let us be diligent to enter that rest, so that no one will fall, through *following* the same example of disobedience.
>
> (Hebrews 4:1,2,9-11)

"Thank you, Nick," Dave said. "For true Christians, this life is a continuous 'Sabbath rest' from working to achieve righteousness, because that is absolutely impossible. We rest in Christ's accomplishments to make us perfect as God is perfect. We, the true believers, 'put no confidence in the flesh.' We place no trust in what we do to gain salvation or keep it.

"There is nothing we can do to be acceptable to God and keep ourselves saved. We simply rest in God, and 'glory in Christ Jesus' and His perfect work! For, regarding salvation, God's holy Word declares that 'the one who has entered His rest has himself also rested from his works, as God did from His.'

"False Christians refuse to enter that rest by faith in Christ's work. These humanists demand to work their own righteousness, as if they could do anything but sin. They refuse to rest from their works, but insist their deeds merit righteousness to keep salvation. They commit the same error unbelieving Israel made by trying to be acceptable to God by doing works. Pam, please read Romans 9, verses 30 through chapter 10, verse 4 for us."

Pam read:

> What shall we say then? That Gentiles, who did not pursue righteousness, attained righteousness, even the righteousness which is by faith;
>
> but Israel, pursuing a law of righteousness, did not arrive at *that* law.
>
> Why? Because *they did* not *pursue it* by faith, but as though *it were* by works. They stumbled over the stumbling stone,
>
> just as it is written,
>
> > "BEHOLD, I LAY IN ZION A STONE OF STUMBLING AND A ROCK OF OFFENSE,
> >
> > AND HE WHO BELIEVES IN HIM WILL NOT BE DISAPPOINTED."
> >
> > (Romans 9:30-33)

> Brethren, my heart's desire and my prayer to God for them is for *their* salvation.
>
> For I testify about them that they have a zeal for God, but not in accordance with knowledge.
>
> For not knowing about God's righteousness and seeking to establish their own, they did not subject themselves to the righteousness of God.
>
> For Christ is the end of the law for righteousness to everyone who believes. (Romans 10:1-4)

"Thank you, Pam," continued Dave. "Ungodly humanists continue to live in utter denial of their heinous, rebellious arrogant filth against the holiness of God, for which they will pay with eternal punishment. These false Christians still maintain that God's 'gift' of salvation, like mountain-climbing gear, requires doing their own climbing to get to heaven. That way, the humanists can try to steal a bit of God's glory for themselves—the very sin of Satan.

"But God's Word urges true believers to be diligent to remain in that state of resting in Christ's work for salvation. 'Christ is the end of the law' of doing works in order to be righteous before God. We must refuse the sinful nature's desire to attempt to usurp God's glory by deceiving our minds that we can be righteous like the Most High. This was the original sin of pride by the devil (Isaiah 14), who succeeded in tempting Eve to fall for the same lie (Genesis 3). But no one is like the Most High God! He declares:

> "I am the LORD, that is My name;
>
> > I will not give My glory to another,
> >
> > Nor My praise to graven images (*margin,* idols). (Isaiah 42:8)

> "For My thoughts are not your thoughts,
> >
> > Nor are your ways My ways," declares the LORD.
>
> "For *as* the heavens are higher than the earth,
> >
> > So are My ways higher than your ways
> >
> > And My thoughts than your thoughts." (Isaiah 55:8,9)

"God will not share His glory with anyone or anything—especially not the idols of humanism—because absolutely nothing in all of creation can possibly compare to the Most High! God is infinitely greater in every respect than everyone and everything else—period! Allow me to read:

> And the twenty-four elders and the four living creatures fell down and worshiped God who sits on the throne saying, "Amen. Hallelujah!"
> And a voice came from the throne, saying,
> "Give praise to our God, all you His bond-servants, you who fear Him, the small and the great."
> Then I heard *something* like the voice of a great multitude and like the sound of many waters and like the sound of mighty peals of thunder, saying,
> "Hallelujah! For the Lord our God, the Almighty, reigns."
> (Revelation 19:4-6)

"The Lord God Almighty reigns sovereignly," praised Dave. "God's **sovereignty** means He has ordained absolutely everything that exists or happens in all of creation for all time. The ungodly humanist refuses to believe this because he has no idea of Almighty God's true identity.

"Thus, though affirming with his words that God is sovereign, the false Christian denies it with his doctrine. The ungodly humanist redefines sovereignty—just as he redefines God—to fit his man-glorifying beliefs. He blasphemes: 'Of course God is sovereign, but He has given man a free will, and made him a free moral agent. God would never interfere with man's decisions, for that would be unloving.'

"We have already destroyed all of these humanistic lies by simply quoting Scripture, just like the Lord Jesus did to Satan in the wilderness (Matthew 4). Man is not a free moral agent, but an enslaved, immoral spiritual corpse—running away from God to remain in his sin. If Almighty God does not interfere by His sovereign choice, man is doomed for his rebellion, and must face the severe, eternal wrath of the holy God.

"Almighty God ordained who would be in His family from before creation. God also made complete provision to satisfy His justice through His Son for these elect, and sovereignly guaranteed every child's salvation through His Holy Spirit.

"The Almighty depends upon nothing outside of Himself—especially spiritually-dead man—to accomplish the salvation of His elect. The ones God chose before creation to be in His family were guaranteed eternal life before they were even born (Romans 9:10-16), because God had sovereignly ordained it.

"Again, and I cannot stress this enough: In true Christianity, man has *absolutely nothing* to do with getting saved or remaining saved. Salvation is the work of God and God alone! Thus, Quiz question 26—'a person who is truly born-again (saved) can lose his salvation—is false because it contradicts God's Word."

First Objection to Eternal Security: The 'I knew a guy who fell away...' Testimony
"But I've known people that I am sure were saved who are no longer walking with the Lord," Jennifer objected. "In real life, they fell away and lost their salvation."

"There are three objections often raised against the true doctrine of eternal security," Dave answered. "First, we have the 'I knew a guy who fell away...' testimony. Second, the doctrine of eternal security is said to lead to '**greasy grace**'—where a person thinks he can continue a life of sin and still be saved. Third, there are the scriptures that are claimed to say salvation can be lost. I'll deal with each of these objections thoroughly.

"Regarding your testimony, Jennifer, remember three very important issues. God's Word is the only standard of truth in the universe—not our finite, sometimes flawed perceptions. Secondly, God's Word says no person can know for sure if another person is saved. But God knows, because He did the choosing and saving. Thirdly, God's Word specifically declares that any person that professes to be a Christian, and then walks away from true Christianity, was *never* a true Christian. He didn't 'lose his salvation'—he was never saved at all, regardless of all outward appearances. Christ will say to him: '"I *never* knew you; DEPART FROM ME!"'

"Jennifer, please read for us the next four passages on the board, beginning with the words of the Lord Jesus to His Father."

Jennifer read:

"Sanctify them in the truth; Your word is truth." (John 17:17)

For who among men knows the *thoughts* of a man except the spirit of the man which is in him? Even so the *thoughts* of God no one knows except the Spirit of God. (1 Corinthians 2:11)

Nevertheless, the firm foundation of God stands, having this seal, "The Lord knows those who are His," and, "Everyone who names the name of the Lord is to abstain from wickedness." (2 Timothy 2:19)

They went out from us, but they were not *really* of us; for if they had been of us, they would have remained with us; but *they went out,* so that it would be shown that they all are not of us. (1 John 2:19)

"Thank you, Jennifer," Dave acknowledged. "I remember Grant telling us what he heard on the radio: A pastor and his wife, after leading a church for more than two decades, testified that they then received true salvation. For the previous 20 years, most of their congregation would have probably insisted that this pastor and his wife were truly saved.

"We, as finite humans, simply cannot know for sure among men who is truly saved. We can only make educated guesses according to spiritual fruit—and sometimes we guess wrongly. But God knows every one of His children intimately, because He chose them, and He guarantees every true child's salvation.

"Those we thought were Christians but 'fell away' most likely were lured by a false gospel making false promises, resulting in a false faith. They never truly repented by giving up this life to Christ for whatever He desired for it, or they would have no reason to leave. They never trusted solely in Christ's work for receiving and keeping salvation, but tried to earn their own righteousness and failed miserably. They finally 'went out from us, but they were never really of us' (1 John 2:19)."

Second Objection: Eternal Security Leads to 'Greasy Grace'

"But, would not believing in the doctrine of 'Once Saved, Always Saved' lead to 'greasy grace?'" asked Ed. "If a person becomes a Christian and is taught eternal security, will he not think he can sin all he wants and still go to heaven?"

"Actually," Dave answered, "the true Christian will think just the opposite. We have, in the modern American church, many ungodly, humanistic ideas. One is the idea of 'greasy grace.' Another is the idea of 'rededicating my life to Christ.'" The class looked stunned.

"Could you imagine," Dave continued, "as we enter the new millennium, a person becoming a Christian in a Muslim-run country, such as Sudan in Africa? The penalties for believing in Christ are torture, enslavement and death! This is a capital crime in many of these countries!

"Announce your conversion to Christ there, and you are not presented with a leather-bound Bible with your name engraved in gold on the cover! No—you are tortured extensively, and then you die! Does anyone really think that the true Christians in Sudan ever have a problem with 'greasy grace'—or ever have to 'rededicate their lives to Christ' after a sinful jaunt into the world? Are you kidding?

"The reason these two ungodly, false doctrines even exist is because they are the fruit of the false gospel which has been taught in the modern church for over a century. 'Just "come on down and make this altar call" and "accept Jesus Christ as your personal Lord and Savior"—and you will be saved!' Sorry—these two false doctrines are nowhere to be found in Scripture.

"What the Lord Jesus Christ does command in Scripture, to the one who comes to Him for salvation, is to 'repent and believe' (Mark 1:15). To **repent** means to change one's mind about who owns this life—and to totally give up this life to Christ for whatever He wants to do with it. The Lord Jesus repeatedly commands this. Paul, would you read the Lord's words in the next two passages for us, please?"

Paul read:

> And He summoned the crowd with His disciples, and said to them, "If anyone wishes to come after Me, he **must** deny himself, and take up his cross and follow Me.
>
> "For whoever wishes to save his life will lose it, but whoever loses his life for My sake and the gospel's will save it." (Mark 8:34,35; *emphasis mine*)

> Now large crowds were going along with Him; and He turned and said to them,
>
> "If anyone comes to Me, and does not hate (by comparison of his love for Me) his own father and mother and wife and children and brothers and sisters, yes, and even his own life, he cannot be My disciple.
>
> "Whoever does not carry his own cross and come after Me cannot be My disciple.
>
> "So then, none of you can be My disciple who does not give up all his own possessions." (Luke 14:25-27,33; *parenthesis from margin*)

> And He was saying, "For this reason I have said to you, that no one can
> come to Me unless it has been granted him from the Father." (John 6:65)

"Thank you, Paul," acknowledged Dave. "The only person who desires to come to Christ is the one in whom God has already placed His Holy Spirit and made spiritually alive (John 6:65). This person had been chosen by God before creation to be His child, and now is eternally saved.

"This person then comes to Christ, and he **must** respond to God's salvation by repenting. He **must** give up this life—denying his ownership, and dying to himself and his own goals and desires. This is what one does on a cross—he dies. He **must** give up this life—giving it back to Christ, its rightful owner, for whatever He desires for it. Any person claiming to be a Christian, but not totally giving this life back to Christ, is a liar and has never been saved.

"Secondly, he **must** believe in Christ—trusting solely in Christ's two-part perfect work to make him legally '"as perfect as the heavenly Father is perfect (Matthew 5:48)."' Any person claiming to be a Christian, but not trusting only in Christ's work, but adding any of his own effort to God's salvation, is a liar and has never been saved. Nick, would you read the next passage from the Apostle Paul in Romans 5, please?"

Nick read:

> But God demonstrates His own love toward us, in that while we were
> yet sinners, Christ died for us.
>
> Much more then, having now been justified by His blood, we shall be
> saved from the wrath *of God* through Him.
>
> For if while we were enemies we were reconciled to God through the
> death of His Son, much more, having been reconciled, we shall be saved
> by His life. (Romans 5:8-10)

"Thank you, Nick," Dave said. "Christ's two-part perfect work includes Christ dying on the cross, taking the wrath of God due to us for our sins. Since we have then 'been reconciled'—having our slate wiped clean—'we shall be saved by His life'—His perfect life imputed to our accounts.

"This is the ***true gospel***. The Father grants salvation to His hateful enemy, against the man's will. God fills the person with the Holy Spirit, who gives the man a new heart and opens the sinner's eyes to his heinous rebellion against God. The sinner experiences remorse for offending God and His holiness. The Holy Spirit empowers the sinner to come to Christ, to be able to repent, and to trust in Christ's work for salvation. Expressly because God gave this person His Holy Spirit, this new child of God is sealed for eternity, guaranteed salvation.

"'***Greasy grace***'—or the idea that a person who is saved can then sin all he wants with impunity—does not exist. God's holy Word specifically says that the person who holds this heresy is not and never was saved, and will certainly perish. This person is a false Christian who has never repented; he never gave up this life to Christ for His use. Kelly, please read the next passages on the board for us."

Kelly read:

Now, on the same occasion there were some present who reported to Him about the Galileans whose blood Pilate had mixed with their sacrifices.

And Jesus said to them, "Do you suppose that these Galileans were *greater* sinners than all *other* Galileans because they suffered this *fate?*

"I tell you, no, but unless you repent, you will all likewise perish.

"Or do you suppose that those eighteen on whom the tower in Siloam fell and killed them were *worse* culprits than all the men who live in Jerusalem?

"I tell you, no, but unless you repent, you will all likewise perish."

(Luke 13:1-5)

What shall we say then? Are we to continue in sin so that grace may increase?

May it never be! How shall we who died to sin still live in it?

Or do you not know that all of us who have been baptized into Christ Jesus have been baptized into His death?

For if we have become united with *Him* in the likeness of His death, certainly we shall also be *in the likeness* of His resurrection,

knowing this, that our old self was crucified with *Him,* in order that our body of sin might be done away with, so that we would no longer be slaves to sin;

for he who has died is freed from sin.

Even so consider yourselves to be dead to sin, but alive to God in Christ Jesus.

Therefore do not let sin reign in your mortal body so that you obey its lusts,

and do not go on presenting the members of your body to sin *as* instruments of unrighteousness; but present yourselves to God as those alive from the dead, and your members *as* instruments of righteousness to God.

For sin shall not be master over you, for you are not under law but under grace.

What then? Shall we sin because we are not under law but under grace? May it never be!

Do you not know that when you present yourselves to someone *as* slaves for obedience, you are slaves of the one whom you obey, either of sin resulting in death, or of obedience resulting in righteousness?

But now having been freed from sin and enslaved to God, you derive your benefit, resulting in sanctification, and the outcome, eternal life.

For the wages of sin is death, but the free gift of God is eternal life in Christ Jesus our Lord. (Romans 6:1-3,5-7,11-16,22,23)

"Thank you, Kelly," Dave applauded. "Those who do not give this life back to Christ for His use—in other words, repent—will most certainly perish. These include the false Christians who embrace a false gospel, continuing to sin while thinking they are saved from God's wrath. On the day of judgment, they will regret they had ever been born.

"As true Christians, we have been freed from slavery to sin and the devil, and can now choose to serve God or sin. The principal desire of the true Christian is to serve and glorify God with every moment of life, not to sin against Him and see how close to the edge of immorality one can walk. 'And if anyone sins, we have an Advocate with the Father, Jesus Christ the righteous' (1 John 2:1). We confess our sins to God, resting in Christ's perfection, and thanking God for His complete forgiveness.

"The true Christian returns to his Holy Spirit-induced desire to obey and please God. If a true Christian continues in rebellion, God declares He will discipline that child and bring him to his knees. God also has the right to take his life. Anna, would you please read the next passages for us?"

Anna read:

> For he who eats and drinks, eats and drinks judgment to himself if he does not judge the body rightly.
>
> For this reason many among you are weak and sick, and a number sleep.
>
> But if we judged ourselves rightly, we would not be judged.
>
> But when we are judged, we are disciplined by the Lord so that we will not be condemned along with the world. (1 Corinthians 11:29-32)

> And you have forgotten the exhortation which is addressed to you as sons,
>
> "MY SON, DO NOT REGARD LIGHTLY THE DISCIPLINE OF THE LORD,
>
> NOR FAINT WHEN YOU ARE REPROVED BY HIM;
>
> FOR THOSE WHOM THE LORD LOVES HE DISCIPLINES,
>
> AND HE SCOURGES EVERY SON WHOM HE RECEIVES."
>
> It is because of discipline that you endure; God deals with you as with sons; for what son is there whom *his* father does not discipline?
>
> But if you are without discipline, of which all have become partakers, then you are illegitimate children and not sons.
>
> Furthermore, we had earthly fathers to discipline us, and we respected them; shall we not much rather be subject to the Father of spirits, and live?
>
> For they disciplined us for a short time as seemed best to them, but He *disciplines us* for *our* good, so that we may share His holiness.
>
> All discipline for the moment seems not to be joyful, but sorrowful; yet to those who have been trained by it, afterwards it yields the peaceful fruit of righteousness. (Hebrews 12:5-11)

"Those whom I love, I reprove and discipline; therefore be zealous and repent." (Revelation 3:19)

"Thank you, Anna," Dave said. "So, the concept of 'greasy grace' is a false idea from a false gospel. Those who think they were saved, and then can live a life of sin with impunity, are false Christians. These false Christians pretend to serve God as a slave to a taskmaster, trying to get away with as much sin as possible. They have never been actually saved, and the proof is that they have never repented.

"The true gospel demands that those who are truly regenerated by the Holy Spirit desire to serve God and not sin. Through the Holy Spirit, true Christians understand the awesome gift of salvation that they have been given, and the enormous price Christ paid to obtain it. True Christians see that the majority of people will burn in hell forever, and that they truly deserve to burn also. True Christians recognize that the only reason they will not burn forever in hell is that God set His love on them, and pulled them from the flames to be in His family.

"True Christians love and serve their Savior in gratefulness and adoration, knowing that His gift of eternal life is forever, and thus by definition can never be lost. Therefore, Quiz question 27—'The doctrine "Once saved, always saved" results in "greasy grace," where a person can sin all he wants and still be saved'—is false because it is unbiblical."

"Why do you say that rededicating one's life to Christ is a lie?" asked Ed.

"Great question," answered Dave. "If I rededicate my life to Christ, the problem is that it is still '*my life!*' This is part of a false gospel that preaches: 'take Jesus along in your life!' It is as if, 'I have this life, and yes, Jesus, You can come along with me. I'm making the decisions, but it would be really great if You bless them and make them prosperous!' This is the utmost in blasphemy and heresy—another example of human idolatry.

"God never commands me to 'rededicate *my* life to Him.' God's Word demands that we *die* to ourselves, and totally give up this life to Christ for whatever He desires. God rules, and we die to our selfish, personal desires. We 'deny ourselves, take up our cross' (Mark 8:34), and follow Christ.

"Any person who keeps his life, and just brings God in to be part of his life, will lose his life and burn in hell forever (Mark 8:35). The person who loses this life by giving it back to its rightful owner, Christ, will be eternally saved from the wrath of God and live in heaven. Those are the words and the promises of the Lord Jesus Christ, the all-righteous and all-powerful Judge of the universe.

"Again, the person who is truly born-again (saved) by God's choice and power can never lose his salvation. Eternal life granted by God is eternal, and it begins now, at regeneration! If this new life ever ends, or is lost, then it cannot be truthfully called eternal life!"

Third Objection: Bible Passages Refute Eternal Security

"But certainly there are scriptures that speak of 'falling away.' Don't these passages mean that one can lose his salvation?" Chelsea asked.

"There are no scriptures that ever say one can lose his salvation," Dave replied. "The meaning of '*falling away*' has nothing to do with losing salvation. Let's begin with the words of the Lord Jesus. Chelsea, would you please read for us the next passages I have written down?"

Chelsea read:

> Jesus presented another parable to them, saying, "The kingdom of heaven may be compared to a man who sowed good seed in his field.
>
> "But while his men were sleeping, his enemy came and sowed tares among the wheat, and went away.
>
> "But when the wheat sprouted and bore grain, then the tares became evident also.
>
> "The slaves of the landowner came and said to him, 'Sir, did you not sow good seed in your field? How then does it have tares?'
>
> "And he said to them, 'An enemy has done this!' The slaves said to him, 'Do you want us, then, to go and gather them up?'
>
> "But he said, 'No; for while you are gathering up the tares, you may uproot the wheat with them.
>
> "'Allow both to grow together until the harvest; and in the time of the harvest I will say to the reapers, "First gather up the tares and bind them in bundles to burn them up; but gather the wheat into my barn."'"
>
> (Matthew 13:24-30)

> When a large crowd was coming together, and those from the various cities were journeying to Him, He spoke by way of a parable:
>
> "The sower went out to sow his seed; and as he sowed, some fell beside the road, and it was trampled under foot and the birds of the air ate it up.
>
> "Other *seed* fell on rocky *soil,* and as soon as it grew up, it withered away, because it had no moisture.
>
> "Other *seed* fell among the thorns; and the thorns grew up with it and choked it out.
>
> "Other *seed* fell into the good soil, and grew up, and produced a crop a hundred times as great." As He said these things, He would call out, "He who has ears to hear, let him hear."
>
> His disciples *began* questioning Him as to what this parable meant.
>
> And He said, "To you it has been granted to know the mysteries of the kingdom of God, but to the rest *it is* in parables, so that SEEING THEY MAY NOT SEE, AND HEARING THEY MAY NOT UNDERSTAND.
>
> "Now the parable is this: the seed is the word of God.
>
> "Those beside the road are those who have heard; then the devil comes and takes away the word from their heart, so that they will not believe and be saved.
>
> "Those on the rocky *soil are* those who, when they hear, receive the word with joy; and these have no *firm* root; they believe for a while, and in time of temptation fall away.

"The *seed* which fell among the thorns, these are the ones who have heard, and as they go on their way they are choked with worries and riches and pleasures of *this* life, and bring no fruit to maturity.

"But the *seed* in the good soil, these are the ones who have heard the word in an honest and good heart, and hold it fast, and bear fruit with perseverance." (Luke 8:4-15)

"Thank you, Chelsea," Dave said. "The Lord Jesus clearly declares that there are two types of people in the church. There are **true believers**—the wheat in His parable; and **false believers**—the weeds, or tares. Almost every book of the Bible deals with this fact: within the physical, visible church, there are the true believers and the false believers. This, by no means, is a side issue. This is a major doctrine of Scripture.

"We have just read passage after passage warning of immoral people, so-called brothers, deceitful workers, and satanic 'angels of light,' as well as false apostles, false brethren, false prophets and false teachers—all within the church (*see pages 258-259*)!

"The Lord says that the visible church will contain both, because He is unwilling to harm one true believer in a purging. Three out of the four groups of people hearing the true gospel will remain unbelievers—even though some may claim to 'believe for a while' and look just like true believers on the outside. As we have learned, many people profess to 'believe.' But if they have not repented by giving this life back to Christ, their beliefs are worthless.

"The Lord Jesus boldly declares that God has granted to His true children the correct understanding of 'the mysteries of the kingdom of God,' including the two primary doctrines: repentance and belief in Christ. But, to those not chosen by God to be saved, this understanding has not been granted.

"False believers lack one critical element: 'an honest and good heart.' All persons born of a human male are born with a spiritually-dead, stone-cold, wicked heart. 'An honest and good heart' must be given by the Lord to replace our hearts of stone, just as we have read today by the prophet Ezekiel (*see page 270*). When God places His Holy Spirit in a spiritually-dead sinner, He makes the corpse alive with a new heart that now desires God.

"Since false believers lack a heart towards God, they are utterly unable to fulfill God's first commandments to the true believer. Grant, would you again read Mark 1:14 and 15, please?"

Grant read:

Now after John had been taken into custody, Jesus came into Galilee, preaching the gospel of God,

and saying, "The time is fulfilled, and the kingdom of God is at hand; repent and believe in the gospel." (Mark 1:14,15)

"Thank you, Grant," Dave replied. "All of the scriptures that speak of 'falling away' specifically involve people who have never repented *and* believed. Remember, one must respond to the Holy Spirit's regeneration of the heart by repenting *and* believing. Both are required responses of the true Christian. Not responding by both repenting and believing in Christ is proof that no regeneration has taken place. The Lord Jesus guaranteed that all persons who do not repent and believe will most certainly perish (Luke 13:1-9, John 3:18).

"I realize I am repeating myself, but these issues are a matter of life and death! To **repent** means to change one's mind about who owns this life, and to totally give back this life to Christ, its rightful owner, for whatever He desires. To **believe** means to trust only in God the Son's two-part perfect work for salvation: Christ's death on the cross to pay the penalty for sins, and God the Son's perfect life credited to the elect's account. Thus, the elect is legally declared as perfect as God is perfect, satisfying God's standard for getting into heaven.

"All false believers lack one or both of these responses to a true regeneration by the Holy Spirit. Some false Christians have never repented—they still maintain their rights to this life. Thus, when God's plans do not live up to their plans—as when experiencing hardship or suffering—they 'fall away' from following Christ. It is not as if they were true believers and then lost their salvation. They never repented, proof that they were never saved at all.

"The Lord Jesus gives prime examples of this in His parable of "The Sower." Those 'beside the road' neither repent nor believe. Those 'on the rocky soil' claim to believe, but are not granted understanding by God, so they never repent. They 'fall away' from following Christ in a time of temptation, which proves they still want to live in their sin. They have not given up this life to Christ. They never repented, a required response from a true believer.

"Those 'among the thorns' have also never repented—'they are choked with worries and riches and pleasures of this life.' These live this life for themselves instead of giving it up to Christ. Three of the four groups hearing the gospel were never saved, because they failed to manifest the Holy Spirit's life-changing power by repenting *and* believing.

"We will see this fact in all passages dealing with the term 'falling away.' Falling away has nothing to do with God's perspective of granting salvation, and the sinner not able to keep it. **Falling away** in Scripture always means man professing to be something he is not—and never was—and in the end, showing his real self to be a liar. **Falling away** always involves people who claim to be Christian—but were never truly saved—and never truly repented and believed.

"This fulfills the clear testimony of God's Word on false believers. Pam, would you read these next two passages please?"

Pam read:

> "Beware of the false prophets, who come to you in sheep's clothing, but inwardly are ravenous wolves.
>
> "Not everyone who says to Me, 'Lord, Lord,' will enter the kingdom of heaven, but he who does the will of My Father who is in heaven *will enter.*
>
> "Many will say to Me on that day, 'Lord, Lord, did we not prophesy in Your name, and in Your name cast out demons, and in Your name perform many miracles?'
>
> "And then I will declare to them, 'I never knew you; DEPART FROM ME, YOU WHO PRACTICE LAWLESSNESS.'" (Matthew 7:15,21-23)

> They went out from us, but they were not *really* of us; for if they had been of us, they would have remained with us; but *they went out,* so that it would be shown that they all are not of us. (1 John 2:19)

"Thank you, Pam," appreciated Dave. "The Lord Jesus, in His parable, says three out of four groups hearing the gospel will not be saved. He also declares that 'many' of those who call Him 'Lord' will not be saved—even though they looked just like true believers on the outside! Eventually, the true colors of these false Christians will show, as they fall away from following the One True God. They were never saved. It was all a lie.

"Let's read the passages that speak of falling away."

The class read:

> But if some of the branches were broken off, and you, being a wild olive, were grafted in among them and became partaker with them of the rich root of the olive tree,
>
> do not be arrogant toward the branches; but if you are arrogant, *remember that* it is not you who supports the root, but the root *supports* you.
>
> You will say then, "Branches were broken off so that I might be grafted in."
>
> Quite right, they were broken off for their unbelief, but you stand by your faith. Do not be conceited, but fear;
>
> for if God did not spare the natural branches, He will not spare you, either.
>
> Behold then the kindness and severity of God; to those who fell, severity, but to you, God's kindness, if you continue in His kindness; otherwise you also will be cut off.
>
> And they also, if they do not continue in their unbelief, will be grafted in, for God is able to graft them in again. (Romans 11:17-23)

"The perishing Jews were 'broken off' from, or no longer included in, God's family tree," Dave explained. "The reason was 'their *unbelief*.' They refused to believe in Christ as their Messiah, and to trust only in His work for their salvation. Believing in Christ is one of the two required responses to God's salvation for a true Christian.

"A person claiming ('you will say then...') to be a true Christian 'stands by his faith' in Christ's work alone for salvation. If this person claiming to be a true Christian does not continue in trusting in Christ and His work alone—but adds his own works to merit or keep salvation—he will no longer considered part of God's family tree by true believers. The fact that he stopped believing in Christ's work alone is proof positive that he was never truly regenerated by God at all. He only claimed to be a true Christian.

"Let's read more passages."

The class continued:

> For it is written that Abraham had two sons, one by the bondwoman and one by the free woman.
>
> But the son by the bondwoman was born according to the flesh, and the son by the free woman through the promise.
>
> This is allegorically speaking, for these *women* are two covenants: one *proceeding* from Mount Sinai bearing children who are to be slaves; she is

Hagar.

But the Jerusalem above is free; she is our mother.

And you brethren, like Isaac, are children of promise.

So then, brethren, we are not children of a bondwoman, but of the free woman. (Galatians 4:22-24,26,28,31)

It was for freedom that Christ set us free; therefore keep standing firm and do not be subject again to a yoke of slavery.

You have been severed from Christ, you who are seeking to be justified by law; you have fallen from grace.

For we through the Spirit, by faith, are waiting for the hope of righteousness. (Galatians 5:1,4,5)

"Those seeking to become righteous before God by doing works of the Law have never believed in Christ's work alone for salvation," Dave expounded. "Thus, they were never truly saved. They are foolishly and rebelliously attempting to be perfect as God is perfect by what they do.

"They have rejected the only method of true salvation—salvation by *grace*, which, by definition, excludes all personal works. These humanists claimed to believe in Christ, but walked away from the only method for true salvation, thereby cutting themselves off from the grace of God. They were never 'children of promise,' and the slavery to their vicious sinful pride eventually became disclosed.

"Let's continue with more passages."

The class continued:

Take care, brethren, that there not be in any one of you an evil, unbelieving heart that falls away from the living God. (Hebrews 3:12)

Therefore, let us fear if, while a promise remains of entering His rest, any one of you may seem to have come short of it.

For indeed we have had good news preached to us, just as they also; but the word they heard did not profit them, because it was not united by faith in those who heard.

For we who have believed enter that rest.

Therefore, since it remains for some to enter it, and those who formerly had good news preached to them failed to enter because of disobedience.

So there remains a Sabbath rest for the people of God.

For the one who has entered His rest has himself also rested from his works, as God did from His.

Therefore let us be diligent to enter that rest, so that no one will fall, through *following* the same example of disobedience.

(Hebrews 4:1-3a,6,9-11)

"The Scripture cannot be more clear!" Dave exclaimed. "The one who 'falls away' refuses to continue on in God's grace because he has 'an evil, unbelieving heart.' These false brethren were never regenerated by God and given a new heart.

"True believers 'enter God's rest' by giving up their futile attempts to be righteous, and trust totally in Christ's work for salvation. These false brethren 'come short of it.' These humanists 'failed to enter because of disobedience.' They pridefully demanded to do it their way, when God's way is the only way to avoid His fierce wrath. They refused to believe in Christ's work alone because God never granted them the faith to believe in Christ—they were never part of 'the people of God.'

"The entire Letter to the Hebrews is dedicated to rooting out the false brethren who sit in the pews and preach in the pulpits. The writer clearly addresses entire congregations made of true Christians and false Christians. These false believers are always shown to have never repented and believed. Let's read the classic passages in Hebrews that the ungodly humanists use to say that true believers can lose their salvation."

The class read:

> Therefore, leaving the elementary teaching about the Christ, let us press on to maturity, not laying again a foundation of repentance from dead works and of faith toward God.
>
> For in the case of those who have once been enlightened and have tasted of the heavenly gift and have been made partakers of the Holy Spirit,
>
> and have tasted the good word of God and the powers of the age to come,
>
> and *then* have fallen away, it is impossible to renew them again to repentance, since they again crucify to themselves the Son of God and put Him to open shame.
>
> For ground that drinks the rain which often falls on it and brings forth vegetation useful to those for whose sake it is also tilled, receives a blessing from God;
>
> but if it yields thorns and thistles, it is worthless and close to being cursed, and it ends up being burned.
>
> But, beloved, we are convinced of better things concerning you, and things that accompany salvation, though we are speaking in this way.
>
> (Hebrews 6:1,4-9)

"The writer to the Hebrews just spent five chapters 'laying a foundation of repentance from dead works and of faith toward God," Dave reviewed. "In case anyone possibly missed his point, the two required responses to a newly regenerated heart are to repent and believe. Because there are still false brethren in the congregations, he goes on to describe their fate.

"Ungodly humanists claim that these passages describe a true Christian. This is impossible because of the use of the word '*impossible*' in verse 6: 'it is impossible to renew them again to repentance.' During the life of Christ, the Apostle Peter committed all six of the sins listed here, but he repented just as Christ prophesied that he would (Luke 22:31,32).

"The writer specifically says in verse 9 that he is not describing true believers in the previous verses. This passage would never even be considered to say true believers can permanently fall away if the readers of the Letter would simply read verse 9!

"The writer turns and addresses true Christians as 'beloved,' and is 'convinced' of their salvation. The writer never says these things about those he is describing in the previous verses."

"It sure sounds like he is describing true Christians," Paul remarked. "He refers to 'those who have once been enlightened, and have tasted of the heavenly gift, and have been made partakers of the Holy Spirit, and have tasted the good word of God, and the powers of the age to come.'"

"What about Judas Iscariot, the one who betrayed the Lord Jesus?" asked Dave. "He was named, with the rest of the disciples in Matthew 10, whom the Lord commissioned and sent out to 'heal *the* sick, raise *the* dead, cleanse *the* lepers, and cast out demons' (Matthew 10:6). But the Lord Jesus called Judas Iscariot 'the son of **perdition**' (John 17:12), a Hebrew idiom meaning 'one destined to perish.' Judas also committed all six of the sins here in Hebrews 6, but was unable to repent because he was never chosen by God to be saved. So, he killed himself (Acts 1:18). Christ had avowed that it would have been better if Judas had never been born.

"God used godless men throughout history to accomplish His plan, from Esau (Hebrews 12:17), Balaam the prophet (2 Peter 2), through all of the wicked kings and rulers of Israel and Judah, and Judas Iscariot. God can use anyone and anything He desires—He is not limited to performing His miraculous power through only true believers. God even used a donkey to get His message to the wicked Balaam (Numbers 22:28)!

"Thus, the Hebrews 6 passages that humanists use to discredit the true doctrine of eternal security are not even talking about true believers. The writer specifically says this in verse 9."

"What about the passages in Hebrews 10?" asked Ed. "I've heard these verses cited to say true believers can lose their salvation."

"Let's read them," Dave replied.

The class read:

> For if we go on sinning willfully after receiving the knowledge of the truth, there no longer remains a sacrifice for sins,
>
> but a terrifying expectation of judgment and THE FURY OF A FIRE WHICH WILL CONSUME THE ADVERSARIES.
>
> Anyone who has set aside the Law of Moses dies without mercy on *the testimony of* two or three witnesses.
>
> How much severer punishment do you think he will deserve who has trampled under foot the Son of God, and has regarded as unclean the blood of the covenant by which he was sanctified, and has insulted the Spirit of grace?
>
> BUT MY RIGHTEOUS ONE SHALL LIVE BY FAITH;
>
> AND IF HE SHRINKS BACK, MY SOUL HAS NO PLEASURE IN HIM.
>
> But we are not of those who shrink back to destruction, but of those who have faith to the preserving of the soul. (Hebrews 10:26-29,38,39)

"Once again, the final verse, here verse 39, destroys the idea that the writer is describing true believers in the preceding verses," Dave explained. "The writer is directly addressing those in the congregations that claim to be true believers, but hold to the false doctrine of 'greasy grace.' In describing their fate in hell, the writer calls them 'the adversaries,' so he is making it very plain they are not friends of God, but enemies.

"The writer clearly says that the reason they are false brethren is because they lack the gift of faith from God. **God's gift of faith—the power to believe in Christ and His work alone for salvation—'preserves the souls' of all true Christians possessing it.** This Scripture guarantees eternal security for true believers, and prophesies eternal torture in hell for false Christians.

"There are other passages speaking of falling away involving the last days of the earth just before the return of Christ. These are found in Matthew 24 and 1 Timothy 4, and each passage mentions that these people rejected Christ in order to follow their evil, deceiving hearts to destruction.

"I think we have seen this obvious pattern in all the passages regarding falling away. These scriptures have nothing to do with being a true Christian and then losing salvation. All of the verses spoke directly of false brethren who claimed to be truly saved, but were living a lie. They were shown to have never been saved at all, the proof being that they never repented and believed in Christ. They never received a new heart from God, so they left the truth of God's grace to pursue their own depraved attempts at being righteous, revealing their real identity as frauds.

"To put the true doctrine of eternal security in a nutshell, let me ask two questions: Is salvation a gift of God?"

"Yes," Anna replied.

"How do you know?" retorted Dave.

"God's Word, the only standard of truth in the universe, says in Romans 6:23: 'For the wages of sin is death, but the free gift of God is eternal life in Christ Jesus our Lord,'" answered Anna, smiling.

"Excellent," praised Dave. "Is salvation a calling of God?"

"Yes," Nick said, "for just last night I read the Apostle Paul's words introducing his First Letter to the Corinthians:

> To the church of God which is at Corinth, to those who have been
> sanctified in Christ Jesus, saints by calling, with all who in every place call on
> the name of our Lord Jesus Christ, their *Lord* and ours:
> Grace to you and peace from God our Father and the Lord Jesus Christ.
> (1 Corinthians 1:2,3)

"Excellent," acknowledged Dave. "Thus, salvation is a gift of God and a calling of God. Let me finish with one more scripture: '**For the gifts and the calling of God are irrevocable**' (Romans 11:29).

"To say we've covered a lot of ground today would be a laughable understatement. Let's do a quick review.

"The Lord Jesus stated that there are 'few' who find the way to life, and 'many' who go the way of destruction.

"About eight out of ten qualifies as many, and definitely two out of ten qualifies as few. Thus, about two out of every ten people that have lived on earth will find eternal life, and eight out of every ten people will burn in hell forever for their sin.

"The Lord Jesus also declares that 'many' people who claim Jesus as their 'Lord' will be rejected by the Lord Himself for entrance into the kingdom of heaven on their day of judgment.

"Scripture definitely warns us that false brothers and sisters are in the church, even ones who teach 'destructive heresies.'

"But we are not to 'yield in subjection to them for even an hour, so that the truth of the gospel would remain.'

"The true gospel of true, biblical Christianity gives birth to true Christians. All false gospels—and there are many of them out there, especially in the churches—give birth to false Christians.

"Throughout all of history and to the end of time, only two faiths exist in the universe: true Christianity and humanism.

"True Christianity preaches the true gospel of the One True God, who alone is able to save a person from the wrath due to him for his rebellion.

"Every other religion preaches the false gospel of humanism, and leads to guaranteed eternal torture in hell.

"Any faith that has man actively participating in his salvation in any way—whether in obtaining or keeping salvation—is the false faith of humanism.

"There are only two methods of salvation, one true—salvation by God's grace—and one false—salvation by man's works.

"Grace and works are mutually exclusive methods. By definition, if one is true, the other is utterly impossible. The reason is that grace means totally unearned or undeserved favor.

"If favor is given as a result of work—such as a paycheck for a job done—then the favor is earned and deserved. This kind of benefit, then, is not by grace.

"God's holy Word specifically states that salvation is by God's grace, and thus absolutely cannot be earned or kept by 'good works.'

"The true gospel is the good news that God Himself, before creation, has chosen a remnant of rebellious sinners to save from the wrath justly due them, and to bring them into His eternal family!

"Though all persons born of a human male deserved eternal punishment for their rebellion against God, He graciously chose an elect few to legally declare as perfect as God is perfect.

"God satisfied His perfect justice by pouring out the chosen sinners' due wrath upon His own holy Son, and transferred God the Son's infinite perfection to the accounts of His elect.

"In true Christianity, these elect sinners 'were dead in their trespasses and sins' (Ephesians 2:1).

"Dead people do not actively participate in anything—they are dead. Spiritually-dead people cannot accept, reach out for, believe in, desire, understand, or think according to God's truth—they are spiritually dead.

"True Christianity therefore demands that God alone must then initiate and complete every detail of salvation into the spiritually-dead corpses He chose to come into His family. The corpse only passively receives the changes wrought by the Divine Hand. Upon becoming alive with a new heart given by God, the born-again man desires for the first time the things of God.

"There is a world of difference between 'accepting' and 'receiving.' In order to accept something, I must actively, willfully choose it.

"The humanistic teaching, 'Just accept the Lord Jesus Christ as your personal Savor, and you will be saved' is false precisely because it requires a spiritually-dead person to do something for salvation.

"God's holy Word specifically states that 'a natural man does not accept the things of the Spirit of God, for they are foolishness to him; and he cannot understand them!' So, how is it that the modern church says that, in order to become a believer, a non-believer must 'accept' Jesus Christ as his personal Savior?

"The answer of the apostles to the question, 'What must I do to be saved?' is to 'Believe in the Lord Jesus.'

"The modern humanistic church would define believing in Christ as something a person must bring up within himself; a decision a person must make based on the facts; choosing to exercise this faith that every person inherently possesses; or something each person must do. Nothing could be further from God's truth!

"Believing in Christ is not something a man does, but is a state of being that a man receives! "A square must have four equal sides because that defines its existence!

"Likewise, believing in Christ is not something a true Christian does, but what he is! Believing in Christ defines the true believer's very existence! It is his state of being. Faith to believe in Christ is granted by the Holy Spirit when He makes a sinner 'a new creation' (Galatians 6:15). A sinner, who is made a believer, believes!

"Biblical salvation is only by God's grace. We cannot do anything to be saved! God's truth cannot be accepted, only passively received.

"To receive something, my will and desires are not even involved. It is something that happens to me. I am utterly passive—I have no choice in the matter.

"'There is none who seeks for God' (Romans 3:11), until God takes out the dead heart of stone, and gives His chosen child a new heart filled with His Holy Spirit.

"True Christians will undergo a judgment, but this judgment has nothing to do with salvation. That has already been decided by God before creation began.

"The true Christian will have his works as a believer tested for rewards.

"Though a true believer's earthly work may be burned up with no reward, still 'he himself will be saved!' The true Christian always was, and always will be God's child.

"All true Christians will spend eternity in heaven with God their Father, because they have been legally declared perfect by God the Son's perfect work on their behalf.

"God started the process of salvation, and God brings it to completion.

"In humanistic false faiths, humans are said to play at least some role in getting and/or keeping salvation in order to steal some of the glory that belongs to God alone for this miracle.

"True Christians, are—present tense—children of God now, beginning at regeneration!

"Eternal means lasting forever, without end.

"Life that can be lost, or ended, cannot truthfully be called 'eternal' life!

"The Lord Jesus guarantees that the sheep that the Father gave to Him 'will never perish.'

"The reason true Christians can never and will never perish is that they are sealed by God Himself, and kept by God for the day of redemption.

"God gave His Holy Spirit to seal His child for eternal life, and to bind His covenant with that child, so that whoever was given the Holy Spirit by God was guaranteed eternal life.

"The false Christian depends on man's decision to be saved.

"Bringing that heresy to its logical conclusion, the ungodly humanist holds that man must also keep himself saved as well.

"But only resting—not working and striving—resting in the work that Christ alone accomplished for salvation is man's only hope for avoiding the wrath of God.

"WARNING: We cannot add anything of our own to God's perfection, or we only taint it—and then we would not be as perfect as God is perfect!

"We must refuse the sinful nature's desire to attempt to usurp God's glory by deceiving our minds that we can be righteous like the Most High. This was the original sin of pride by the devil (Isaiah 14), who succeeded in tempting Eve to fall for the same lie (Genesis 3).

"The Lord God Almighty reigns sovereignly, and God's sovereignty means He has ordained absolutely everything that exists or happens in all of creation for all time.

"Though affirming with his words that God is sovereign, the false Christian denies it with his doctrine. The ungodly humanist redefines sovereignty—just as he redefines God—to fit his man-glorifying beliefs.

"He blasphemes: 'Of course God is sovereign, but He has given man a free will, and made him a free moral agent. God would never interfere with man's decisions, for that would be unloving.'

"However, man is not a free moral agent, but an enslaved, immoral spiritual corpse—running away from God to remain in his sin.

"The Almighty depends upon nothing outside of Himself, especially spiritually-dead man, to accomplish the salvation of His elect.

"The ones God chose before creation to be in His family were guaranteed eternal life before they were even born (Romans 9:10-16), because God had sovereignly ordained it.

"There are three objections often raised against the true doctrine of eternal security. First, we have the 'I knew a guy who fell away...' testimony. Second, the doctrine of eternal security is said to lead to 'greasy grace'—where a person thinks he can continue a life of sin and still be saved. Third, there are the scriptures that are claimed to say salvation can be lost.

"Regarding the 'I knew a guy who fell away...' testimony, there are three very important issues.

"Firstly, God's Word is the only standard of truth in the universe—not our finite, sometimes flawed perceptions.

"Secondly, God's Word says that no person can know for sure if another person is saved. But God knows, because He did the choosing and saving.

"Thirdly, God's Word specifically declares that any person that professes to be a Christian, and walks away from true Christianity, was never a true Christian. They didn't 'lose their salvation.' They were never saved at all, regardless of all outward appearances.

"The second objection to eternal security is the idea of 'greasy grace'—where a person thinks he can continue a life of sin and still be saved.

"God's holy Word specifically says that the person who holds this heresy is not and never was saved, and will certainly perish. This person is a false Christian who has never repented; he never gave up this life to Christ for His use.

"Equally as false as the idea of 'greasy grace' is the idea of 'rededicating my life to Christ.'

"If I rededicate my life to Christ, the problem is that it is still 'my life!'

"God never commands me to 'rededicate my life to Him.' God's Word demands that we die to ourselves, and totally give up this life to Christ for whatever He desires.

"This ungodly teaching and the false idea of 'greasy grace' exist because they are the fruit of the false gospel which has been taught in the modern church for nearly a century.

"There are no scriptures that ever say one can lose his salvation. The meaning of 'falling away' has nothing to do with losing salvation.

"The Lord Jesus clearly declares that there are two types of people in the church: true believers—the wheat in His parable; and false believers—the weeds, or tares. This is a major doctrine of Scripture.

"False believers lack one critical element: 'an honest and good heart.' All persons born of a human male are born with a spiritually-dead, stone-cold, wicked heart.

"'An honest and good heart' must be given by the Lord to replace our hearts of stone.

"Since false believers lack a heart towards God, they are utterly unable to fulfill God's first commandments to the true believer: to 'repent and believe' (Mark 1:15).

"All of the scriptures that speak of 'falling away' specifically involve people who have never repented and believed. Both are required responses of the true Christian.

"Not responding with both is proof that no regeneration has taken place, for the Lord Jesus said those who do not repent and believe will perish (Luke 13:1-9, John 3:18).

"'Falling away' in Scripture always means man professing to be something he is not—and never was—and in the end, showing his real self to be a liar.

"The Lord Jesus says three out of four groups hearing the gospel will not be saved. Christ also declares that 'many' of those who call Him 'Lord' will not be saved—even though they looked just like true believers on the outside!

"Finally, Scripture declares that salvation is a gift of God and a calling of God. And the Apostle Paul delivers humanistic false Christianity its fatal blow: 'For the gifts and the calling of God are irrevocable' (Romans 11:29).

"I hope that everyone now understands that the sovereign Almighty God has ordained everything that comes to pass in His creation—especially salvation," Dave concluded. "Man has absolutely nothing to do with salvation, because man was not around when God made His sovereign choices before the foundation of the world (Ephesians 1:3-6).

"The humanistic heresy of false Christianity fails miserably because it rejects God and His Word. The humanist claims that salvation is man's choice, and must be kept by man's obedience in doing good works.

"Scripture, however, declares that man's will to choose is absolutely not involved in salvation (John 1:12,13; Romans 9:16). Scripture also makes keeping salvation by man's works an impossible feat, as the standard for being accepted by God is clearly presented by the Lord Jesus: "'Therefore you are to be perfect, as your heavenly Father is perfect'" (Matthew 5:48).

"God sovereignly chose those He wanted to be in His family. God can do that. Everything belongs to Him, and He can do whatever He wishes with it. God sovereignly chose only a few—a remnant—in order to bring the highest glory and honor to God the Son Jesus Christ, the only Savior of the universe. And these elect ones whom God chose before creation were guaranteed eternal life before they were even born (Romans 9:10-16)!

"God made many promises in His holy Word to His true children. God declares that He keeps, guards and protects His children; He confirms His child blameless until the end; He seals His child for the day of redemption; He begins the good work of salvation and perfects it; He will bring to pass our complete preservation; He will bring us safely to His heavenly kingdom; and He will raise us up on that day and lose not one of His children!"

"Thank God that He is the one bringing me to heaven," Nick said. "Because if it was up to me, I'd blow it for sure! I want God to sovereignly ordain my future. That way I can rest in God's power and promises—not my own failures and shortcomings! Why would anyone want to hang his eternal destination on finite human inadequacies, instead of on the sovereign, immutable, omnipotent Word of Almighty God?"

"No truer words have ever been spoken!" applauded Dave. "Nick, would you close our class with prayer?"

"Almighty God and Father, we praise You and thank You for Your glorious truth—Your holy Word! We thank You that You guide us by the power of Your Holy Spirit through the muck and mire of man-made humanistic lies designed to steal the glory that only belongs to You! You are the sovereign Creator who sustains everything, and You deserve all of our praise and all of our worship.

"Thank You for sending Your Son to be the only Savior of the universe. We thank You for making us Your own, even though we were rebellious sinners deserving of nothing but eternal torment. We cannot thank You enough.

"Fill us with Your Holy Spirit, and empower us with Your love. Let us know Your ways, that we may know and love You more intimately every day. Let Your awesome love shine through us to a dark world, and use us to bring glory to Your holy Name. In Jesus' Name we pray, amen!"

13

The Law of God

"Hi, Dave!"

"Hey, Nick!" Dave responded as his brother-in-Christ entered the dormitory room. "How is it going?"

"Excellent!" replied Nick, embracing Dave and taking his usual seat. "My grades are up this semester, and I think I'm ready for final exams next week. Even more importantly, I'm learning more about my heavenly Father, so I'm falling more in love with Him every day!"

"All right! Would you open our Bible study with prayer?"

"Dear heavenly Father, we praise and adore You, for You deserve all of our worship. We thank You so much for saving us from ourselves, and pulling us out of the mire of our rebellion against You. Thank You for such incredible love.

"Thank You for sending Your holy Son, Jesus, and for His awesome sacrifice on the brutal cross at the hands of His own creation. Thank You, Lord, for crediting us with Your perfect life, so that we may enjoy eternity in Your glorious paradise.

"Fill us now, we pray, with Your blessed Holy Spirit. Give Dave the wisdom and knowledge, straight from Your throne, to teach me Your ways. Empower us to hear and understand Your Word, and give us the overwhelming desire to obey Your commands. In Jesus' Name we pray, amen!"

Obeying God Is the Key

"That's very interesting that you asked the Lord for the desire to obey Him," Dave began. "Obedience to God's commands—regardless of man's traditions, or even our own sinful desires—is the key to the fulfilled Christian life. So many people who call themselves Christians read God's Word, and hear God's commands, but still insist to live life their own ways by their own opinions. This is living in rebellion against God. Let's read some passages on obedience."

Nick read:

> But Peter and the apostles answered, "We must obey God rather than men." (Acts 5:29)

> *We are* destroying speculations and every lofty thing raised up against the knowledge of God, and *we are* taking every thought captive to the obedience of Christ,
>
> and we are ready to punish all disobedience, whenever your obedience is complete. (2 Corinthians 10:5,6)

> Peter, an apostle of Jesus Christ,
>
> To those who reside as aliens, scattered throughout Pontus, Galatia, Cappadocia, Asia, and Bithynia, who are chosen
>
> according to the foreknowledge of God the Father, by the sanctifying work of the Spirit, to obey Jesus Christ and be sprinkled with His blood: May grace and peace be yours in the fullest measure.
>
> As obedient children, do not be conformed to the former lusts *which were yours* in your ignorance,
>
> but like the Holy One who called you, be holy yourselves also in all *your* behavior;
>
> because it is written, "YOU SHALL BE HOLY, FOR I AM HOLY."
>
> (1 Peter 1:1,2,14-16)

"True Christians were chosen by God the Father specifically 'to obey Jesus Christ,' bringing honor and glory to His Name," Dave stated. "This is a true saying worth remembering: '**Do it God's way, and He will bless you for your obedience. Insist on doing it your way, and God will frustrate this life!**'

"Obedience to God's commands is the key for God's grace and peace 'in the fullest measure.' Obedience is so critical that the Apostle Paul commands us to take 'every thought captive to the obedience of Christ.'

"The Apostle Peter's command for obedience is based on God's standard for acceptance: '"YOU SHALL BE HOLY, FOR I AM HOLY."' God repeatedly reinforces this command in the book of Leviticus, chapters 11, 19 and 20. This is the very scripture the Lord Jesus quotes in Matthew 5:48: '"Therefore you are to be perfect, as your heavenly Father is perfect."'

"In talking to many Christians, and finding those not experiencing God's peace and joy in this life, one fact became very clear. Almost every one of them were not obeying any, or all, of God's Four Basic Commands: praying and studying His Word every day, as well as going to church and fellowshiping with committed Christians as often as possible. Please read Acts 2:41 through 43."

Nick read:

> So then, those who had received his word were baptized; and that day
> there were added about three thousand souls.
>
> They were continually devoting themselves to the apostles' teaching and
> to fellowship, to the breaking of bread and to prayer.
>
> Everyone kept feeling a sense of awe; and many wonders and signs
> were taking place through the apostles. (Acts 2:41-43)

"The 'apostles' teaching' today is found in the Bible," Dave continued. "We 'break bread' as a church body, as the Lord Jesus broke bread with His disciples, at the Lord's Supper during the worship service. Also, 'they were continually devoting themselves...to fellowship...and to prayer'—the Four Basics.

"These Four Basics are commanded by God to bring about God's will for man: to get on His Lap, and get to know Him intimately. But for those continuously obeying the Four Basics, and desiring to go deeper into following Christ, the question must be asked: 'What is next? What else does God command me to obey?'"

"Great question!" said Nick.

God Is Eternal, Perfect and Unchanging

"Here we come to the Law of God," Dave stated. "As I promised you in our personal study last week, we will define the Law of God, and the Law of Moses, and discuss their relevance to the Christian."

"That's good, because I'm using the guideline in my Bible to read through the Bible in a year," Nick replied. "So, I'm reading through the Law of Moses in the Old Testament, and I am very confused as to how all of that relates to me."

"As we studied God, we found our heavenly Father declaring Himself to be eternal, perfect and unchanging," Dave began. "In other words, God's holy character is eternal, perfect and unchanging.

"God's sovereign will, as well as His eternal purpose (or plan) for creation, come forth from His eternal, perfect and unchanging character.

"The Law of God for His creation also comes forth from His eternal, perfect and unchanging character. Thus, God's sovereign will, His purpose (or plan), and the Law of God are also eternal, perfect and unchanging.

"**God can never and will never change His character, sovereign will, purpose, or His Law—because they are already perfect!** To say that God changes any of these things commits blasphemy for many possible reasons. Either God and His character are not perfect, and He is changing to something better; or, they are perfect, and He is changing to something less than perfect! Since God's character, will, plan and Law are eternally perfect, they can never and will never change. If they change, they are not eternal, for they stopped being what they were, and changed to something different.

The Law of God Is the Law of Christ

"***The Law of God*** is the collection of rules that God imposes upon His creation by His own authority. God created everything that exists, and everything belongs to Him. Thus, God has the right to do whatever He wishes with what is His own. This right includes commanding man to obey His rules, and administering punishment for man's refusal to do so."

"That makes sense," agreed Nick. "Even human fathers expect that right in dealing with their kids."

"Exactly," Dave applauded. "Scripture mentions three names of Law given by God: the Law of God, the Law of Moses and the Law of Christ. What I am about to say now is the critical point in understanding the Law of God properly. **The eternal, perfect, unchanging Law of God** *is one and the same as* **the Law of Christ**.

"The common assumption is that the Law of God came first, then God gave the Law of Moses, and then the Lord Jesus brought the Law of Christ when He took on a human nature. This idea is entirely false.

"Jesus Christ *is* God. Thus, Christ's character, sovereign will, purpose and Law are God's character, sovereign will, purpose, and Law. There is only one God, and the Father, Son and Holy Spirit are that one God (*see chapter 6*). And since God's character, sovereign will, purpose and Law are eternal, perfect and unchanging, those of Christ are eternal, perfect and unchanging as well. Therefore, the Law of God is one and the same as the Law of Christ.

"Christ, being fully God, always existed eternally. When Christ became a man, He simply added humanity to His deity. Christ's Godhood never changed at all. Christ's purpose—to create man and save some of them for His family—was an *eternal* purpose. This eternal plan always existed in the mind of Christ. God's holy Word states this with precision. Please read these two passages, Nick."

Nick read:

> ...so that the manifold wisdom of God might now be made known through the church to the rulers and the authorities in the heavenly *places*.
> *This was* in accordance with the eternal purpose which He carried out in Christ Jesus our Lord,
> in whom we have boldness and confident access through faith in Him.
> (Ephesians 3:10-12)

> Therefore do not be ashamed of the testimony of our Lord or of me His prisoner, but join with *me* in suffering for the gospel according to the power of God,
> who has saved us and called us with a holy calling, not according to our works, but according to His own purpose and grace which was granted us in Christ Jesus from all eternity. (2 Timothy 1:8,9)

"The *eternal* purpose of God—the Father, Son and Holy Spirit—was to create in order to bring glory to its Creator. The Law of Christ, which rules that creation, existed eternally as well. From that creation, God eternally planned to take an elect group of people to bring into His family. These chosen ones were saved in order to obey Christ and His Law, thus bringing honor and glory to God the Son.

"Again, and this is key: The eternal, perfect, unchanging Law of God is one and the same as the Law of Christ. Read the next passages I have written down, beginning with the words of the Lord Jesus."

Nick read:

> "Heaven and earth will pass away, but My words will not pass away."
>
> (Matthew 24:35; Mark 13:31; Luke 21:33)

> Therefore as you have received Christ Jesus the Lord, *so* walk in Him.
> For in Him all the fullness of Deity dwells in bodily form,
> and in Him you have been made complete, and He is the head over all
> rule and authority. (Colossians 2:6,9,10)

> So then you are no longer strangers and aliens, but you are fellow
> citizens with the saints, and are of God's household,
> having been built on the foundation of the apostles and prophets, Christ
> Jesus Himself being the corner *stone.* (Ephesians 2:19,20)

> All Scripture is inspired by God and profitable for teaching, for reproof,
> for correction, for training in righteousness;
> so that the man of God may be adequate, equipped for every good work.
>
> (2 Timothy 3:16)

"*The Law of Christ* consists of the Lord Jesus' words—all of His eternal commands—and all of His commands sovereignly communicated through His apostles and prophets by the Holy Spirit," Dave explained. "Thus, the Law of Christ is God's holy Scripture—the Bible. The Law of Christ is the Law of God, which is eternal, perfect and unchanging. The Law of Christ is perfect because God the Son is perfect; it is eternal, existing in the mind of Christ in eternity past; and it can never and will never be changed, or 'pass away.'"

God Writes His Law on Man's Heart

"So, God creates the human race, beginning with Adam and Eve," observed Nick. "You are saying that the Law of Christ existed then?"

"Absolutely," Dave answered. "The Law of Christ is the perfectly complete, full expression of the Law of God, and it existed in eternity past in the mind of Christ. The Law of Christ was not created by the Lord Jesus during His incarnation here on earth.

"Remember, after He had finished creation by making man, 'God saw all that He had made, and behold, it was very good' (Genesis 1:31). Man, at that time, had the ability to obey or disobey God. What exactly of God could Adam and Eve obey or disobey? God's commands, otherwise known as the Law of God, which is one and the same as the Law of Christ.

"God gave man a spirit into which God programmed His eternal Law. Before The Fall of Adam and Eve into sin, God's Law was clearly and easily communicated to their minds and consciences. There was no inherent, rebellious, sinful nature that obscured God's message.

"Since The Fall, man became separated from the holy God, spiritually dying, being cursed with a sinful nature. Man's mind and conscience are now defiled from conception, and his heart is darkened. Man can no longer choose to obey or disobey God, but is sold into slavery to sin and to the devil (2 Timothy 2:24-26). Man is born spiritually dead.

"Scripture later tells us that God has written His Law on 'the hearts' of man. As we have studied, 'the heart' is symbolic of the man's spirit, which controls man's conscience and man's mind (*see page 180*). As a reminder, man's human nature ultimately controls man's mind, which generates desires that control his will and emotions. Let's read some passages explaining that God placed His Law on man's mind and conscience."

Nick read:

> For the wrath of God is revealed from heaven against all ungodliness and unrighteousness of men who suppress the truth in unrighteousness,
>
> because that which is known about God is evident within them; for God made it evident to them.
>
> For even though they knew God, they did not honor Him as God or give thanks, but they became futile in their speculations, and their foolish heart was darkened.
>
> And just as they did not see fit to acknowledge God any longer, God gave them over to a depraved mind, to do those things which are not proper,
>
> and although they know the ordinance of God, that those who practice such things are worthy of death, they not only do the same, but also give hearty approval to those who practice them. (Romans 1:18,19,21,28,32)

> For when Gentiles who do not have the Law do instinctively the things of the Law, these, not having the Law, are a law to themselves,
>
> in that they show the work of the Law written in their hearts, their conscience bearing witness and their thoughts alternately accusing or else defending them,
>
> on the day when, according to my gospel, God will judge the secrets of men through Christ Jesus. (Romans 2:14-16)

"Since man became a slave to sin and to the devil, he can no longer clearly 'read' the Law of God on his heart. God gives every person the knowledge of His existence, authority, law and coming judgment. But man purposely suppresses this knowledge to continue in his rebellious, sinful lifestyle.

"Truthfully, man rarely considers all of the ramifications of violating God's perfect Law. But every man knows in his heart that God exists (Romans 1:21), and that God will condemn him to eternal, conscious punishment for being evil and offending God's eternal holiness (Romans 1:32). Let's read the scriptures denoting the effects of The Fall of man."

Nick read:

> "For from within, out of the heart of men, proceed the evil thoughts, fornications, thefts, murders, adulteries,

deeds of coveting *and* wickedness, *as well as* deceit, sensuality, envy, slander, pride *and* foolishness.

"All these evil things proceed from within and defile the man."

(Mark 7:21-23)

"This is the judgment, that the Light has come into the world, and men loved (desired) the darkness rather than the Light, for their deeds were evil." (John 3:19; *parenthesis mine*)

Because the mind set on the flesh is hostile toward God; for it does not subject itself to the law of God, for it is not even able *to do so*.

(Romans 8:7)

Among them we too all formerly lived in the lusts of our flesh, indulging the desires of the flesh and of the mind, and were by nature children of wrath, even as the rest. (Ephesians 2:3)

To the pure, all things are pure; but to those who are defiled and unbelieving, nothing is pure, but both their mind and their conscience are defiled. (Titus 1:15)

The Lord's bond-servant must not be quarrelsome, but be kind to all, able to teach, patient when wronged,

with gentleness correcting those who are in opposition, if perhaps God may grant them repentance leading to the knowledge of the truth,

and they may come to their senses *and escape* from the snare of the devil, having been held captive by him to do his will. (2 Timothy 2:24-26)

God's Plan of Redemption Unfolds

"The Fall caused a most abysmal state of affairs," concluded Nick.

"Yes," Dave agreed somberly. "But God promised Adam that He would send a Redeemer to save a people for Himself out of the lost human race. This was all part of God's eternal plan to bring all honor and glory to God the Son Jesus Christ, the only Savior of the enslaved universe.

"A brief overview of history would be extremely helpful here. Many years after Adam's fall, God chose a pagan from Ur of the Chaldees named Abram, and eventually renamed him Abraham.

"God sovereignly reckoned—or credited—righteousness to Abraham's account, and gave him the power to repent. God then granted Abraham faith in God's promise to be his Savior. Abraham gave up this life to God—*repenting*—by leaving his relatives and country of birth. Abraham trusted God's Word by obeying His commandments—*believing in Him*—and followed Him throughout the land God promised to his descendants. Thus, Abraham demonstrated the proof of being a true child of God by repenting and believing in God his Savior.

"As God had dealt with Adam and Noah beforehand with covenants, God also administered His promises to Abraham by means of covenants. A *covenant* is an agreement, dictated by a greater being to a lesser party, sealed with a blood sacrifice to underscore the life-and-death nature of violating it. God is obviously the 'greater being,' and the person or persons with whom He chose to confer His blessings are the 'lesser parties.'

"So God set Abraham apart from the pagans to become the father of a great nation which would later be called Israel. One of God's covenants with the 75-year-old patriarch had promised him many descendants. But Abraham and his wife Sarah were childless, and well beyond child-bearing years.

"Ten years passed with no child, so Sarah tried to manipulate a solution because of the absence of God's answer. The Almighty, Sovereign Creator and Sustainer of the universe 'obviously' needed her help. So, she gave to Abraham her maid, Hagar, who promptly bore him a child named Ishmael. This was the beginning of centuries of trouble. Whenever sinful, impotent man feels like he must 'help the Almighty God out'—just like in the humanistic method of salvation—disaster is inevitable.

"Ishmael, the product of man's sinful arrogance and impatience—'the son of the flesh'—was not to be Abraham's heir of God's promises. Thirteen years later, God revisited Abraham and Sarah, telling them that within one year God's promise of a son would be fulfilled by a miracle of God Himself. Sarah then gave birth to Isaac, 'the son of the promise of God.' Through Isaac, all of God's promises to Abraham would be administered by God.

"By God's orders, Ishmael—'the son of man's arrogant attempt to do what only God can do'—was sent away with his mother Hagar to live toward the east. Isaac married Rebekah, and she gave birth to twins—Esau and Jacob. Esau again represented the son of the flesh. God chose Jacob before they were born—before either boy had done anything good or bad—to be the heir of God's promises to Abraham (Romans 9:6-13).

"God visits Jacob in Bethel, and changes Jacob's name to Israel, which means 'one who strives with God.' There God reiterates to Israel the promises He had made to Abraham and Isaac concerning their physical descendants, and the promise of a homeland.

"Jacob and his wives have 12 sons, the fathers of the 12 tribes of Israel. Although these sons lead treacherous lives, including selling their brother Joseph into slavery in Egypt, God continues to sovereignly execute His eternal plan and not destroy them.

"When God brings about a severe famine, Israel and all of his family move to Egypt where food was abundant. God had already made Joseph second-in-charge to Pharaoh the king, and Joseph welcomed and provided for his family there. The Israelites multiply in Egypt. But years later, a Pharaoh who did not know Joseph abhors and enslaves the Israelites.

"True to His promise to Abraham, God raises up Moses to deliver the Israelites from slavery in Egypt and bring them back to the Promised Land. During the journey from Egypt, God made a covenant with Moses and the descendants of Israel, giving them *the Law of Moses* to regulate almost every detail of their lives.

"But this Mosaic covenant, given 430 years after God made His covenants with Abraham, did not invalidate or replace God's covenants with Abraham. All later covenants with the physical descendants of Abraham—Isaac, Israel, Moses and King David—were simply added on to the original 'physical' covenant with Abraham.

God's Two Covenants with Abraham

"This point is critical: **God made two distinct covenants with Abraham—one 'physical' and one 'spiritual.'**

"God established one covenant with Abraham and his 'physical' descendants, and God promised to give the 'physical' nation of Israel a 'physical' homeland. The 'physical' sign that made these 'physical' descendants legal participants in this 'physical' covenant was a very 'physical' seal—circumcision (Genesis 15:7-17:27).

"The second covenant God made with Abraham was a 'spiritual' covenant. This covenant was by far the more important of the two, because only this covenant involved salvation (Genesis 22). Let's read the description of the two covenants in God's holy Word."

Nick read:

> Tell me, you who want to be under law, do you not listen to the law?
>
> For it is written that Abraham had two sons, one by the bondwoman and one by the free woman.
>
> But the son by the bondwoman was born according to the flesh, and the son by the free woman through the promise.
>
> This is allegorically speaking, for these *women* are two covenants: one *proceeding* from Mount Sinai bearing children who are to be slaves; she is Hagar.
>
> Now this Hagar is Mount Sinai in Arabia and corresponds to the present Jerusalem, for she is in slavery with her children.
>
> But the Jerusalem above is free; she is our mother.
>
> And you brethren, like Isaac, are children of promise.
>
> So then, brethren, we are not children of a bondwoman, but of the free woman. (Galatians 4:21-26,28,31)

"Again, the Apostle Paul tells us that God made **two** distinct covenants with Abraham.

"God established His first covenant with Abraham and his 'physical' descendants, the future Israelites. God promised to give Abraham's blood descendants a 'physical' homeland, which 'corresponds to the present Jerusalem.' The 'physical' sign that certified these 'physical' descendants as participants in this 'physical' covenant was circumcision—a very 'physical' seal (Genesis 15:7-17:27).

"The Savior of fallen man that God promised to Adam would eventually come as a physical descendant of Abraham. Just as Adam was the head of the *physical* race of humans, the Savior would be the head of the *spiritual* race of humans whom God chose to become members of His heavenly family. Though these elect people are part of the *physical* human race, God's choice made them also a part of the *spiritual* race of God's true children.

"During the Old Testament and until the promised Savior came, God would choose the majority of His true children from circumcised Israel, though some were chosen from the

Gentiles (Hebrews 11:31). But, even among the Israelites, God chose only a small remnant of the total number of Israelites to be His true children (Romans 9:1-33).

"This was a vicious issue with the Jews—as the Israelites became known—and so they argued with the Lord Jesus in the Gospel of John, chapter 8. These Jews wrongly assumed that, as *physical* descendants of Abraham, they automatically inherited God's *spiritual* promises to Abraham regarding salvation. The Jews greatly erred in assuming that God only made one covenant with Abraham. These Israelites wrongly maintained that if they were circumcised, they were guaranteed God's eternal blessings.

"But God made two covenants with Abraham. The second covenant was the 'spiritual' covenant, and only this covenant involved salvation. It is definitely possible that a physical Jew—circumcised according to God's physical covenant with Abraham—could be chosen by God to become His true child, and thus be a part of the spiritual covenant as well. In fact, the great majority of the Christians in the first decades of the church were Jews who became true Christians. But, by no means did a physical connection to Abraham guarantee participation in God's spiritual covenant. God alone decided whom He wanted in His family before creation.

"God's 'spiritual' covenant with Abraham is found in Genesis 22. Abraham spent the better part of a century with his wife Sarah, and they were childless. After God called him out of his pagan roots to travel to an unknown country, and after 25 years of waiting for God's promise of a son with Sarah, Isaac was finally born. And then God commands of Abraham the unthinkable:

> He said, "Take now your son, your only son, whom you love, Isaac, and
> go to the land of Moriah, and offer him there as a burnt offering on one of
> the mountains of which I will tell you."
>
> So Abraham rose early in the morning and saddled his donkey, and took
> two of his young men with him and Isaac his son; and he split wood for the
> burnt offering, and arose and went to the place of which God had told him.
>
> (Genesis 22:2,3)

"Abraham had finally understood the power and majesty of Almighty God," Dave continued. "After seeing God's miracle of the birth of Isaac to two people well beyond child-bearing years, Abraham learned that the omnipotent Almighty God needed no help of any kind from any finite human being to accomplish His eternal purposes.

"The writer of the Letter of the Hebrews tells us:

> Therefore there was born even of one man, and him as good as dead at
> that, *as many descendants* AS THE STARS OF HEAVEN IN NUMBER, AND
> INNUMERABLE AS THE SAND WHICH IS BY THE SEASHORE.
>
> By faith Abraham, when he was tested, offered up Isaac, and he who had
> received the promises was offering up his only begotten *son*;
>
> *it was he* to whom it was said, "IN ISAAC YOUR DESCENDANTS SHALL BE
> CALLED."
>
> He considered that God is able to raise *people* even from the dead,
> from which he also received him back as a type. (Hebrews 11:12,17-19)

"I'm sure Abraham could not sleep that night, wondering what God had in store," Dave observed. "So, he 'rose early in the morning' and proceeded to obey God. But Isaac noticed that something was missing. Read Genesis 22, verses 7 and 8."

Nick read:

> Isaac spoke to Abraham his father and said, "My father!" And he said, "Here I am, my son." And he said, "Behold, the fire and the wood, but where is the lamb for the burnt offering?"
>
> Abraham said, "God will provide for Himself the lamb for the burnt offering, my son." So the two of them walked on together.
>
> (Genesis 22:7,8)

"Yes," Dave mused, "Abraham finally understood his sovereign, Almighty God. Abraham did not know it, but God led him to sacrifice his only son of promise in the exact same area where, 2000 years later, God Himself would give His only Son to die for the sins of His children of promise. God set up His dealings with the physical world, and especially with the physical descendants of Abraham, as a picture—a *type*, or ***foreshadow***—of His spiritual truths.

"God stopped Abraham from killing Isaac on the altar, and indeed provided a ram caught in a nearby thicket for the sacrifice. Then God establishes His 'spiritual' covenant with Abraham. Read verses 14 through 18."

Nick read:

> Abraham called the name of that place The LORD Will Provide, as it is said to this day, "In the mount of the LORD it will be provided."
>
> Then the angel of the LORD called to Abraham a second time from heaven,
>
> and said, "By Myself I have sworn, declares the LORD, because you have done this thing and have not withheld your son, your only son,
>
> indeed I will greatly bless you, and I will greatly multiply your seed as the stars of the heavens and as the sand which is on the seashore; and your seed shall possess the gate of their enemies.
>
> In your seed all the nations of the earth shall be blessed, because you have obeyed My voice." (Genesis 22:14-18)

"In this very spiritual moment," Dave expounded, "Abraham builds a monument to the truth that 'The LORD Will Provide.' Exactly what 'The LORD will provide in the mount' is the ultimate sacrifice of God the Son, on a mount called Golgotha, for the sins of God's people.

"This 'spiritual' covenant is not the same as God's 'physical' covenant.

"God made His 'physical' covenant with Abraham and his physical descendants in Genesis, chapter 15, verse 7 through the end of chapter 17. God began His 'spiritual' covenant with Abraham and his spiritual descendants in Genesis 15:1-6, but completed the details of the covenant in Genesis 22.

"The words 'your seed' in chapter 22, verse 18, do not refer to Abraham's many physical descendants, but to one specific Descendant—singular—who is Christ Jesus, the ultimate sacrifice. Likewise, the words 'your seed' in verse 17 do not refer to Abraham's many physical descendants, but to God's true children of promise—the ones He chose to come into His family as a result of Christ's ultimate sacrifice."

"How do we know this?" asked Nick.

"Though the entire Bible is God's holy Word, the New Testament gives the fully revealed explanations of God's dealings in the Old Testament. Read the Apostle Paul's explanation of these verses in his Letter to the Galatians."

Nick read:

> Christ redeemed us from the curse of the Law, having become a curse for us—for it is written, "CURSED IS EVERYONE WHO HANGS ON A TREE"—
>
> in order that in Christ Jesus the blessing of Abraham might come to the Gentiles, so that we would receive the promise of the Spirit through faith.
>
> Brethren, I speak in terms of human relations: even though it is *only* a man's covenant, yet when it has been ratified, no one sets it aside or adds conditions to it.
>
> Now the promises were spoken to Abraham and to his seed. He does not say, "And to seeds," as *referring* to many, but *rather* to one, "And to your seed," that is, Christ.
>
> What I am saying is this: the Law, which came four hundred and thirty years later, does not invalidate a covenant previously ratified by God, so as to nullify the promise.
>
> For if the inheritance is based on law, it is no longer based on a promise; but God has granted it to Abraham by means of a promise.
>
> Why the Law then? It was added because of transgressions, having been ordained through angels by the agency of a mediator, until the seed would come to whom the promise had been made.
>
> And if you belong to Christ, then you are Abraham's descendants, heirs according to promise. (Galatians 3:13-19,29)

"In the 'spiritual' covenant established with Abraham, God's promise of His eternal inheritance of salvation was made specifically to Abraham's seed, Christ Jesus," Dave explained. "Thus, every person who is in Christ—every person chosen and made by God a born-again, true believer—receives the promised inheritance of eternal salvation in Christ! Please reread the Apostle Paul's words here in Galatians 4."

Nick read:

> Tell me, you who want to be under law, do you not listen to the law?
>
> For it is written that Abraham had two sons, one by the bondwoman and one by the free woman.
>
> But the son by the bondwoman was born according to the flesh, and the son by the free woman through the promise.
>
> This is allegorically speaking, for these *women* are two covenants: one

proceeding from Mount Sinai bearing children who are to be slaves; she is Hagar.

Now this Hagar is Mount Sinai in Arabia and corresponds to the present Jerusalem, for she is in slavery with her children.

But the Jerusalem above is free; she is our mother.

And you brethren, like Isaac, are children of promise.

So then, brethren, we are not children of a bondwoman, but of the free woman. (Galatians 4:21-26,28,31)

False Salvation vs. True Salvation

"The Apostle Paul here, believe it or not, is describing the age-old fight between man-made humanism and God-ordained, true Christianity," Dave commented. "This is a continuously recurring theme throughout the entire Bible. The Apostles labor in their letters to warn of the destructive lies of the humanistic heresy.

"As we just studied in Sunday school, in all of history there are only two methods of salvation—one false, which guarantees eternal hell; and one true, which guarantees eternal life in heaven. Humanism is false, because this method requires man to be actively involved—'to do something'—in order to be saved and/or to keep salvation. This is salvation by works: the arrogant, sinful attempt by man to do what only God can do.

"The example here is Sarah, thinking that she needs to 'help out' the Almighty God by giving her maid to Abraham. The Apostle Paul's allegory compares the cursed fruit of Abraham's union with the bondwoman Hagar to the cursed spiritual fruit of the physical Jews living under the Law of Moses. They are trying to be righteous before God by 'doing the works' of the Mosaic Law.

"But they are in continuous bondage to sin, never fulfilling the Law of Moses' requirements. The problem is that the commandments in the Mosaic Law are impossible to do: '"YOU SHALL BE HOLY, FOR I AM HOLY"' (Leviticus 11:44,45; 19:2; 20:7,26). Again, this is the very scripture the Lord Jesus quotes in Matthew 5:48 as God's standard for being acceptable to Him and going to heaven: '"Therefore you are to be perfect, as your heavenly Father is perfect."'

"This command in the Law of Moses is absolutely impossible to fulfill for any person born with a sin nature, which is any person born of a human male. As the Apostle James explains Leviticus 18:5 of the Mosaic Law: 'For whoever keeps the whole law and yet stumbles in one *point,* he has become guilty of all' (James 2:10). Attempting to obey the Law of Moses—in order to gain salvation, or keep it, or to be righteous before God—is a lost cause for human beings. All persons born of a human male are already guilty at conception.

"Many in the modern church have bought into the lies of humanism," Dave continued. "Any attempt by sinful man to be righteous before God—to gain or keep salvation by doing 'good works'—commits the same sin of Abraham and Hagar. They arrogantly tried to do what only God can do. The Almighty God does not need the 'help' of spiritually-dead, sinful man to accomplish His eternal plan.

"Sinful man's attempt to usurp the glory and power that belongs only to God is nothing less than the heinous crime of idolatry. Again, humanism guarantees eternal torment in hell, because it fails to produce God's required perfection in sinful man.

"But read the great news of the true gospel of true Christianity in Romans 8."

Nick read:

> Therefore, there is now no condemnation for those who are in Christ Jesus.
>
> For the law of the Spirit of life in Christ Jesus has set you free from the law of sin and of death.
>
> For what the Law could not do, weak as it was through the flesh, God *did*: sending His own Son in the likeness of sinful flesh and *as an offering* for sin, He condemned sin in the flesh,
>
> so that the requirement of the Law might be fulfilled in us, who do not walk according to the flesh but according to the Spirit.
>
> (Romans 8:1-4)

"What sinful man could never accomplish in attempting to obey the Law of Moses, 'God did!'" Dave repeated. "To pay the just penalty for all of the sins of His children, The Father sent His Son to die on the brutal cross, while legally transferring Christ's infinite perfection to the accounts of His elect!"

"Amen!" Nick shouted. "Thank You, God! So, we can't obey the Law of Moses in order to please God. Then how can we, as His true children, do anything to please God?"

"Great question!" Dave applauded. "For salvation—standing perfect before God—we do nothing. God does it all in making us righteous. But, once we are saved by God, then we obey the Law of Christ. Christ immediately commands us to respond to His new life by repenting, and then believing in His accomplished work (Mark 1:15).

"When we repent, we give this life back to Christ, its rightful owner, for whatever He desires for it. As true believers with eternal life that can never end, we are no longer doing good works in order to earn or keep salvation. We have already been made legally perfect in God's eyes.

"By believing in Christ, we trust only in that two-part perfect work Christ Himself accomplished for our total salvation. As God's children, we do not 'do' to become righteous, but we 'rest' in what Christ has already done.

"Then, instead of immediately taking true believers to heaven, God has condescended to use His children in His eternal plan for the universe. Thus, we are to be doing what Christ wants done, because this is His life now! In other words, we are to obey the rest of the Law of Christ. But, these works have absolutely nothing to do with gaining or keeping salvation. Anyone who can do deeds that are acceptable to God *must be already saved*. This person already possesses eternal life, for anything an unbeliever does is sinful rebellion against God.

The Law of Christ

"Again, the Law of Christ *is* the Law of God—which is perfect, eternal and unchanging. The Law of Christ is also called 'the law of the Spirit of Christ Jesus' and 'the law of liberty.' Let's read the scriptures on the Law of Christ."

Nick read:

> For the law of the Spirit of life in Christ Jesus has set you free from the
> law of sin and of death. (Romans 8:2)

> To the Jews I became as a Jew, so that I might win Jews; to those who
> are under the Law, as under the Law though not being myself under the Law
> (of Moses), so that I might win those who are under the Law;
> to those who are without law, as without law, though not being without
> the law of God but under the law of Christ, so that I might win those who
> are without law. (1 Corinthians 9:20,21; *parenthesis mine*)

> Bear one another's burdens, and thereby fulfill the law of Christ.
> (Galatians 6:2)

> But one who looks intently at the perfect law, the *law* of liberty, and
> abides by it, not having become a forgetful hearer but an effectual doer, this
> man will be blessed in what he does. (James 1:25)

> So speak and so act as those who are to be judged by *the* law of liberty.
> (James 2:12)

"***The Law of Christ*** consists of the Lord Jesus' words: all of His eternal commands, and all of His commands sovereignly communicated through His apostles and prophets by the Holy Spirit," Dave continued. "The Law of Christ is God's holy Word, the Bible.

"***The New Testament*** is the fully revealed explanation of the perfect Law of Christ, which has existed eternally in the mind of Christ. ***The Old Testament*** is also the Law of Christ, but God's originally intended meanings of His words and actions in the Old Testament are defined and clarified in the New Testament.

"Now, as true Christians, we obey the eternal Law of Christ—being 'effectual doers' of His commands—for this life now belongs to Christ for His use. And God blesses our obedience to God's holy Word with His 'grace and peace in the fullest measure' (1 Peter 1:2)."

"Reading through the Bible beginning with Genesis, it is very easy for me to forget that the Law of Christ came first," Nick noted. "The Law of Moses came during this world's history, but the Law of Christ existed eternally in the mind and character of Christ. So, if the Law of Moses could not be obeyed by sinful man, why did God add it to the covenant of promise made with Abraham?"

"God did not add the Law of Moses to the second Abrahamic covenant, the 'spiritual' covenant of promised salvation. God added the Law of Moses only to the first covenant, the 'physical' covenant with Abraham and his physical descendants," Dave clarified.

"So, if we as God's true children are to obey the Law of Christ as fully explained in the New Testament, why would God even give the Law of Moses at all?" Nick wondered.

The Law of Moses as a Foreshadow

"God gave the Mosaic Law for three major reasons," Dave answered. "Firstly, the Law of Moses was a foreshadow of the Law of God. Secondly, the Mosaic Law declared the holy and righteous perfection of Almighty God. Thirdly, the Law of Moses demonstrated the total depravity of man.

"Abraham's sacrifice of his only son was a picture—a *type*, or *foreshadow*—of the ultimate sacrifice God would make of His only Son. In like manner, the Law of Moses is a type, or foreshadow of the eternal Law of God, which is the Law of Christ.

"God's holy Word is replete with physical examples, visible pictures—*types* and *foreshadows*—of eternal, invisible spiritual truths. One of God's chosen ways of teaching His truth is by using everyday, visible examples. The Lord Jesus often did this in His parables.

"The Law of Moses is very real, but it is a weak copy—a mere shadow—of the complete fullness of the Law of Christ. God the Son came in human flesh, giving us the fullness of the Law of God in Christ while explaining the meaning of God's Law to us. We no longer need the mere shadow of the Law of Moses to hint at God's true intentions. The best analogy I can give is our own physical bodies.

"When we are glorified in heaven, our present, weak, deteriorating physical bodies will be changed by God to incorruptible, glorified bodies. When we are given these eternal, imperishable, glorified bodies, we will no longer have any desire or need to return to these present, weak, perishing bodies. These physical bodies that we inhabit for 70 or 80 years are a weak copy—a mere shadow—of the glorified bodies we will have for eternity.

"Let's read the Apostle Paul's description of this glorious change."

They read:

> But someone will say, "How are the dead raised? And with what kind of body do they come?"
>
> You fool! That which you sow does not come to life unless it dies.
>
> So also is the resurrection of the dead. It is sown a perishable *body*, it is raised an imperishable *body*;
>
> it is sown in dishonor, it is raised in glory; it is sown in weakness, it is raised in power;
>
> it is sown a natural body, it is raised a spiritual body. If there is a natural body, there is also a spiritual *body*.
>
> Now I say this, brethren, that flesh and blood cannot inherit the kingdom of God; nor does the perishable inherit the imperishable.
>
> For this perishable must put on the imperishable, and this mortal must put on immortality. (1 Corinthians 15:35,36,42-44,50,53)

"Thus, our present perishable bodies are just a weak copy—a type, or foreshadow—of our eternal, imperishable glorified bodies," Dave concluded. "The same is true of the Law of Moses. The Mosaic Law was given by God as a copy, or foreshadow, of the fullness of the Law of God, which is the Law of Christ. The following points are critical to understanding the relationship between the Mosaic Law and the Law of God: **The Law of Christ was not based on the**

Law of Moses. God based the foreshadow, the Law of Moses, on the eternal Law of Christ!

"This is precisely why the New Testament writers quoted the Law of Moses to prove their teachings. God's eternal principles in the Law of Christ were foretold and foreshadowed by God, both in the Mosaic Law and through His prophets. The New Testament writers were simply saying, 'God told you so! And here, in the Old Testament, is where He told you!'

"Read the passages I have written that explain that the Law of Moses is a type, or shadow, of the Law of God."

Nick read:

> Therefore no one is to act as your judge in regard to food or drink or in respect to a festival or a new moon or a Sabbath day—
>
> things which are a *mere* shadow of what is to come; but the substance belongs to Christ. (Colossians 2:16,17)

> Now the main point in what has been said *is this*: we have such a high priest, who has taken His seat at the right hand of the throne of the Majesty in the heavens,
>
> a minister in the sanctuary and in the true tabernacle, which the Lord pitched, not man.
>
> Now if He were on earth, He would not be a priest at all, since there are those who offer the gifts according to the Law;
>
> who serve a copy and shadow of the heavenly things, just as Moses was warned *by God* when he was about to erect the tabernacle; for, "SEE," He says, "THAT YOU MAKE all things ACCORDING TO THE PATTERN WHICH WAS SHOWN YOU ON THE MOUNTAIN."
>
> But now He (Christ) has obtained a more excellent ministry, by as much as He is also the mediator of a better covenant, which has been enacted on better promises.
>
> For if that first *covenant* had been faultless, there would have been no occasion sought for a second.
>
> When He said, "A new *covenant*," He has made the first obsolete. But whatever is becoming obsolete and growing old is ready to disappear.
>
> (Hebrews 8:1,2,4-7,13)

> For the Law (of Moses), since it has *only* a shadow of the good things to come *and* not the very form of things, can never, by the same sacrifices which they offer continually year by year, make perfect those who draw near. (Hebrews 10:1; *parenthesis mine*)

The Law of Moses Cannot Be the Law of God

"The Mosaic Law 'has *only* a shadow of the good things to come *and* not the very form of things,'" Dave repeated. "These scriptures clearly sum up God's teaching on the Law of Moses.

The Mosaic Law decreed 'things which are a *mere* shadow of what is to come; but the substance belongs to Christ.' The **substance**—the fullness, the complete reality, not the mere glimpse, copy, shadow or refection—'belongs to Christ.'

"So, the Law of Moses was given by God as a picture, a foreshadow of the full Law of God found in the Law of Christ. Thus, **the Law of Moses cannot be the Law of God**. Why? Because, by definition, the foreshadow cannot be the object being foreshadowed.

"Look at the sacrifice of Isaac by Abraham. God commanded Abraham to do this as a picture of the sacrifice of God's only Son, Jesus Christ. Is Isaac Jesus Christ? No! The foreshadow—Isaac—cannot be the object being foreshadowed—Christ. But they share many similar circumstances. God ordained, and still uses, those similarities to teach His children about His eternal truths. But the foreshadow and the object foreshadowed cannot be one and the same thing, or it would not be a foreshadow at all.

"This is why the Law of Moses cannot be the Law of God. The scriptures we just read repeatedly say that the Law of Moses is a type, a foreshadow of the Law of God expressed fully in the Law of Christ.

"As another example, we just read the Apostle Paul's analogy of the two covenants God made with Abraham (*see pages 308-309*). Paul equates Hagar, the bondwoman, with the earthly city of Jerusalem. The Apostle also equates Sarah, the free woman, with the heavenly city of Jerusalem. These women, types and foreshadows, are obviously not the cities themselves. They are used as examples with similarities to teach God's truth.

"Therefore, the foreshadow cannot be the object being foreshadowed. Thus, the Law of Moses cannot be the Law of God—it is a foreshadow of it. So, one reason God gave the Mosaic Law was to give a picture of His eternal Law as instruction for the true believer.

The Law of Moses Shows God's Righteousness

"Another reason the Law of Moses was given by God was to show God's righteousness. The Mosaic Law displays the perfection and righteousness of the holy, blessed Almighty God. The Law of Moses is a foreshadow, or reflection, of God's perfect, holy and upright character. God is eternally holy. He is perfectly righteous and good. Therefore, the Law He gave to Moses is holy, righteous and good. Let's read the scriptures regarding the Law of Moses.

Nick read:

> So then, the Law is holy, and the commandment is holy and righteous and good. (Romans 7:12)

> But we know that the Law is good, if one uses it lawfully,
>
> realizing the fact that law is not made for a righteous person, but for those who are lawless and rebellious, for the ungodly and sinners, for the unholy and profane, for those who kill their fathers or mothers, for murderers
>
> and immoral men and homosexuals and kidnappers and liars and perjurers, and whatever else is contrary to sound teaching,
>
> according to the glorious gospel of the blessed God, with which I have been entrusted. (1 Timothy 1:8-11)

The Law of Moses Shows Man's Utter Depravity

"God never gave the Law of Moses for man to obey, and thus be righteous—because man does not have any righteousness at all!" Dave reviewed. "Remember that since The Fall, unregenerate man can only sin, because he is born spiritually dead. The Lord Jesus declared: '"No one is good except God alone"' (Luke 18:19). Unless man is given a new heart by God, man can not, and thus will not, obey God and His Law. Sinful man is utterly rebellious, running away from God and His Law as fast as he can run.

"If man were inherently righteous and desired to do good, law would be completely unnecessary. The ungodly humanist preaches continuously that 'man is basically good.' But it is precisely because man is inherently and totally evil that man needs law books that fill law libraries designed to protect society! As Scripture declares, 'law is not made for a righteous person, but for those who are lawless and rebellious, for the ungodly and sinners, for the unholy and profane.' This is simply a description of every single person born from a human father.

"The actual effect that the righteous and good Law of Moses has on the heart of sinful man is **not** to inspire obedience in the man. Quite the opposite! The effect is for rebellious man to do exactly what the Law forbids!

"Sports played by man against man is an excellent example. Tell most professional athletes that they cannot do something, and they will make it a personal obsession to prove you wrong. Tell a basketball player he cannot make 20 free throws without missing, and he will immediately go to the line and start shooting.

"While this pride may be an admirable trait in sports played by man against man, it is deadly when it comes to morality and the Law of God. This pride is deadly because sinful man can never fulfill God's law 'to be holy (perfect) as He is holy (perfect).' Man always loses this match. Let's read the passages declaring the effect of the Law of Moses on sinful human beings."

Nick read:

> For while we were in the flesh, the sinful passions, which were *aroused* by the Law, were at work in the members of our body to bear fruit for death.
>
> What shall we say then? Is the Law sin? May it never be! On the contrary, I would not have come to know sin except through the Law; for I would not have known about coveting if the Law had not said, "YOU SHALL NOT COVET."
>
> But sin, taking opportunity through the commandment, produced in me coveting of every kind; for apart from the Law sin *is* dead.
>
> I was once alive apart from the Law; but when the commandment came, sin became alive and I died;
>
> and this commandment, which was to result in life, proved to result in death for me;
>
> for sin, taking an opportunity through the commandment, deceived me and through it killed me. (Romans 7:5,7-11)

"The Apostle Paul makes its very clear here," Dave continued, "that the effect of the Law of Moses on a man with a sinful nature is total disobedience and rebellion. The righteous and good Mosaic Law—one of the Ten Commandments—commands, '"YOU SHALL NOT COVET."' Our flesh's 'sinful passions, which were aroused by the Law...produced in us coveting of every kind!'

"Command a sinful, rebellious person to not do something, and he or she will seek out any and every way possible to do it. This defines our fallen, sin nature. This also shows the weakness of the Law of Moses. The Mosaic Law manifested the holiness of God. But, in requiring man to be as holy as God is holy, it condemned man to eternal damnation. In displaying God's righteousness, the Law of Moses conspicuously revealed the sin and depravity of man. Let's read the passages on the results of the effect the holy Law has on sinful man."

Nick read:

> Now we know that whatever the Law says, it speaks to those who are under the Law, so that every mouth may be closed and all the world may become accountable to God;
> because by the works of the Law no flesh will be justified in His sight; for through the Law *comes* the knowledge of sin. (Romans 3:19,20)

> For if those who are of the Law are heirs, faith is made void and the promise is nullified;
> for the Law brings about wrath, but where there is no law, there also is no violation. (Romans 4:14,15)

> For what the Law could not do, weak as it was through the flesh, God *did*: sending His own Son in the likeness of sinful flesh and *as an offering* for sin, He condemned sin in the flesh,
> so that the requirement of the Law might be fulfilled in us, who do not walk according to the flesh but according to the Spirit. (Romans 8:3,4)

> "Therefore let it be known to you, brethren, that through Him forgiveness of sins is proclaimed to you,
> and through Him everyone who believes is freed from all things, from which you could not be freed through the Law of Moses." (Acts 13:38,39)

> "Nevertheless knowing that a man is not justified by the works of the Law but through faith in Christ Jesus, even we have believed in Christ Jesus, so that we may be justified by faith in Christ and not by the works of the Law; since by the works of the Law no flesh will be justified.
> "I do not nullify the grace of God, for if righteousness *comes* through the Law, then Christ died needlessly." (Galatians 2:16,21)

> For, on the one hand, there is a setting aside of a former commandment
> because of its weakness and uselessness
>
> (for the Law made nothing perfect), and on the other hand there is a
> bringing in of a better hope, through which we draw near to God.
>
> (Hebrews 7:18,19)

"The Law of Moses was weak because it was an incomplete copy—a mere shadow—of the Law of Christ, the full expression of the Law of God," Dave explained. "The Law of Moses could not justify sinful man in order to make him acceptable to God. The Mosaic Law could not free man from his bondage to sin and the devil. Even worse, it put man's depravity right in the spotlight! It screamed that man was utterly unable to obey even one statute: '"YOU SHALL BE HOLY, FOR I AM HOLY"'(Leviticus 19:2). The Law of Moses could not make man perfect as God is perfect, and it condemned man to the eternal wrath of the holy God.

"The response of the ***elect***—the man chosen by God to come into His family—to the Law of Moses is totally different than the response of the ungodly humanist. The humanist, upon receiving the Mosaic Law, would respond in prideful arrogance. Like some athletes, the humanist would insist that he could fulfill those commandments. He would demand that holiness was up to him. He would die trying to be righteous by doing it his own way, insisting all the while that his 'good' deeds kept him acceptable to God. This response guarantees God's fierce wrath.

"The elect, however, would receive the Law of Moses and fall on his face before the holy God. This man would realize that he could never be as perfect as God is perfect, and he would cry out to God for mercy. The Holy Spirit reveals to the elect his utter depravity, and all the man can do at that point is throw himself on the mercy of the Judge of the universe. This is the only response that pleases God. God then declares the sinner whom He has chosen to be righteous by applying Christ's perfection to his account.

"The Lord Jesus tells a parable that expressly details God's response to these two types of individuals. Read the next passages, please."

Nick read:

> And He also told this parable to some people who trusted in themselves
> that they were righteous, and viewed others with contempt:
>
> "Two men went up into the temple to pray, one a Pharisee and the other
> a tax collector.
>
> "The Pharisee stood and was praying this to himself: 'God, I thank You
> that I am not like other people: swindlers, unjust, adulterers, or even like this
> tax collector.
>
> "'I fast twice a week; I pay tithes of all that I get.'
>
> "But the tax collector, standing some distance away, was even unwilling
> to lift up his eyes to heaven, but was beating his breast, saying, 'God, be
> merciful to me, the sinner!'
>
> "I tell you, this man went to his house justified rather than the other;
> for everyone who exalts himself will be humbled, but he who humbles
> himself will be exalted." (Luke 18:9-14)

"The sinful tax collector, who recognized his own depravity and repented, 'went to his house justified by God,'" Dave expounded. "The sins of the self-righteous Pharisee remained on his account. If he never repented and believed in Christ, he paid for those sins with God's eternal wrath.

"Therefore, the Law of Moses sets forth God's standard for entering heaven and avoiding His wrath—to be perfect as God is perfect. The Mosaic Law is weak because it is only an incomplete copy of the Law of Christ, which contains the only remedy for man's enslavement to sin.

The Only Lawful Use of the Law of Moses

"However, 'the Law of Moses is good, if one uses it lawfully' (1 Timothy 1:8). **The only lawful use of the Law of Moses is to drive the man seeking mercy to Christ Jesus, who alone is able to save the man from his sin**. Christ alone has the answer to man's lost condition.

"The true believer uses the Law of Moses to explain God's standard for going to heaven to unbelievers. The Lord Jesus and the Apostles quoted the Mosaic Law extensively for this very purpose. The Christian points to God's requirement of absolute perfection. The unbeliever must recognize the impossibility of God's command, and that the Almighty will never compromise. The sinner is left with the only option of falling down before the holy God and begging for mercy.

"The Lord Jesus commands sinful man in the Law of Christ to *repent*—utterly surrendering this life to God—and to *believe* in Christ's perfect work alone for salvation. The sinner who is given a new life by God is set free from slavery, granted the power to repent and believe, and is justified before God.

"Thus, the only lawful use of the Law of Moses is to display to unbelievers the righteousness of God and man's utter depravity. Any person attempting to obey the commands in the Mosaic Law in order to be righteous before God is using the Law of Moses illegally, and committing the great sin of idolatry. Read the words of the Apostle Paul here."

Nick read:

> But the Scripture has shut up everyone under sin, so that the promise by faith in Jesus Christ might be given to those who believe.
>
> But before faith came, we were kept in custody under the law, being shut up to the faith which was later to be revealed.
>
> Therefore the Law has become our tutor *to lead us* to Christ, so that we may be justified by faith.
>
> But now that faith has come, we are no longer under a tutor.
>
> (Galatians 3:22-25)

"Since the 'tutor'—the Law of Moses—did its job in driving the unbelieving man seeking mercy to Christ the Savior," Dave noted, "we no longer need 'the tutor.' Once a sinner becomes a true believer, he is 'no longer under' the authority of the Law of Moses. He now is under the Law of Christ, the full and complete expression of the Law of God!

The True Christian Dies to the Law of Moses

"Let's read God's holy Word on the end of the Law of Moses as the true believer's authority for living."

Nick read:

For Christ is the end of the law for righteousness to everyone who believes. (Romans 10:4)

For sin shall not be master over you, for you are not under law but under grace. (Romans 6:14)

For the law of the Spirit of life in Christ Jesus has set you free from the law of sin and of death.

For what the Law could not do, weak as it was through the flesh, God *did*: sending His own Son in the likeness of sinful flesh and *as an offering* for sin, He condemned sin in the flesh. (Romans 8:2,3)

Therefore, my brethren, you also were made to die to the Law through the body of Christ, so that you might be joined to another, to Him who was raised from the dead, in order that we might bear fruit for God.

For while we were in the flesh, the sinful passions, which were *aroused* by the Law, were at work in the members of our body to bear fruit for death.

But now we have been released from the Law, having died to that by which we were bound, so that we serve in newness of the Spirit and not in oldness of the letter. (Romans 7:4-6)

To the Jews I became as a Jew, so that I might win Jews; to those who are under the Law, as under the Law though not being myself under the Law, so that I might win those who are under the Law;

to those who are without law, as without law, though not being without the law of God but under the law of Christ, so that I might win those who are without law. (1 Corinthians 9:20,21)

For through the Law I died to the Law, so that I might live to God.

I have been crucified with Christ; and it is no longer I who live, but Christ lives in me; and the *life* which I now live in the flesh I live by faith in the Son of God, who loved me and gave Himself up for me.

(Galatians 2:19,20)

For He Himself is our peace, who made both *groups into* one and broke down the barrier of the dividing wall,

by abolishing in His flesh the enmity, *which is* the Law of commandments *contained* in ordinances, so that in Himself He might make the two into one new man, *thus* establishing peace,

and might reconcile them both in one body to God through the
cross, by it having put to death the enmity. (Ephesians 2:14-16)

For this Melchizedek, king of Salem, priest of the Most High God,
who met Abraham as he was returning from the slaughter of the kings and
blessed him,

to whom also Abraham apportioned a tenth part of all *the spoils*, was
first of all, by the translation *of his name*, king of righteousness, and then
also king of Salem, which is king of peace.

And those indeed of the sons of Levi who receive the priest's office
have commandment in the Law to collect a tenth from the people, that is,
from their brethren, although these are descended from Abraham.

Now if perfection was through the Levitical priesthood (for on the
basis of it the people received the Law), what further need *was there* for
another priest to arise according to the order of Melchizedek, and not be
designated according to the order of Aaron?

For when the priesthood is changed, of necessity there takes place a
change of law also. (Hebrews 7:1,2,5,11,12)

Therefore, holy brethren, partakers of a heavenly calling, consider
Jesus, the Apostle and High Priest of our confession. (Hebrews 3:1)

A Change of Priesthood Means a Change of Law

"The Lord Jesus is now our High Priest in the presence of God," Dave explained. "When
there is a change of the priesthood, 'of necessity there takes place a change of law also.' We see
this in the political arena as well. When one nation conquers another nation, the conquered now
live under the law of the new rulers. The conquered nation's laws are defunct and extinct.

"The Law of Moses appointed Aaron and his sons, descendants of Levi, to be the only tribe
eligible to serve as priests before God. The law of this Order of the Levitical priesthood was the
Mosaic Law. **If the Mosaic Law is still in force, then Christ could not be a priest at all**
(Hebrews 8:4). Christ was a descendant of Judah, not Levi.

"But God's Word declares that now a change of priesthood has taken place. Christ Jesus
has become the High Priest of all true believers. Christ now serves as the only High Priest
according the Order of Melchizedek, not the Levitical Order. With the change of priesthood,
there *must* come a change in law. The Law of Moses is replaced by the eternal, perfect and
unchanging Law of Christ.

"The true believer, according to the many scriptures we just read, has been set
free—released—from the Mosaic Law. Being 'in Christ,' the true believer is commanded 'to *die*
to the Law of Moses'—'for Christ is the end of the law for righteousness to everyone who
believes.' The Mosaic Law—the weak, incomplete, mere shadow of the eternal, perfect,
unchanging Law of God—is no longer necessary, since we now have the fullness of God's Law
in the Law of Christ.

"When Christ died on the cross, He fulfilled the Law of Moses by living a perfect life. Jesus Christ, fully God with added humanity, obeyed the commandment to be as holy as God is holy. Thus, upon His death, the Lord Jesus 'abolished' the Law of Moses as a means for true believers to obey God and be acceptable to Him."

Christ Came to Fulfill the Law of Moses

"But I've read books by teachers that say that the Lord Jesus Himself taught that the Law of Moses will never pass away," objected Nick.

"The Law of Moses still exists, and it 'is good, *if one uses it lawfully*' (1 Timothy 1:8). Again, the only lawful use of the Mosaic Law by true believers is to explain to unbelievers God's standard for going to heaven, and man's utter inability to achieve it. Any other use is an unlawful use.

"The Law of Moses was never intended as a set of commandments for true believers to obey in order to live righteously before God. The purpose of the Mosaic Law was to show *God's* righteousness, and the impossibility of man to live up to it. The effect of the Mosaic Law upon sinful man was to arouse the desire to disobey the very same commandments. The results of that effect guaranteed the eternal wrath of God upon every person born of a human male.

"Thus, the ultimate design of the Law of Moses was to drive the man seeking reconciliation with God to Christ Jesus, who alone is able to save a man from the wrath of God. Let's see what the Lord Jesus declares in Scripture on the subject."

They read:

> "Do not think that I came to abolish the Law or the Prophets; I did not come to abolish but to fulfill.
>
> "For truly I say to you, until heaven and earth pass away, not the smallest letter or stroke shall pass from the Law until all is accomplished.
>
> "Whoever then annuls one of the least of these commandments, and teaches others *to do* the same, shall be called least in the kingdom of heaven; but whoever keeps and teaches *them,* he shall be called great in the kingdom of heaven.
>
> "For I say to you that unless your righteousness surpasses *that* of the scribes and Pharisees, you will not enter the kingdom of heaven."
>
> (Matthew 5:17-20)

"The Jews wrongly assumed that when their promised Messiah (Savior) arrived, He would release them from the strict regimen of the Mosaic Law. The Apostle Peter described the prevailing Jewish opinion of the Law of Moses as 'a yoke which neither our fathers nor we have been able to bear' (Acts 15:10).

"It was in this context that Christ declared that His Messianic purpose was not to abolish the Mosaic Law, but to fulfill it. The Jews did not understand that God the Son *Himself* was going to complete the requirements of the Law of Moses. God's promised blessings of that fulfillment would then go to those chosen to be 'in Christ.' These elect respond with repentance and faith in Christ's work alone, not with any futile attempts to obey the Mosaic Law.

"Thus, the Mosaic Law still stands as the standard of God's righteousness. But it is abolished as a means for man to become righteous and live uprightly before God. God never gave it for that purpose. It was sinful, humanistic man who tried to manipulate God's holy Law illegally to serve his arrogant pride.

"The Lord specifically ends this discussion by saying that the righteousness of those men aspiring to go to heaven must 'surpass that of the scribes and Pharisees.' These were men thought by the Jews to be the holiest people alive because of their knowledge of, and strict adherence to, the Mosaic Law. The Jews mistakenly thought that the Mosaic Law was given by God to attempt to obey in order to be accepted by God. But Christ Jesus declares that these men 'will not enter the kingdom of heaven' for their pathetic, idolatrous, finite attempt to be as perfect as the infinitely holy God is perfect.

"The only righteousness that exists is in God—period. The Lord declared that 'not the smallest letter or stroke shall pass from the Law until all is accomplished.' Christ is referring to His accomplishing the fulfillment of the righteous perfection required by the Mosaic Law. He completed His mission, testifying to that fact, as He died on the cross, by announcing: '"It is finished"' (John 19:30)!"

"So, in effect, Christ did abolish the Law of Moses as a means for man to become righteous and accepted by God," Nick summarized.

"Correct," Dave affirmed. "The Mosaic Law still stands as a manifestation of the holiness of God, and is to be used by God's true children to declare to unbelievers God's requirement of absolute perfection for going to heaven.

"But, from its inception, the Law of Moses had no bearing on making man righteous—it never could, and never was designed to accomplish that feat. Only Christ Jesus can make a man perfectly righteous as God is righteous.

"Thus, 'Christ is the end of the Law (of Moses) for righteousness to everyone who believes' (Romans 10:4). True believers do not go to the weak and incomplete copy, the Mosaic Law, to find their heavenly Father's commands. True believers go to the complete, fully revealed Law of Christ as explained in the New Covenant by the Lord Jesus and His inspired writers."

Error in the Modern Church on the Law of Moses

"There are some denominations in Christendom that teach that true believers are still under the authority of the Law of Moses, right?" asked Nick.

"That is true, but this position has insurmountable biblical and logical problems to scale," Dave replied. "A typical synopsis of this position would be as follows:

> The character of God is eternal, perfect and unchanging. God's Law for His creation comes from God's character, so God's Law is eternal, perfect and unchanging.

> Christ Himself said that He did not come to abolish the Law of Moses, but to fulfill it. The Lord also said that not even the smallest stroke of the Law of Moses will pass away until all is accomplished. Christ also gave strict warnings not to annul even the least of these commandments, but to keep them and teach them.

Until the coming of Christ, the Law of Moses was the most complete revelation of the Law of God. The Law of Moses is the Law of God. Since it is God's Law, only God can change it. If God did not change something in His administration of the Law of Moses, then it is still binding today on man, and especially true believers.

The Mosaic Law is divided in three parts: civil, ceremonial, and moral. True, the Lord Jesus repealed the civil and ceremonial statues. For example, Jesus declared 'all foods clean' (Mark 7:14-23), whereas the Law of Moses declared entire classes of animals to be unclean, or off-limits. Jesus can do that because He is God. In stopping the ceremonial sacrifices, Christ fulfilled those requirements by being the final sacrifice. But the moral part of the Law of Moses—the Ten Commandments—remains binding.

To say that the 'moral' part of the Law of Moses is no longer binding leads to an antinomian position—derived from the Greek words meaning 'against law.' Since obedience to God is a major doctrine in the New Testament, having no Law of God leaves nothing to obey. Leaving sinful man to do what is right in his own eyes, instead of God's eyes, leads only to utter rebellion.

"The problems with these teachings are many, and they are insurmountable, in that they are unbiblical and illogical," Dave maintained. "First, it is illogical to reason as follows: God's character is eternal, perfect and unchanging. His Law, which proceeds from His character, must then be eternal, perfect and unchanging. So, only God can change His Law.

"If God's Law is eternal and thus unchanging, then not even God can change it! If He did, God would either have lied in calling His Law eternal and unchanging—which is impossible for God to do (Hebrews 6:18); or, He would have sinned against Himself by denying Himself, which would make God imperfect (2 Timothy 2:13)!

"It is blasphemy to say that God can change His eternal, perfect character. If God changes His character one bit, then either He was not perfect and is changing to something better, or He was perfect and has become imperfect. The same principle applies to God's Law. God's Law is the very expression of His eternally perfect and unchanging character toward His creation.

"To plead the case that God's Law stays the same, but God's 'administration of His Law' has changed, is only using verbal gymnastics to try to get around an insurmountable problem.

"The Mosaic Law absolutely demands that the physical descendants of Abraham keep the Sabbath—the seventh day of the week, Saturday—according to God's detailed rules. But, the Apostle Paul declares that, in the New Covenant, such rules are not mandatory (Romans 14:5; Colossians 2:16,17). Why? Because the physical observance of the Sabbath in the Mosaic Law was a type, a foreshadow of God's eternal principle regarding the Sabbath.

"The writer to the Hebrews expressly declares God's eternal meaning of the Sabbath. God says that true believers 'who have believed enter—*present tense*—that rest' (Hebrews 4:3). God's rest is a continuous rest for the believer, beginning at the moment of regeneration, from working in order to be righteous before God. The true believer rests in what Christ has already done for salvation. The physical Sabbath was a foreshadow of God's continuous rest for His children.

"Thus, to its human recipients, obviously the requirements of the Law of Moses have been canceled or changed. This is impossible for the eternal, perfect and unchanging Law of God.

"The theological position we are examining errs greatly by equating the Mosaic Law with the Law of God. Passage after passage clearly declare that 'the (Mosaic) Law...has only a shadow of the good things to come and not the very form of things' (Hebrews 10:1; Colossians 2:17; Hebrews 8:5). The New Testament gives the full explanation of the identity of the Law of Moses, defining it as an incomplete copy—or a mere shadow—of the Law of God. The eternal, perfect and unchanging Law of God is fully revealed in the Law of Christ.

"Christ did say that He came not to abolish the Law of Moses, but to fulfill it. So, what happens to an agreement that is fulfilled? Let's say I am a home builder, you are a nail salesman, and we sign a contract. I agree to pay you $500 to provide me with, say, one million nails. You show up with all of the nails, and I give you $500.

"What happens to that fulfilled agreement? Do you then take back those nails, and I take back the money, and we do it all over again? No! When an agreement is fulfilled, it is by necessity abolished. It is over, completed, fulfilled, ended. Christ fulfilled God's standard for righteousness in the Law of Moses. That makes the Law of Moses over, completed, ended as a means of righteousness before God.

"Another insurmountable problem is the position that 'if God did not change something in His administration of the Law of Moses, then it is still binding on man today.' The books of Romans, First Corinthians, Galatians, Ephesians and Hebrews all specifically say repeatedly that 'Christ is the end of the law for righteousness to everyone who believes' (Romans 10:4).

"The Letter to the Hebrews specifically explains that when Christ became the High Priest of true believers, with that change of priesthood, by necessity a change of law had to take place (Hebrews 7:12). 'When He said, "A new *covenant*," He has made the first (the Mosaic Law) obsolete. But whatever is becoming obsolete and growing old is ready to disappear' (Hebrews 8:13). Any law that God says is going to 'disappear' cannot possibly—by definition—be the eternal, perfect and unchanging Law of God.

"Thus, God did declare very explicitly in His holy Word that the Law of Moses went out with the Levitical priesthood, and is now obsolete—no longer to be erroneously considered the expression of His Law. The entire seventh and eighth chapters of the Letter to the Hebrews are completely dedicated to explaining this fact. The Mosaic Law is no longer necessary because it was only a weak copy, or shadow, of the Law of God.

"Another grave error of this position is the compartmentalizing of the Law of Moses. Theologians, like biologists, love to slice things up and categorize parts in order to better understand the whole. This is not a problem, unless the theologian forgets to put the pieces back together when he is done!

"These theologians teach that the Mosaic Law is divided in three parts: civil, ceremonial, and moral. The civil and ceremonial parts were stopped, or fulfilled, by Christ. But, since God, according to these theologians, has not specifically repealed the moral part—also known as The Ten Commandments—then they are still binding.

"In naming one part of the Law of Moses 'moral,' are these theologians saying that the laws in the 'civil' and 'ceremonial' parts were not commandments with 'moral' implications? In other words, if a Jew broke a 'civil' law, did he not sin against God as when he broke one of the Ten Commandments? Obviously, the entire Law of Moses defined God's unreachable standard of morality until the fullness of the Law of Christ was revealed. Breaking any law in the Mosaic Law—whether in the 'civil,' 'ceremonial' or 'moral' parts—was a moral offense against God.

"According to the Apostles Paul and James, the Law of Moses stands or falls as a whole. James says 'whoever keeps the whole law and yet stumbles in one *point,* he has become guilty of *all*' (James 2:10). Some theologians would say that James' two examples of the Law of Moses in the very next verse were from the Ten Commandments. Thus, these teachers claim that James is only referring to the moral part of the Law that was claimed to be still binding. So, James must mean 'all' of the moral part only.

"But, the Apostle Paul clearly reveals that the true believer is to die to the Law of Moses, and that he is released from the Law of Moses. Immediately, in the next verse, the Apostle gives, as his example from the Law of Moses, the last of the Ten Commandments! So, the Apostle Paul obviously considered the Ten Commandments as part of the whole Law of Moses to which true believers are to die, and from which they are released!

"Let's read these four verses in Romans, chapter 7."

Nick read:

> Therefore, my brethren, you also were made to die to the Law through the body of Christ, so that you might be joined to another, to Him who was raised from the dead, in order that we might bear fruit for God.
>
> For while we were in the flesh, the sinful passions, which were *aroused* by the Law, were at work in the members of our body to bear fruit for death.
>
> But now we have been released from the Law, having died to that by which we were bound, so that we serve in newness of the Spirit and not in oldness of the letter.
>
> What shall we say then? Is the Law sin? May it never be! On the contrary, I would not have come to know sin except through *the Law*; for I would not have known about coveting if the Law had not said, "YOU SHALL NOT COVET." (Romans 7:4-7)

"The Apostle Paul undeniably states, in quoting the Tenth Commandment, that the Ten Commandments are part of the Law of Moses from which true believers are released," Dave reasoned. "Lest there be any question as to God's command that true believers are to consider themselves 'dead' to the Law of Moses, the Apostle uses the same idea five paragraphs earlier in Romans: 'Even so consider yourselves to be dead to sin, but alive to God in Christ Jesus' (Romans 6:11). Paul's obvious meaning is that sin is to play absolutely no part in the true believers' lives.

"The Apostle declares that the exact same principle is true regarding the Law of Moses in the true believer's life. '...Law is not made for a righteous person, but for those who are lawless and rebellious, for the ungodly and sinners' (1 Timothy 1:9). The Mosaic Law declares God's righteousness, and by contrast glaringly shows the unrighteousness of sinful man."

"Does this mean true believers are no longer under any Law of God, and that they can covet all they want, and not be sinning?" asked Nick.

"That is the very charge of 'antinomianism,' a term coming from Greek words meaning 'against or without law,'" Dave answered. "The charge of ***antinomianism*** suggests that without the 'moral' part of the Mosaic Law, then there is no Law of God at all.

"This is a very poor argument. It is an obvious logical fallacy that guarantees the reasoning of such teachers here to be abjectly unsound. Just because the true believer is no longer under the Law of Moses does not mean they are under no Law of God at all. Their erroneous assumption that the Mosaic Law is the Law of God, and that they have to rescue some part of it in order to have any Law at all, leads to many poor conclusions.

"This position falsely assumes that the Law of Moses is the Law of God, and points to many Old Testament passages to show that the two are equated in some way. But, the complete explanation of Old Testament truths is found in the New Testament. Repeatedly, these New Covenant, Holy Spirit-inspired writers declare that the Law of Moses is only an incomplete, weak, mere shadow of the full Law of God.

"But the New Testament also declares that the eternal, perfect, and unchanging Law of God is the Law of Christ, not the Law of Moses. The true believer is under the authority of the Law of Christ, so he is under the Law of God, and he goes to the Law of Christ for God's commandments to obey. It bears repeating: **the Law of Christ was not based on the Law of Moses, but God based the temporary Law of Moses on the eternal Law of Christ!**

"If these other theologians are correct—saying the moral part of the Law of Moses is still the authority over the true Christian—then the Apostle Paul lies, and God's holy Word is no longer infallible and inerrant. For the Apostle Paul declares:

> To the Jews I became as a Jew, so that I might win Jews; to those who
> are under the Law, as under the Law though not being myself under the Law,
> so that I might win those who are under the Law;
>
> to those who are without law, as without law, though not being without
> the law of God but under the law of Christ, so that I might win those who
> are without law. (1 Corinthians 9:20,21)

"How could the Apostle possibly say that he is not under the Law of Moses, if true Christians are supposed to be under the authority of the 'moral' part of the Law of Moses?" Dave questioned. "The answer is clear. Paul declares that the true believer is not under the Mosaic Law. But, he is not without the Law of God, because he is now under the authority of the Law of Christ.

"The final nail in the position requiring true believers to obey the 'moral part' of the Law of Moses comes in ***the meanings*** of the commandments. The Apostle Paul clearly demonstrates my point here by explaining God's true meaning of a commandment in the 'civil part' of the Law of Moses. Let's read these passages."

Nick read:

> Or do only Barnabas and I not have a right to refrain from working?
> Who at any time serves as a soldier at his own expense? Who plants a

vineyard and does not eat the fruit of it? Or who tends a flock and does not use the milk of the flock?

I am not speaking these things according to human judgment, am I? Or does not the Law also say these things?

For it is written in the Law of Moses, "YOU SHALL NOT MUZZLE THE OX WHILE HE IS THRESHING." God is not concerned about oxen, is He?

Or is He speaking altogether for our sake? Yes, for our sake it was written, because the plowman ought to plow in hope, and the thresher *to thresh* in hope of sharing *the crops.*

If we sowed spiritual things in you, is it too much if we reap material things from you? (1 Corinthians 9:6-11)

"The immature Corinthians were complaining about financially supporting the ministry of the Apostles," Dave reviewed. "So the Apostle Paul defends his position by quoting Deuteronomy 25:4: 'YOU SHALL NOT MUZZLE THE OX WHILE HE IS THRESHING.' Some of those Corinthians had to be scratching their heads at that quote!

"But the Apostle immediately explains that, in this law of the Mosaic Law, God is not even talking about oxen! God's truly intended meaning of this law, Paul says, is that the minister doing God's work is worthy of financial support from those benefitting from the ministry. Does anyone think that the Jews—who had that law for almost 2000 years—understood God's real meaning of this commandment from the Law of Moses?

"The aforementioned theologian would probably say that the true meanings of the Ten Commandments—the only 'part' of the Mosaic Law he claims is still binding—are self-evident and clear. But the Lord Jesus Christ declared just the opposite.

"All of Christ's explanations of the Ten Commandments in His Sermon on the Mount—beginning with 'You have heard that it was said,' and ending with, 'but I say to you'—astounded the Jews. 'When Jesus had finished these words, the crowds were amazed at His teaching; for He was teaching them as *one* having authority, and not as their scribes' (Matthew 7:28,29). The crowds were not only stunned by Christ's assumption of authority, but that His authoritative teachings on God's true meanings of the Ten Commandments were totally different than what they had understood for centuries!

"Let's read the passages where Christ gives God's true meanings of the Law of Moses." Nick read:

"You have heard that the ancients were told, 'YOU SHALL NOT COMMIT MURDER' and 'Whoever commits murder shall be liable to the court.'

"**But I say to you** that everyone who is angry with his brother shall be guilty before the court; and whoever says to his brother, 'You good-for-nothing,' shall be guilty before the supreme court; and whoever says, 'You fool,' shall be guilty *enough to go* into the fiery hell.

"You have heard that it was said, 'YOU SHALL NOT COMMIT ADULTERY';

but I say to you that everyone who looks at a woman with lust for her has already committed adultery with her in his heart.

"It was said, 'WHOEVER SENDS HIS WIFE AWAY, LET HIM GIVE HER A CERTIFICATE OF DIVORCE';

but I say to you that everyone who divorces his wife, except for *the* reason of unchastity, makes her commit adultery; and whoever marries a divorced woman commits adultery.

"Again, you have heard that the ancients were told, 'YOU SHALL NOT MAKE FALSE VOWS, BUT SHALL FULFILL YOUR VOWS TO THE LORD.'

"**But I say to you**, make no oath at all, either by heaven, for it is the throne of God,

or by the earth, for it is the footstool of His feet, or by Jerusalem, for it is THE CITY OF THE GREAT KING.

"You have heard that it was said, 'AN EYE FOR AN EYE, AND A TOOTH FOR A TOOTH.'

"**But I say to you**, do not resist an evil person; but whoever slaps you on your right cheek, turn the other to him also.

"You have heard that it was said, 'YOU SHALL LOVE YOUR NEIGHBOR and hate your enemy.'

"**But I say to you**, love your enemies and pray for those who persecute you,

so that you may be sons of your Father who is in heaven; for He causes His sun to rise on *the* evil and *the* good, and sends rain on *the* righteous and *the* unrighteous."

(Matthew 5:21,22,27,28,31-35,36,37,43-45; *emphasis mine*)

"These were radical teachings!" Dave exclaimed. "The point I am laboring to make is that God's originally intended meanings of all Old Testament passages—including the Law of Moses—*must* be found in the Law of Christ. The Jews had no idea that simply lusting after a woman in one's mind was the same abomination to God as having sexual intercourse with a woman who was not one's spouse.

"**The true meaning of God's Word is *not* what it means to man, but what it means to God!** If any theologian, as well as any student of Scripture, must go to the fully-revealed New Testament in order to correctly understand the shadowy Old Testament—including the Law of Moses, beginning with the Ten Commandments—why would the 'disappearing' shadow still be necessary?

"God gave these Mosaic laws as foreshadows of the eternal, imperishable standards that reflect God's eternal, unchanging, holy character. The fullness of these foreshadows—God's complete explanations and intended meanings—is found only in the eternal Law of Christ.

"I know I'm repeating myself, but this is crucial to avoiding error, unsound doctrine and even heresy: The Law of Christ is the eternal, full expression of the Law of God. The Law of Moses was only a weak copy—a mere shadow of God's eternal, perfect and unchanging Law—designed to lead us to Christ.

"The Mosaic Law cannot be the Law of God, because a foreshadow cannot be the object being foreshadowed. Again, the Law of Christ was not based on the Law of Moses, but God based the temporary foreshadow of the Law of Moses on the eternal Law of Christ. There are similarities, because the very function of a type or foreshadow is to teach eternal truths based upon similarities.

"But, the meanings man applies to God's law can be wrong, as the Lord Jesus aptly demonstrated. God's Word is only the meanings God intended, and these truths are only found in the eternal Law of Christ in the New Testament.

"The Law of Christ declares that the Mosaic Law went out—became obsolete—with the change from the Levitical priesthood to the reign of Christ. Righteousness before the face of Almighty God is only found in Christ, the only High Priest of all true believers. All true believers were saved to obey the Law of Christ, bringing all honor and glory to God the Son!

"Thus, Quiz questions 28 and 29 are false. Please read them."

"Okay," Nick replied. "Question 28: 'Christians are still under the authority of the Law of Moses.' Question 29: 'Christians are still under the authority of the Ten Commandments.'"

"The Ten Commandments are only the first ten laws of the Law of Moses, which has over 600 ordinances," Dave said. "Since the Mosaic Law is merely a shadow of the eternal Law of God, Christians are under the authority of the real Law of God as expressed in the Law of Christ.

"Since God has fully revealed His real meanings to His Law in Christ, the weak and worthless shadow is useless as a rule for true believers to obey. The only lawful use of the Mosaic Law is to show unbelievers the perfection of God, and His requirement to be as perfect as He is perfect. But the Law of Moses is utterly worthless to attain to that perfection."

"So, please sum up the teaching of God's holy Word on the Law of God," Nick asked.

"Okay," assented Dave. "We were chosen by God the Father specifically 'to obey Jesus Christ' (1 Peter 1:1,2), bringing all honor and glory to God the Son.

"Obedience to God's commands is the key for God's grace and peace 'in the fullest measure.'

"This is a true saying worth remembering: 'Do it God's way, and He will bless you for your obedience. Insist on doing it your way, and God will frustrate this life!'

"Almost every Christian not experiencing God's grace and peace were not obeying any or all of God's Four Basic Commands: praying and studying His Word every day, as well as going to church and fellowshiping with committed Christians as often as possible.

"Being as God's holy character is eternal, perfect and unchanging, God's sovereign will, His eternal purpose (or plan) for creation, and the Law of God—which are expressions of God's character—are also eternal, perfect and unchanging.

"To say that God changes any of these things commits blasphemy for one of two reasons: either God and His character are not perfect, and He is changing to something better; or, they are perfect, and He is changing to something less than perfect!

"The Law of God is the collection of rules that God imposes upon His creation by His own authority.

"Jesus Christ is God. Thus, the eternal, perfect, unchanging Law of God is one and the same as the Law of Christ.

"The Law of Christ consists of the Lord Jesus' words—all of His eternal commands—and all of His commands sovereignly communicated through His apostles and prophets by the Holy Spirit.

"Thus, the Law of Christ is God's holy Scripture—the entire Bible, though God's true meanings of all Old Testament passages must be found in the fully-revealed New Testament.

"Scripture tells us that God has written His Law on 'the hearts' of man. Thus, God gives every person the knowledge of His existence, authority, law and coming judgment.

"But man purposely suppresses this knowledge to continue in his rebellious, sinful lifestyle.

"God promised Adam that He would send a Redeemer to save a people for Himself out of the lost human race.

"As God had dealt with Adam and Noah beforehand with covenants, God also administered His promises to Abraham by means of covenants.

"A covenant is an agreement, dictated by a greater being to a lesser party, sealed with a blood sacrifice to underscore the life-and-death nature of violating it.

"Abraham had two sons, Ishmael and Isaac, who represented the two covenants God made with Abraham.

"By God's orders, Ishmael—'the son of man's arrogant attempt to do what only God can do'—was sent away with his mother Hagar to live toward the east.

"Isaac married Rebekah, and she gave birth to twins—Esau and Jacob.

"God chooses Jacob to inherit His promises to Abraham, rejecting Esau before the twins were even born.

"God visits Jacob in Bethel, and changes Jacob's name to Israel, which means 'one who strives with God.' Israel moves his family to Egypt to escape the famine in Canaan.

"True to His promise to Abraham, God raises up Moses to deliver the Israelites from slavery in Egypt and bring them back to the Promised Land, giving them the Law of Moses to regulate almost every detail of their lives.

"But this Mosaic covenant, given 430 years after God made His covenants with Abraham, did not invalidate or replace those covenants with Abraham. All later covenants with the physical descendants of Abraham—Isaac, Israel, Moses and King David—were simply added on to the original 'physical' covenant with Abraham.

"God made two distinct covenants with Abraham.

"God established one covenant with Abraham and his physical descendants, and God promised to give the physical nation of Israel a physical homeland. This covenant was sealed by circumcision (Genesis 15:7-17).

"The second covenant God made with Abraham was a spiritual covenant. Only this covenant involved salvation (Genesis 22).

"In the age-old fight between humanism and true Christianity, there are only two methods of salvation—one false, which guarantees eternal hell; and one true, which guarantees eternal life in heaven.

"Humanism is false, because this method requires man to be actively involved—'to do something'—in order to be saved and/or to keep salvation. This is salvation by works—the arrogant, sinful attempt by man to do what only God can do.

"The commandments in the Mosaic Law—in order to be accepted by God—are impossible to do: '"YOU SHALL BE HOLY, FOR I AM HOLY (Leviticus 11:44,45; 19:2; 20:7,26).'"

"What sinful man could not accomplish in attempting to obey the Law of Moses, 'God did!' The Father sent His Son to pay for all of the sins of His children on the cross, while legally transferring Christ's infinite perfection to the accounts of His elect.

"As true believers with eternal life that can never end, we are no longer doing good works in order to earn or keep salvation, but we are to be doing what Christ wants done, because this is His life now! In other words, we are to obey the Law of Christ.

"The Law of Christ is God's holy Word, the Bible.

"The New Testament is the fully revealed explanation of the perfect Law of Christ, which existed eternally in the mind of Christ. The Old Testament is also the Law of Christ, but God's true understanding of the Old Testament is defined in the New Testament.

"Until the promised Savior came—during the Old Testament—God would choose from circumcised Israel the majority of His true children, though some were chosen from the Gentiles (Hebrews 11:31).

"But, God chose only a small remnant of the total number of Jews—as the Israelites became known—to be His true children.

"Again, God made two covenants with Abraham, the first with his physical descendants, and the second one being the spiritual covenant.

"By no means did a physical connection to Abraham guarantee participation in God's spiritual covenant. God alone decided whom He wanted in His family before creation.

"Abraham learned that the omnipotent Almighty God needed no help of any kind from any finite human being to accomplish His eternal purposes.

"Abraham did not know it, but God led him to sacrifice his only son of promise in the exact same area where, 2000 years later, God Himself would give His only Son to die for the sins of His children of promise.

"God set up His dealings with the physical world, and especially with the physical descendants of Abraham, as a picture—a type, or foreshadow—of His spiritual truths.

"In the 'spiritual' covenant established with Abraham, God's promise of His eternal inheritance of salvation was made specifically to Abraham's seed, Christ Jesus.

"Thus, every person who is in Christ—every born-again, true believer chosen by God—receives the inheritance of eternal salvation in Christ.

"The Law of Moses is very real, but it is a weak copy—a mere shadow—of the complete fullness of the Law of Christ.

"Since God the Son came in human flesh, and gave us the fullness of the Law of God in Christ, and explained this full meaning to us, we no longer need the mere shadow of the Law of Moses.

"The Law of Christ was not based on the Law of Moses, but God based the Law of Moses on the Law of Christ!

"The Mosaic Law decreed 'things which are a mere shadow of what is to come; but the substance belongs to Christ' (Colossians 2:16,17).

"The 'substance'—the fullness, the complete reality, not the mere glimpse, copy, shadow or refection—'belongs to Christ.'

"The Law of Moses was given by God to show God's righteousness.

"God never gave the Law of Moses to man to show man's righteousness, because man does not have any righteousness at all!

"The ungodly humanist preaches continuously that 'man is basically good.' But it is precisely because man is inherently and totally evil that man needs law books that fill law libraries throughout the world!

"The Law of Moses still exists, and it 'is good, if one uses it lawfully' (1 Timothy 1:8).

"The only lawful use of the Mosaic Law by true believers is to explain to unbelievers God's righteousness, giving His perfect standard for going to heaven. Any other use is an unlawful use.

"The Law of Moses was never intended as a set of commandments for true believers to obey in order to be perfectly righteous before God.

"The effect of the Mosaic Law upon man was to arouse the very desire to disobey the commandments. The results of that effect guaranteed the eternal wrath of God upon sinful man.

"Thus, the ultimate design of the Law of Moses was to drive the man seeking reconciliation with God to Christ Jesus, who alone is able to save a man from the wrath of God.

"The Law of Moses appointed Aaron and his sons, descendants of Levi, to serve as priests before God. The law of this Order of the Levitical priesthood was the Mosaic Law.

"But now a change of priesthood has taken place. As Christ Jesus has become the High Priest of all true believers, He serves according the Order of Melchizedek.

"With the change of priesthood, Scripture states there must be a change in law. The Law of Moses is replaced by the eternal, perfect and unchanging Law of Christ.

"The true believer has been set free—released—from the Mosaic Law. Being 'in Christ,' the true believer is commanded 'to die to the Law of Moses' (Romans 7:4).

"Christ abolished the Law of Moses as a means for man to become righteous and accepted by God. The Mosaic Law still shows the holiness of God and His standard of perfection.

"But, from its inception, the Law of Moses had no bearing on making man righteous—it never could, and never was designed to accomplish that feat. Only Christ Jesus can make a man perfectly righteous as God is righteous.

"It is illogical to argue that God's character is eternal, perfect and unchanging; His Law which comes from His character then is eternal, perfect and unchanging; so only God can change His Law.

"If God declares that His Law is eternally unchanging, then not even God can change it!

"It is blasphemy to say that God can change His eternal, perfect character—or His eternal, perfect Law which is the expression of His character.

"If the Mosaic Law says eating certain animals is unclean, and Christ Jesus declares those animals and all foods clean, then the Law of Moses, to its human recipients, has changed. This is impossible for an eternal, perfect and unchanging Law of God.

"Another great example is God's Sabbath. The Mosaic Law absolutely demands that the physical descendants of Abraham keep the Sabbath—the seventh day of the week, Saturday—according to God's detailed rules.

"But, the Apostle Paul declares that, in the New Covenant, such rules are not mandatory

(Romans 14:5; Colossians 2:16,17). The physical observance of the Sabbath in the Mosaic Law was a type, a foreshadow of God's eternal principle regarding the Sabbath.

"God now says that true believers 'who have believed enter—present tense—that rest.'

"The New Testament gives the full explanation of the identity of the Law of Moses, defining it as an incomplete copy, or a mere shadow, of the Law of God—which is fully revealed in the Law of Christ (Hebrews 10:1; Colossians 2:17; Hebrews 8:5).

"Christ did say that He came not to abolish the Law of Moses, but to fulfill it. When an agreement is fulfilled, it is by necessity abolished!

"The entire seventh and eighth chapters of the Letter to the Hebrews are completely dedicated to explaining the fact that the Law of Moses went out with the Levitical priesthood, and is now obsolete—no longer to be erroneously considered the expression of God's Law.

"Some theologians teach that the Mosaic Law is divided in three parts—civil, ceremonial, and moral—only the 'moral' Ten Commandments still binding on man.

"But, according to the Apostles Paul and James, the Law of Moses stands or falls as a whole.

"The Apostle Paul considered the Ten Commandments as part of the whole Law of Moses to which true believers are to die, because he uses the Tenth Commandment as his example of the Mosaic Law.

"The charge of antinomianism suggests that without the 'moral' part of the Mosaic Law, then there is no Law of God. But this is a very poor argument, as it is a logical fallacy.

"The true believer is under the authority of the Law of Christ, so he is under the Law of God, and he goes to the Law of Christ for God's commandments to obey.

"God's true meanings of all Old Testament passages—including the Law of Moses—must be found in the Law of Christ, because the Law of Christ is the eternal, full expression of the Law of God."

"Now that makes total sense of how the Law of God, the Law of Christ and the Law of Moses all fit together," praised Nick. "Now I can understand God's purpose for the Mosaic Law, and how I am to use it as a Christian. The Law of Christ—the eternal, perfect and unchanging Law of God—is where I go to find God's commandments for me, His child."

"Excellent!" Dave responded. "Would you like to close our Bible study with prayer?"

"Dear heavenly Father, as this semester draws to a close, I just want to thank You for Your unchanging love. You have truly raised me from the dead, and You have used Your servant Dave to help me to know You and love You intimately.

"Continue to bless us by letting us know Your ways, and let us draw closer to You every day. Thank You for Your holy Word, and the eternal, perfect and unchanging Law of Christ. Fill us now with Your Holy Spirit, and enable us to love others as You have commanded. In Your precious Son Jesus' Name we ask, amen."

"Amen!" Dave echoed. "I'll see you Sunday for our last College & Career Bible study of the semester."

"You bet! I'll see you then, brother!"

14

Last Things Last

"Here we go!" Dave exclaimed to bring the College & Career Sunday school class to order. "Let's begin the final class of the semester with prayer to our heavenly Father. Paul, would you do the honors?"

"Dear Father, we praise You and exalt Your holy Name. You are our God, our Creator, our Sustainer, and our precious Father. You deserve all of the glory, and we bow before You in worship. We thank You for the gift of Your Son, and the awesome work of salvation that He completed for Your children.

"Fill us now with Your Holy Spirit, and bless us with ears to hear and minds to understand Your Word. We desire to know Your ways, so that we may love You more intimately than ever possible.

"Thank You for the friendships You have given to us, and for all of Your blessings during this past semester. Bless the efforts of the students as they take final exams this week. Finally, bless Dave, our teacher and Your servant, for his sacrifice and hard work for the glory of Your kingdom.

"We praise You, O Lord, for You alone are worthy of all the glory and honor. In Jesus' Name, amen."

"Thank you, Paul," Dave said. "I'm sure, after a semester of studying God's holy Word, your answers to the Pop Quiz have changed. That probably means that we have learned a great deal about our heavenly Father and His ways of ruling His creation. Are there any questions that have come up during your study of God's Word with which I may help?"

Does God Regret, Repent or Change His Mind?

"Yes," Grant interjected. "I was listening to a program on Christian radio last week, and a professor was teaching an opposing view of God. This instructor claimed that many places in the Bible say that God changes His mind. He concluded that God must not know the future exhaustively, and that God is not immutable. How would you answer his claims?" Intense

"There are many passages saying that God regretted doing something, changed His mind, or relented from carrying out an action," Dave replied. "Remember in past classes, we read dozens of scriptures clearly teaching that God is sovereign. Everything that happens or exists in creation has been ordained by God—even the 'bad' things. God ordains what He hates in order to accomplish what He loves.

"God's primary reason for creation is to bring total honor and glory to God the Son, Jesus Christ. In His infinite understanding, God deemed necessary the sacrifice of His only Son on the brutal cross—the worst of all 'bad' things. But, this horrific act resulted in the eternal salvation of God's people, bringing total honor and glory to Christ as the only Savior of the universe.

"God takes absolutely no pleasure in wickedness (Psalm 5:4). God is truly grieved by man's sin and its inevitable consequences of great suffering. But, in His infinite wisdom, God deemed evil necessary in order to fulfill His ultimate purpose of bringing total glory to the only Deliverer from such evil. Everything God ordained in this creation is geared to accomplish His ultimate purpose of glorifying Jesus Christ, the only way out of slavery to evil.

"Thus, when God regrets something, this does not change His perfect character or His eternal purpose for creation. An excellent example is found in the life of Saul, Israel's first human king. Grant, please read this passage."

Grant read:

> Then the word of the LORD came to Samuel, saying,
>
> "I regret that I have made Saul king, for he has turned back from following Me and has not carried out My commands." And Samuel was distressed and cried out to the LORD all night.
>
> Samuel rose early in the morning to meet Saul.
>
> As Samuel turned to go, *Saul* seized the edge of his robe, and it tore.
>
> So Samuel said to him, "The LORD has torn the kingdom of Israel from you today and has given it to your neighbor, who is better than you.
>
> "Also the Glory of Israel will not lie or change His mind; for He is not a man that He should change His mind."
>
> Then Samuel went to Ramah, but Saul went up to his house at Gibeah of Saul.
>
> Samuel did not see Saul again until the day of his death; for Samuel grieved over Saul. And the LORD regretted that He had made Saul king over Israel. (1 Samuel 15:10-12a,27-29,34,35)

"Thank you, Grant," Dave said. "The prophet Samuel clearly understood that, though God regretted making Saul king, 'the Glory of Israel will not lie or change His mind.' The rejection of Saul was a necessary, preordained occurrence for King David to take the throne. Though Saul's disobedience grieved God, it was all part of God's eternal plan for the Son of David, Christ Jesus, to come and establish His eternal kingdom.

"When Scripture does say that God changes His mind, these passages always reflect man's point of view, not God's point of view.

"A good analogy would be a mother refusing to let her two-year-old son touch a hot stove. Though he persists, she continually stops him. Finally, she decides to let him go. Through the eyes of the child, his mother must have changed her mind about the matter. But she never changed her ultimate concern. Though the mother took no pleasure in the slight burn her child received, she knows he has learned a valuable lesson.

"God deals with man as a parent deals with a toddler. If man repents of his wickedness, God's mercy deems to respond with forgiveness instead of deserved wrath. To man, it may look like God changed His mind about threatened punishment. But God's mercy toward the repentant sinner is an eternal attribute of His character.

"But, remember!" Dave announced. "Sinful man can only repent after God grants repentance (2 Timothy 2:24-26). Repentance must be granted by God through His sovereign choice."

"Now, that explains it," appreciated Grant. "God truly grieves, regrets, and relents. But this has no bearing on His eternal character and purpose. And when Scripture says that God changed His mind, it is meant from the vantage point of the human writer."

"You've got it!" Dave applauded. "'Every good thing given and every perfect gift is from above, coming down from the Father of lights, with whom there is no variation or shifting shadow' (James 1:17). Any other questions?"

We Know God's Will on Specific Decisions

"Yes," Ed offered. "How do I know if God wants me to go to school here, or in the next state? I guess I am asking how any child of God knows God's specific plan for this life."

"Excellent question," Dave replied. "Absolutely every decision that we as Christians will ever make in this lifetime is covered in God's holy Word." The class appeared stunned at this statement.

"Do you mean that God tells me the type of car to buy, where to go to school, or whom I should marry?" Matt asked.

"Absolutely. Every one of those decisions, as well as every other decision, is covered," Dave answered. "God tells us that His children are to *know* His will. We are not to guess, or call some psychic hotline, or get real quiet and listen for some inner impression or imaginary voice in our heads. Rely on any of those ungodly methods, and we are directly disobeying God's Word.

"Let's read some passages instructing us that we are to know the will of God."

The class read:

> And do not be conformed to this world, but be transformed by the renewing of your mind, so that you may prove what the will of God is, that which is good and acceptable and perfect. (Romans 12:2)

So then do not be foolish, but understand what the will of the Lord is.
(Ephesians 5:17)

For this reason also, since the day we heard *of it*, we have not ceased to
pray for you and to ask that you may be filled with the knowledge of His will
in all spiritual wisdom and understanding,
so that you will walk in a manner worthy of the Lord, to please *Him* in
all respects, bearing fruit in every good work and increasing in the knowledge
of God. (Colossians 1:9,10)

"We are not to 'be foolish,' but we are to know the will of God, so that we may 'please Him
in all respects,'" Dave continued. "In the New Covenant, God set up His moral will for believers
like two pillars. On one pillar are all of the things God commands us *to do*. On the other pillar
are all of the things God commands us *not to do*. In the middle is a 'grey area.' Look at this
diagram on the chalkboard.

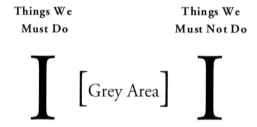

"Chelsea, please read the next three passages, which are some examples of things God
commands His children to do."
Chelsea read:
"But you, when you pray, go into your inner room, close your door and
pray to your Father who is in secret, and your Father who sees *what is done*
in secret will reward you." (Matthew 6:6)

Finally, be strong in the Lord and in the strength of His might.
Put on the full armor of God, so that you will be able to stand firm
against the schemes of the devil. (Ephesians 6:10,11)

Be diligent to present yourself approved to God as a workman who does
not need to be ashamed, accurately handling the word of truth.
(2 Timothy 2:15)

"Thank you, Chelsea," Dave said. "These are obvious things God commands us to do. Now, Anna, would you please read for us scriptures about some things God commands us not to do?"

Anna read:

"Do not store up for yourselves treasures on earth, where moth and rust destroy, and where thieves break in and steal." (Matthew 6:19)

"So do not worry about tomorrow; for tomorrow will care for itself. Each day has enough trouble of its own." (Matthew 6:34)

And do not get drunk with wine, for that is dissipation, but be filled with the Spirit. (Ephesians 5:18)

"Thank you, Anna," Dave replied. "We can see that there are two obvious 'bookend' pillars to the moral will of God. God commands things we are definitely to do, and things we are definitely not to do. The middle area is the 'grey area,' and this is the area which seems to cause the greatest confusion within the church, but really provides the greatest blessings.

"The grey area is where we find the matters of conscience, otherwise called matters of Christian liberty. The commandments regarding the grey area are found in Romans 14 and First Corinthians 8. **If a matter is not specifically commanded or forbidden by God, then God declares it a matter of personal conscience**. I can do it or not do it, and God will totally support my decision either way, provided I make my decision by the following guidelines:

1) The foremost consideration of any decision made by a true believer is the glory of God, for this is His life we are living.

2) The second consideration is that any decision must not violate related commandments of God.

3) The third consideration is that any decision must not violate the believer's conscience.

4) The final consideration is that any decision must not violate a weaker brother's conscience.

"The glory of God should be the focus of every minute of the true believer's existence. Upon repenting, we gave up this life to Christ for whatever He desires to do with it. If going to an R-rated movie would fill your mind with worldly profanity, sensuality and violence, one can hardly imagine how that activity could possibly glorify God.

"Any decision on one matter must not violate another of God's commands. We are totally free to buy a $10,000 car or a $60,000 car. If buying the more expensive car prevents us from providing for our own families, for example, then we have violated another of God's commands (1 Timothy 5:8). Buying the higher-priced car would then be sinful.

"A decision must not violate one's own conscience. For example, I may have a glass of wine with dinner. God nowhere commands to drink or not to drink, only that it is a sin to get drunk. However, a believer whom God saved from a life of alcoholism may not be able to ever drink again. For him to have any wine would sin against his own conscience, and as a result, sin against God.

"Lastly, we must not violate a weaker brother's conscience. I know I can have a glass of wine with dinner with God's full approval. But, if I go to dinner with my brother who was saved out of alcoholism, seeing me drink wine must cause him to stumble. We must put our brother's conscience ahead of our own freedoms as a Christian, and refuse to drink alcohol in his presence.

"Thus, loving God first and foremost, and loving our brothers and sisters in Christ, provide the parameters for making decisions on matters of conscience. God gave us brains so that we will use them. If deciding to go to State University or Podunk College is the issue—a grey area matter—listing the positives and negatives for each might help. If they are still equal, then whatever decision you make, God will fully support you.

"Many immature Christians do not like God's method for making decisions, because it requires them to take responsibility for their choices. They would much rather have God tell them which way to go. The problems with this are twofold.

"First, God rarely speaks audibly, even on the greatest of decisions. If the immature Christian resorts to sinful methods, such as trying to get an inner impression from the spiritual realm, he is violating God's commandment to already know His will.

"God's truth is not subjective. God's truth is an objective, universal standard. God set up His moral will like two pillars for a reason—so that His children *know* His will on any issue. God clearly commands us to do things and not do things. If the matter falls in the grey area, God's will is that we are free to choose either option. God will totally support our decision, as long as that decision is made with God's four guidelines.

"Attempting to 'hear God's voice' through inner impressions is sinful in that it disobeys God's command to know His will. It is also very dangerous. Impressions from the spiritual realm can come from God, Satan, or our own minds. Two out of those three are fraught with rebellious tendencies or downright destruction.

"This is why the Bible commands: 'Beloved, do not believe every spirit, but test the spirits to see whether they are from God, because many false prophets have gone out into the world' (1 John 4:1). How do believers 'test the spirits?' By judging such information by the only standard of truth in the universe, the Word of God.

"Thus, we have to go back to Scripture anyway, even with 'convincing impressions.' Scripture then tells us that God set up His moral will like two pillars, with a grey area for Christian freedom. God commands that we are to know His will, not guess or seek inner impressions.

"Many immature Christians seeking inner impressions defend their behavior by claiming that they are seeking God's 'still, small voice.' They mistakenly base this thinking on the story of God's prophet Elijah, who was running away from the wicked king Ahab and his wicked wife Jezebel. Jennifer, would you please read these passages for us?"

Jennifer read:

> Then he came there to a cave and lodged there; and behold, the word
> of the LORD *came* to him, and He said to him, "What are you doing here,
> Elijah?"

He said, "I have been very zealous for the LORD, the God of hosts; for the sons of Israel have forsaken Your covenant, torn down Your altars and killed Your prophets with the sword. And I alone am left; and they seek my life, to take it away."

So He said, "Go forth and stand on the mountain before the LORD." And behold, the LORD was passing by! And a great and strong wind was rending the mountains and breaking in pieces the rocks before the LORD; *but* the LORD *was* not in the wind. And after the wind an earthquake, *but* the LORD *was* not in the earthquake.

After the earthquake a fire, *but* the LORD *was* not in the fire; and after the fire a sound of a gentle blowing ("still, small voice" *in the King James version*).

When Elijah heard *it,* he wrapped his face in his mantle and went out and stood in the entrance of the cave. And behold, a voice *came* to him and said, "What are you doing here, Elijah?"

(1 Kings 19:9-13; *parenthesis mine*)

"Thank you, Jennifer," Dave said. "Some teacher somewhere must have equated the 'gentle blowing'—or 'still, small voice' as the King James version translates it—to getting real quiet, and listening for an inner voice from God. What an error!

"God's voice in the Bible always originates from outside of the person. God was not speaking *within* Elijah. God was speaking '*to* him' from the outside. Elijah was not getting real quiet on his bed to hear God's inner voice. The prophet was standing on a mountain with tornadoes and earthquakes going on!

"God teaches us by His Holy Spirit (John 16:13; 1 John 2:27). The Holy Spirit illuminates our minds with the truth, giving us knowledge by illuminating God's Word. God certainly can speak audibly anytime He sovereignly desires. But, even in the Bible, these instances were not only rare, they came unexpectedly. The person addressed by God was not getting quiet and seeking His voice.

"There is a second reason the immature Christian would rather have God make the decisions involving grey area matters. If anything goes wrong, he can just blame God for making him go that direction. This is simply childish behavior. 'Brethren, do not be children in your thinking; yet in evil be infants, but in your thinking be mature' (1 Corinthians 14:20).

"When I was a young Christian, I went into missionary work in an inner city. I 'felt' through inner impressions that God wanted me there, and that 'full-time ministry' was the 'best' way to serve God. I had not yet learned God's Word concerning His will, and specifically how to know it. I was also ignorant that every moment of a true believer's life is to be dedicated to God and His ministry, regardless of occupation. Needless to say, I was miserable. Even though God did some great things, within one year I was completely exhausted and burned out.

"Career choices are in the grey area. Concerning ministry, God explicitly says: 'It is a trustworthy statement: if any man aspires to the office of overseer, it is a fine work he desires *to do*' (1 Timothy 3:1). The *person* is doing the aspiring and desiring here. One may claim that

God gave him the desire to go into ministry. But God leaves it up to every person to decide the grey area of occupation.

"Ministry work, as one's occupation, is a matter of personal desire, not compulsion from God. God gives us the choice. God may give us gifts with which to serve Him, but that service can be effectively done in a variety of ways, including 'part-time' ministry while gainfully employed elsewhere.

"So, God has provided a simple way to know His will, which gives true believers the blessing of freedom and creativity. But **God's freedom definitely requires that we diligently study His Word to know what He commands and forbids**. As the Apostle Paul commands: 'Be diligent to present yourself approved to God as a workman who does not need to be ashamed, accurately handling the word of truth' (2 Timothy 2:15).

"If a decision falls in the grey area, such as whether or not to marry, we make our decision using our brains and God's biblical guidelines. God will totally support our decisions in matters of conscience, but He requires that we take responsibility for our choices. With freedom always comes responsibility.

"Many Christians are under a grave misconception that they have to find God's one and only one plan, and if they miss it, they miss God's best. This is a heinous lie, because not only is it impossible to accomplish, but God never set it up that way at all! The decisions we make in the grey area, under the biblical guidelines, will always be supported by God, for this is His moral will for His children.

"I have one last and most important concern regarding matters of conscience. **WARNING: God absolutely condemns anyone passing judgment on the 'grey area' decisions of any true believer**. Pam, would you please read for us these next passages I have marked?"

Pam read:

> Now accept the one who is weak in faith, *but* not for *the purpose of* passing judgment on his opinions.
>
> One person has faith that he may eat all things, but he who is weak eats vegetables *only.*
>
> The one who eats is not to regard with contempt the one who does not eat, and the one who does not eat is not to judge the one who eats, for God has accepted him.
>
> Who are you to judge the servant of another? To his own master he stands or falls; and he will stand, for the Lord is able to make him stand.
>
> One person regards one day above another, another regards every day *alike.* Each person must be fully convinced in his own mind.
>
> But you, why do you judge your brother? Or you again, why do you regard your brother with contempt? For we will all stand before the judgment seat of God.
>
> Therefore let us not judge one another anymore, but rather determine this—not to put an obstacle or a stumbling block in a brother's way.
>
> For if because of food your brother is hurt, you are no longer walking according to love. Do not destroy with your food him for whom Christ died.

Therefore do not let what is for you a good thing be spoken of as evil;

for the kingdom of God is not eating and drinking, but righteousness and peace and joy in the Holy Spirit.

For he who in this *way* serves Christ is acceptable to God and approved by men.

So then let us pursue the things which make for peace and the building up of one another.

Do not tear down the work of God for the sake of food. All things indeed are clean, but they are evil for the man who eats and gives offense.

The faith which you have, have as your own conviction before God.

Happy is he who does not condemn himself in what he approves.

(Romans 14:1-5,10,13,15-20,22)

"Thank you, Pam," Dave continued. "God's declared goal in His kingdom is 'righteousness and peace and joy in the Holy Spirit.' God gives His children the freedom to make decisions in any 'grey area' matter of conscience. The Lord explicitly forbids anyone to condemn another believer's decisions in this area of Christian freedom. We are not our Christian brother's master. The Lord Jesus Christ is the only Master in true Christianity.

"In the modern church, people condemn others all the time for 'grey area' matters, not even realizing that it is the one who condemns that is sinning against God! The problem is that so few people in the church know God's Word well enough to handle it accurately. In ignorance, these people open their mouths, passing judgment by their own blind opinions on things about which they know nothing (1 Timothy 1:6,7). This idolatrous sin causes nothing but evil, all the while claiming to be serving God (John 16:2).

"Regarding the holy essentials of the Christian faith given by God in His Word, true believers are to 'contend earnestly for the faith which was once for all handed down to the saints' (Jude 1:3). In dealing with the lies of heretics, we must 'not yield in subjection to them for even an hour, so that the truth of the gospel would remain with you' (Galatians 2:5).

"BUT, if a person is going to open his mouth—or write a book—in condemnation, he had better be able to prove by the Word of God that the issue is an essential of the Christian faith. Again, if anyone condemns another for his decisions regarding 'grey area' matters of conscience, the person doing the condemning is the one committing a most heinous sin against God.

"I hope that makes the will of God regarding all decisions crystal clear," Dave concluded. "Are there any other questions?"

Is Tithing in the Law of Christ?

"Yes," chimed Nick. "In our Tuesday Bible study, we examined the Law of God, the Law of Christ and the Law of Moses. While reading through the Mosaic Law during the week, I had a question regarding tithing. Since true believers are no longer under the authority of the Law of Moses, are we still required to give an exact percentage of our incomes to God?"

"Superior question," Dave replied. "There has been a vast amount of man-made tradition taught on this subject in the past decade. Let's see what God Himself has to say on **tithing**, the giving of one-tenth of one's income to the work of God. Nick, would you please read for us, in the Law of Moses, Leviticus 27:30, 32 and 34, as well as Deuteronomy 14:24 and 25?"

Nick read:

> "Thus all the tithe of the land, of the seed of the land or of the fruit of the tree, is the LORD'S; it is holy to the LORD.
>
> "For every tenth part of herd or flock, whatever passes under the rod, the tenth one shall be holy to the LORD."
>
> These are the commandments which the LORD commanded Moses for the sons of Israel at Mount Sinai. (Leviticus 27:30,32,34)

> If the distance is so great for you that you are not able to bring *the tithe,* since the place where the LORD your God chooses to set His name is too far away from you when the LORD your God blesses you,
>
> then you shall exchange *it* for money, and bind the money in your hand and go to the place which the LORD your God chooses.
>
> (Deuteronomy 14:24,25)

"Thank you, Nick," Dave said. "The Law of Moses demanded that the children of Israel bring one-tenth of their produce and livestock to the Temple and give it to the priests for their service to God. The Israelites were under compulsion to tithe by God. If they did not tithe, God would bring judgment upon them. Thus, tithing was not a gift so much as it was a tax, so that the priests who served day and night in the Temple had food and provisions.

"The tithe cannot be a New Covenant concept! This must come as a shock to churchgoers who have heard it preached for years. But, it is absolutely impossible for tithing to be practiced by Christians, as this would directly violate God's commands. Let's read God's Word on God's method of giving in the New Covenant."

The class read:

> "In everything I showed you that by working hard in this manner you must help the weak and remember the words of the Lord Jesus, that He Himself said, 'It is more blessed to give than to receive.'" (Acts 20:35)

> Now this *I say,* he who sows sparingly will also reap sparingly, and he who sows bountifully will also reap bountifully.
>
> Each one *must do* just as he has purposed in his heart, not grudgingly or under compulsion, for God loves a cheerful giver.
>
> And God is able to make all grace abound to you, so that always having all sufficiency in everything, you may have an abundance for every good deed. (2 Corinthians 9:6-8)

"Giving in the New Covenant is considered by the Lord Jesus as a 'blessed' position," Dave reiterated. "And since all true believers have given this life back to Christ for His use, then real Christians should be known by their generous giving.

"But notice several commands by God on giving. Each one must give cheerfully, 'not grudgingly or under compulsion.' Also, each one must give 'just as he has purposed in his heart.' These commands expressly declare why tithing is impossible in the New Testament.

"God placed the Israelites *under compulsion* to tithe. The tithe had to be given, or they were living in sin against God. In the New Covenant, God commands that giving must *not be under compulsion*, the exact opposite of tithing!

"In the Law of Moses, the Israelites were compelled to give exactly a tithe, one-tenth of their grain and livestock. In the New Covenant under the Law of Christ, God places the responsibility for the amount one gives on the giver. This responsibility comes with limitations and blessings.

"God says if one gives but a little, God will bless him but a little. If one gives greatly, God promises to bless him greatly. God does not specifically promise financial blessing here, but financial blessing is certainly not excluded! Ask any mature believer, and he will proclaim that peace of mind and closeness with God are blessings that are priceless.

"God also promises the cheerful giver of 'always having all sufficiency in everything,' plus an abundance in order to give more. Are you sufficiently supplied in 'everything' you need, or do you find yourself lacking in several areas—especially in your relationship with God and others? Take a look at your giving, and not just in financial areas, but in time and talent as well. For God promises to supply the cheerful giver sufficiently in every way."

"But I've heard preachers defend tithing in the New Covenant," Nick commented. "They claim that tithing was practiced before the Law of Moses was given. Their point is, if something was practiced from the beginning of humanity, then unless God specifically repeals it, it should be practiced by Christians today."

"I've heard those arguments for tithing also," Dave replied, "but there are several serious problems with that line of reasoning. First, marrying more than one wife was practiced from the beginning of humanity, hardly something these preachers would recommend today.

"But, most importantly, God does repeal tithing in the Law of Christ. Remember, tithing was compulsory and the amount was exact. In the New Covenant, God specifically says that giving must not be compulsory, and that the amount is totally up to the giver. The more generous a person gives, the more generous God blesses. God lets the giver decide the amount.

"Also, Abraham (Hebrews 7:1-10) and Jacob (Genesis 28:22) practiced tithing long before the Mosaic Law made it compulsory. But Abraham and Jacob did not give one-tenth because they were *commanded* to give one-tenth. There was no Law of God at the time commanding a tithe. They gave a tithe of their possessions because they cheerfully *wanted* to give it. Had they chose to give five percent or fifty percent, God would have loved their generosity and cheerfulness!"

"Well, these principles on godly giving have been a great help to me," Pam remarked. "But I still can't help feeling guilty when I see a homeless person on the side of the road with a sign expressing his need. I just don't know how to handle that situation, especially when I sometimes don't have anything extra to give him even if I wanted to help."

"Great point Pam," Dave responded, "and God has a great way to solve this problem without any guilt! First, read God's Word on the subject for us."

Pam read:

> But now finish doing it also, so that just as *there was* the readiness to
> desire it, so *there may be* also the completion of it by your ability.
>
> For if the readiness is present, it is acceptable according to what *a person*
> has, not according to what he does not have. (2 Corinthians 8:11,12)

"Thank you, Pam," Dave said. "These verses alone may not help, but the context will certainly shed a lot of light. The Apostle Paul informed the new Gentile churches in Europe and Asia that there was great poverty and financial hardship upon the believers in Israel, and that he was taking a collection.

"In this and the following chapter, the Apostle outlines many great principles for effective giving. God commands that giving 'is acceptable according to what *a person* has, not according to what he does not have.' Each believer should determine for himself the percentage of his income that he can give. This is now Christ's life, and He demonstrated infinite generosity!

"If God has blessed a person greatly with money, than that person can certainly afford to give a greater percentage, because he still has plenty on which to live. If God has blessed a person in other ways, but with little money, than that person could be just as cheerful and generous with a much smaller percentage. But God allows the giver to decide.

"Any guilt can be replaced with cheerfulness by following these two simple steps:

    1. Determine a "***Definite Percentage of Income***" to give.

        ✧   Remember that this is Christ's life, and giving generously is His practice.

        ✧   Try a specific percentage, and reevaluate after a month or two, adjusting up or down as necessary.

    2. Within that "Definite Percentage of Income," allocate what percentage you will give to each of the following "***Four Biblical Areas for Giving***":

        ✧   Your family (1 Timothy 5:8)—for example, 40%

        ✧   Your church (Galatians 6:6)—for example, 30%

        ✧   Believers in need (Galatians 6:10)—for example, 20%

        ✧   Unbelievers in need (Galatians 6:10)—for example, 10%

"This provides a great model for Christian giving," Dave continued. "The 'Four Biblical Areas for Giving' are listed in the order of the importance attributed in God's Word. Adjustments can always be made. For example, if you have a family member in great need, such as an ailing parent, you might raise that percentage from 40% to 60% or even 80%, depending on your situation.

"Let's say you decide to give 10% of your income to God's work—"

"Isn't that a tithe?" Nick questioned.

"Believe me, if you decide to give one-tenth of your income to God's work, that's great!" Dave answered. "Just don't say God *commanded* you to give exactly 10%! Under the Law of Moses, the tithe was commanded by God. It was compulsory, and was exactly 10% whether the Israelites liked it or not. And, there were other tithes commanded by God as well.

"Under the Law of Christ, giving is to be without compulsion, and the amount is to be cheerfully determined by the giver. One-tenth is a nice, round figure, and easy to compute. Believe me, if all true believers gave 10% of the money with which God has blessed them, the Christian church would have missionaries in every inhabitable square mile on the earth!"

"So, do we give one-tenth of our gross income or our net income?" asked Ed.

"How generous do you want to be?" Dave replied. "The amount is totally up to you. Work it out so that you will give it cheerfully. To the extent that you give generously, God promises to bless you. And, after a while, if God blesses so that you can give a greater percentage, you can decide if you want greater blessings."

"I can see that this is a very organized way to give to the Lord's work," Pam added. "But how does this help with my feelings of guilt when I see people in need?"

"Here is how it works," Dave explained. "For example, if you make $2000 per month, and want 10% to go toward giving, then you have $200 every month to give. Take whatever "Definite Percentage of Income" you established—for example, that $200—and divide it up into the "Four Biblical Areas for Giving." Remember, you can always readjust next month.

"If you decide to give 20% of your "Definite Percentage of Income" to the needs of unbelievers, that gives you $40 every month to give to people you see in need. When you have given out all of that money, you no longer have to feel guilty if you have nothing left in that category to give. You can rejoice in that God has used you to bless all of the others that you have helped. And, you can pray that God will use other believers to help anyone you cannot help that month.

"Thus, you have given generously; others have been blessed by you; you can rejoice over how God has used you; the false guilt is no longer a part of your giving plan; and finally and most importantly, God is pleased and promises to bless you for your obedience!"

"Thanks!" Pam said. "I think God's method of giving can be a real blessing!"

"Great! Any more questions?"

God's Word for the Last Days

"I've been hearing a lot about the last times," Paul said as he raised his hand. "Shows about prophesy abound on Christian radio and television, and the best-selling books in Christendom usually involve eschatology. Do you have a clear understanding of the pre-millennial or post-millennial positions?"

"What is eschatology?" Pam intervened.

"***Eschatology*** is the study of last things, such as the end of this universe as described in the Book of Revelation," Dave answered. "Most Christians have heard the theories tossed around on the pre-, mid-, or post-tribulation returns of Christ. We have also been inundated with the theories of pre-, post-, or even amillennialism.

"Let's read the Lord Jesus' words on the matter."

The class read:

> "But be sure of this, that if the head of the house had known at what hour the thief was coming, he would not have allowed his house to be broken into.
>
> "You too, be ready; for the Son of Man is coming at an hour that you do not expect." (Luke 12:39,40)

So when they had come together, they were asking Him, saying, "Lord, is it at this time You are restoring the kingdom to Israel?"

He said to them, "It is not for you to know times or epochs which the Father has fixed by His own authority;

but you will receive power when the Holy Spirit has come upon you; and you shall be My witnesses both in Jerusalem, and in all Judea and Samaria, and even to the remotest part of the earth." (Acts 1:6-8)

The Revelation of Jesus Christ, which God gave Him to show to His bond-servants, the things which must soon take place; and He sent and communicated *it* by His angel to His bond-servant John,

who testified to the word of God and to the testimony of Jesus Christ, *even* to all that he saw. (Revelation 1:1,2)

"We know for certain that the Lord Jesus' words concerning the end times are very clear," Dave expounded. "The Lord specifically tells us that He will return 'at an hour that you do not expect.' Therefore, all of the attempts by Christians to figure out how the prophecies in Revelation are going to shake out is a complete waste of time.

"The second that any person thinks he has figured it out, and expects Christ's return at a certain point in time, he can immediately know that he is dead wrong. Christ said very clearly that 'the Son of Man is coming at an hour that you do not expect.' If you expect Him before the tribulation, for example, then He isn't coming then!

"Not only are the attempts to figure out the end times a complete waste of time, they are also abject sin against God. Christ directly answered the queries of His disciples by saying, 'It is not for you to know times or epochs which the Father has fixed by His own authority.' If our Commander explicitly tells us that something is off-limits, and we persist in delving into the matter, are we not utterly guilty of rebellion? Will God not discipline such sin?

"I have heard lame excuses for such behavior. One person tried to justify his obsession with eschatology by saying that, after all, it is in God's Word, and we are supposed to study God's Word diligently. I would answer by saying that *adultery* is also in God's Word, but God is not advocating diligent study of all the possibilities of that sin.

"The problem with the obsession of eschatology is a fundamental error of totally misunderstanding God's reason for giving prophecies like the Book of Revelation. This book begins with the words, 'The Revelation of Jesus Christ, which God gave Him to show to His bond-servants.' This is not the Revelation of John, or of the last days, or of anything else. It is the revelation of *Jesus Christ*.

"The total focus of the Book of Revelation is Jesus Christ Himself! Christ is the One being revealed here. Again, God's entire purpose for creation is to bring total honor and glory to God the Son. This book is replete with angelic praises to His majesty, and filled with awesome demonstrations of His power. Revelation shows Christ's suffering servants that He wins! And if we are in Him, as true children of God, we win with Him!

"As Christ has explicitly told us, the minute we think we have figured out when to expect

His return, we are immediately wrong! Instead of focusing on God and His holy character when studying the Law of Moses, the Jewish lawyers and scribes spent hours trying to discern when their Messiah would come. These extremely bright minds studied every prophecy to its smallest detail. And they completely missed the Lord, the Messiah, as He stood right in front of them.

"The reason for the Book of Revelation was never for Christians to waste time trying to figure out future events that, as the Lord already commanded, are not for us to know. Instead of spending hours piecing together a puzzle with a conclusion that Christ says is guaranteed to be wrong, God would much rather have us spend those hours getting to know Him! We would fall more intimately in love with the Lord by focusing on Him. We would become better followers, and would be more effectively used by Christ to bring Him glory!

"We would then be empowered to fulfill Christ's command to 'be ready' (Luke 12:40), at whatever time He decides to return. This is God's will concerning the end times: 'Be ready!'

"I'm not sure who said it first, or I would give him proper credit. The best position to hold in eschatology is to be a *pan-millennialist*. That means it will all pan out in the end! God will fulfill His prophecies down to the last detail, because He ordained everything that happens or exists in creation. God knows the future because He ordained the future.

"God commanded us to do the Four Basics, not for some ritualistic reason, but to draw closer to Him in order to know Him better. As we pray and read God's Word every day, as well as fellowshiping with committed Christians and going to church as often as possible, God works His plan through us.

"If we disobey Him by delving into areas He has forbidden, God will certainly not bless our sin. God never blesses sin. Our decisions as true children of God are first and foremost to glorify our heavenly Father by obeying our Lord Jesus Christ through the power of His Holy Spirit.

Knowing God Intimately

"Becoming a child of God, however, is not a decision we make. That decision was made before creation by God and God alone. We are born as sinners, rebelling against God and running away from Him as quickly as possible. Many false Christians claim to desire God, but they are only after God's benefits—blessings for a life that they refuse to give back to Christ.

"If you greatly desire to be reconciled to God, then it is highly likely you have already been born anew by the Holy Spirit, because the sinful nature never desires God. If God has chosen you, at His preordained moment He placed His Holy Spirit inside of you to raise you from spiritual death. Then you will experience remorse for offending God and His holiness—for stealing this life, that belongs to Him, to serve yourself. Come to Christ. Admit your rebellion and sin against Him.

"*Repent*, which means to give this life back to Christ for whatever He desires for it. *Believe* in Christ's two-part work to make you acceptable to God. Christ died on the cross to pay for your sins, cleaning your slate. Then, to make you as perfect as God is perfect, our heavenly Father transferred God the Son's perfect life to your account. *Come to Christ* in prayer, receiving His miracle of new life, and thanking Him for the awesome privilege of knowing the awesome, Almighty God.

"Understanding the awesome miracle of eternal life which God has given to His children leads to great thankfulness, worship and honor to God. The Lord Jesus said it best during His prayer to the Father: 'This is eternal life, that they may know You, the only true God, and Jesus Christ whom You have sent (John 17:3).' Get to know God intimately, for He alone *is* the Source of eternal life.

"Seek the Lord earnestly in prayer, and develop a close relationship with Him. 'Draw near to God and He will draw near to you' (James 4:8a). Get on the Father's Lap and stay there. A Christian will never be effective in this life without staying on the Father's Lap. A believer may accomplish his own great goals in his own strength, and claim it for God's Name. But, without God Himself bringing *His* work to pass through us, all of our efforts will be wood, hay and straw that will be burned up in the fire (1 Corinthians 3:10-15).

"Anna, would you please read the passages on the chalkboard for us?"

Anna read:

> One of them, a lawyer, asked Him *a question,* testing Him,
> "Teacher, which is the great commandment in the Law?"
> And He said to him, "'YOU SHALL LOVE THE LORD YOUR GOD WITH ALL YOUR HEART, AND WITH ALL YOUR SOUL, AND WITH ALL YOUR MIND.'
> "This is the great and foremost commandment.
> "The second is like it, 'YOU SHALL LOVE YOUR NEIGHBOR AS YOURSELF.'" (Matthew 22:35-39)

"Do not pass by the great and foremost commandment, assuming as a Christian that it is automatically done, and move on to the second commandment. Loving our Father with every ounce of our beings requires time spent in intimate communion with Him. God's will for every child is to know His ways intimately, and to love Him deeply.

"If you have found yourselves exhausted by doing, doing, doing for the Lord—stop. God can, and will, accomplish more with you on His Lap than you could ever do for Him in your own strength. God is the Source of all life and power. Go to Him. Stay with Him. Fall deeply in love with Him, and this life will never be the same.

"I hope this semester has drawn you closer to our loving, heavenly Father. I hope you know God better, and understand more of His ways. Almighty God is sovereign. He alone ordained creation, and everything that comes to pass in creation. God will also roll up the skies like a scroll, and destroy the earth with intense heat. At that moment, we will all step into eternity.

"'We will all stand before the judgment seat of God' (Romans 14:10b). Instantly at death, every person is given a glorified body which will last for eternity. For those chosen by God to enter His heavenly kingdom, we will hear the words for which we long: "'Well done, good and faithful slave. You were faithful with a few things, I will put you in charge of many things; enter into the joy of your master'" (Matthew 25:21b).

"For the evildoers, it will be a terrifying sight. They will wish that they had never been born. Those who claimed to be Christians, but relied on their own merits to be accepted by God, will be utterly shocked. These will hear the horrifying words: "'Throw out the worthless slave into the outer darkness; in that place there will be weeping and gnashing of teeth'" (Matthew 25:30).

"Paul, please read our Lord's dire words."

Paul read:

> "Not everyone who says to Me, 'Lord, Lord,' will enter the kingdom of heaven, but he who does the will of My Father who is in heaven *will enter.*
>
> "Many will say to Me on that day, 'Lord, Lord, did we not prophesy in Your name, and in Your name cast out demons, and in Your name perform many miracles?'
>
> "And then I will declare to them, 'I never knew you; DEPART FROM ME, YOU WHO PRACTICE LAWLESSNESS.'" (Matthew 7:21-23)

"Thank you, Paul," acknowledged Dave. "The Lord warns that 'many' who claimed to be Christians will be cast into hell. The Apostle Paul warns: 'Test yourselves *to see* if you are in the faith; examine yourselves! Or do you not recognize this about yourselves, that Jesus Christ is in you—unless indeed you fail the test' (2 Corinthians 13:5)?

"Many people have been deceived by the humanism that has crept into the modern church. They believe what someone told them, instead of examining the very words of God in the Bible to find truth. These people may have attended a church service, or evangelistic crusade, and 'made a decision for Christ.' They may have walked down to the altar or platform, and prayed a 'sinner's prayer.' They may have 'accepted Jesus as their personal Lord and Savior.' But their lives never changed.

"None of these 'ways to get saved' are taught in the Bible. The Lord Jesus is very explicit concerning His Word and eternal salvation. Let's read the passages."

The class read:

> "Heaven and earth will pass away, but My words will not pass away."
> (Mark 13:31)

> "He who rejects Me and does not receive My sayings, has one who judges him; the word I spoke is what will judge him at the last day."
> (John 12:48)

> "The time is fulfilled, and the kingdom of God is at hand; repent and believe in the gospel." (Mark 1:15)

> "But unless you repent, you will all likewise perish." (Luke 13:5)

> "He who loves father or mother more than Me is not worthy of Me; and he who loves son or daughter more than Me is not worthy of Me.
>
> "And he who does not take his cross and follow after Me is not worthy of Me.
>
> "He who has found his life will lose it, and he who has lost his life for My sake will find it." (Matthew 10:37-39)

> "Therefore you are to be perfect, as your heavenly Father is perfect."
> (Matthew 5:48)

"Do we really believe that, on Judgment Day, the Lord Jesus will say: 'You know, I didn't really mean it when I said that, to be My follower, you must give up everything, including your life, to Me'"? Dave asked. "Have we become so deceived that we think the Lord God Almighty will say: 'You know, I fibbed. It was okay for you to continue living your own life, with your own goals and opinions, and not to submit to My Word. I guess I was a little harsh with those commands to repent'?

"'Test yourselves to see if you are in the faith.' The true Christian faith, the only faith that can save a person from the wrath of God, requires man to repent and believe. To repent means to change one's mind about who owns this life, and to give this life back to Christ, its rightful owner, for whatever *He* desires for it.

"To believe means to trust only in Christ's two-part perfect work for salvation. Christ died on the cross to pay for our sins, and the Father credited His perfect life to our account. That is the only way to meet God's standard for entering heaven. God's eternal standard for entering heaven applies to everyone: to be as perfect as God is perfect.

"If anyone adds *anything* to Christ's perfect work for salvation, like one's own goodness or good works, then we humans only taint God's gift of perfection. Then we are no longer as perfect as God is perfect, and will be rejected by Christ Himself on Judgment Day. Repenting, and trusting only in what Christ has already done, is man's only hope for salvation.

"'Test yourselves to see if you are in the faith.' Have you given this life back to Christ, its rightful owner, for whatever He wants with it? Or do you still consider this life to be your life, working your own agenda, with your own goals and opinions? Are you trusting solely in Christ's work for salvation, or are you really relying on your own 'goodness,' or your 'good' works?

"Do you think you are really a good person, and that your good deeds outnumber your bad deeds? The sovereign Judge of the universe, the Lord Jesus Christ, declares that '"no one is good except God alone"' (Luke 18:19). Are you still deceived in thinking that God uses some sliding scale—comparing you to other humans—to determine your eternal fate? Or do you know that the standard for entering heaven is to be as perfect as God is perfect; that you are a sinner from birth; and that your only hope is to fall at the feet of Christ in repentance, and to trust in Him and His work alone?

"Eternal life in God's glorious presence is defined by God the Son: '"This is eternal life, that they may know You, the only true God, and Jesus Christ whom You have sent"' (John 17:3). Not religion...not 'churchianity'...but knowing God Himself intimately—this *is* eternal life! And it begins now for the one chosen by God who repents, believes, and comes to Christ!

"I hope this semester's Bible study has answered many of your questions, and brought you to examine your relationship to Almighty God. And to think we have only scratched the surface of the infinite depths of our heavenly Father! I close with the words of the Apostle Paul:

Oh, the depth of the riches both of the wisdom and knowledge of God!

How unsearchable are His judgments and unfathomable His ways!

For WHO HAS KNOWN THE MIND OF THE LORD, OR WHO BECAME HIS COUNSELOR?

Or WHO HAS FIRST GIVEN TO HIM THAT IT MIGHT BE PAID BACK TO HIM AGAIN?

For from Him and through Him and to Him are all things. To Him
be the glory forever. Amen. (Romans 11:33-36)

"Nick, would you please end this semester's study of the Word of God with prayer?"
Nick answered, "I can think of only one prayer:
Lord,
If I, as Your child, have found favor in Your sight,
Let me know Your ways,
So that I may know and love You intimately,
And may forever find favor with You.
Let this life bring exceedingly great glory to You,
For otherwise it is not worth living. Amen.

Bibliography

Due to the conversational style of this book, I am unaware of directly quoting any particular work. However, many great works by mighty people of God were indispensable in putting all of God's truths together. I am gratefully indebted to the following works and their authors.

Bahnsen, Dr. Greg L. *Higher Thoughts: A Theological Exposition of Isaiah 55:8-9.* Covenant Media Foundation, cassette.

Bahnsen, Dr. Greg L. *The Great Debate; Does God Exist?* Covenant Media Foundation, cassette.

Bahnsen, Dr. Greg L. *The Problem of Evil.* Covenant Media Foundation, cassette.

Bahnsen, Dr. Greg L. *Arguments for the Existence of God.* Covenant Media Foundation, cassette.

Bahnsen, Dr. Greg L. *Difficult Doctrines.* Covenant Media Foundation, cassette.

Copi, Irving M., and Carl Cohen. *Introduction to Logic,* 9 ed. New York: Macmillan, 1994.

Danker, Frederick William. *A Greek-English Lexicon of the New Testament and Other Early Christian Literature,* 3 ed. (BDAG). Chicago: University of Chicago Press, 2000.

Friesen, Garry, and J. Robin Maxson. *Decision Making & the Will of God.* Portland, Oregon: Multnomah Press, 1980.

Green, Jay P., Sr., ed. *Interlinear Greek-English New Testament,* 3 ed. Grand Rapids, Michigan: Baker, 2000.

Mathison, Keith A. *Dispensationalism: Rightly Dividing the People of God?* Phillipsburg, New Jersey: Presbyterian and Reformed Publishing, 1995.

Owen, John. *The Death of Death in the Death of Christ.* Carlisle, Pennsylvania: Banner of Truth Trust, 1995.

Pink, Arthur W. *The Attributes of God.* Grand Rapids, Michigan: Baker, 1975.

Pink, Arthur W. *The Sovereignty of God.* Grand Rapids, Michigan: Baker, 1983.

Robertson, O. Palmer. *The Christ of the Covenants.* Phillipsburg, New Jersey: Presbyterian and Reformed Publishing, 1980.

Sproul, R. C. *The Consequences of Ideas: An Overview of Philosophy.* Ligonier Ministries, 1999, cassette.

Sproul, R. C. *Essential Truths of the Christian Faith.* Wheaton, Illinois: Tyndale House, 1992.

Steele, David N., and Curtis C. Thomas. *Romans, An Interpretive Outline.* Phillipsburg, New Jersey: Presbyterian and Reformed Publishing, 1984.

Tabletalk. Lake Mary, Florida: Ligonier Ministries, 2000, 2001, 2002.

The Open Bible. Nashville: Thomas Nelson Publishers, 1978, 1979.

The Westminster Confession of Faith. Atlanta: Committee for Christian Education & Publications, 1990.

Thomas, Robert L., ed. *New American Standard Exhaustive Concordance of the Bible, Hebrew-Aramaic and Greek Dictionaries.* Nashville: Holman Bible Publishers, 1981.

Webster's New Universal Unabridged Dictionary, Fully Revised and Updated. New York: Barnes & Noble, 1996.

Index

To order more copies,
please contact:

KGI Publishing
2232 South Nellis Blvd.
Suite #103
Las Vegas, Nevada 89104
(702) 457-7237
www.kgipress.com

"Knowing God Intimately"